THE FRENCH FOREIGN
LEGION
DOUGLAS BOYD

Ian Allan
PUBLISHING

What attracts men from 136 different nations to embrace the harsh military code of an army that requires them to lay down their lives for a country not their own, if ordered to do so by politicians whose language many of them hardly speak?

'You legionnaires have become soldiers in order to die,' one French general told his men - and that has been the Legion's lot many times. Founded in 1831 to fight France's colonial wars without spilling French blood, this mysterious army is today a world-class fighting force. Unlike most Western armies, it admits no women, but one woman - the English mistress of a colonel - defied the men-only rule and served with distinction.

Training is so tough that five recruits out of six are rejected, never to wear the coveted white képi. This is a world where fact exceeds the wildest fiction: men fighting literally to the last bullet at Camarón in Mexico in 1863; cooks and clerks with no parachute training volunteering to be dropped into beleaguered Dien Bien Phu in 1954 with the intention of dying alongside their comrades abandoned by the government that had sent them there; the paras who mutinied in Algeria to bring down the government of France; the heroes who dropped on Kolwezi to rescue thousands of European hostages.

The Legion is all those things and much more, so it is fitting that this history of it reads at times like a thriller - with the difference that everything is true!

About the Author

After serving as a Russian linguist in the RAF, Douglas Boyd has been an international businessman, an impresario and a BBC Television Producer/Director. He has been writing full-time since setting up home in a medieval farmhouse in south-west France thirty years ago.

His published fiction and non-fiction, translated into many languages, includes three novels set against a Legion background. English-speaking ex-legionnaires so appreciated this history of their unique army that they elected him an honorary ex-legionnaire!

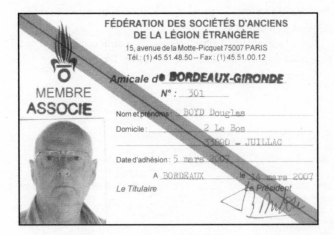

The French Foreign Legion
Douglas Boyd

ISBN 978 0 7110 3500 3

All rights reserved. No part of this book may be reproduced or transmitted in any form or by any means, electronic or mechanical, including photocopying, recording, scanning or by any information storage and retrieval system, on the internet or elsewhere, without permission from the Publisher in writing.

First published by Sutton Publishing 2006

© 2010 Douglas Boyd

The right of Douglas Boyd to be identified as author of this work has been asserted by him in accordance with the Copyright, Designs and Patents Act 1988.

Published by Ian Allan Publishing

an imprint of Ian Allan Publishing Ltd, Hersham, Surrey KT12 4RG.

Printed in England by CPI Mackays, Chatham, Kent ME5 8TD.

Visit the Ian Allan Publishing website at www.ianallanpublishing.com

Distributed in the United States of America and Canada by BookMasters Distribution Services.

Copyright
Illegal copying and selling of publications deprives authors, publishers and booksellers of income, without which there would be no investment in new publications. Unauthorised versions of publications are also likely to be inferior in quality and contain incorrect information. You can help by reporting copyright infringements and acts of piracy to the Publisher or the UK Copyright Service.

Sans honneur? Ah, passons. Et sans foi? Qu'est-ce à dire?
Que fallait-il de plus et qu'aurait-on voulu?
N'avez-vous pas tenu, tenu jusqu'au martyre,
la parole donnée et le marché conclu?

They say that you're without honour or faith,
But what more could they have asked?
Did you not fulfil unto death
the sworn duty with which you were tasked?

Legion Captain Borelli, to his legionnaires
who died at Thuyen Quang in 1885

Contents

Foreword   10
Introduction   12

Part I: THE END OF AN EMPIRE
1:    A bullet for my pal: Vietnam, 1949-53   20
2:    You gotta die sometime: Dien Bien Phu,
      November 1953-April 1954   38
3:    Terrorism and torture: Algeria, 1954-7   56
4:    Dare call it treason: Algeria, 1957-62   68

Part II: BUILDING AN EMPIRE WITH BLOOD
5:    The legion of the lost: France, 1813-31   86
6:    The scarecrow soldiers: Algeria, 1831-5   100
7:    No pay, no bullets, no mercy: Spain, 1835-9   112
8:    Blood on the sand: Algeria, 1835-40   123
9:    A head on a spear: Algeria, 1840-9   132
10:   Chaos in the Crimea: 1851-5   143
11:   Theirs not to reason why: Crimea,
      1855-6; Italy, 1859   153
12:   Myth and madness in Mexico: 1862-3   166
13:   Death in the afternoon: Mexico, 1863-7   178
14:   With rifle-butt and bayonet: France, 1866-70   192
15:   Blindfolds and bullets on the boulevards:
      France, 1870-71   202
16:   Tweaking the dragon's tail: Algeria, 1871-82;
      Vietnam, and Formosa, 1883-5   212
17:   As good as it gets: Vietnam, 1885-92   224
18:   War on the belly of Dan: Dahomey, 1892-4   234
19:   The cut-price campaign: Madagascar, 1895   243
20:   Miracle and massacre at Taghit: North Africa, 1901-3   252

21:   In the kingdom of the west: North Africa, 1901-3   261
22:   Chaos and confusion: France, 1914   274
23:   Guns and gas in the trenches: France, 1915   283
24:   Rendezvous with death: France, 1916-18   296
25:   Identity crisis: North Africa, 1918-40   309
26:   At both ends of the Med:
      North Africa, 1918-33; Syria/Lebanon, 1918-27   322
27:   Veterans and volunteers:
      France, 1939-40; Norway, 1940   335
28:   Whose side are we on, sergeant?
      France-North Africa-Syria, Britain, 1940   343
29:   Which side did you say, Miss? West Africa, 1940   351
30:   'La Miss' and the heroes of Bir Hakeim:
      Western Desert, 1942   361
31:   The stormy re-marriage: North Africa, 1942-3;
      Europe 1944-5; Vietnam 1945-9   374

PART III: THE POST-IMPERIAL PERIOD

32:   Who needs the Legion now?   390
33:   The Legion reborn   394
34:   The Dove that was a Tiger: 12-16 May 1978   401
35:   Go! Don't go! Go! Operation Leopard,
      17-19 May 1978   408
36:   Kill or be killed at Kolwezi: 19 May-6 June 1978   418

Acknowledgements   432
Appendix A: Equivalent ranks   433
Appendix B: Glossary   434
List of illustrations   437
Further Reading in English   439
Notes and Sources   440
Index   453

Foreword

by Brigadier Anthony Hunter Choat, OBE

Since King Louis Philippe created the French Foreign Legion in 1831, thousands of books and articles have been written and countless films made about this mysterious, myth shrouded body of men which has been almost continuously in combat in Africa, Asia, Europe and the Americas ever since. Legionnaires – I was one myself – have always loved a fight, man against man, section against section, company against company. The other characteristic that makes them good soldiers is their craving for the satisfaction of duty done and orders obeyed.

Their motto *Legio patria nostra* means 'the Legion is our country' and tens of thousands of legionnaires have fought for this adopted country, winning themselves worldwide respect and admiration. Many have died and many more been wounded performing deeds of the most amazing valour, but until now little has been known of the social and geopolitical circumstances in which they were achieved.

Living in France and speaking French like a native, Douglas Boyd has long been fascinated by the Legion and explored the subject in earlier writings. He understands what motivates the French and what motivates the Legion. The two are not always the same. This major work weaves French political warp with the weft of the Foreign Legion to produce a comprehensive, tight and fascinating history. Boyd's knowledge of French politics over a span of nearly two centuries, particularly in Indochina and North Africa, gives him a clear perspective on the Legion's activities, and throws light on the reasons for its successes and failures, and for its sometimes recalcitrant attitude.

For the greater part of its existence, the Legion has been unashamedly used by French governments for operations overseas that attracted little support or interest at home and for which the average Frenchman had no taste. Legionnaires have accepted this so long as the deal was fair and honest. Although France's treatment of the Legion now is excellent - perhaps because Paris has at last realised that it is an asset not to be wasted or disparaged - in the past, the deals have sadly often been far from fair and honest. Nonetheless, legionnaires have carried out their mission whatever the cost. Reading the accounts of the battles of Camerone, of Highway Four and Dien Bien Phu will tell the reader just how high that cost has been.

As a former legionnaire, I welcome this book, for both its depth and clarity. It will greatly enhance the Legion's already superb reputation.

Tony Hunter Choat
(formerly 116798 Sergeant Choat of 1 REP)
Hereford, September 2005

Introduction

While researching this book, I met at the bar of a West London cricket club a former SAS sergeant and naturally asked him whether he had ever bumped into the Legion during his service years. Not exactly a chatty guy, he eyed me suspiciously before admitting that he had - several times.

I asked, 'When was the last time?'

'A while back,' he replied.

'Where?'

Luckily, I was with a mutual friend - with whom I served in the RAF - so the man of few words took another draught of beer and said, 'Western Sahara.'

The disputed territory to the south of Morocco? That sounded promising, so I pushed my luck and asked, 'What was the Legion doing there?'

By now, he had had enough of my questions, and muttered, 'Same as us, like.'

'And what was that?' I asked innocently.

He finished his beer, said, 'Don't be f---ing daft,' and left.

It can be difficult, researching the Legion. As Brig Hunter-Choat says, it is a mysterious, myth-shrouded body of men which has been in combat somewhere on the globe more or less continuously for nearly two centuries. So, where does one begin?

Well, the most famous Frenchman of all time was a soldier who was not even born in France, but on Corsica when Italian was its first language. The two best-known French presidents of the twentieth century were both military men. Marshal Philippe Pétain was the Hero of Verdun in World War I who became the Traitor of Vichy in World War II, after which his former protégé and wartime enemy General Charles De Gaulle sentenced his senile ex-patron to death, and commuted the sentence before turning France from 'the sick man of Europe' into an independent nuclear super-power.

In a country where politics and the military are so closely interwoven it is no surprise to find that one branch of the armed forces has provided many generals, marshals and high-ranking politicians up to Prime Minister. That it should be the Foreign Legion gives cause for thought.

What makes the French Foreign Legion different from any other army - apart from its unequalled mixture of races - is that it numbers in its ranks men from all social and educational backgrounds: musicians like American Cole Porter, philosophers like Hungarian-born Arthur Koestler, writers like Switzerland's Blaise Cendrars and the grand old man of German letters Ernst Junger. Poets, painters and professional sportsmen have served alongside bemedalled veterans prepared to work their way up again from the lowest rank after donning Legion uniform.

For 179 years jobless, homeless and loveless men have found a sense of purpose worth all the rigours and risks of serving in the world's longest-standing mercenary army, but so too have many born in palaces. Royal legionnaires include King Peter I of Serbia, Prince Louis II of Monaco, Crown Prince Sisowath Monireth of Cambodia and princes Aage of Denmark and Amilakvari of Georgia. Of slightly lesser pedigree was Prince Napoleon, son of Princess Clementine of Belgium and great-grandson of the Legion's founder King Louis-Philippe. The Prince served as Legionnaire Blanchard, No 94707. His haughtier cousin the Count of Paris enlisted as engagé volontaire D'Orliac with the number 10681. Maxim Gorky's adopted son rose from enlisted rank to general's stars, yet chose to be buried beneath a stone inscribed simply Legionnaire Zinovi Pechkoff.

Twenty-first century recruits are unlikely to be motivated by the romance of Edith Piaf's hit-song about her legionnaire lover, whose skin 'smelt deliciously of hot desert sand'.[1] Fewer still will ever have read the Beau Geste novels or watched 1930s black-and-white films in which legionnaires dying from booze and boredom inside remote Saharan mud-brick forts snap out of it just in time to rescue rich and glamorous lady tourists from the rapacious veiled warriors of the sands.

So what is it that attracts men still unborn when the USA disengaged from the Vietnam conflict to accept the harsh discipline of this legendary army with a Code of Honour that sounds like the Boy Scouts' pledge? Every other legionnaire is your brother. In combat, you act without passion or hate but with respect for your vanquished enemy. You never abandon your dead, your wounded or your weapons...

Some join in search of adventures you can't find in civilian life. For others, it's a fresh start after unemployment, a police record, family- or girl-trouble. For many, the reward is French citizenship at the end of their service, with all the freedoms of the European community theirs to enjoy. In the words of one of the Legion's many poets, Pascal Bonetti, they become sons of France not by inheriting French blood, but by spilling theirs for France.[2] Whatever his reason for joining, every legionnaire knows that for the rest of his life he will never have to prove himself among fighting men. To have worn the white képi is proof that he is as tough as they come.

The term 'legionnaire' strictly means the ordinary soldier, not his NCOs and officers. But all ranks swear on oath that their mission is sacred, however tough it may be. In 1881 General De Négrier famously told his men 'You legionnaires have become soldiers in order to die and I am sending you where people die.'[3] A Harvard graduate who died at Belloy-en-Santerre just off the A1 motorway in Picardy during the catastrophic month of July 1916, Legionnaire Alan Seeger was a Romantic poet in search of a heroic death. He wrote, 'I have a rendezvous with Death at some disputed barricade when Spring comes back with rustling shade and apple-blossoms fill the air ... I to my pledged word am true. I shall not fail that rendezvous.'

Exploring the high mortality rate among legionnaires early in the twentieth century, Dr Jean Robaglia and Commandant Paul Chavigny equated the desire to enlist in the Legion as a death-wish. Although France had been anti-clerical since the Revolution, Robaglia went on to say that the strict discipline and harsh punishments served as a school of expiation for those who could not carry the burden of their guilt through civilian life.

Psychobabble or truth? On today's battlefield a soldier with a death-wish is a danger to many people besides himself, so seekers of a heroic death are now weeded out in the initial battery of psychological tests. A tough interrogation in his own language also ensures that, contrary to popular belief, a violent or confirmed criminal will not make it through the rigorous selection process - although minor brushes with the forces of law and order in one's home country are taken as indicators of masculine spirit.

Today's engagés volontaires have an average age of twenty-three with well above-average intelligence. The Legion has its own education service, and is less interested in previous academic education than a keen brain and a fit body. The first thing it teaches recruits is basic French - the language of command. The second is a trade - which may be jumping out of helicopters in mid-air without a parachute, driving a computer to fire artillery or something useful in civilian life like cookery or motor maintenance.

The French Ministry of Defence ruled in 1960 that women are entitled to join any branch of the armed forces for which their intelligence and physique fitted them. This was partly political correctness and also a solution to the recruiting crisis that besets most Western regular armies. However, the Legion has no problem attracting sufficient male recruits; on the contrary, five out of six are rejected. So far, only one woman has managed to penetrate its ranks. The extraordinary British nurse Susan Travers became a Warrant Officer when selected by her lover General Pierre Koenig as his personal driver during the North African campaign of 1942.

In this otherwise all-male world, every man gets the chance to start life anew, enlisting as Bill Gates or Mickey Mouse if he wishes and receiving the appropriate papers for his new persona. While insisting on knowing his true origins, the Legion respects forever his anonymity as far as the outside world is concerned. This can make research even more difficult. Another major difficulty in compiling a history of this unique army is the conflict between accredited sources and the image of their corporate past that many legionnaires take as gospel. There may be a tendency in men who are given a new identity to shrug off the reality they are escaping and live in a world of fantasy where anything is possible, but that does not make for objective history.

There are a number of basic truths, one of which is that the

Legion does not recruit outside French territory. Anyone pretending otherwise for money is, as the succinct website of the French Embassy in Chile warns, 'a crook'. Nor are there any funds to defray travel expenses of would-be legionnaires. They have to reach a recruiting office on French soil under their own steam. Most simply buy an air ticket, but one Armenian in his early twenties whom I rescued from the frontier police in Hendaye had walked from the Caucasus to the Atlantic to join the Legion, slipping over borders at night and sleeping rough with other illegal immigrants living on scraps thrown away at fast-food joints and markets because he was wary of being picked up by the police, if caught begging.

If the Armenian made it through basic training, he will have found himself in a world where life is tough and punishments hard. Just once a year the Legion relaxes and the veil of mystery is allowed to drop. On 30 April, the anniversary of its great defeat at the battle of Camarón, the Legion throws open the doors of its bases and invites the local population to spend the day as its guests. There are sideshows for the kids and a chance to scramble over the ready-to-go vehicles, painted in green and brown camouflage, grey urban warfare zigzags or desert sand colour, depending for where they are on alert. Pretty girls eye the smart young soldiers with exotic accents. The mums appreciate the gallantry of the immaculately uniformed officers. The dads try out under supervision a version of the FAMAS assault rifle.

The Bastille Day crowd on 14 July in Paris, watching the pride of France's armed forces march down the Champs Elysées, reserves its loudest cheer for the men wearing white képis. Yet in the palaces and ministries inhabited by civil servants and politicians there reigns a constant mistrust of this self-contained army of highly-trained men who will follow their own NCOs and officers to hell and back. During the colonial era, metropolitan France was a no-go area for the Legion, which policed an empire stretching from the Caribbean to the Indian Ocean, Indo-China and the Pacific. Only in the dire days of three German invasions was it posted to French soil in 1870, 1914 and 1939.

Based in France since 1962, the elements of the Legion are dispersed, all at a safe distance from Paris. The paras are confined to Corsica - as far from Paris as you can get on French soil because in 1962 they came within an ace of dropping on Paris and overthrowing the government. In a bar at the port of Calvi, a few kilometres from their base at Camp Rafalli, I overheard a frighteningly fit corporal and sergeant arguing over whose team should have won a shooting competition that morning. The umpire, it was plain, had been blind, stupid and probably deaf as well. Every other word began with f, but no French was required to follow the post-mortem discussion because the corporal was a Geordie and the sergeant a Cockney. Both were among France's elite soldiers, although their loyalty was not to the government or president in faraway Paris, but to their own officers. Their motto *Legio patria nostra* says it all.

It is a paradox that most people want to live as long as possible, yet professional soldiers take the ultimate gamble in signing a contract by which they stake their lives. Men have always done this to protect their wives and children, but what makes the men of the Foreign Legion want to serve, and if necessary die for, a country that is not theirs, whose language many of them hardly speak - and which cannot make up its mind whether they are magnificent heroes or dangerous thugs?

I hope this history of France's mysterious mercenaries provides answers to some of the questions.

Douglas Boyd
Gironde, France, Summer 2010

PART I

THE END OF AN EMPIRE

INSTITIÚID TEICNEOLAÍOCHTA
AN LEABHARLANN
LEITIR CEANAINN
355
35 40 0

500 38728

Chapter 1

A BULLET FOR MY PAL

Vietnam 1949-1953

There are few battles that military historians and lecturers in staff colleges worldwide can use to illustrate all the mistakes a general can make in one operation. Dien Bien Phu is one.

It is also an extraordinary example of hundreds of men in uniform *choosing* to die together, rather than forfeit their honour by abandoning their comrades. And these were not legendary Bronze Age heroes or gung-ho kids but campaign-hardened veterans of the Second World War serving in Foreign Legion uniform in Vietnam, which was then a colony of France.

The French plan at DBP was to trick the wily guerrilla leader Gen Vo Nguyen Giap into throwing the uncounted thousands of his Viet Minh guerrillas into a pitched battle against an impregnable fixed position where they would all be wiped out. Yet the generals in Paris and Hanoi already knew that Giap was a master of guerrilla strategy, unlikely to fall into such a trap. They also knew that he was supported by the Communist regime, which came to power in 1949 at the end of the Chinese civil war, and afforded the Viet Minh safe training bases on the Chinese side of the common border, plus apparently limitless supplies of materiel, smuggled along the jungle trails.

Four whole years before DBP, French Chief of Staff Gen Georges Revers read a Top Secret report to the National Defence Committee in Paris on 25 July 1949, informing them that a *vital* communications axis designated Highway Four[1] in Vietnam would have to be abandoned because the French garrisons along it were otherwise inevitably going to be overwhelmed by Giap's guerrillas.

Highway Four was the strategic road twisting and turning between the hills for 116km parallel with the Chinese frontier in

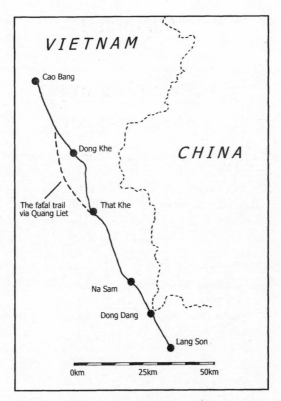

Vietnam: the strategic Highway Four, 1949

the northeast of Vietnam. From Lang Son to Dong Dang was 15km; at Kilometre 33 was Na Sam; at Kilometre 63, That Ke; at Kilometre 88, Dong Khe; at Kilometre 101, Nam-Nang and so on to Cao Bang, marking Kilometre 116. On many stretches of the road, the frontier was an easy two-hour stroll distant and Highway Four also crossed several historic invasion routes from China. To save needless loss of life, Revers recommended the posts be swiftly evacuated, together with the thirty-odd way-stations in between. His report became embarrassingly public when a Spanish ex-legionnaire using the name Tomás Pérez was arrested for assaulting on a Paris bus two Vietnamese students who had been

21

attending the Communist-front World Youth Congress in Budapest. Police investigating the incident 'happened to find' copies of the Revers Report in their possession, which justified subsequent enquiries revealing scores of duplicated copies of the report among the Left-Wing Vietnamese student community. Claiming that he had been paid by French Intelligence to expose top-level leaks in government ministries, Pérez was allowed to disappear - possibly by re-enlisting in the Legion - before the cases came to court.

Of all the garrisons on Highway Four that Revers had recommended for evacuation, Dong Khe was the weirdest. Situated at the start of the 28km stretch known as the Road of Spilt Blood between there and Cao Bang, it was held for a time by two companies of the Legion's 3rd Régiment Etranger d'Infanterie, designated 3 REI, whose commander Maj De Lambert was a mad dog without a bone to chew on - in other words a first-rate soldier frustrated to the core by the lack of sufficient forces to do anything about the vast numbers of Viet Minh moving in from China all around him. His mission was to stay put and keep Dong Khe a safe overnight stop for convoys heading north along Highway Four before they tackled the lethal final stage of their journey. He therefore put all his considerable energies into making Dong Khe the best possible place for men to spend their last night on earth.

He built a nightclub casino with a difference, hacked out of the cliffs within the base and called Le Hublot - the Porthole. Since the men entering its portals were aware that the money in their pockets might never be spent anywhere else in this life, the stakes were high and the banker's share distributed among the garrison was proportionate.

Poker, chemin de fer, baccarat, *backuan* - one could play them all, smoke a few pipes, get blind drunk or have a dozen women, one after the other. There were only two prohibitions. A notice on the door signed by Lambert read: *Following the death of Cpl Négrier and the deaths of* - here followed names of six legionnaires - *the games of Buffalo and Cuckoo are henceforth forbidden in this establishment.*

These were the games played by those who wanted the

strongest buzz of all. Buffalo involved two 'players'. On the bar were placed two bottles of aperitif, usually Cinzano or Dubonnet. Each man swallowed a bottle of his poison and then the two charged each other heads down and hands behind their backs like two buffaloes clashing their heads together at full speed. If neither was knocked out in the collision, they both drained another bottle of aperitif before repeating the confrontation. On occasions the players had been known to down two bottles of aperitif each before one was taken to the sick bay with severe concussion. On other occasions one collision was enough to crack a man's skull.

Cuckoo was, if anything, madder still. In the empty basement two men were given Colt 45s with nine rounds each. The lights switched out, one called out, 'Cuckoo,' meaning, 'Is anyone there?' He then jumped as smartly as a very drunken man can to one side, so that the bullet of the other player missed him. If it missed, the other called, 'Cuckoo,' and this continued until all eighteen bullets had been fired - in theory. In practice hardly any one ever got that far, which is why Lambert eventually banned the two most popular games in Le Hublot.

A legionnaire who knew Dong Khe at this time said, 'So we were crazy? We wouldn't have been there otherwise, would we?'[2] You did have to be crazy. The forts and way-stations along Highway Four were trip-wires, existing not to attack or even slow down the enemy, but simply to be wiped out by any important incursion and thereby signal its presence. Sanity was in short supply on both sides. The reinforced concrete way-stations were used as training grounds by the Viets, testing the effects on concrete of different explosives and experimenting with different ways of blasting a passage through the wire by human suicide torpedoes and bamboo tubes stuffed with plastic explosive.

Experimenting? The most surreal attack came at a way-station near Dong Khe known only by the elevation of the hill on which it stood. At midnight early in 1950 the garrison of six legionnaires and eight anti-Viet guerrillas commanded by Sgt Maj Gianno from Italy was awoken by the sentinels when what seemed to be a sparkling home-made bomb arched over the wall and fell into the courtyard. It was a petrol-soaked cat with a bundle of smouldering tinder tied to its tail. Before the first cat had exploded in a ball of flame, another landed in the courtyard, followed by another and another until the courtyard was a mass of demented, flaming cats.

The hope of the Viets was that one or more of the desperate animals would run into the ammunition store and blow the whole place sky-high, which is what happened. The sole survivor of the explosion who managed to creep away through the jungle to Dong Khe was a Dutchman by name of Strast. Recounting his story next morning, he could hardly have expected to be believed anywhere else. Along Highway Four, everything was possible. The method of attack was never used again, probably because capturing enough cats and preparing them was harder work than chucking home-made bombs over the wall.

Before 3 REI took over Dong Khe, at 0645hrs on 27 May 1950 the garrison of French-officered Moroccan colonial infantry awoke to the sound of exploding shells from five beautifully camouflaged 75mm guns hauled clandestinely into position on the hills above them. Forty-eight hours later, Gen Giap's elite 308th Brigade took the place by storm, to be driven out within hours by the drop of a battalion of colonial paras, whose success engendered a false confidence within the French command, along the lines of 'one battalion of our boys is worth a brigade of theirs'.

On 24 June Communist North Korea invaded South Korea with Chinese backing and what little space the international press had allocated to the French war in Vietnam dwindled to nothing. Believing that Giap would now go all-out to win his war, marching in step with North Korea, the new C-in-C Vietnam Gen Marcel Carpentier defied Revers and decided that the frontier posts along Highway Four must be held at all costs to block Viet reinforcements and supplies coming in from China.[3] Events moved swiftly. Less than three months later Carpentier was planning to evacuate one of them before mid-October.

Cao Bang was a tin-mining town surrounded by Viet Minh territory at the nodal point where Highway Three, leading to the capital Hanoi, intersected Highway Four, which ran from the coast northwards. It also lay astride an historic Chinese invasion route only 24km from the frontier of Guangxi Zhuang province. The town was garrisoned by two companies of legionnaires from 3 REI under 40-year-old Col Pierre Charton, a wiry little man who stood so straight that he appeared tall, and whose reputation as a soldier's soldier had spread well beyond the regiment.

The only way to evacuate Cao Bang on the ground was via Highway Four, passing through Dong Khe, now garrisoned by 5th and 6th Companies of 3 REI. However, at 0700hrs on 16 September Giap repeated the previous treatment. After two days of bombardment from concealed artillery, the post was again overrun with so many casualties that only nine legionnaires made it through the jungle to the neighbouring post at That Khe, where they arrived with uniforms in shreds, nearly dead from hunger and thirst.

With Cao Bang more isolated than ever, Carpentier reinforced its garrison by air with a battalion of Moroccan infantry. At Lang Son to the south on Highway Four Lt Col Marcel Lepage was ordered to retake Dong Khe again and hold it until the Cao Bang garrison could rendezvous with him there. After that, the combined forces could march safely south. That was the plan, but Charton was not supposed to know in case it leaked out and the Viet Minh got to know. To lull his suspicions, Carpentier paid Cao Bang a lightning visit by air to reassure him that everything was under control. Two days later Gen Alessandri, C-in-C North Vietnam, came on the same mission, but took Charton into his confidence. Charton was furious because he knew there was no way the Viets positioned all along Highway Four would let him and the garrison just walk away, even if all the scorched-earth destruction was left undone until the last minute to avoid giving them prior warning.

Two weeks passed before Lepage set out from That Khe on 30 September after the Legion's 1st Bataillon Etranger de Parachutistes - abbreviated to 1 BEP - dropped in to reinforce his force of 8th Moroccan Infantry Regiment, making a total of 3,500 men on the post. Their mission was to retake Dong Khe by 1200hrs on 2 October. In Cao Bang, Charton was fuming at the order radioed to him to abandon the fortress at 0001hrs on 4 October - a time chosen to wrong-foot the Viets.

'To set an exact time for an operation like this is crazy,' he retorted. 'Who knows what the weather will be like? And without air cover, we haven't a chance.'[4]

The order was unshakeable. According to Hanoi, relayed by radio from Lang Son, Lepage was advancing and Dong Khe would be in the bag in a matter of hours. So what was Charton worried about?

'In that case, make the RV nearer me,' snapped Charton over the static interference. 'Make it Kilometre 22 and not Kilometre 28. I'm going to be slowed down by our wounded and sick civilians, pregnant women and children, people in all stages of malaria, people with dysentery.'

He had already told the population they could leave and join the Viets, stay and see what happened after the French withdrawal, or come with him. Nung, Meo and other minority-race locals had good reason to fear genocide from the Vietnamese after the French pull-out and the town's whores faced the same fate on moral grounds. As a result the withdrawal would include 1,500 civilians.

Charton was effectively told he was losing his nerve. How could he imagine that a few lousy Viet guerrillas would dare attack the combined force of his garrison and Lepage's column? From the safety of Hanoi, that was unthinkable.

And so the plan went ahead. South of Cao Bang in a basin surrounded by forested hills, 1 BEP's two companies under Capt Pierre Jeanpierre and Lt Roger Faulques were tasked with retaking the apparently abandoned citadel of Dong Khe on the morning of 2 October. It was a trap. Snipers, mortars and heavy artillery on the surrounding hills exacted a severe toll before the decision was taken to retreat after suffering 30% casualties.

In Cao Bang at midday Charton obeyed orders, ordering his garrison to blow the charges already laid under the magazines and start destroying stores, burning everything that could not be moved and at the same time stashing anything edible and drinkable in their packs. Before they had finished this orgy of destruction, Lepage's retreating column reached an abandoned way-station called Na Pa around 1400hrs. Suddenly mortar and large-calibre artillery shells were landing in profusion on the 2,000-plus men trapped in the valley. Lepage was scornfully called 'the gunner' by the paras of 1 BEP, but as an artilleryman he knew that the fire was coming from a Viet force several times as big as any forecast by Intelligence. With movement forward or back along Highway Four impossible, if he stayed where he was, the entire column could be wiped out in a couple of hours.

It seems that only then was Lepage informed from Lang Son by radio that the purpose of his mission was to link up with the break-out from Cao Bang.[5] Since a further attack on Dong Khe was out of the question until the very low cloud lifted so that he could have fighter cover - which, at that time of year, could be days away - he replied that on no account must Charton leave Cao Bang.[6] This was more or less what Charton had been yelling into a microphone for the last two weeks.

Lang Son did not agree. Looking at the maps, it seemed possible for Lepage to drive across country on a trail shown as a dotted line to Quang Liet, by which he could link up with Charton west of Dong Khe in the Coc Xa valley. Lepage therefore ordered 1 BEP to hold the enemy at Na Pa, while he led the Moroccans along the dotted-line trail, as ordered by Lang Son. Nobody as yet understood they were up against odds of at least ten to one. That came when Jeanpierre at Na Pa observed through binoculars a company of Moroccans wiped out by an entire regiment of Viets before they could reach tree cover. A single survivor made it back to Na Pa.

At that moment Jeanpierre understood that 1 BEP was not being more heavily attacked because the main body of Viets had gone after Lepage, trapped in the jungle on an overgrown trail. It seemed that his only hope was for 1 BEP to draw them off. So, at 2200hrs, 1 BEP went over to the attack and took the crest between Na Pa and Lepage, somewhere in the jungle below them. By now 1 BEP was down to 350-400 men, who had not slept for two days and nights, had neither food nor water and were asleep on their feet as they hacked a way with an unreliable compass towards where they thought Lepage was.

At midnight, precisely as ordered, Charton's column of 1,000 men of 3 REI and 600 Moroccans drove and marched out of the smoking ruins of Cao Bang, dragging the long tail of refugees with them.

At 1700 on 3 October Lepage managed to raise Lang Son by radio to give a situation report, but learned to his horror that

Charton had left Cao Bang and was much too far along Highway Four to retreat. By dusk Charton's column had covered 16km in nineteen hours without major incident. A few shells had come their way from guns mounted on the crests of the hills, but Charton was not convinced the Viets' failure to follow up with a ground attack meant that they lacked any sizeable infantry in the immediate vicinity. He confided his uneasiness to Maj Forget, who detailed six legionnaires under Sgt Kress to bring up the rear, isolated from the vanguard, but with a walkie-talkie that had a 5km range at best.

The men set off cheerfully enough despite Kress forbidding them to even taste the many bottles of spirits offered by refugees eager to show gratitude to their protectors. Arriving at the rear of the column, two legionnaires asked permission to *tirer leur coups* with the prostitutes just ahead of them. Kress gave permission - for thirty minutes only.[7] During a local radio check minutes later, Snolaerts the radio man pretended that Kress had sent the two legionnaires on a brief reconnaissance, but they came back sooner than expected. The Chinese girls had been prepared to do a quick turn in the bushes, but the North African madam had forbidden it on the grounds they needed to save their energy for walking the next day! If the men wanted sex, she said in the unambiguous language of her trade, they should use each other.[8]

At 0500hrs a jeep patrolled the length of the column, with orders for everyone to get moving again. At 1000hrs Charton radioed the rear guard with the news that he had at last got through to Lang Son and been ordered to leave the highway and follow the dotted-line trail on the map to Quang Liet and the new RV because Dong Khe was still in Viet hands. The problem was that his map did not correspond with the topography. Kress was ordered to ask the locals whether anyone knew where the trail was.

Through one of the Chinese prostitutes who spoke French and the local languages, they discovered an old man who said he could guide them and drove him to the head of the column, where all the vehicles were being burned and the field artillery that Charton had brought along against orders was being rendered useless.

The trail turned out to be unused for many years, so that the point men had to hand their rifles to comrades and hack a passage through thick secondary growth jungle with *coupe-coupe* jungle knives. Kress was ordered to make sure the rear guard kept the column tightened up, with stragglers being left to their fate, although they would be killed by the Viets for having sided with the French.

Kress was a tough veteran of the Second World War, but even so, he remonstrated, 'What about the kids and pregnant women?'

'Leave them,' Charton ordered.[9]

Disregarding that, first one legionnaire took a child being carried on its pregnant mother's back, then another did the same, until they were all carrying at least one child. For the old and ill, they could do nothing. The laggards gathered into little groups, to have the comfort of not dying alone. Some slit open wrist veins to bleed to death before the Viets got them.

From the south they could hear intermittent gunfire as Giap's artillery harassed Le Page's column fighting its way towards the new RV. The survivors of 1 BEP also converged on it towards nightfall, to find that they were at the top of a 300-metre precipice. After several men fell to their deaths trying to find a way down in the darkness, it was decided to spend the night at the top.

At daybreak, Jeanpierre and Faulques did not like what they saw. The Coc Xa valley was cut in two by a narrow gorge in the middle. All the Viets had to do was wait until Lepage's column entered at one end and Charton's at the other - and wipe them out before they could join forces.

Neither Jeanpierre nor anyone else then knew how many Viet Minh battalions were closing in on them. Sustained harassment for the rest of the day reduced 1 BEP to less than 300 men. The wounded who could not walk received a French bullet in their skulls as a last favour from a comrade. Meanwhile, the Viets were biding their time and building their strength to an unprecedented 20,000-30,000 men with both field and heavy artillery, waiting for Charton to arrive.

That night, Lepage received the first direct radio transmission from Charton, with the news that he hoped to reach Coc Xa next evening, or at latest by dawn on 6 October. From his reaction, Jeanpierre and Faulques realised that 'the gunner' was hoping to be rescued by the people he was supposed to rescue. Repeatedly their men had to strengthen his Moroccans wherever they were under most pressure. Moving at night in single file along a narrow trail in thick jungle, more than 30 paras were unnervingly grabbed one after another and had their throats cut in total silence.

Counting the losses at dawn, 1 BEP was ordered to spearhead a breakthrough to link up with Charton. Without air cover, they were mown down by well-sited mortars and machine guns. Running out of ammunition and resorting to grenades and bayonets, they finally made contact with their fellow-legionnaires of 3 REI in Charton's advance party. Once the panic of Lepage's Moroccans had infected their compatriots in Charton's column the only troops still effectively under control were 3 REI and 1 BEP. Despite fighting against appalling odds in the way that had become traditional in the Legion, their valour was not enough to halt the confusion and slaughter in the Coc Xa valley.

Approximately 6,600 men were killed or taken prisoner. Nobody counted the civilian dead. Twelve officers and 475 men made it safely to That Khe on 8 October, including three officers, three NCOs and twenty-three men of 1 BEP - among them Jeanpierre and Faulques, both wounded. The scale of the disaster at Coc Xa was observed that day by a Morane spotter aircraft piloted courageously down through the clouds into the valley to find signalling panels spread meaninglessly among the debris, from which long columns of prisoners were already being herded away through the jungle into the Viet prison camps.

The toughest officers and men taken prisoner would remain there during four years of watching their less robust comrades growing fewer in number each week, owing to untreated diseases and forced marches from camp to camp on rations of rice, political indoctrination and little else. One of the few 'lucky' ones at Coc Xa was Legion Cpl Zurell. Picked up in the jungle so badly wounded that he seemed bound to die, he was exchanged by the Viets. Repatriated to Algeria, he wanted to live, and somehow pulled through, to volunteer for Vietnam a second time.

In concert with the massacre in the Coc Xa valley, Giap launched attacks all along Highway Four, as Revers had foreseen. Two companies of legionnaires were told to hold That Khe as a base for survivors of the two columns to home in on, but forbidden to go to their rescue under any pretext. On 18 October Carpentier ordered a military and civil evacuation of Highway Four from Lang Son all the way south to the coast. This was sheer panic. Although there was no immediate risk, in some cases magazines and artillery pieces were not even blown up or rendered unserviceable and the Viet Minh, always short of medicine, received in this way a present of 150 tonnes of medicine and surgical supplies.[10]

The arrival of the refugees in Hanoi had people in the terrace cafes talking openly of abandoning the colony. In Paris, the Communist credentials of Giap and his political master Ho Chi Minh made them heroes of the Left Wing, which organised blockades to halt ambulances carrying the repatriated wounded and incited blood donors to refuse their blood to soldiers. Nervous that conscripts would refuse to report for military service en masse, the government passed a law prohibiting any conscript being sent to a war zone[11] - a law that was conveniently forgotten when Algeria erupted in 1954.

A strong man was evidently required to halt the panic in Vietnam. He was found in the person of the universally popular 'King John', correctly known as Gen Jean De Lattre De Tassigny, the most senior Vichy officer to rally to De Gaulle in the Second World War. To counter the Viet Minh promise to take Hanoi by 19 December, his arrival and that of Minister of State Letourneau was marked by a parade of 5,000 troops in the city that evening to show the population who was in charge. Since the VIPs could not drive in from the airport without the route being secured by 2 BEP, it was a debatable point. The legionnaires had so little time to prepare for the parade that they arrived in combat gear and donned their képis only at the last moment for the ceremonies, lit by the headlamps of trucks parked around the parade ground.

That was PR to calm the civilians. De Lattre's personality also calmed the troops. 'I have come,' he said to the captains and the lieutenants, while their seniors kept discreetly to the rear of the reception, 'so that from now on you will have a commander who commands'.[12] His manner and his words went a long way to reassure the fighting soldiers with no respect for the REMFs who had ordered the retreat from Highway Four. They also approved

De Lattre's recipe for combating the Viet Minh by implanting quick-build 'hedgehog' fortresses deep in Viet Minh areas which Giap would have to attack and where he would incur such heavy losses that they would collectively bleed him white. The hedgehogs were not linked by roads because there was no time to build them and anyway the Viets would have cut them, so resupply and reinforcement were by air. Perhaps the real heroes were the pilots who daily risked their lives juggling their Second World War Junkers aircraft between the clouds and mountains in areas where the maps often bore little resemblance to what they could see of the terrain, dropping supplies to the outposts and both men and ammunition into positions under enemy attack. They also dropped napalm, which De Lattre introduced to Vietnam.

For a while, it seemed to be working, so long as one did not look at what the planners called the 'pox map', whose red blotches of Viet Minh-controlled areas grew week by week. With De Lattre's requests for more men never satisfied, he had to plunder the rear to use every man at the front in this new aggressive warfare. In this way 13th Demi-Brigade de le Légion Etrangère - abbreviated to 13 DBLE - lost three of its four battalions, posted to the north.

Changing the rules, Giap stepped up terrorist atrocities in the poorly defended towns and cities. The need to protect civilians in the towns so that business could continue - it was, after all, the reason for being there, especially the rubber plantations so vital for the huge Michelin company - meant abandoning many of the new bases. So Giap won that round.

The forces deployed against him were numerically impressive. At its peak, the expeditionary force numbered 235,721 officers and men including French-officered colonial troops fromVietnam, Laos, Cambodia and North Africa. Of the 18,710 men drawn from Legion regiments around 50% were German. In many units instruction and orders had to be translated into German, or given directly in the language. A government policy to exclude ex-SS men would have been impossible to enforce, since many had had their under-arm blood-group tattoos removed - not that the Legion worried too much about government policy.

Less than 25% of the French population was in favour of what

Le Monde already called 'this dirty war',[13] which was costing France the equivalent of all the Marshall Aid the country was receiving, with the result that its post-war recovery was slower than that of any other European state. Washington had made it clear that more aid would not be forthcoming until France agreed to grant Vietnam complete independence.

That Christmas the legionnaires of 2 BEP had a surprise visitor. De Lattre came in person, not to wish them peace and goodwill but to assure them of his concern. The visit was particularly effective because he came not in a throng of senior officers but with an escort of just two aides-de-camp. None of the men whose spirits he lifted were aware that their C-in-C was dying of cancer, and would be replaced by Gen Raoul Salan in 1952.

In any case, 2 BEP was not in Vietnam when Salan arrived, but in Tunisia, where Habib Bourguiba, who would become president of the country, had been arrested by the French yet again. Commanded by Maj Albert Brothier, who had begun his Legion career in the 22nd Regiment of Foreign Volunteers in 1940, the battalion was not jumping out of aircraft, but tasked with keeping order among a population that wanted the French out. Based in the busy port of Sfax, Lt Bernard Cabiro's company had more trouble with desertion than rioting natives. The Italian legionnaires especially were targeted by local compatriots, who offered to smuggle them on board ships heading for home.

The boredom continued after they were posted back to Sétif in eastern Algeria. Desperate for some action, in August they hitched a lift aboard some US C-119 cargo planes that landed at Annaba[14] so they could make some practice jumps. It was with enormous relief that Cabiro was posted to 1 BEP in Vietnam, where Gen Salan had been replaced for political reasons in May 1953 by Gen Henri Navarre.

Navarre's brilliant career in Intelligence and counter-espionage did not equip him for the job. It is required of commanders whose predecessors have failed in their mission that they should have a 'better idea'. Navarre's was so simple that his masters in Paris had had no trouble grasping it. He explained that De Lattre had done the right things, but on too small a scale. In place of the many 'hedgehogs', so costly in manpower, Navarre planned to build one huge super-fortress in a strategic corner of northwest Vietnam to block Giap's route into neighbouring Laos, where two offensives had been driven back that spring.

The attraction of his master plan over a Paris conference table was that it sounded very 'modern', combining air supremacy, air transportation, air-mobile and parachute troops. Yet officers who knew the country could not believe their ears because they knew the Viets were like ants in their ability to find a way round any obstacle. Navarre did not listen. He was convinced that Giap would be unable to bypass the super-fortress and would therefore go on attacking it until he ran out of men. In a telling metaphor, he explained at every briefing that his super-fortress would be an anvil so big that it would shatter the Viet Minh hammer for good. And the place where this was to happen was called Muong Thanh, but went down in history as Dien Bien Phu - a translation of the French for 'Administrative Centre of Frontier Region'.

Navarre was appointed expressly 'to create the circumstances for a resolution of the Vietnam conflict'. His political masters' confidence in him and his ability to impress the Joint Chiefs of Staff in Washington[15] was reflected in his portrait as Man of the Moment on the 28 September 1953 cover of Time magazine. While he did accelerate the resolution of the conflict, it was in the way opposite to what they had hoped.

To take command of the super-fortress, Navarre brought with him to Vietnam a distinguished commander, who has been called his 'golden boy'. Col Christian Marie Ferdinand de la Croix De Castries was, however, an odd choice - a 51-year-old cavalryman whose strengths did not lie in defence of fixed positions - a fact he repeatedly gave away at DBP by screaming, 'This is an offensive operation,' long after that had become impossible.

The location Navarre chose for his anvil was less than a day's walk from the Laotian border, in a shallow valley dominated by high ground on all sides. Building a base in a valley overlooked by high ground all around defies a basic rule of warfare, but the jovial, self-assured gunner Col Charles Piroth assured the new C-in-C that the 600km of mountain and jungle lying between DBP and Giap's usual supply sources in China meant he could not possibly bring in any heavy artillery. So the anvil was bound to break the hammer, wasn't it?

The valley boasted an abandoned airstrip, last used during the Japanese occupation. However, it lay 300km from Hanoi and 400km from the naval air base at Cat Bi near Haiphong - and thus at the limit for resupply without refuelling by the Dakotas and C-119 'Flying Boxcars', on which the garrison would depend for every bullet, weapon, kilogram of food and litre of clean water. With Piroth's bland reassurance about artillery, nobody was expecting much in the way of Viet anti-aircraft fire, but Col Nicot, responsible for air transportation in Vietnam, warned Navarre that the weather would prevent him flying in anything like the minimum necessary flow of supplies for the garrison once the monsoon broke.

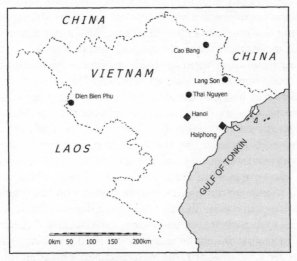

Province of Tonkin, North Vietnam

The cardinal principle of any operation is for the commander to have a clear objective. De Castries seems to have been unclear from the outset. Was he there to reinforce local minority-race anti-Viet Minh guerrillas? They were to be abandoned anyway, as they would later be by the US. If he was there simply to defend the valley and block Viet Minh incursions into French-held Laos, that would have required not the thirteen battalions under his command but roughly fifty battalions.[16]

The battle began with Operation Castor starting at 1030hrs on 20 November 1953 when 65 DC3s and C47s dropped their human cargoes in two zones near the village of Muong Than. The drop of 200 metres was short enough. However, the paras were encumbered not only with their own weapons but also heavy equipment such as parts of mortars and sacks of ammunition. Waddling forward in overloaded aircraft bucking in the morning heat rising from the ground, they were slow out of the side doors of the Dakotas, whose minimum ground speed of 170kph meant each stick of 24 men being spread out over 3km when they hit the ground.

At exactly the same time Navarre was in his office in Hanoi being informed by Rear-Admiral Georges Cabanier, the assistant secretary-general of the Committee of National Defence who had just flown in especially from Paris, that the government expected diplomatic negotiations for ending the war to start in Geneva the following month.[17] Navarre was therefore to do nothing that put the expeditionary force at unnecessary risk.

Somehow, Navarre talked Cabanier round, relying on the traditional freedom of action given to French commanders in the field. Paris did not learn that Castor had been launched until 1630hrs Vietnam time. Why did Navarre not halt this operation and order the men already on the ground to march out via Laos, since the airstrip was unserviceable - or make it serviceable and then evacuate them by air? Did he believe himself capable of resolving the entire Vietnam conflict single-handedly despite Cabanier's message from Paris? Or, was he in a 'no win' situation, under pressure to gain leverage for the talks, yet without taking any risks? Was that why he launched a large operation code-named Atlante in south central Vietnam and other lesser operations all at the same time, thus depriving himself of any reserves for DBP?

Thereafter, his reaction to every setback was to order more of the same - until he and Gen Cogny, commanding the military area in which DBP lay, were not on polite speaking terms. At one point, Cogny told Navarre that the only thing stopping him punching his superior in the face was respect for the stars he wore.

Whatever Navarre's reasoning, his underestimation of the

enemy was to cost thousands of lives. The scene was set for tragedy, but on 29 November there was a chance to avert it when Ho Chi Minh told a Swedish journalist that he was prepared to end the conflict, providing the French would discuss complete independence. Since they had already, however insincerely, promised this to their corrupt Vietnamese puppet-emperor Bao Dai[18], there was no reason not to sit down immediately and talk. But they didn't - and the tragedy became inevitable.

Chapter 2

YOU GOTTA DIE SOMETIME

Dien Bien Phu: November 1953-April 1954

Since it was used to save French lives, the Legion often drew the short straw, but at DBP all the straws were short. Casualties were incurred before the first stick of paras reached the ground. What had looked from the air like black-clad peasants working their fields turned out to be Viet Minh *bo-doi* soldiers training with Chinese AK 47s and US machine guns and mortars from stocks supplied to Chiang Kai-Chek's Kuomintang forces in China or recovered from Korean battlefields. With their instructors, they sacrificed themselves so that the HQ staff of Giap's 148th Regiment could escape. As the gunfire died away, the valley fell eerily silent.

Navarre had not entrusted the establishment of the camp to De Castries, but to Brigadier Jean Gilles, the veteran commander of one of De Lattre's 'hedgehogs' at Na Son. He jumped into DBP on Day Two, bringing with him a bad heart problem exacerbated by constant overwork, to do a job he had not wanted. On paper, it was bad enough. Once on the ground, during Cogny's first visit Gilles told his boss that the sooner he was replaced, the better he would like it. Having spent six months living mainly underground in the command bunker of the Na Son 'hedgehog', he knew what he was talking about.

Na Son had been a conventional fortress with artillery, minefields and concrete strong-points all within a defensible perimeter, but DBP was a mess. The plan in Gilles' hand showed a number of *separate* strong-points on various raised parts of the valley bottom, all bearing names of women important in Navarre's life. Around the main airstrip were clustered Claudine, Dominique, Eliane and Huguette. Northwest of Huguette was a complex of defensive positions manned by White Thai colonial troops. Gabrielle and Béatrice lay 2km to the north of Huguette, and were to be manned by 450 legionnaires of 3/13 DBLE. Protecting the secondary airstrip 6km to the south, would be more legionnaires at Isabelle under Col André Lalande, a veteran of 13 DBLE throughout the Second World War. The distances between them meant that, although they had interlocking fields of fire, each could be surrounded separately.

On Day Eight 675 paras of 1 BEP under Maj Guiraud dropped in to contribute their various skills to the clearing of the airstrip and securing of the valley. With the thickly forested hills all around, their first reactions were negative. Zurell - now a sergeant in 4th Company - was reminded of Dong Khe, where he had lost one of every three comrades. His swarthy company commander Bernard Cabiro, now promoted to captain and nicknamed 'Le Cab', stood a moment looking west after gathering up his 'chute. 'That,' he announced to his men, 'is the only way out of this dump - on foot, via Laos.'

The Black Thais living in Muong Thanh - a picturesque collection of thatched long-houses on stilts beside the Nam Youm river - returned to the valley after the initial battle, women and children first. The men were more cautious, suspicious of occupiers, whether Viet or French. Like troops all over the world, the paras spoiled the wide-eyed kids clothed all in black with sweets and chocolate. The Vietnamese paras of Col Marcel Bigeard's 6th Battalion of Colonial Parachutists had dropped in with kilos of sea salt in their packs. Here in the highlands, it was a commodity worth its own weight in opium and Muong Thanh was the biggest opium market in Vietnam.

For the first weeks all was relatively quiet in the surrounding hills. The Viets were there all right, because 1 BEP's probing patrols found plenty of freshly dug trenches and bunkers. The trails were obviously well-frequented and they heard the ceaseless sound of distant chopping as Giap's men hacked out new ones. So effective was the Viets' camouflage and use of tree cover that no one in the valley had any idea he was mobilising 260,000 civilians as coolies and requisitioning 20,000 bicycles, each transporting a load up to 250 kilos, which would otherwise have required five porters at least. In this way, he brought to DBP more than 200 artillery pieces bigger than 57mm broken down into parts and several batteries of Soviet Katyusha rocket launchers.[1] Against this, Piroth had six batteries of six 105mm guns and a single battery of four 155mm howitzers, plus three heavy mortar companies. For reconnaissance there were two Cricket light aircraft, supported by a handful of Bearcat fighters for local air cover.

With bulldozers dropped from the C-119s - one which escaped its parachutes on the way down dug itself inextricably deep into a rice paddy to everyone's amusement - the airstrip of interlocking metal strips was usable on 25 November, three days ahead of schedule. On the same day a Legion patrol noticed a stiffening of Viet resistance and the Thais of Muong Thanh took off with their French Catholic missionary to build a new village several kilometres to the south, where the para medics ran a free clinic in the mornings, giving vaccinations and simple medical care.

The anti-Viet White Thai guerrillas manning outlying posts around the valley were the first to be attacked. On 10 December, one company of them under Sgt Blanc in Muong Pon, a village north of DBP, radioed for help. Capt Erwan Bergot commanded the main relief column which was finally halted at 1800hrs the following day after fighting its way through 11km of ambushes, forced to leave the road and go cross-country through hilly jungle, criss-crossed with watercourses, mostly dry. They were still 10km - or thirty-six precious hours' march - short of Muong Pon, when a Piper Cub spotter plane overhead signalled significant concentrations of Viets ahead. Sgt Blanc radioed that the garrison had only six rounds left per man. From DBP he was promised a munitions drop at dawn. Bergot decided to make the final push at 0400hrs, hoping to catch the Viets off-balance with several renegade former *bo-dois* at the point of his column to confuse the opposition in the dark.

At dawn on 13 December, they were sleepwalking from sheer exhaustion when the sound of heavy firing warned them that the final assault was being made. With them under observation all the way, the timing was no accident. At 1100hrs they still had one kilometre to go, when the Viets melted away. At noon Bergot's men finally entered the village, to find it empty but for piles of cartridge cases, dirty field dressings and blood-soaked bandages. No trace of Sgt Blanc or the White Thais, living or dead.

Shuddering at the familiar scene, Sgt Zurell said, 'This is how it all started at Dong Khe.'[2]

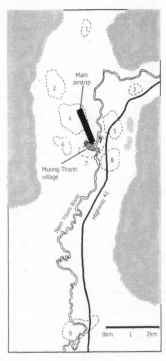

French positions at Dien Bien Phu, November 1953-May 1954

Shaded areas show surrounding high ground. Dotted outlines are the French positions:

1 - Gabrielle; 2 - Anne-Marie; 3 - Béatrice; 4 - Huguette;
5 - Dominique; 6 - Françoise ;
7 - Claudine; 8 - Eliane; 9 - Isabelle

As demolition of existing buildings and excavation of bunkers in the main valley progressed, the visitors came in droves, driving Lt Col Gaucher of 13 DBLE to swear, 'I'm a bloody tourist guide.

I know what they're all going to say. The ministers ask whether we can hold on. The vote-collecting politicians murmur, "France is counting on you." As for the Yanks, they poke a stick in the roofs of the dugouts to measure the thickness of earth and then look worried.'[3] Gilles wanted to finish the job and be off. He left on 8 December and the stream of VIP visitors continued with Castries showing them round. Lesser mortals were farmed out to his colonels.

On 24 December there was not a single para in the valley because 1 BEP and the rest were across the border in Laos on Operation Regattas - a link-up with a Laotian column from Luang Prabang. Hard on the paras' trail, the Viets gave them just time to shake hands with the Laotians before harassing them all the way home across country, every track being mined and ambushed. That was the last regular offensive patrol.[4] From then on, DBP was an entrenched camp, fighting for its life.

Navarre's Christmas present was three Chaffee M-24 tanks with 75mm guns, flown in as spare parts on 28 December and rebuilt in twenty-four hours by mechanics of 13 DBLE in underground workshops. Seven more M-24s were to follow. The majority of legionnaires being German, their delayed Christmas was celebrated with decorated branches, home-made cribs and small presents - and the singing of *Lili Marlene, Deutschland über Alles and Stille Nacht, heilige Nacht* ringing out across the valley to the godless enemy. In return, echoing from psywar loudspeakers in the Viet front-line trenches came the voices of deserters speaking French, German, Arabic and all the other languages of the colonial troops, with the Christmas message, 'Comrades, why do you go on fighting? Do you want to die for Michelin?' Rubber from the Michelin plantations was the most important single export of the country.

As a reminder that soldiers can also be hurt by personal tragedy, Maj Pégot of 3/13th had lost his wife, swept overboard from the ship bringing her to Vietnam earlier in the year. Keeping him company on his first New Year's Eve as a widower, Gaucher was discussing the report of Sgt Maj Fels in 11 Company, who had just returned from a night recce with three other LURPs. Only 8km from DBP they had observed not a few porters struggling along a trail under heavy loads but convoys of trucks running through the darkness with headlights full on.[5]

On 27 January the French positions were completely surrounded, and resuppliable only by air. Yet, 31 January was VIP day with Colonial Secretary Marc Jacquet flying in with Ambassador Maurice Dejean and Navarre himself. Even Under-Secretary of State for War Chevigné came to rubberneck, and was advised like all the others to leave before 1600hrs when, punctual as a church clock, a single gun in the hills always fired a few rounds. The defenders dubbed it 'the lone Jap', believing it a solitary relic from the Japanese occupation that had fallen into Viet hands.

Giap was in no hurry because he needed time to build up supplies and train his troops. A network of trails beneath the jungle canopy had to be constructed. Most importantly, by waiting for the start of the monsoon - during the six-month rainy season the valley received more than 1.5 *metres* of rainfall - the low cloud and heavy downpour would make air support and resupply impossible on most days. By the second week of March, when Giap was still offering to talk[6], the Viets had dug more than 100km of trenches around the northern strong-points of Anne-Marie, Béatrice and Gabrielle. At this point, De Castries had 13,000 men - a cocktail of Algerian, black Senegalese and Vietnamese infantry, three Legion infantry battalions plus 1 BEP and 2 BEP and other French and colonial paras - all surrounded by four Viet divisions.

'Soldier's comforts' amounted to not much more than stacks of much-thumbed old French magazines until the arrival of the BMC - *bordel mobile de campagne*. The pioneers had constructed an underground brothel with cubicles. The pretty girls in *ao-dais* arrived with their madam, a slim and elegant lady whose golden sandals were soon begrimed with the ubiquitous dust, above which she delicately held the folds of her pink satin *kai hao* with one hand while the other kept the sun off her face with a large black umbrella. They were welcomed by the MO of 1/2 REI, whose job would now include the VD checks. Once they were installed, Standing Orders specified the hours for different units and ranks.[7] As one legionnaire remarked seeing the girls totter down the steps of their DC3 on their high heels, all the camp lacked now was a garrison cinema.

Wounded in a minor operation on 5 March, Cabiro lost consciousness after seeing his right foot apparently attached to the leg only by a strip of muscle. He came to in a hospital bed in Hanoi, too horrified at the thought of being crippled for life to ask an orderly to pull back the sheets and show him the damage. As a fair example of military humour, when the orthopaedic surgeon did his rounds and showed the patient some toes sticking out of the plaster, Cabiro asked if that meant he still had a right foot and was informed that the nurses always stuck some spare toes into the plaster, so as not to traumatise amputee patients.

The anaesthetist for his first operation was the fiancée of Roger Faulques who, on turning up at the bedside to announce his imminent returning to DBP, was told by the normally positive Cabiro, 'Don't go. It's a fuck-up.' Faulques landed back in the camp next day in the middle of a fire-fight.

On the afternoon of 13 March Giap's ally the monsoon arrived and the humidity turned to a sticky drizzle that magicked out of the dirt buzzing swarms of blue flies hungry for the feast that awaited them. Every six seconds a shell landed on the French positions from the 105mm and 75mm howitzers dug in on the reverse slopes of the surrounding hills. Once the French artillery had been neutralised, they would move to the forward slopes and fire 'down the tubes'. Later still, they would be inside the French positions.

On Béatrice, held by 3/13 DBLE, Lt Col Gaucher and Maj Pégot were watching the Viet trenches closing around them like a pincer. It was the last thing they saw. They and most of the headquarters staff were killed when the command post took a direct hit. Casualties rose to thirty-six dead and wounded as the ruins of the position became a scrap-yard of steel fragments in knee-deep mud with the air stinking of cordite and the vaporised contents of dead men's bowels.

Simultaneously Giap launched between 5,000 and 6,000 *bo-dois* in waves against Gabrielle, whose outlying blockhouse was captured, retaken by a battalion of legionnaires and lost again. The next target was Gabrielle itself. Instead of human waves, this time Giap used artillery and infiltration. A direct hit on the command post from a 75mm wheeled bazooka dragged to within 150 metres killed all the command team. Anne-Marie fell in turn. By 1600 the airstrip was closed to traffic, with the control tower and radio beacon destroyed. The Bearcat fighters had been destroyed on the ground by Viet artillery, with only two of the light observation craft able to take off and make it back to Hanoi.

The 'lone Jap' had turned out to be one gun of each Viet battery in turn registering its allotted targets in the valley. The resultant accuracy caused an appalling toll among the crews of the French gun-pits, ringed by sandbags for protection against mortars, but neither dug in nor covered. Having lost two 105mm guns, a quarter of his 75s and a third of the 120mm mortars, one-armed Col Piroth went from pit to pit, apologising to the survivors - and then retired to his quarters, where he pulled the pin out of a grenade with his teeth and held it to his stomach.

On 14 March 1954, the second day of the Viet offensive, De Castries was so out of control that he ceased to function as commander, but isolated himself in his bunker, dining off the family porcelain in a dream-world of denial. Instead of sacking him and parachuting in a replacement, Navarre promoted him to Brigadier. The forceful para Lt Col Pierre Langlais became the *de facto* commander. When criticised afterwards, his answer was typically para: the brass in Hanoi could have dropped in another commander any time, if they did not like what he was doing![8] It is largely to his credit that the valley was held for fifty-four days in the face of overwhelming enemy superiority.

On 15 March communication with the legionnaires on Béatrice was lost as one radio after another was silenced with the loss of 326 men. The last call came from an operator of 9th Company, calling in the fire on himself as the Viets overran his position. It is no exaggeration to say that this was felt by the entire garrison to be an omen: if the Legion could not hold, what hope was there for the rest of them? By the evening, Anne-Marie and Gabrielle, defended by Algerian *tirailleurs*, had also been overrun.

Within days, the main strip was unusable in the daytime owing to accurate shelling on each aircraft that landed in daylight. Medical evacuations continued at night, thanks to a handful of pilots and a team of specialised and very courageous nurses, one of whom was to become the heroine of DBP. By 23 March the road linking the French positions, and along which all supplies had to pass, was also unusable in daylight, even for the volunteer ambulance drivers from 13 DBLE.

The former Resistance hero Col Bigeard, whose Vietnamese paras had dropped in on 20 November and been withdrawn at the end of December, dropped in with them for a second time. On 10 April Cabiro was lying on a stretcher at Bach Mai airbase, waiting to be flown to Saigon en route for France when several former comrades from 2 BEP broke ranks and crossed the hard standing to shake his hand with that peculiar duck-walk imposed by wearing two 'chutes and bulky gear. Shortly afterwards they were in the air heading for DBP in support of their comrades in 1 BEP, eroded by being used as a mobile reserve from the day they dropped in.

They were not the last legionnaires to parachute into the beleaguered camp. A unique if irregular flow of volunteers materialised from the strangest sources, including 120 men from 1st Company of 3 REI and 207 officers and men from 5 REI who had no parachute training. Oddly, the rate of casualties on landing was no higher than for regular paratroops. The voluntary reinforcements continued to arrive until 6 May, even though the later volunteers knew they had a one-way ticket. Their motto was '*Crever pour crever, autant crever avec les copains.*' You gotta die sometime, it might as well be with your mates.

In a Saigon military hospital, Cabiro met the elegant wife of Gen Gambiez, whose own son had been killed when an Evasan helicopter in which he was being evacuated after being wounded at DBP was blown out of the air by a Viet shell. In the tradition of service wives, Madame Gambiez had put aside her own grief to come and comfort the pilot, who had lost a leg and was in the room next door to Cabiro.

It was only a matter of time until even medical evacuations from DBP became impossible. On 26 March the last aircraft managed to take off with a load of badly wounded men. The next Evasan flight was not so lucky: 28-year-old *convoyeuse* nurse Geneviève de Galard could not fly back to Hanoi with her wounded men after a direct hit prevented their Dakota from taking off. Reporting for duty to Surgeon-Major Paul Grauwin, operating twenty-three hours out of twenty-four in mud over his ankles, naked to the waist in the stifling humid heat of the underground operating theatre, she then calmly supervised the main surgical ward of forty beds, with frequent electricity cuts and drugs and even dressings in short supply. Personally nursing the most severely wounded men, she was constantly being asked by blinded multiple amputees who had been healthy young men, *'Vais-je vivre, mademoiselle?'* Am I going to live, miss? Mam'zelle became her nickname. And Grauwin, the senior surgeon on the post, who never asked whether the body on the table in front of him was French or Viet, received the nickname from his Cambodian patients of *bac-si kim* - the doctor who stitches.

He wrote of this time: 'Blood, vomit and faeces mixed with the mud made up a frightful compound that stuck to the boots in thick layers. I shall never forget the martyrdom of men wounded in the thorax, trying in vain to get into their lungs the air and oxygen on which their lives depended; and my oxygen cylinders were emptied at a crazy rate. I had to put these patients in the farthest of the Air Commandos' shelters, where the main passage was not covered over. When I saw them again, a pleural effusion was gently taking them to their deaths.'[9]

'I saw a long line of muddy statues - but they were moving, groping their way along the walls. Under their layers of mud they were quite naked. One of them had a leg missing. How had he managed to get here? Another had only one eye. Then men with plaster on their shoulders, their thorax, their legs. There was mud over everything, dressings and plaster.'[10]

'After the last operation I staggered half-conscious towards the rectangle of grey light down there at the end of the passage. Then I heard a small voice whispering somewhere behind me, "Oh, I would like to go to sleep and never, never wake up again." I turned and saw Geneviève leaning against the wall behind me, quietly crying.'[11]

From the night of Geneviève's arrival air drops of supplies brought in about twelve tons daily, or one-fifth of the minimum requirement. The pouring rain and low cloud forced aircraft to fly in low where they were sitting ducks for the anti-aircraft batteries.

By the end of the battle, the French had lost sixty-two aircraft with another 167 damaged. So short of machines and men were they that crews were hired from US-operated Civil Air Transport Company, whose pilots said the intensity of Viet Minh anti-aircraft fire over the approaches to the valley was worse than they had known in Korea or the Second World War over Germany.

One counter-attack by tanks and infantry including men from 13 DBLE was made to take out some of the anti-aircraft positions in the hills near Claudine. Five 20mm guns and various machine guns were destroyed and 300 enemy killed, but it made no difference. And when Claudine was abandoned, one of the last men of 13 DBLE to leave said, 'We killed masses, but always more came, jumping over the bodies of the others.'[12]

Knee-deep in water, slipping and sliding in the mud, the Viet Minh sappers inched their trenches nearer and nearer to Dominique and Eliane. On 30 March when the final human wave came in, the colonial gunners depressed the barrels of their guns to fire horizontally. This and the scything fire from the quad-fifties - a Second World War mating of four .50 calibre machine guns with synchronised feeds - caused the Viets to retreat blindly into a newly laid minefield. Survivors of 2 BEP, 8th Assault Regiment and 6th Colonial Paras managed to retake the hill called Eliane 2 at the cost of several hundred lives. They need not have bothered. Under cover of a mortar barrage, the Viets retook it anyway.

From the west, Huguette was the next to be assaulted. There, the surgical station was overwhelmed with more than 1,000 men needing attention. Such was the stench of unburied corpses, rotting body parts removed during surgery, the maggots pastured on wounds in place of unobtainable antibiotics and the excrement everywhere underfoot that many walking wounded preferred to return to their companies, where at least they could breathe the air.

Between 2,000 and 3,000 Thai, Algerian, Moroccan, Vietnamese and European soldiers deserted. Since North African and European would-be deserters could not hope to pass through the lines, they dug holes in the banks of the river where they were unlikely to be shelled, and lived there on food scrounged from the daily drops. Known as the rats of the Nam Youm, they even organised a brothel for non-European troops without any interference because nobody had the energy or time to police the area. The Legion too had its deserters. 13 DBLE recorded seventy-seven during the siege. If they could make it through the lines without getting shot or blown to pieces, those who were Germans stood a good chance of being repatriated by the Viets to Communist East Germany.

Resupply was way below critical level. Owing to the ring of anti-aircraft batteries, the drops were made from a not-always-safe altitude of 8,500 feet, so that frequently men, ammunition and food landed in Viet territory. Many of the 105mm shells that landed in the valley to telling effect had been acquired by the Viets in this way. C-119 Flying Boxcars dropped six-ton loads of napalm on the Viet trenches. Had this been the dry season, the hills would have been alive to the sound of crackling flesh, but in the monsoon conditions only local damage resulted, as Giap had foreseen.

On 23 April the last counter-attack was made by 2 BEP as State Department counsellor Douglas MacArthur II was listening in Paris to a plea that US Navy planes be painted in French colours, with their pilots temporarily enrolled in the Legion, to bombard the Viet positions around DBP for two or three days without formally involving the USA.[13] The Pentagon, in response to French pleas for aid, also worked out Operation Vulture involving the use of Arclight bombardments by eighty B-29s flying out of the Philippines to drop conventional HE bombs and also nuclear weapons.[14] Given the intermingling of French and Viet positions by this stage, let alone the political implications, nothing came of either plan.

On the night Huguette 1 was overwhelmed, Castries came to life and ordered 2 BEP to lead the counter-attack, crossing the exposed main landing strip in small groups. A snafu with the battalion commander having his radio tuned to the wrong frequency left the legionnaires unable to 'turn off' a friendly bombardment, in which they took 150 casualties. The survivors were subsequently merged with 1 BEP.

On 29 April Geneviève de Galard was ordered to report to Castries, who personally invested her with the Légion d'Honneur and Croix de Guerre, the citation describing her as 'a pure incarnation of the heroic virtues of French nursing'.[15] The following day the Legion made her an honorary legionnaire first class - as they did Col Bigeard at the same time. *Paris Match* called Geneviève the only woman at Dien Bien Phu, omitting to mention the score of Vietnamese prostitutes from the BMC who also nursed the wounded.[16]

One day later, with the monsoon in full, drenching power, the French positions had been reduced to parts of Huguette, Dominique and two high points of Eliane. Active combatants were down to fewer than 2,000, mostly wounded at least once. On Huguette, Col Guiraud had a total of 500 legionnaires from 1 BEP and 2 BEP, plus 140 Moroccans. A stranger mixture was holding the outpost Juno on the banks of the Nam Youm: 150 White Thais and twenty aircrew, marooned there since their planes had been destroyed on the strip by Viet guns.

The French artillery had enough shells left for twenty-four hours. Malnutrition and dysentery were taking their toll. One tank was still in running order and a few guns still firing. At Isabelle, the southern strongpoint, another 1,000 men in similar condition were defending a quarter of a square mile. De Castries kept muttering that a twelve-hour break would mean a relief column could be got through to them.

That evening the Viet radio operators monitoring the French frequencies were surprised to hear, not terse orders and pleas for support or ammunition in code or the legionnaires' slang that passed for a code, but a message in clear grammatical French, delivered in the measured tones of the senior Legion officer Col Lemeunier. Speaking into a 300 military communications set, he read a story for all to hear: 'The French army was besieging Puebla in Mexico. The Legion was ordered to patrol and make secure 20km of roads used by supply convoys…'

All the legionnaires listening knew by heart this story of a battle at Camarón in Mexico that ended, 'The Emperor Napoleon III decided that the name of Camerone should be inscribed on the flag of the Foreign Regiment and that in addition the names of Danjou, Vilain and Maudet should be carved in gold on the walls of Les Invalides in Paris.'

Clean-shaven for the first time in weeks, legionnaires able to hear the message toasted the Legion in whatever was still drinkable. Had all their comrades in misfortune been fellow-legionnaires, many would have been tempted to *faire Camerone* and go down fighting as their predecessors had done in Mexico. But that would have been to condemn also all the other men in French uniform. Many wondered whether the Viets would be as gallant victors as the Mexicans at Camarón had been.

They were not to know, but the siege had only lasted so long because Giap too had his problems: he was short of even untrained conscripts and running out of ammunition for the artillery. The huge losses of men and materiel were worrying Ho and the Party Central Committee. To raise morale, commissars gave rousing lectures on agrarian reform, promising that every peasant would be the master of his own land after the French were driven out.

The international Communist holiday of 1 May was the day chosen by Giap to launch the final push. After a heavy bombardment from Katyusha rocket launchers and guns now sited well within what had been the French positions, suicide volunteers threw themselves on the wire to make a human bridge for the men following. Wave after wave of Viets pressed relentlessly into the shrinking camp. Too late, Navarre considered implementing Operation Albatross - a last-ditch breakout, which would have meant leaving the wounded and medical staff for the able-bodied to escape through the Viet lines. But eastwards that was out of the question and lately Giap had deliberately increased the depth of the siege lines to the west, between DBP and friendly Laos.

On 4 May the combined Legion paras on what remained of Huguette went down under a final human wave attack by Giap's so-called Iron Division that had taken Dong Khe. On the evening of 6 May, with the French holding only part of the central area and Isabelle, the final assault was launched as overhead five Dakotas carrying the last 100 men to volunteer for DBP turned back, unable to make it through the anti-aircraft fire.

Dominique and Eliane finally fell on 7 May. With the Viets within grenade-throwing range of Castries' HQ, he finally ordered a cease-fire for 1730hrs, which was communicated to Giap. Those still able to do so destroyed any serviceable weapons

51

and ammunition, burying parts like mortar base plates that could not be destroyed. The two M-24 tanks still working had their oil drained and the engines run until they seized up. An unaccustomed silence assaulted the ears. Men crawled out of holes and collapsed bunkers to enjoy the forgotten pleasures of standing up bare-headed or urinating in the open air. Others refused to emerge until a shouted warning was followed by a burst of automatic fire into whatever hole was their refuge. Despite the thousands of armed male and female Viet Minh soldiers rounding them up, some soldiers were so deep in denial that one MP threatened to place on a charge a Nam Youm rat he recognised as having filched medical supplies during an air drop - until forcibly reminded by a French-speaking *can-bo* commissar that he had no authority over anyone, including himself, from then on.

A relatively small number of prisoners were shot, bayoneted or beaten to death, some for threatening their captors, others because of a linguistic misunderstanding or threatening gesture. Given the bitterness of the fighting and the scale of casualties suffered by the Viet Minh, it is a tribute to their discipline that more prisoners were not summarily executed. Vietnamese prisoners in colonial regiments were immediately segregated for re-education.[17] Those in French regiments were treated as French. Most, if not all, of the whores who had helped Geneviève nurse the wounded were killed. Some, it is true, had borne arms at the end, but they were killed because they were women and thus the natural target of angry men with weapons in their hands.

Only Isabelle held out until 0800hrs on 8 May, to allow a party from 3rd Battalion of 3 REI to get away through the lines in darkness. About 600 men managed to escape, but the price was high: many of the wounded manning weapons to cover their leaving were afterwards shot for having contravened the cease-fire arrangement. That day at Legion HQ in the Quartier Viénot of Sidi bel-Abbès Col Paul Gardy ordered every man to present arms in honour of the lost colours: 2nd and 3rd Battalions of 13 DBLE, 2nd and 3rd Battalions of 3 REI, 1st battalion of 2 REI, 1st and 2nd BEP. That was not the full list, because the volunteers had come from many other units, but it was enough.

Ho and Giap had gone all out to end the siege by 8 May, aware that it was the ninth anniversary of VE Day - the Allied victory over Nazi Germany - and that a major French defeat on such a date would be taken in Asia and many other parts of the world as a sign that the days of European colonialism were over.

Red Cross Dakotas evacuated 858 severely wounded men and brought in medical supplies. As the long columns of POWs were herded out of the valley, even those with leg and foot wounds had to ford the Nam Youm because the still intact Bailey bridge across the river was a filming location. An East European film unit was recording a dramatised re-enactment of the last assault. Offered cigarettes to play the parts of themselves, the prisoners refused - although later they would take part, waving white flags as they shambled past the cameras near their prison camps, for reasons that can be guessed. Leaving DBP, some men were not fully dressed or lacked head covering or shoes; others had prudently packed food and toilet articles and changes of underwear in kitbags. One surprise punishment was to find that shaving was forbidden because their Vietnamese captors considered it a sign of intention to escape, no natives having facial hair.

One small group of legionnaires from Isabelle fought their way out and walked through the jungle into friendly Laos, only to find that it was not so friendly. At the first French post they encountered, they were accused by the Deuxième Bureau major in command of being deserters because they were not properly dressed in uniform with clean weapons, their clothes and footwear having been torn to pieces on the journey. Stunned to be locked up behind bars after all they had been through, they learned that the real reason he wanted them out of the way was in case they had seen too much of a drugs cartel he was running. Killing their guards with their bare hands, they grabbed their confiscated weapons and walked back into Vietnam.

Geneviève de Galard refused both indoctrination and repatriation offers, saying that she preferred to stay and nurse the wounded. Against her will, she was liberated on 24 May. Dressed in para fatigues with sandals on her bare feet, coming down the steps of the Red Cross Dakota at Luang Prabang in Laos, she showed less emotion at being released than three of her fellow-nurses who had come to greet her. Besieged by astronomical offers from French and American press agencies for her exclusive story, she refused, saying that her job was to nurse the men, not make money out of their suffering.

A one-on-one personal war was still ongoing. Aged ten, Eliahu Itzkowitz was the sole survivor when his family and 53,000 other Jews of Kishinev in Rumania were massacred after the German occupation of Moldavia in 1941. In 1945, still an adolescent, Itzkowitz tracked down the son of the man he blamed, an Iron Guardist named Stanescu, and killed him. After serving five years in prison, Itzkowitz emigrated to Israel and joined the paras. From a French immigrant who had served in the Legion he learned of a Rumanian NCO who answered to Stanescu's description. Applying for a transfer to the Israeli navy, Itzkowitz jumped ship in Genoa and made his way to Marseille to enlist.

Choosing his time, for he had no wish to spend more time in prison, he was in 3 REI during June 1954 patrolling Highway Three northeast of Hanoi when an ambush forced the patrol to take cover. Alone with his corporal, Itzkowitz asked him in Rumanian during a lull in the firing, 'Aren't you Stanescu?'

Caught off-guard, the corporal admitted that he was, and asked, 'Who are you?'

'I'm one of the Jews you missed in Chisinau (the old name for Kishinev).'

Nobody noticed that the wounds which killed the corporal had come from a French weapon. Itzkowitz finished his service with a certificate of good conduct, and returned to Israel.

The defeat at DBP brought down the government of Joseph Laniel on 12 June. Pierre Mendès-France became Prime Minister with the brief to end the war and get the POWs home, cost what it may. By now few voters wanted anything to do with Vietnam. A producer who wanted to make a film of Geneviève's story with Leslie Caron as lead got the same brush-off she had given the glossy magazines, but government pressure forced her to undergo a ticker-tape welcome on 26 July in New York and a visit to the White House in an attempt to fan the dying embers of US support.

They call it the art of the possible. Mendès-France ordered the French spokesman at Geneva not to raise problems by trying to protect the non-French anti-Viet guerrillas and racial minorities who had sided with France. They had to be written off - for the same reasons that nobody asked the Viet Minh delegation why, if they had taken 11,721 prisoners on 8 May, they were returning only 3,290 in August.

What happened to the other 8,431? A comrade of Cabiro's who had been in the camps for four years since the debacle of Highway Four was only returned in September because fellow officers bombarded the French armistice commission with specific enquiries about him. A few incredibly tough individuals trickled back to France over the years with stories of their suffering that no one wanted to hear. Others returned smeared with the stigma of having become indoctrinated, whether by political conviction or in the hope of better rations or other favourable treatment. Outsiders who expected the men who had suffered under these turncoats in the camps to attack them physically or in print were disappointed.

They simply said, 'We're the only ones who can judge them, and we're not going to.' No outsider had any idea what the pressures had been in this war that had cost the lives of so many legionnaires.

Erwan Bergot, commanding the heavy mortar company of the combined BEP, was comparatively lucky. Taken prisoner on 8 May, he was placed in a POW column designated *Convoi 42* which left Dien Bien Phu 400-strong. During the 700km march to Re-education Camp 42, eighty-three men died of wounds and disease. A further 250 succumbed to malaria, dysentery and malnutrition in the camp. He and seventy-two others survived to be liberated.[18]

Chapter 3

TERRORISM AND TORTURE

Algeria, 1954–1957

The lucky legionnaires who survived the Viet Minh POW camps soon had reason to recall the *can-bos* announcing during obligatory political 'education' classes that the banner of worldwide anti-colonial revolution would next be raised in Algeria. Like much of what they had to listen to in these sessions, the idea seemed preposterous: Tunisia and Morocco were protectorates with increasing internal autonomy, but Algeria was administratively French territory, as well as being the home of the Legion. It was unthinkable that an insurgency could wrest away control of the three *départements* of Oran, Algiers and Constantine, which had been part of France for thirty years longer than mainland Savoie – and never been annexed by a neighbour, as had Alsace and Lorraine from 1871-1919 and 1940-1944.

That it all happened so bloodily was partly because, whereas the French colonial administration had governed Morocco, like the Romans, through the existing power structure, Algeria had not been a homogeneous nation before the French conquest, during which all traditional authority had been eradicated. There was thus no curb on the generation of political activists whose violence was directed 1954-1962 not only against Europeans but also other factions in the revolutionary camp.

To be exact, the violence started on 8 May 1945 when the VE Day[1] parade in Sétif – a market town in eastern Algeria – was disrupted by a demonstration of young Muslims waving independence banners. The heavy-handed Gendarmerie riposte, in which several demonstrators were shot dead, led to two days of rioting, rape and arson that left 100 Europeans dead and many more wounded. Before detachments of legionnaires and other military units succeeded in completely restoring order three weeks later, at least 1,500 Muslims had been killed.[2] When military governor Gen Duval afterwards warned the European diehards that their attitudes would have to change, he foreshadowed a three-way war between the army, the settlers and the Arabs, in which each side fought both the others.

It seemed for several years of sporadic violence that Duval had been pessimistic. Then, exactly as prophesied by the *can-bos* in the camps, the violence broke like a storm a few months after their warnings. Between midnight and 0200hrs on 1 November 1954, thirty synchronised terrorist attacks on police and military installations woke people all over Algeria to the realisation that they were living in a war zone. Responsibility was claimed by Le Front de Libération Nationale.

Most of FLN's 20,000 members – from a population of nine million – were hesitant about their extremist leadership. Later that day, a couple of French teachers from an Arab school were dragged off a bus in the Aurès Mountains and machine-gunned, together with the *caïd* or local official they had been sitting with. The wife survived her wounds after lying beside her dead husband on the mountainside for several hours.

The idea of two European civilians being randomly murdered like this sent a shiver through peoples' spines. With only 37,000 troops in Algeria – before the end of the emergency, half a million soldiers would be sent or raised there – Paris played down the events of All Saints Day, so that they made only two columns in *Le Monde* and even less in *L'Express*. On 12 November Prime Minister Pierre Mendès-France stated categorically that, whereas the secession demanded by the FLN was impossible, reforms would be introduced to improve living and political conditions of Muslim Algerians. To this end, the new liberal governor Jacques Soustelle was prepared to talk with all sections of the population. Yet, less than two months after his arrival in February, a state of emergency was declared on 31 March 1955, placing the Aurès Mountains under military law, with the army authorised to destroy villages and move the inhabitants into 'resettlement areas'.[3]

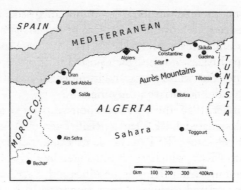

The Algerian war 1954-62

The reply of the Armée de Libération Nationale – ALN was the armed wing of FLN – came on 20 August with attacks all over eastern Algeria claiming the lives of seventy-one Europeans and fifty-two Arab 'collaborators'. As in May 1945, the forces of order reacted with speed and savagery, assisted by armed settlers' vigilante groups. At the end there were so many corpses that nobody could seriously contradict the FLN's claim of 12,000 Arab deaths.[4] On 24 August the government began calling up thousands of reservists. The war was on.

Where was the Legion in all this?

To avoid reporters tracking them down for interviews, the surviving POWs had been discreetly flown from Vietnam to North Africa in aircraft chartered by SDECE – French Intelligence. Few were fit enough for light duties, let alone patrolling. The discovery that a ration allowance had been docked from their back-pay, on the grounds that the Viets had fed them during their captivity, was hardly calculated to restore discipline and morale in men who had lived through the nightmare of Dien Bien Phu and eaten only rice for three months, let alone those who had been in Viet hands for four years, since the fiasco on Highway Four.

Ostensibly to check them out for tropical infections, they were confined to barracks and given lectures on how to behave in North Africa in case they had become infected with the easier way of life with wives and children during their years in Vietnam.

Those sent out on missions too soon simply collapsed. Only 1 REI was combat-ready in November 1954, to be joined by 3 REI on its return from Indochina, with 13 DBLE returning in May 1955 and 2 REI shipped back to Tunis, then posted to Morocco, where it remained until the country received its independence. The newly formed 4 REI did not arrive in Algeria until 1957.[5]

In December 1955 the para battalions expanded to become regiments designated 1 REP and 2 REP. There had been talk of making 3 BEP into 3 REP; instead, its officers and men were absorbed into 1 REP, which was commanded by Pierre Jeanpierre, promoted colonel. After fighting the Allies with 5 REI in Syria, he had been repatriated to France, was caught with the Resistance and sent to Mauthausen concentration camp before rejoining the army after the war and serving two tours in Vietnam with distinction. In Algeria until his untimely death he exhausted himself and his men constantly in the effort to beat the guerrillas at their own game. His story epitomises that of 1 REP during the next six years, not that he was alive to share its final disgrace.

After independence was granted to Morocco in November 1955 and to Tunisia in March 1956, Algeria's new tough-line Resident Minister Robert Lacoste divided the country into 'pacification areas' where the army was to *protect* the civil population; 'operational areas', where it had carte blanche to crush the rebels known as *fells*[6] and 'forbidden areas' whose population was forcibly resettled elsewhere, turning them into free-fire zones.

Four days later on 16 March the first series of explosions rocked Algiers itself. Since the ALN bombers had their caches of explosives and bolt-holes in the *casbah* or native town, on 27–28 May the first *ratissage* or manhunt took place there, with troops and police combing every street. So many buildings were centuries old with intercommunicating passages and tunnels that the manpower required was massive.

The ALN's riposte was a wave of individual assassinations. In case anyone was wondering why France was so intent on hanging onto Algeria after freeing its neighbours, the reason sprang for the first time from beneath the sands of Hassi Messaoud on 26 June. The oil pipeline to the coast was patrolled by 1 REI in rapid-response units aboard GMC trucks. On 10 August the first outrage of the nascent settlers' secret army was an 'anti-terrorist' bomb that killed scores of Arabs and maimed many more in the rue de Thèbes. On 30 September the FLN launched a wave of bombings, to which French Intelligence officers of SDECE replied by using fighter aircraft to force down in Algerian territory a Moroccan aircraft, on board which Ahmed Ben Bella and other FLN leaders were returning to their base in Cairo after a conference in Morocco with ALN leaders. Ignoring international protests, Paris kept them imprisoned for six years.

It gives an idea of what life was like for civilians that Thierry and Geneviève Delannoy – a girl aged ten and a boy of twelve – sat up on one of these nights of violence with their uncle, listening to the explosions coming nearer and nearer their home. Their father, an army officer, was with his unit. Their mother was visiting a sick relative in France. And the uncle was more than a baby sitter. He had been entrusted not just with his brother's loaded service revolver, but the sworn duty to shoot his nephew and niece in the head, should *les fells* break into the apartment.

In Biskra, teenager Hélène Auclair said goodbye to a boy in her class one Friday afternoon. Forty-eight hours later she was being driven in a long convoy to the farm on which he and his father had been murdered while working their fields. All his classmates were made by their parents to look at the burned bodies, and told, 'This is the work of ALN. This is what they want to do to us all.'[8]

Pieds noirs were not the sole victims of the ALN terror campaign. Arab teachers and civil servants who worked with the French authorities received the same treatment. Interpreters had their tongues and upper lips routinely hacked off, while the *harki* interpreters who accompanied the French military on operations suffered sexual mutilations when captured, allegedly in punishment for the rapes inflicted on women in lonely *mechta* farmhouses, whose menfolk were away or had been taken prisoner. The level of terror escalated until the violent but legal *ratissages* turned into lynch-law *ratonnades*, meaning rat-hunts, where armed European civilians killed Muslims on mere suspicion.

The political and financial support which the ALN derived from Cairo and the anti-French broadcasts of the Voice of the Arabs radio station in Cairo were the main reasons why France joined the Suez invasion in November 1956. The joint UK–France–Israel operation was qualified by Prime Minister Sir Anthony Eden as not a war, but just an armed conflict.[9] On 6 November 1 REP landed at Port Fuad with 2nd Squadron of 2 REC in AMX 13 tanks to take part in operations along the Canal Zone until the withdrawal. After the fighting was over a young para lieutenant by the name of Jean-Marie Le Pen – later to be famous as the leader of France's Right-Wing Front National party – was put in charge of burying Egyptian dead, which he did with respect, insisting on all the bodies being lined up with heads towards Mecca.

Whatever the hopes of French Intelligence, the Suez invasion did nothing to calm the situation in Algeria. To stamp out the urban terror, on 7 January 1957 Gen Jacques Massu was ordered by Lacoste to restore order in Algiers using 10th Parachute Division, which included 1 REP. Patrols of paras in full battle order became a part of the everyday urban scene. On 26 January three ALN bombs killed twenty people and mutilated many others in downtown Algiers as a warning to obey FLN instructions for a general strike in two days' time. Opening shops by crowbar, sitting in classrooms to ensure teachers taught and ordering bus drivers at gunpoint to choose between getting behind the wheel or 'coming along for a chat', the paras broke the strike after three days.

Introducing a programme of *quadrillage intensif*, Massu divided the *casbah* into grid squares with files for every person. Heads of families and landlords were made answerable for the actions of those in their households. The files were used to check out every unemployed bricklayer by *interrogations poussées* – in other words, torture – until one of them was driven to admit he had bricked up the secret bomb factory. Thus located, it was destroyed on 19 February.

Because it saved French lives, Chaplain Delarue of 1 REP called torture in Algeria a necessary evil, like the Allies' terror bombing in the Second World War.[10] At the other end of the moral spectrum, Gen Paul Aussarès, a shadowy figure in the universally feared Action Service, claims to have been explicitly ordered at the start of the emergency by François Mitterand – as

Minister of the Interior, he was responsible for Algeria – to use every means *legal and illegal* to obtain information from ALN/FLN suspects.[11]

In colonial Vietnam it had been accepted that torture was used to extract information from prisoners, but Deuxième Bureau officers distanced themselves by claiming that it was applied by their interpreters in their absence. In Algeria torture became normal practice. Faced with the atrocities of FLN terror, few on the French side objected. On 28 March 1957 Gen Jacques Paris de Bollardière – veteran of Narvik, 13 DBLE throughout the Second World War and Vietnam – resigned, rather than sanction more torture. He received sixty days' imprisonment for supporting the allegations on the subject made by his former subordinate Jean-Jacques Servan-Schreiber, editor of *L'Express*.[12] In September of the same year Paul Teitgen, a Catholic Resistance hero appointed Secretary-General of the Algiers police, resigned after being sickened by the sight of prisoners who had patently 'been subjected to the same tortures I suffered in the cellars of the Gestapo at Nancy'.[13]

Which side began first to torture its prisoners is impossible to untangle, but it became such a normal way of exacting information that the French army issued the Code of Humane Torture. There had to be 'reasonable grounds' for suspicion, but what constitutes 'reasonable grounds' for torturing another human being? Often people known to be personally innocent of any act of violence were tortured because they *might* have some useful information, which could only be pried out of them by a fear greater than that of being murdered as a traitor by *les fells*. Other rules were that children must not be tortured and that an officer must be present at each session to halt the torture immediately suspects started to talk.

Whether it was used by a particular unit or not depended, it seems, on the officer in command. Sensible legionnaires who had learned early on to keep their noses out of other people's business did not ask what happened to prisoners handed over to Deuxième Bureau officers and their *harki* interpreters for interrogation.[14] The practice was so widely known that journalist Henri Alleg published a book in January 1958 entitled simply *La Question* and everyone knew to which question he was referring. Before the book was withdrawn by the publishers under pressure from the government, 60,000 copies were sold.

So many torture sessions were witnessed by 19-year-old conscript Pascal Chauvin that he had no idea of the number. The method, he explained, was simple. After a *ratissage*, a mixed bag of 'suspects' including innocent men who had had the bad luck to be in the wrong place at the wrong time were brought back to the MT section at the rear of his barracks, where there was a large metal workbench, which was so hot under the afternoon sun that it burnt his hand on contact. Stripped naked, the 'suspects' were handcuffed and thrown bodily onto the scorching metal. A moment of relief came from the cold water with which they were hosed down – to make a better electrical contact, as Chauvin explained. Then the crocodile clip electrodes were attached to the moist skin of scrotum and lips and the para whose turn it was to operate the *gégène* field generator started it up. As the current flowed, sphincters loosened and more water was hosed over the writhing bodies until someone could take it no more.

Asked by the author thirty years later, 'What did you feel, doing that?' Chauvin did not bat an eyelid. '*Fallait qu'ils parlent*,' he shrugged. We had to make them talk …[15]

Jean-Marie Le Pen spent some months with 1 REP in Algiers in 1957 as a reservist lieutenant. Accused by *Libération* in October 1984 of having tortured terrorist suspects, he was acquitted on appeal, the Court accepting that he had not personally tortured anyone. This was in line with the claim by one young officer attached to Massu's staff that electric shock and water 'treatment' was not administered by officers, but in their presence by *harkis* and ex-*fellouzes* who had themselves cracked under torture and changed sides.

Whatever the truth of that, the paras' victims were not only Arabs. A particular malevolence was reserved for *les porteurs de valises* – the European Left-wing sympathisers of the FLN who took the voluntary subscriptions, the blackmail and the protection money collected in cash by activists in mainland France and brought it to North Africa in their personal baggage, hoping not to be searched. Some also carried weapons and explosives in

Algeria for the ALN, believing they could talk their way through police and military cordons. When these men and women were caught, the sadism, sexual abuse and gang-rapes they endured meant that they could not be allowed to walk free and talk about it. As with Maurice Audin, a Communist lecturer at Algiers University who disappeared off the face of the earth after being arrested in his home on 11 June by paras of 1 RCP, the bodies were never found.

In April 1957 C-in-C Gen Salan cut the ALN's supply routes from the training bases in Tunisia by erecting La Ligne Morice. Named for the Minister of Defence, the barrier consisted of lines of barbed wire carrying 5,000-volt and 12,000-volt current running along the frontier, back up by tangles of wire, minefields and ground-sweeping radar linked to batteries of remote-controlled artillery, which theoretically could wipe out any border-crossing group without a single soldier's life being risked. This was not incursion-proof, but anyone cutting the wire risked electrocuting himself and also triggered a signal to rapid-response units of 2 REP, detachments of 3 REI and the tanks of 1 REC, who tracked the reinforcements coming from the training camps across the border and called down air strikes on them before they could get far.

On one typical operation, British Legionnaire James Worden thought that his company from 3rd Battalion of 3 REI was the only unit chasing a column of *fells*. Without, as usual, any clear knowledge of where he was, he saw a group of men in what appeared to be Legion camouflage fatigues running in a bleak and rocky valley below him, one of them carrying an AA 52 light machine gun, the rest with rifles and machine-pistols. Only when the three men with the machine gun were mown down by a Legion sergeant who had cut them off, did Worden realise they were the enemy.

Other legionnaires appeared over the skyline and advanced into the valley. Worden was so startled when an ALN officer with stars on his shoulder straps emerged from a bush thirty paces away with his carbine held above his head in a gesture of surrender that he would have shot the man, had not his captain pushed down the barrel of his machine-pistol in time.

After the bodies of the dead *fells* were arranged in rows for photographing by Deuxième Bureau officers, Worden noticed that their uniforms and boots were brand new, and found the ammunition in their pouches shining, straight from the factory, and the soap and toothpaste in their packs unopened, proving that their column had not travelled far before being wiped out.[16]

Back at the trucks, he had a further shock on finding several thousand men from regular regiments who been blocking parties in the operation. By early afternoon, he was back in camp eating his lunch, kept piping hot by the German cook. As he says, no legionnaire had any idea what part he played in the war, or even how effective 3 REI was. His world was not even 3rd Battalion, but restricted to its 2nd Company, outside which he knew only a handful of legionnaires in 5th and 6th Companies.

He described without any emotion the normal way of dealing with prisoners. In mountainous country where every litre of water and spoonful of coffee had to be carried on one's back, no one was prepared to share his carefully hoarded provisions. So, on one occasion a group of *fells* were told to clear off by the section sergeant, while his men were enjoying a well-earned coffee break. Casting anxious glances behind them, the Arabs shuffled away, breaking into a run after twenty or thirty paces. Only then did the legionnaires cut them down with automatic fire, without even bothering to stand up. The report on the incident noted that they had been shot while trying to escape.[17]

Similar treatment was occasionally meted out to the Legion's own, as when a young sergeant deserted near the Tunisian frontier. Had he gone without his rifle, it is probable that the Legion would not have wasted time looking for him, but to avoid it being used to kill other legionnaires, he was hunted down by his own section. Foolishly, he opened fire on them as they neared his hideout, and was shot dead. His pack contained not only family photographs, but also bars of chocolate and a spare water bottle, indicating that his desertion was not the result of a momentary impulse. The men shared out the chocolate, only Worden refusing his share.[18]

A more serious case involved a legionnaire who had deserted from 12 DBLE and spent six months with the *fells* as a weapons instructor. Taken prisoner alive, he was court-martialled by a captain who acted as his defence and prosecution. The trial was over in less than thirty minutes, with sentence immediately following: the captain ordered the deserter to kneel in the dirt, gave him two minutes to make his peace with God and fired a bullet from his revolver into the back of the man's head. The only concession made was burial of the body; the bodies of dead *fells* were left where they died, and the places are now marked by monuments all over Algeria.[19]

Occasionally a female *fell* was captured in the field. For obvious reasons, Worden does not name the captain involved when a wounded ALN paymaster was taken prisoner. The captain ordered her wound dressed by the company medic before she was delivered to his tent 'for interrogation'. Intent on his own pleasure, he overlooked until it was too late what was happening to her satchel of notes in various currencies, of which Worden's share was $2,000 and £800.[20] So he says …

As in the east of the country, so in the west. During 1958 half-tracks of 1 REI patrolled the minefields and three-metre-high wire tangle along the Moroccan frontier for 260 consecutive nights.

War in the mountains, war in the cities … . At close quarters in the *casbah* of Algiers the Legion paras were in an alien world where everyone was the enemy. Through 'information received in the usual way', legionnaires from 1 REP captured local ALN commander Yacef Sa'adi and his chief bomber Zohra Drif there on 23 September 1957. After Col Jeanpierre and Sgt Maj Tasnady were wounded by a hand grenade thrown by Sa'adi, he climbed out of the hideaway choking from the smoke of all the paperwork on fire behind him. The French-educated FLN leadership had a bureaucratic obsession with minutes of meetings, lists of membership and copies of written orders that came in very useful for the Intelligence analysts when found intact.

On 8 October a notorious ALN assassin with the Runyonesque name of Ali La Pointe was run to earth in another *casbah* hideout, allegedly by Tasnady dressed as an Arab woman. La Pointe refused to emerge, his comrade-in-arms Larbi Ben M'Hidi having been 'suicided' in a French prison at the same time as Ali Boumendjel by Gen Aussarès – allegedly on orders from François Mitterand, then Minister of Justice.[21] Still bandaged from his grenade wound and in no mood to risk his men's lives, Jeanpierre ordered the neighbouring properties evacuated so that the hideout could be blown up. Lt Simonot, two German legionnaires and Cpl Ray Palin from Liverpool set charges against the false wall behind which La Pointe was hiding. Unaware that the terrorist's store of plastic explosive was on the other side of the wall, they found out when the entire block blew up with them inside. Palin lost an eye, but La Pointe lost his life, along with seventeen Muslims in neighbouring houses.

Massu never apologised for the incidental deaths, nor for the torture, instead justifying the acts of his men by saying that if they had used conventional means of fighting the ALN every suspect would have been killed, whereas the victims of torture were still alive decades later. The body count of 1 REP in this dirty seven-and-a-half-year war ran to about 2,000 killed or captured, in the course of which the regiment lost 123 dead and 350 wounded. Given a regimental strength of about 850 superbly fit trained soldiers, the casualty figures testify that they were not fighting only innocent civilians.

Chapter 4

DARE CALL IT TREASON

Algeria 1957–62

Always leading from the front, Jeanpierre broke with Legion tradition by inventing what he called *le rouleau compresseur*. This particular steamroller minimised French losses by a drill of 'movement by sections' using massive concentrations of artillery, automatic fire on the ground and a liberal employment of grenades. After 1 REP installed itself in the strategic market town of Guelma in an ALN no-go zone near the Tunisian border on 21 January 1959, the steamroller's first run three days later accounted for ninety-two border-crossers killed before breakfast. Day after day, buzzing around in his Alouette personal command helicopter and heliportering his men in Shawnee H-21 Flying Bananas to where they were least expected, Jeanpierre carved up the enemy.

A latter-day crusader who never let up the pressure on himself or his men, his end was inevitable. By Camerone Day of 1958, his hard-driven 1 REP had been in action almost continuously for eight months. It may be that the ALN chose 1 April to launch a major offensive in the hope that all the Legion regiments would be hung-over after their annual Camerone celebration. Jeanpierre at least was one jump ahead, having trucked and heliportered his men overnight to Souk Ahras, one day's walk from the Tunisian frontier, to reinforce 9 RCP under Col Buchoud, tasked with surrounding and wiping out a large group of border-crossers hiding in the network of underground Roman cisterns near there, whose exact locations were unknown to Europeans – not that there were many left in that part of Algeria.

Some legionnaires had consumed a fair amount nevertheless. As Pierre Sergent described the battle, Jeanpierre's paras did not bother to take cover, but lurched into battle singing their marching song *Le Boudin* at the top of their voices. The jollity ended with bullets, blood and knives one-on-one. Only eight prisoners were taken for interrogation, but the haul of six MG 42s, thirty-seven sub-machine guns and seventy-five rifles is a fair indication how many were killed.

Living at that pace, something had to give. On 19 May Jeanpierre – in his habitual, but then revolutionary, way of directing a battle – was overflying an engagement in mountainous country in his Alouette. On the ground, Capt Ysquierdo decided that the substantial force of *fells* hiding in caves could not be dislodged without wasting lives. After artillery had failed to penetrate the interior of the caves, he wanted to call in an air strike with napalm to asphyxiate them.

Jeanpierre fell victim to the we-can-do-it syndrome and made another extremely low pass over the enemy positions out of stubborn pride and with his judgement impaired by exhaustion. An ALN bullet cut the Alouette's fuel lead. In the brief comparative silence, the legionnaires on the ground could hear the last rounds of the burst of automatic fire that had done the damage. The Alouette vanished from sight behind a ridge, whence came the sound of a crash. Reaching the site to find several *fells* about to loot the wreck, Ysquierdo and Lt Simonot drove them off, to find their colonel and his pilot dead. The news was broken to the Legion by Ysquierdo's terse radio message, '*Soleil est mort.*' It was almost poetic: the sun is dead.

The massive turn-out of 30,000 people at the funeral on 31 May in the presence of generals Salan and Massu honoured not only the man in the plain coffin with the colonel's gold-braided képi on it, but also the 111 legionnaires killed and 272 wounded in four months of combat around Guelma.[1] There were too many funerals, but the war was going well and the enemy were losing far more men and supplies than they could afford.

In July 1 REP was posted to Algiers, where Massu himself was made an honorary corporal and downed the regulation quarter-litre of *pinard* before singing the sixteen rather monotonous verses of *Le Boudin*. Replacing Salan as C-in-C Algeria, the amiable pipe-smoking air force officer Gen Maurice Challe decided that with 80,000 highly trained men very effectively blocking the frontiers it was time to mop up the ALN in the interior. An all-out offensive spearheaded by the paras claimed 1,600 dead and 460 prisoners in the Saïda region alone. On the other side of the coin the Legion also contributed to the SAS. Unlike the British forces known by that acronym, the Sections Administratives Spécialisées was a hearts-and-minds operation, sending teachers, medics, midwives and other social workers into remote villages without even running water. Sometimes this backfired, as when an ALN unit cut off the arms of all the children who had been vaccinated. The cost was high for SAS personnel also, with seventy-three officers, thirty-three NCOs, forty-two civilians and 612 Algerian home guards being killed during the emergency.[2]

Laslo Tasnady had learned the lessons of soldiering with the Legion in Vietnam and put them to good effect in Algeria. 'Tunnel rats' were not invented by the Americans in Vietnam. Tasnady used an Arab boy nicknamed Ouled, who would go into any hole with a torch and yell, 'No one here,' if he found signs of life. As soon as he was out, legionnaires blocked the entrance after throwing in one or more chlorine gas grenades. This was not Geneva Convention territory.

A marksman who once coolly took out six running targets with six bullets, Tasnady volunteered on 14 May 1959 to be lowered head-down on a rope over a cliff as the only way of reaching an FLN cave refuge. Into it he swung a basket of explosives including a primed grenade, which gave at most seven seconds[3] for his comrades on the cliff-top to haul him clear of the blast.

Tasnady's upside-down exploit was his last. Minutes before climbing into the trucks waiting to take them back to base that afternoon, his men heard a single shot. With a home-moulded shotgun pellet lodged in his neck vertebrae, the soft-spoken Hungarian was dead. His body was carried back to bel-Abbès and lay in state alongside two other Hungarian sergeant-majors from 3 REI and 5 REI who died the same week.

All the Legion regiments were in it together. Infantry, cavalry, para – the routine on operations was much the same for all: long days of scrambling up and down mountains with everyone including the officers carrying heavy Bergens when too far from a road for clothing and sleeping bags to be transported by truck.

In August 1959, ordered to relinquish command of 1 REP, Col

Dufour joined a hard core of deserters planning to kidnap or assassinate President De Gaulle on his imminent *tournée des popotes* – a whistle-stop tour of officers' messes in Algeria to remind the army that it existed to enforce his will. Nothing came of the assassination plan, but hostility to the president rose when 1 REP learned while on operations in the Aurès that the green-and-white star and crescent ALN flags they seized in the packs of dead *fells* were to be flown publicly in Algiers during a universal suffrage referendum on the country's political future. The regiment went on strike, refusing to leave its quarters. The strike was broken by the simple but tactless expedient of posting all the senior officers to other regiments. Many deserted instead.

On 16 September 1959 De Gaulle, the champion of the army that had brought him back to power and the great hope of the European settlers, was hinting openly at the possibility of independence for Algeria. As a gesture 7,000 ALN prisoners were released and promptly went underground again. They had no choice, for refusal meant execution by their erstwhile comrades. Many voters in France would have given Algeria away at the first chance, had they been asked – including every farmer who could not compete with the cheap Arab labour of his competitors there – but the Gaullist officers of 1 REP were sure that their president would never abandon the *pieds noirs*. Had he not voiced their much-chanted slogan *Algérie française* many times?

They had yet to learn that, like the utterances of the Pythia at Delphi, De Gaulle's could be construed in many ways. For telling a German journalist what he thought of the amnesty, Massu was summoned to Paris and sacked. The European inhabitants of Algiers rose in support of their man and barricaded the town in a citizens' revolt. De Gaulle ordered the forces of order to crush them, with the result that 1 REP was hauled in from the field and ordered to restore order in the capital.

Traditionally, the army in North Africa was not greatly respected by the settlers, and the Legion with its history of welcoming all-comers least of all. Certainly no *pied noir* wanted his daughter to marry a legionnaire. But the times, they were a-changing: welcomed as saviours by the settlers who had just killed fourteen over-zealous gendarmes, the legionnaires fraternised freely, accepting flowers and kisses from the pretty girls and feeling naturally good, for these were, after all, the people they were in Algeria to protect. Beneath the overt bonhomie on the streets many of the officers were privately making last-ditch promises, from which the Organisation Armée Secrète was later born.

On 1 February 1960 the very Gaullist commander of 2 REP, Col Darmuzai, was furious at the arrival in 2 REP's camp at Chefka of men from 1 REP who had been arrested on the barricades in Algiers. He had no objection to running a work camp for mutineers, but feared the prisoners might 'infect' with partisan sympathies his officers and men, especially the few married to local girls. In fact, their stay of one month would have passed off without incident, had not the government broken its word that no one would be singled out for especial punishment. Ten days after their arrival, the new colonel of 1 REP, Maurice Guiraud, arrived by helicopter to take two of them away for trial, and even the more Gaullist officers saw this as a breach of honour.

Against the background of political manoeuvring in preparation for the government's volte-face, the war in the mountains continued, its goals becoming as muddy as the hillsides on which the legionnaires slipped and slid and died for the rest of that winter. As 1 REP's padre said at a funeral, speaking in front of ten coffins, each bearing a képi, 'We no longer know what we are dying for.'

In his second tournée des popotes during March 1960, with De Gaulle talking openly of *Algérie algérienne* – Algeria for the Algerians – the listening officers knew that independence would mean a mass exodus of the settlers or a bloodbath with a million European victims. Only by constantly changing his itinerary did their president escape four assassination attempts in the space of a few days. Intelligence officers of SDECE were meanwhile turning one ALN faction against another. When Si Salah, the commander of *willaya* IV, was received with two of his adjutants by De Gaulle at the Elysée Palace on 9 June, the talks came to nothing, but SDECE made sure the ALN high command got to hear about them, which resulted in the would-be go-betweens being purged by their own comrades in Algiers.

Maj Elie Denoix de St-Marc was named acting CO of 1 REP after Guiraud left on sick leave, of which the main cause was seeing too many of his men die in a war that was as good as won militarily for a government that was turning the achievement into a defeat for political reasons. Yet the military machine went on turning nevertheless. British Legionnaire Simon Murray joined up in February 1960 and fortunately kept a day-by-day diary of his experiences. At the time there were probably no more than fifty British legionnaires, whose 'club' was the Foot Bar – 'foot' meaning football – in bel-Abbès, where several of them regularly drank and used the notice board to keep in touch with compatriots based elsewhere.

After parachute training, Murray was posted in November to 2 REP at Skikda,[4] just over 100km from the Tunisian frontier. At first sight, the immaculately kept beachside depot with its flower beds and sports facilities looked like a Club Med resort, apart from the barbed wire perimeter, but this was no holiday camp. For what seem trivial offences, or simply getting on the wrong side of an NCO, a man spent eight days' in *taule*, during which his pay went into company funds. Nor did the days count for service, so that a frequent recidivist risked finding his demob date extended again and again.

Heads shaven, dressed night and day in the same stinking fatigues, for the slightest infringement of the draconian rules, prisoners were awarded 'musical' press-ups with the hands clapped in front of the body on each 'up'. The bruises to the face each time it collided with the concrete floor accounted for the rumour that the prison NCOs beat up prisoners. The worst of the punishment was not the physical hardship, but being unable to keep clean. Cleanliness was so dinned into every recruit that spending a week in the same dirty clothes, without being allowed to wash or even clean his teeth, was the strongest deterrent.

There were eight companies in 2 REP, four rifle companies, one for transport, an assault company, the *compagnie d'appui* with its mortars and the rejects and skivers in the depot company back in base. On joining 3rd Company in the Aurès Mountains, Murray was surprised to find the whores of the company brothel toughing it out under canvas for the same rates as their sisters back at base:

£1 for a quickie or £5 for the night. At the funerals of 2 REP, Cabiro records the madam of the BMC and her girls standing side-by-side with the officers' wives, their presence offending no one.[5]

Under an ex-SS sergeant-major and two German sergeants, Murray was on patrol next day. A three-hour truck drive into the mountains of the Djebel Chélia was followed by a climb of 1,000 metres for an operation with 1st Company combining dive-bombers, artillery and helicopters. His Christmas holidays were spent on ops with 13 DBLE high in the Djebel Chélia, which he described as being as bleak and cold as Dartmoor in winter, with the German legionnaires singing *Stille Nacht* and everyone getting drunk to keep out the sub-zero wind.[6]

New Year saw him right on the other side of the country, patrolling the fortifications along the Moroccan frontier. In March 1961 all four companies were back in the Aurès with 13 DBLE and 3 REI after an overwhelming endorsement by plebiscite of De Gaulle's plans for Algeria caused hard-line settlers and officers in Algeria to form the underground Organisation Armée Secrète, together with Legion deserters of all ranks, their numbers swollen by comrades who had deserted from regular regiments in France and clandestinely returned to North Africa. The most important returnees were generals Challe and Zeller, who were smuggled aboard an air force flight from France to Algeria in the evening of 20 April.

St-Marc's hesitation about joining the growing anti-government movement vanished next morning when he met them in a suburban villa, flanked by all the officer-deserters of 1 REP. Suspecting that the civilians of OAS would use an uprising as cover for settling personal scores, St-Marc's condition for supporting their coup was that it be executed under military discipline, and not as a popular uprising. It has been suggested that 1 REP and 2 REP became the most 'political' regiments in Algeria because they were never rotated back to France as regular army regiments were, but the true reason for their prominence in the putsch lies in the unqualified loyalty of most legionnaires toward their commanders. Legally, too, it could be argued that the legionnaires were not guilty of treason, since France was not their country.

Whatever the niceties, towards midnight 1 REP was paraded in full combat gear at the magnificent base it had built for itself at Zeralda on the coast 20km west of Algiers. Openly joined by their officers who had been underground for three whole months, they sped off in a convoy of trucks to occupy downtown Algiers almost without bloodshed. It was a tribute to 1 REP's training and discipline that the only casualty was an over-zealous infantry sergeant at the radio station. Prisoners loyal to De Gaulle included Délégué-Général Morin, Prefect of Police Jannin and the C-in-C Gen Gambiez. The military commander of Algiers district, Gen Vézinet, was arrested by Lt Godot of 1 REP, who bluffed his way into HQ with a handful of men and overrode Vézinet's protests that protocol forbade him to surrender his sidearm to a lieutenant. So polite in every case were the paras that the Minister of Public Works Robert Buron was confined to his room at the Palais d'Eté, but allowed to use the telephone, by which he immediately advised Paris what was going on.

Generals Salan, Challe, Jouhaud and Zeller persuaded Gen Gouraud to bring two of the colonial para regiments over to the side of the putsch. Next morning, the legionnaires and men of 14 RCP and 18 RCP were the idols of every European in Algiers. Oran came over to their side immediately, although Constantine declared for De Gaulle. In Paris, he condemned the leaders of the putsch on television as a quartet of superannuated generals out of their depth. Although the rest of the Legion had made no move, he was facing the nightmare of every French government since 1831: that the entire mercenary army of Louis-Philippe would get out of hand and blindly follow its officers in a new revolution.

At the naval base of Mers el-Kebir outside Oran, Admiral Querville was hostile to the putsch and stationed a cruiser offshore with its heavy guns trained on Zeralda camp. At Blida air base, just outside Algiers, men refused to obey their officers and hoisted the Red Flag. At the same time, aircrew loyal to De Gaulle ignored appeals by their former master Gen Challe and flew twenty Noratlas transports empty to the mainland, so that they could not be commandeered. In France, commanders of several fighter bases made it known that they would shoot down the paras, should they attempt to fly into French airspace in the remaining planes.

A measure of the confusion among officers and men of the other Legion regiments is conveyed by Cabiro's account of the heated debates that day in 2 REP's officers' mess at Camp Pehau. As a staunch Gaullist, Col Darmuzai was 100% convinced that the president would never actually give independence to Algeria after a war that was all but won militarily. He was, however, unable to calm his subordinates who argued for joining their brother-officers in 1 REP while the iron was hot.

Cabiro's wife having just had their second child, he was given permission to collect mother and daughter from the hospital and take them back to their married quarters. When he returned to the mess, confusion reigned, with the majority of the other officers in favour of joining the coup. His wife was relieved to see him return for dinner, but at 2230hrs a jeep arrived in front of their apartment with an invitation from his brother officers to take command of the regiment, en route without Darmuzai's knowledge to join the rebellion in Algiers.

This, Cabiro agreed to do after asking his wife to tell his colonel in the morning what had happened and reassure him that the regiment was still his to command, should he chose to rejoin it in Algiers. Not seeking to usurp his authority, Cabiro was furious with the other officers when he caught up with them at Sétif for placing him in this position. He had no wish to mutiny, but they were metaphorically marching their NCOs and men into great danger, and his place was with them to calm the more belligerent officers. He thus became a mutineer out of loyalty to the men he commanded.[7]

At that stage, the legionnaires still had no clear idea what was going on. They were obeying orders, as usual. Simon Murray recalled 2 REP's progress in soft-topped trucks from the Aurès to Algiers on 23 April, greeted along the way by cheering crowds of Europeans. Once again, the legionnaires enjoyed their popularity. In the capital, they were hailed as heroes by the ecstatic population in the streets to the exuberant accompaniment of motor horns beeping the rhythm of the slogan *Al-gé-rie fran-çaise*. Murray and his comrades still had no idea which side they were supposed to be on because their NCOs had not passed on the gist of the officers' deliberations.

Cabiro, the reluctant acting colonel, went from office to office seeking news. Everybody welcomed him with open arms, regarding 2 REP's arrival as presaging a wholesale support for the coup. It did not come. From Sidi-bel-Abbès there came not a solitary signal indicating what the rest of the Legion was doing, but as the day wore on it became apparent that the paras stood alone. In vain, Challe worked the telephones from his temporary HQ in Algiers, to find all the promises of support he had received from other regiments fading away in the hour of need.[8]

On 24 April 2 REP was ordered to take over the Maison Blanche civil airport from the Gaullist marines occupying it, but without using violence! Murray recalled being issued with pick handles, with which the marines were, none too gently, shoved out of the way and rounded up without a shot being fired. At the time, he and his fellow-legionnaires thought they were at the airport preparatory to being dropped on Paris in a nationwide revolution.[9]

Confusion in the French capital was such that Prime Minister Michel Debré was panicked into asking the population to go to the Paris airports 'on foot or by car as soon as the sirens sound'.[10] What they were supposed to do once there, except lie down and prevent the paras landing by covering the ground with their bodies, he did not say. More to the point were De Gaulle's orders to ring the airports by armoured units. The president who had started his political career with the famous broadcast from London on 18 June 1940 calling on all French men and women to rally against the German invaders now used the microphone again to forbid every citizen to have anything to do with the mutineers. By Tuesday 25 April, it was all over. Challe announced that he was surrendering himself to De Gaulle. Aghast at the implications for the men who had followed him and their other officers in rebellion, Capt Sergent went to the radio station and begged all military personnel to defy orders from Paris and live up to their moral responsibilities and the memory of all their comrades who had died. Nobody listened.

When Challe gave himself up, Salan and others were changing into civilian clothes for a clandestine life. Col St-Marc was driven back to Zeralda, there to await his fate. His officers clambered into a bus heading for prison. Their men threw away their berets and képis to the crowd as souvenirs and departed under guard on open trucks, firing their weapons in the air and singing Edith Piaf's hit *Non, Je ne regrette rien* – I regret nothing.

Among units tasked with sorting out this mess was 3 REI. James Worden recalled being detailed off to guard 1 REP's brothel. The expected 'favours' did not materialise. That was business and had to be paid for, but the girls did press the men's uniforms and cook for the ones they liked.[11] By then, 2 REP was back in its trucks, heading for the depot at Skikda. Summoned into Darmuzai's office, Cabiro and the other officers found their colonel refusing to speak to them. Instead, he played them a carefully worded pre-recorded message, lecturing them on their duty and requiring them to make a full report of their actions.

After the others had left, he turned to Cabiro and spat at him, 'You will be shot! D'you hear me? Shot! Whatever got into your head, to do such a thing?'

Cabiro replied, 'If you don't understand that, there's no point in me telling you. I'll write you a letter before I am shot.'[12] At that moment, it seemed almost certain that he would be.

Camerone Day 1961 was a sad feast. The story of the heroes of the battle at Camarón was read out at every Legion base and camp, but with none of the usual festivities. Col Guiraud of 1 REP was recalled from sick leave by Minister of the Armed Forces Pierre Messmer – himself a former legionnaire – and obliged to watch his political master issue the order dissolving the regiment for good, together with the two other para regiments directly involved in the mutiny: 14 RCP and 18 RCP.

On 3 May Cabiro and four other officers of 2 REP were arrested at Skikda and flown to Paris, where they found the officer core of all the rebellious para regiments locked up in the military prison at the Fort de l'Est. After seeing De Gaulle finally announce on television that Algeria was shortly to be given its independence, their anger was not that of the settlers losing their homes and livelihood, but of officers who had spared neither themselves nor their men, watching them die day after day, month after month, in obedience to orders from a president who had now made all the suffering and the deaths pointless.

Transferred to the Santé prison the following day and expecting to be shot after his trial, Cabiro asked for a typewriter and a teach-yourself typing manual, so that he could leave a full explanation of his actions for his children. His defence was undertaken free of charge by the celebrated barrister Maître Bondoux, a former *chef de cabinet* of Gen De Lattre at 1st Army. The hardest thing for Cabiro was to be visited by his wife, 6-year-old son and baby daughter, whose mother had told the boy that their father was in the prison to work on some very secret papers. Faced with the near-certainty of execution or at least a long prison sentence for 'unauthorised abuse of command', Cabiro asked her not to bring the children again.

The enforced inactivity was hard on men of action, who had literally been working day and night for years. The high of rebellion swiftly faded into depression tainted by bitterness against the comrades who had 'gone sick', taken leave or otherwise welched on promises of support, and then covered their arses one way or another. Yet, so impeccable was the discipline of the imprisoned officers that they were well treated by the prison staff, allowed to take their meals together and exceptionally not even handcuffed on the journeys through Paris for interviews with the examining magistrates.

Brought back to prison on the evening after their trials, Challe and Zeller knocked on all the cell doors in turn to announce their sentences of sixteen years apiece. 'If they don't shoot us, they won't shoot you,' was the message. Other sentences ranged from fifteen years down to five or less. When his turn came, Cabiro stood wearing all his many medals before the highest judges and generals in the land at the High Court, gazing out of its windows at the stunning view of the Sainte Chapelle, unable to credit his ears when he heard the verdict: a suspended sentence of one year.[13]

By an irony that caused few smiles, those still in prison in May 1968 were released thanks to a section of the community for which the military traditionally had scant respect – the Left-Wing students under 'Red Danny' Cohn-Bendit who tore up the cobble-stones of Parisian streets to use as missiles against the tear-gas and fire hoses of the CRS riot squads and took De Gaulle to the brink of the Fourth Revolution.

In the immediate aftermath of the failed Algiers coup, with OAS mounting thirteen 'near miss' assassination attempts on De Gaulle's life, every Paris policeman on traffic duty carried a loaded sub-machine gun. Tourists were warned not to ask them for directions in case they got shot accidentally by officers unaccustomed to handling anything more lethal than the service-issue pistol. Whose side the armed *flics* were on was made clear when thousands of North Africans and Left-Wing sympathisers took to the streets of Paris on 17 October. Several hundred of the demonstrators were deliberately drowned in the Seine or killed and then dumped into the river by CRS and other police units under Prefect Maurice Papon, who later faced trial not for this but for sending Jews to their deaths while Under-Secretary of the Gironde *département* during the German occupation of France. In Algeria the OAS was committing outrages against Muslims, but its victims also included some defeatist army officers.

For 2 REP and the rest of the Legion, the war continued right up to the very last day. Murray recorded living permanently under canvas during those last months, the regiment being forbidden entrance to its barracks at Skikda in case they blew them up as the men of 1 REP had done at Zeralda. In November 1961 he was with 2 REP *inside* Tunisian territory, driving the border-crossers back into the training camps and killing them there, where they had formerly been safe from pursuit except in a few rare cases that caused international repercussions. A freezing Christmas was spent under canvas near Sétif, with the German legionnaires making and decorating cribs with home-made *papier maché* figures of the Infant, Mary and Joseph and the three wise men in attendance, singing carols while suspects were being tortured elsewhere in the same camp.[14]

By February Murray noted a distinct rise in the rate of desertion as more and more officers, NCOs and men went underground to adopt the lost cause of the settlers, their lethal military skills being welcomed by the OAS, which was threatening to kill any European who tried to leave the country, and had spies in travel agencies to finger the would-be runaways. On one day there were 300 *plasticages* in Algeria, some committed by ALN, others by OAS,[15] whose most murderous arm was Delta Force, commanded by Lt René Degueldre from Belgium, a Legion deserter who had sworn an oath on Jeanpierre's coffin that he would die rather than let the FLN have Algeria.

Whatever their motivation, his group of around 100 mainly German fellow-deserters committed over 300 sordid murders in the month of February 1962. On one day they targeted postmen. The next day cleaning ladies were killed. It was a campaign of pure terror using an arsenal of plastic explosives, automatic weapons, mortars and anti-tank grenades stolen from army stores. De Gaulle's riposte was to unleash Gen Aussarès' Action Service, which despatched teams of equally ruthless assassins known as *barbouzes* to wipe them out. The result was an undercover street war worthy of Chicago in the Thirties – with men, women and children machine-gunned from passing cars, or maimed and killed by booby-trapped parcels.

The defiance of the European civilians turned to despair. Pro-OAS graffiti on the walls were reduced to one: *La valise ou le cercueil*. A suitcase or a coffin, was indeed the choice for the Europeans of Algeria. A million civilians were forced into exile from what had been their homeland for four or five generations, leaving behind them everything except what they could carry in two suitcases per adult. They departed in bitterness and hatred of the president and government that had reneged on its promises to them, with traders destroying family businesses inherited from their grandparents and farmers setting fire to their crops and homes rather than leave them. Although promised a derisory compensation for their homes and businesses, they never received it all.

The country they had thought theirs continued tearing itself apart until a ceasefire was announced on 18 March 1962 to take effect at noon the following day after seven and a half years of war. When the Legion marched out of its headquarters in Sidi bel-Abbès, it left a town of 102,000 inhabitants, completely laid out and partly built by Legion architects and engineers. The newly appointed Inspector General of the Legion, Gen Jacques Lefort closed the hall of honour. The bronze Monument aux Morts had already been dismantled and removed by the pioneers. The banners and standards were taken down, and the black banners from the siege of Thuyen Quang ceremonially burned in compliance with the oath sworn by Capt Borelli, who had brought them back from Vietnam. The other precious relics – the ashes of US legionnaire William Moll; the wooden hand of Capt Danjou, hero of the battle of Camarón in Mexico; three coffins containing the remains of the Father of the Legion Gen Rollet, Prince Aage and the Unknown Legionnaire – were all transported on a special flight to Aubagne, the Legion's new HQ near Marseille.

The official statistics compiled by the Bureau d'Etudes et de Liaison record 24,614 army and police deaths during the emergency against 141,000 *fells* killed. Officially 3,663 European civilians went missing or were known to have been killed during the war and 7,541 seriously injured.[16] An estimated 50,000 Algerian civilians were incidentally murdered by the ALN for alleged or real political reasons that included collaboration.[17]

Before one judges the manner in which the French forces, including the Legion, fought the Algerian war, it is worth reflecting that immediately after the French expulsion, the Arab liberation movement split in two with bloody results for supporters of both sides. Ahmed Ben Bella, the first president of Algeria, was not only ousted by his rival Houari Boumoudienne, but imprisoned by him for 15 years. Released in 1980 after Boumoudienne's death, he lived in exile fearing for his life for another ten years. Of the other wartime leaders, Hocine Aït Ahmed and Mouhammed Boudiat also lived in exile, with Mohammed Khader murdered in Madrid in 1967 and Krim Belkacem strangled in a Frankfurt hotel room in 1970. These men and their killers were the enemy the Legion had been fighting.[18]

As though to balance the equation of misery, set against the tragedy of one million *pieds noirs* refugees forced to abandon their property, homes and businesses after a century and more in North Africa, the French departure unleashed a countrywide groundswell of violence among the descendants of the native Algerians who had been dispossessed by the European influx. Apart from a small minority of university-educated doctors, lawyers, teachers and pharmacists like the revolutionary leader Farhat Abbas, who was now President of the Constitutional Assembly, Algerians had been repressed as second-class citizens in their own country.

Five generations of hatred fuelled the violence latent in North Africa. Between 12,000–15,000 people fell victim to the internecine power struggles of the several armed political factions,[19] during which 1,800 Europeans were murdered and approximately 150,000 Algerians 'executed' for collaboration by their fellow-citizens.[20] Mayors who had done nothing more than accept office and negotiate for roads and schools and medicine for their constituents were attached to four tractors and pulled limb from limb in front of their families; policemen were disembowelled, kneecapped, blinded or had limbs amputated.

The worst fate was reserved for 25,000 *harkis* who had served in the Algerian regiments or as interpreters with the Legion and other French forces in the fight against the ALN. Whether guilty or not of torturing suspects or the rapes of women and girls living in unprotected *mechtas*, whose menfolk had already been arrested or were in the maquis with the ALN, they died most often with their penises and testicles stuffed into their mouths. Three years later the Red Cross counted 13,500 other *harkis* still languishing in Algerian prisons. In 1964 Algeria and Morocco were at war, each claiming it was the other's fault.[21]

The people of France heaved an enormous sigh of relief that their Algerian war was over. Reservists in the regular army, navy and air force were demobilised to pick up the pieces of their interrupted lives. Conscripts and regulars were posted back to France where, typically, the 21st Marine Regiment numbered only 700 men. The question being debated by the politicians in chauffeur-driven cars shuttling along the embankment of the Seine between their ministries and the Elysée Palace was what to do with the Legion.

De Gaulle was not noted for generosity to his enemies. Having already disbanded 1 REP and the other para regiments which had mutinied against his authority, why should he keep in existence a single company of the world's largest mercenary army, whose campaign-hardened soldiers were noted for following their officers to hell and back? Divested of her empire except for a few remaining tropical territories[22], what further need did France have for the army of foreigners that had fought her colonial wars across the globe for 130 years?

PART II

BUILDING AN EMPIRE WITH BLOOD

Chapter 5

THE LEGION OF THE LOST

France 1813–1831

Rome conquered the entire known world by not spilling Roman blood if it could use someone else's. That awesome war machine the legion ran equally well on Spanish, German, Scythian or African blood. In the early Republic, brutally thorough training turned 3,000 men into a single-minded fighting machine that marched, pitched camp, fought and whored as one man. In Caesar's day the number increased to 4,800 men and was up to 5,000-plus in Augustus' time.

The root of the word legion is the same as that of selection. It implies picking the best. Men in the peak of physical condition from any part of the Empire, whom their patrician overlords considered illiterate savages, were deployed in another province far from the land where they had been recruited, and there fought for the might of Rome against people with whom they had no family or tribal constraints – and usually no common language.

After the Empire's peak of expansion the 5,000–6,000 heavy infantry of the Augustan legion were augmented by cavalry units necessary to fight off invasions of mounted barbarian incomers. With its auxiliaries including archers, slingers and javelin-throwers, the legion acquired its own artillery in the shape of up to ten mobile catapults and sixty ballistae, making it truly a self-contained army, the mere thought of whose approach terrified not only the enemy but also its own distant masters.

Most foreign-recruited legionaries never made it back home. Although the lucky ones who survived thirty-five years' service were granted Roman citizenship and a piece of ground to call their own wherever in the Empire they happened to be demobilised, few ever got to see Italy. Fewer still had any idea for what strategic reason they were posted from Britain to Spain, from Spain to the ever-restive *limes* in the far north of the Empire, and from there perhaps to Syria or Africa.

Throughout the known world they fought and died in return for regular meals, free clothing and lodging, medical care and a mean level of pay, including the daily allowance of salt that gave the word salary its first syllable. Even their burial arrangements were paid for by the legion's burial clubs, as witness the memorials of German legionaries on Hadrian's Wall, Spaniards on the Danube and Scythians in Spain. To desert the legion in which they served merited the death sentence. It had become their country, to which they belonged body and soul. They knew no other loyalty than that towards their NCOs and officers – which is why Rome mistrusted them on Italian soil. Only on the rare occasions of a triumph were any legionaries allowed within the gates of the City whose wealth came from the empire they had built and policed.

After the Roman Empire collapsed, the infrastructure of civilisation necessary to organise and pay mercenary armies did not exist in Europe until the early Middle Ages, when the imposition of monarchy and the shift from feudal knight service to scutage tax gave rulers the money once again to hire professional warriors who would stay until the end of their contract and not go home at the end of forty days' feudal obligation. In the early twelfth century King Stephen brought mercenaries from Brabant to England for his civil war against his cousin Matilda the Empress. For his campaigns both north and south of the Channel, Stephen's successor Henry II hired mercenaries from Wales, Flanders and Navarre. His bellicose son Richard Coeur de Lion went further afield, hiring specialist slingers from the Balearic Islands and crossbowmen from Genoa.

So long as discipline was tough and the pay regular, the system worked, but Richard's unpaid Navarrese mercenaries took their revenge by sacking his city of Bordeaux on the way home in 1176. His similarly cheated Flemings looted, pillaged and raped their way home across northern France in 1199. A few years later, during the campaign of his brother John that lost the duchy of Normandy to Philip Augustus of France, John's mercenaries under their warlord Louvrecaire robbed and raped the very people for whom they were ostensibly fighting, treating them like enemies, according to the chronicler.[1] At Crécy in 1346 Genoese crossbowmen broke and ran before the superior range of the English longbows and were subsequently made scapegoats for the French defeat. The same century saw the unpaid *almogovar* mercenaries from Spain turn on their Byzantine masters and ravage Thrace and Macedonia for two whole years.

After the Hundred Years' War ended at the battle of Castillon in 1453, much of western Europe was at the mercy of bands of men who offered to the highest bidder the only skill they possessed: soldiering. In the fifteenth century the 'free companies' of professional French, Swiss, Italian and German mercenaries were loyal so long as the pay lasted. When unpaid, they deserted on the eve of battle or, worse still, changed sides and betrayed their former employers, supporting themselves by living off the land and supplementing their irregular revenues by plunder.

Not until the seventeenth century did a European military leader return to the Roman model of what a legion should be. In the second Anglo-Dutch war after New Amsterdam had been captured by the English and renamed New York, Maurice of Nassau was rewarded with loyal and efficient service by his mercenaries in return for regular pay. Soldiering was respectable again – as exemplified by the Swiss mercenaries hired out by their own cantonal governments to anyone who could pay them, and who came to enjoy such a high reputation that they are still entrusted with guarding the Holy See and the Pope's person.

In pre-Revolutionary France, the *ancien régime* monarchs recruited a quarter of their army from foreign sources. Of 102 line infantry regiments, eleven were Swiss, serving under long-standing *capitulation* agreements with the cantonal governments; twelve other regiments were also composed of foreigners. The courage and loyalty of these units to the Crown at the time of the Revolution caused the Constituent Assembly to place an early ban of foreign units in the 'new' French army. However, with revolutionary anarchy being inimical to what soldiers term 'good order and discipline', when Austria invaded on 20 April 1792, the part-militia French army broke and ran on several occasions.

With Paris threatened in that September, the government recalled approximately 4,000 of the trustworthy Swiss mercenaries who had finally been discharged only a month before. Their numbers were swollen by Dutch and Belgian deserters enticed to the French side by the slogan *Liberté, Egalité, Fraternité!* and incorporated in the *Légion franche étrangère*, open to all comers, and the *Légion germanique* for German-speakers.

Under the Directory government 1795–99, foreign recruitment continued, helped by a new *capitulation* agreement with the cantons bringing another influx of Swiss mercenaries. Napoleon, ever-hungry for new blood to replace the enormous losses he incurred in his army of over half a million men, recruited foreign regiments from Liège, Ireland, Germany, Italy, Switzerland and the Vistula Legion from Poland – even Coptic and Greek units for use in his unfortunate Egyptian expedition 1798–1801. From 1802 onwards, his *bataillons étrangers* expanded to *régiments étrangers*, in which prisoners and deserters from different countries were deliberately mixed to minimise the risk of them conspiring to mutiny when their collective interest lay in turning their coats again. Mistrusting nevertheless their general level of competence, the Emperor preferred to use them for garrison and defence purposes, freeing French regiments for the more crucial roles.

After the Bourbon Restoration in 1814 the traditional reliance on foreign soldiery uninvolved in French politics continued partly because the enormous casualty rate of Napoleon's campaigns had lowered the French birth-rate at a time when most other European nations were expanding. In addition to the overpaid guards regiments, the paranoid Bourbon king Louis XVIII and his successor Charles X kept themselves in power by employing six regiments of Swiss mercenaries, plus the Hohenlohe Regiment, manned by foreigners from many countries. Being paid twice as much as their equivalent ranks in the French army and having far better conditions of service made the Swiss so unpopular that friction exploded into a regimental-scale war between them and 2nd Grenadiers at Versailles in November 1828.

Two years later, after several attacks on their men by civilians revenging themselves for the Swiss firing on the mob while defending Louis XVI in August 1792, the colonels of the mercenary regiments were obliged to obtain safe-conducts from the provisional regional commanders and move their troops out of the country as swiftly as possible. The scene was set for the creation of a truly foreign legion, which might, however, never have been created except for a tangled story known as *L'Affaire Bacri*.

In 1796 two Jewish merchants of Algiers named Bacri and Busnach had furnished grain to the Directorate to combat starvation, owing to peasants neglecting their fields during the Revolution. In gratitude for the grain, a June edition of *Le Moniteur* informed Parisians that, 'While all Europe stands against a free France, Algiers in Africa remains loyal, recognises the Republic and swears friendship to it.'[2]

Fine words, but business is business. Bacri and his partner subsequently sold the French debt at a discount to Dey Omar, the Turkish governor of Algiers. Napoleon, intending to conquer North Africa in the near future, could see no point in repaying the debt and went so far as to despatch a sapper major by the name of Boutin in 1808 to make a reconnaissance of Algiers for a possible invasion. About this time, Busnach was killed in an anti-Jewish riot that also cost the life of his protector Dey Ahmed Khodja. After the Bourbon Restoration, Louis XVIII settled accounts with the heirs of Bacri and Busnach, but their French creditors seized the money against their continental debts, leaving the Algerian debt still unpaid.

Fourteen of the thirty deys who ruled Algiers between 1710 and 1830 were assassinated, so it was no surprise when the current dey was strangled in a palace intrigue during 1817 and replaced by Ali Khodja, known to Europeans as Crazy Ali. He died of the plague the following year and was replaced by Dey Hussein – the man indirectly responsible for the Foreign Legion's long connection with Algeria.

On 29 April 1827, the eve of the Muslim feast of Id el-Seghir, Consul Deval representing French interests in Algiers called on Dey Hussein in his palace overlooking the Casbah, as was the custom each year to present the French government's compliments. Reminded by Hussein of the outstanding debt due, Deval replied less than courteously and was rewarded for his insolence by a glancing blow from Hussein's fly-whisk. Construed as an insult to France, the incident was used to justify a blockade of the port by the French navy, preparatory to an invasion.

With many domestic worries on his plate, Charles X hesitated for three years, so it was not until 16 May 1830 that his Minister of War Count Louis de Bourmont embarked 36,450 men in a fleet of 675 vessels at the port of Toulon. After a storm drove them back into harbour, they eventually landed at Sidi Ferruch 15km west of Algiers at 0100hrs on 14 June 1830. Fifty minutes later, the Turkish artillery on the hills overlooking the invasion beaches fired its first shell that killed a sailor on board the *Breslaw*, but could not prevent the French establishing a bridgehead, where men and equipment were landed during the next four days.

Hussein had at his disposal an army of 7,000 Turkish janissaries, 13,000 men sent by his ally the Bey of Constantine, 6,000 from Oran and 18,000 Kabyles – all encamped at Staoueli, a strategic position blocking the road to Algiers. Too wary of the warships' cannon to attack the bridgehead at its most vulnerable, this large but ill-coordinated army waited until the evening of 18 June before marching down to Sidi Ferruch. In this engagement and the counter-attack on the camp at Staoueli next day, the French suffered fifty-seven dead and 473 wounded. Once his supplies and reserves of munitions had caught up, Bourmont pressed inland, following the plan prepared by Napoleon's spy Boutin twenty-two years before.

He had a deadline for the capture of Algiers, but the Turks and their allies fought back hard in bloody hand-to-hand combat, selling every inch as dearly as possible. The bloodiest combats of 26–28 June brought Bourmont's force onto the plateau of El-Biar. The fort called Bordj Taos, manned by 2,000 janissaries, was blown up by the despairing defenders, enabling Bourmont to send a despatch to Paris that he had taken the city on the anniversary of the storming of the Bastille, although the surrender document was not signed until the following day in the palace of Djenane er-Raïs.

Back in Paris, Charles X had already dissolved the troublesome Chamber of Deputies in March of that year. Receiving the good news from Algiers on 9 July, he overestimated his subjects' enthusiasm for overseas possessions. The newspaper *Le Globe* summed up popular feeling about the invasion of Algeria thus: 'The motives are futile, the purpose suspect and the result uncertain to say the least.'[3]

Riding for a fall, Charles issued four repressive ordinances including the suppression of press freedom just over a fortnight later. It was the last straw. The ensuing revolution of the three 'Glorious Days' at the end of July not only saw him forced to flee to asylum in England with the liberal Duke Louis-Philippe of Orleans chosen by the bourgeoisie as replacement monarch, it also rang the death knell of the hated guards regiments that had kept Charles X in power. In the six weeks between 14 August and the end of September 1830 the Swiss were paid off, leaving only one foreign regiment, composed of a mixture of nationalities.

The Hohenlohe Regiment was stationed near the old port of Marseilles in the Fort St Jean, which coincidentally would see many later generations of Foreign Legion volunteers killing time within its walls until they were shipped out to Algeria to begin training. Apart from giving band concerts to entertain the townsfolk in the afternoons, the regiment had kept a low profile during the July Revolution, in return for which the Marseilles National Guard commander declared them naturalised Frenchmen with the honour of sporting a regimental number on their shakos instead of the H for Hohenlohe, which indicated foreign status.

The government did not agree and decided on 12 December to despatch these embarrassing aliens to the French garrison of Morea near Patras, which was supporting Greek independence fighters in western Greece. Less than a month later the government changed its mind and ordered the regiment disbanded on 5 January 1831. For a brief period, France had no foreign soldiers in her pay.

At the time, Paris could claim literally to be the City of Light, with several streets lit by gas lamps. Victor Hugo was campaigning against the death penalty after witnessing a public guillotining that went hideously wrong. Louis Braille had invented his system of embossed dots enabling blind people to 'read'. A nation-wide daily postal service was starting. The Academy of Sciences was divided by the debate over the theory of the origin of species.

An outbreak of cholera in Stains on the outskirts of Paris claimed fifteen victims, but for those with money the capital offered distractions a-plenty. Virginie Dejazet, an actress specialising in male roles, was playing Bonaparte to full houses. Rossini had just produced his opera *William Tell* at the Peletier Hall and Hector Berlioz heard the first performance of his *Symphonie Fantastique* after marching in the streets during the July Revolution.

From all corners of Europe, deserters and dissidents were flooding into France, whose post-Revolutionary governments had made it a *pays d'accueil*, or country of asylum, by unilaterally revoking the extradition treaties with the monarchist governments of Europe, imposed by the Congress of Vienna. Penniless, homeless and workless, the newcomers were tinder awaiting a spark. Riots, broken glass and burning buildings had been everyday scenes towards the end of Charles X's reign, and Louis-Philippe's government was all too well aware that violence could break out again.

Napoleon's veteran Marshal Soult, having expiated his loyalty to the Emperor by his own exile after the Hundred Days, was appointed Minister of War. It is he who is generally credited with the idea of creating the Foreign Legion, much as the English preferred to hire unemployed and dispossessed Scots and Irishmen or British-officered colonial forces to fight their imperial wars, rather than waste their own industrial manpower. The Indian army had been recruiting since 1765 and Britain's famous Gurkha mercenaries had been fighting for the Crown since 1817 when the Cuttack Legion was raised.

Soult was a soldier who had taken a leading part in the greatest military gamble since Rome. Yet, with the growth in political and military power of the German states, it was obvious that France's much-reduced army could not hope to extend French influence in Europe again in his lifetime.

Additionally, the army had lost so many French lives under Napoleon that it was understandably not popular since his fall, whereas the comparatively unbesmirched French navy held the key to the next phase of French expansion, with the Ministère de la Marine or Admiralty controlling the transport facilities and having the weaponry and the know-how to bombard and seize major seaports around the world, and then to put ashore *les marins-soldats* of its marine regiments who could garrison the captured cities and thus win colony after colony for France.

By creating under the War Ministry a regiment exclusively for deployment abroad composed of foreigners with previous military experience, Soult was giving the army a new lease of life in the only area of expansion still open to France: the winning of an overseas empire to replace Napoleon's lost European one. Put another way, he was playing the old game of inter-service rivalry at the same time as ridding France's cities of their dangerous dross. However, to get around the anti-military feeling of the time, he argued publicly for a legion of foreigners as a good way of getting off the streets and into uniform the dissidents with military experience who had been so prominent in the riots that unseated Charles X.

On 9 March 1831 the Chamber of Deputies passed his Bill and the following day Louis-Philippe signed the ordinance creating a legion of foreigners, to be officered by Frenchmen. All recruits had to be aged between 18 and 40 and not less than 1.52 metres (five feet) in height. As with line infantry regiments, each battalion was to have eight companies of 112 men, whose uniform was to be a royal blue tailcoat with red piping, and crimson trousers, with a heavy – and very hot – black shako. The iron-grey greatcoat was to be carried rolled up in a ticking cover atop the back-pack.

The stipulation in the Bill that the new corps should serve only outside France somehow got lost between Louis Philippe's desk and the drafting of the ordinance, but was taken as read from the outset – and continued to be so except for emergencies until 1962. On 18 March 1831 a supplementary order barred enlistment by Frenchmen and married men.

Overseas service at the time embraced the French garrisons in Greece, at Ancona in Italy and on the islands of Guadaloupe and Martinique. Thanks to Dey Hussein's ill-judged gesture with the fly-whisk, it would also include the little war in Algiers. However, the Foreign Legion's first home was in Champagne at Langres, a safe 300km from Paris. There, unemployed foreigners already living in France and men honourably discharged from the Hohenlohe Regiment were turned away by the commanding general of the 18th Military Division, into whose jurisdiction

Langres fell. The Legion, he made clear, would accept only immigrants.

His ruling reinforces historians' opinion that the Legion was intended by Soult as nothing more than a sink for dissidents, as does a letter written three years later to Gen Voirol, C-in-C Algiers, who had suggested that the mediocre performance of legionnaires in his jurisdiction would be improved if their initial engagement was raised from three years to five. The venerable Marshal replied tersely, 'As the Foreign Legion was set up with the sole purpose of … giving a destination to foreigners flooding into France and who might cause trouble, we have no need to consider your suggestion. The government has no desire to look for recruits for this Legion. This corps is simply an asylum for misfortune.'[4] The Marshal was either being disingenuous, or simply disillusioned with the performance of the Legion until then.

In 1831 social unrest in France was reaching dangerous heights. In Lyon 600 workers were killed or seriously injured when a mob of 15,000 confronted the National Guard. The Ariège region was torn by a revolution of peasants and shepherds. Disguised as women to hide their identity and calling themselves Les Demoiselles, they attacked gamekeepers who confiscated their flocks for illicit pasturing. In Paris, tailors fearing unemployment were smashing the new-fangled sewing machines in a lingerie factory in the rue des Sèvres. Even workers with jobs lived meanly, the capital's building labourers being paid just enough to live in dormitories with fewer beds than bodies and one stinking earth-closet toilet among sixty men.

From all the border cities, especially those in the northeast, came warnings to Paris that the flood of foreign trouble-makers was increasing, not drying up. So why was the Legion allotted a barracks in Langres that could only accommodate 385 men, if it was intended to soak up many thousands of potentially troublesome refugees?

Towards the end of March 1831 Soult ordered the depot for primarily German-speaking deserters entering France from the northeast to be moved to the depressed textile town of Bar-le-Duc in Lorraine, overriding the protests of the Prefect of the *département* on behalf of local inhabitants who had no desire for their town's economic troubles to be aggravated by an influx of destitute deserters. Two other towns with similar problems were Auxerre in Burgundy – which had a depot for the reception of Italian-speakers imposed upon it – and Agen, midway between Bordeaux and Toulouse, which became the base to which Spanish refugees were directed.

By July 1832, 15 months after it had been set up, the Langres/Bar-le-Duc depot had attracted a total of 1,164 legionnaires[5], as they were coming to be called. This does not seem like a significant contribution to the refugee problem, but it was far in excess of the number that could be accommodated in barracks – which makes the choice of the Legion's second home even more questionable. With the majority of legionnaires billeted in private homes in the unwalled town, discipline was impossible to enforce and normal garrison duties difficult to organise. In any case, most of the men had neither arms to drill with, nor uniforms to clean and polish.

Eleven hundred restive men need to be kept busy. It had been envisaged that Legion officers and NCOs would be drawn from the regular army, which was itself in upheaval. Denunciations of officers allegedly disloyal to the July monarchy, usually by subordinates who wanted their jobs, resulted in thousands of dismissals including the colonels of forty-four of the sixty-four infantry regiments and out of the twelve regiments of dragoons[6]. Lower down the scale, revolutionary democracy saw junior officers replaced by NCOs, which in turn caused a shortage of experienced NCOs.

The government's solution was to recall the *demi-soldes* – Napoleon's officers retired to their country estates on half-pay. Like many political answers to military questions, it caused as many problems as it cured, the return of senior officers meaning their subordinates kissing goodbye to any chance of promotion. In addition, after their years in retirement on their country estates, the *demi-soldes* tended to be poor disciplinarians and were out-of-date in the drills and manoeuvres that served as tactics at the time.

Not surprisingly, service in the hotch-potch Legion of refugees attracted only those officers and NCOs who had no family connections or were simply not wanted elsewhere. Its first commander, Baron Christophe Antoine Jacques Stoffel complained soon after the move to Bar-le-Duc, 'Of the twenty-six officers here, only eight are competent. The others have been retired for some time, are foreigners or cavalrymen. It is imperative that we be sent good *German-speaking* line officers.'[7]

One of the twenty-six was labelled 'the worst officer in the army' by an inspecting general. Col Stoffel's admin staff were either incompetent or corrupt, or both, lining their own pockets by selling supplies instead of distributing them. Even he complained that his companies were commanded by second-lieutenants who stole the pay of their men and spent it themselves, while in many cases their NCOs neither understood French nor could keep accounts, and so had no idea what stores had been issued to whom.

Ignoring the resistance of the French officer corps to the employment of foreign officers, the government set about recruiting foreigners who would make a better job than Stoffel's original staff. It was not easy. Of the many Spanish officers who had fled to France, only six were enticed to Bar-le-Duc, and all of them resigned within months. In the first four years of its existence, the Legion saw 107 foreign officers come and go – mainly Swiss, German and Polish. Nor was the inspecting general much impressed by poor Stoffel. By background a Swiss staff officer, he was assessed as lacking military experience and familiarity with French army regulations, although it was admitted that he was popular with his men and genuinely concerned for their welfare.

Stoffel's two battalion commanders – Maj Clavet Gaubert and Maj Salomon de Musis – did not conceal their poor opinion of him. Although their sarcastic comments went over the heads of the men, few of whom could speak French, the colonel's habit of reviewing his motley Legion on parade accompanied by his mistress dressed as a man must have seemed unusual. The inspecting general thought so, and required it to stop – which did not prevent a later commanding officer of the Legion from indulging a similar habit.

It is a truism that all armies are run by their sergeants. The dearth of experienced NCOs in the Legion therefore led to a decision to promote the more educated German-speaking refugees to serve as corporals. This was a disastrous choice, for academic intelligence has little to do with wielding authority over men from different countries and very different social backgrounds. The rank-and-file objected to what they saw as the airs and graces of the new corporals, whose precarious authority was undermined by men who had themselves been NCOs in previous armies, while the corporals' middle-class sensibilities made it hard to share dormitories with illiterates who habitually sold any article of equipment or clothing – their own or stolen from a comrade – in order to buy drink.

The educated men were therefore segregated into two separate companies, where they clustered, refusing new 'promotions' in the hope that their superior education would lead to them being collectively nominated as the two elite companies of grenadiers and skirmishers to which a normal line battalion was entitled. With no such provision in the Legion until April the following year, their premature addition of grenade badges to their shakos had to be expressly forbidden.

Arrests owing to drunken brawling resulted in the local prison having to accommodate up to fifty-six legionnaires per communal cell, with a can for its only sanitation. The prison authorities had no funds to feed military prisoners, but provisions from the Legion commissariat were intermittent at best, with the defaulters' quartermasters often unaware they were in the cells.

By mid-May of 1831 the Legion was in a state of mutiny so acute that the two battalion commanders had to call out a hundred men of the National Guard to protect civilian police charged with arresting the ring-leaders. Even this attempt to impose normal military discipline turned to farce because twenty of the arrested men could not be court-martialled. Not having been formally inducted and made to sign enlistment papers, they were officially civilians not subject to military law.

The decision in November to despatch this travesty of an army to North Africa had little to do with its military value in the campaign around Algiers. Stoffel's men were being sent there to die. Understandably, he foresaw massive desertions on the march to Toulon for embarkation on 25 November. Probably the only happy people in Bar-le-Duc were the local inhabitants, watching Stoffel's ill-dressed ragtag army shambling away towards the distant Mediterranean. In the event, few men went missing during the 700km march – perhaps because they had already discovered that life as a penniless deserter was even harsher than in the Legion with all its problems. Or perhaps they simply had no idea of the hell that awaited them south of the Mediterranean.

Chapter 6

THE SCARECROW SOLDIERS

Algeria 1831–1835

The French navy did not waste its single prestige steamship, the paddle-steamer *Sphynx*, on shipping across the Mediterranean several hundred men who were going to die. It was from wooden troopships, pitching and tossing abominably in the teeth of the December gales that the landlubber legionnaires gained their first impression of their new home. It was not comforting.

After 120 years of Turkish rule the *casbah* of El Djazaïr[1] – the name was soon be Europeanised to 'Alger' in French and 'Algiers' in English – was a medieval city of 15,000 homes jammed together within its imposing walls, protected by a deep dry moat. Outside the Bab Azoun, or southern gate, where Stoffel's men were drawn up to impress the natives, rows of hooks on the walls showed where the heads of executed men had been impaled until recently. As to impressing the natives, the author Camille Rousset – one of the few European civilians present – commented, 'To clad this mob, which comprised of men of every age from sixteen to sixty and over, we appear to have scraped the bottom of army supplies to procure the oldest rags. They were a bizarre sight that would have delighted a circus crowd. But, their heads high, their banner before them, their drums beating to the rhythm of the famous war-song *La Parisienne*, they proudly paraded through the crowded city streets.'[2]

The banner to which Rousset refers was a cock rampant with its talon on a globe marked 'France'[3] and they were marching at the slow pace of eighty-eight paces to the minute, as taught by their NCOs from the Hohenlohe Regiment – as they obstinately continue to do today, making problems for any unit behind them in a parade. Obviously not a military man, Rousset mistook the popular ditty the legionnaires were singing for a marching song, but his remarks on their dress were accurate: in complete defiance to the Ordinance, the quartermasters had issued just about every cast-off uniform the army wanted to get rid of, from 1789 National Guard, Imperial Guards, Royal Guards, Swiss Guards, infantry, cavalry and artillery.

There was little that was familiar to the legionnaires' European eyes in a walled city dominated by the palace of the former *dey*, from the topmost tower of which fluttered the tricolour flag that had replaced Charles X's fleur-de-lys banner after the July Revolution. The main thoroughfare later known as the rue Bab Azoun was lined with arcades of shops and stalls from which, thanks to the mixture of blood from centuries of slaving, all the male faces of Africa north of the Equator peered out at the newcomers while veiled women followed by their African slaves made their way to the baths and markets. There were also the *kouloglis* of mixed Turkish and native blood.

Founded by the Phoenicians, captured by Carthaginians and from them by the Romans, Algiers had been destroyed by the Vandals in the fifth century, to be revived as a Berber dynasty in the tenth long before the Turks arrived. Now the Turks too were gone, chased out by these fair-skinned foreigners who would one day also go, as they had come, in blood and fire and grief.

The slave market was a reminder that the city had been built largely by Christian slaves of the Barbary corsairs, who levied a toll on all vessels passing through the southern Mediterranean. In default of payment, they took the vessels as prizes, selling off their cargoes, enslaving their crews, ransoming the passengers and selling any female captives to the harems of North Africa and the Middle East. This traditional privateering had gone too far in 1804 when the US frigate *Philadelphia* was taken prize and naval officer Stephen Decatur was despatched to wreak retribution on the corsair harbour of Tripoli and burn *Philadelphia* at her mooring. Succeeding in his objective and escaping under fire with only one man wounded won him a captain's commission and a sword of honour from the Congress – an adventure still commemorated in the US Marine Corps hymn, *From the halls of Montezuma to the shores of Tripoli.*

Relieved to be on land again, the legionnaires saw the scars of cannonry from the recent French attack on the city walls and on the white marble Roman columns with Ionic capitals of the 'barracks of the whey drinkers', just inside the walls. Fresh milk was supplied to the city-dwellers by peasants who drove herds of goats or donkeys through the city gates to milk them at the customer's door and the barracks' recently departed teetotal janissary inmates had been in the habit of levying an unofficial extra tax in kind on them each morning, to guarantee themselves a permanent cost-free supply of milk.

In all, the city boasted seven Turkish barracks capable of housing 9,722 janissaries, but the Legion was not to be accommodated within the walls at all. Like a politically unreliable ally, it was based 5km away in a palace of the former *dey* at Moustafa. In this Moorish/Turkish extravaganza of marble floors, pillars and fountains with fine fixtures and fittings, from which the furniture had been pillaged during the invasion, there was plenty of space for the legionnaires to sling their hammocks.

The Maghreb[4], or North African littoral, is today divided into the countries of Morocco, Algeria, Tunisia and Libya, but was then an unmapped confusion of tribal territories. The writ of the *dey* had run in the cities of Algiers and a few towns, but the surrounding countryside was ruled by local chieftains whose traditional independence would give the French colonists problems intermittently for the next ninety years.

As though it were a unified country on the European model, the new masters of Algiers created in 1839 the name 'Algeria' to define geographically and politically that part of the North African littoral they sought to control. The inhabitants were politely called 'Arabs', despite the Berbers living mostly in the Atlas Mountains having their own language, script and customs, as did the Tuareg of the Sahara.

In the Oranais – the western third of the region that would become French Algeria – the tribes were loosely united under a religious leader, the saint or *sidi* Mahdi ed-Din. Imam of a religious school near Mouaskar, he decided that he was too old to undertake the military harassment of the French based in Oran and delegated this task not to his eldest son, but to his second son,

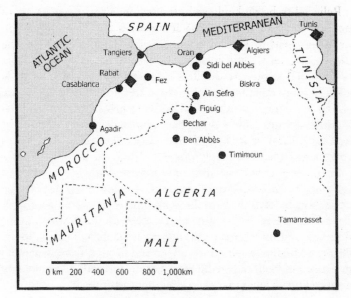

The Maghreb / French North Africa

Abd el-Kader. Already renowned for both piety and military prowess this charismatic 24-year-old would become the greatest thorn in the side of successive French generals.

Through 1832 his spies watched the occupation forces under Gen Pierre Berthezène occupy Algiers, Oran and Bejaïa, noting that their quality was extremely uneven. A quasi-militia corps calling itself *les Volontaires de la Charte*, but also known as the Parisian Volunteers, was nicknamed 'the French Bedouin'. Universally detested for its thieving, ill discipline and debauchery, the Volunteers were dissolved by Berthezène, its less unsavoury members transferred to the Zouaves. Originally intended as a native light infantry, the distinctively attired Zouaves became a European force, but retained their mock-Turkish uniforms. Others of the Volunteers were drafted into 67th Infantry Regiment in the traditional military way of breaking up bad units.

1st, 2nd and 5th battalions of the Legion stayed near Algiers when 4th Battalion was posted to Oran and the Belgians of 6th Battalion went east to Annaba. The 7th Battalion was being formed

103

in France, of Polish immigrants, but when it did eventually arrive in Algeria 35 men were missing at the first roll-call. Two days later an entire company got drunk and attacked its officers, resulting in the court-martialling of two ring-leaders.[5]

The fine-sounding title of the light cavalry corps known as the Chasseurs d'Afrique, created in November 1831 just before the arrival of the Legion, concealed a similar problem that led to two mutinies in its first three years, ending with executions of the ring-leaders and cashiering of officers considered responsible.

The unrest in the soldiery mirrored that in metropolitan France. In cycle after cycle of strikes and bloody repression, even the rag-and-bone men of Paris struck to protest against organised garbage collection. With a national census numbering the population at 32,500,000, a new law enfranchised anyone reaching the tax threshold of 200 francs per annum, thus doubling the electorate. Branding with hot iron, the pillory and cutting off the hand of thieves were abolished on 28 April, but the increasing liberty of the citizen at home had little effect in occupied Algiers. The conditions under which European soldiers served there were appalling, starting with the poor food and Napoleonic uniforms with high black shakos quite unsuitable for the heat of the Maghreb summer. Disease was rife, especially malaria and dysentery, but in France too the cholera epidemic was claiming up to 13,000 lives in one month, with black tea recommended as the only cure.

In the fashionable salons on the banks of the Seine, gossip was not of such depressing subjects, but the astounding revelation of the identity of author George Sand. Madame Aurore Dudevant was a liberated woman who dressed as a man on occasion, had left her husband and openly flaunted the lover whose name she had borrowed to get her first newspaper articles published in Le Figaro. Her first novel Indiana was about ... a free-thinking woman who abandoned her husband to find true love.

When Napoleon's only son known as the Young Eagle[6], died outside Vienna in the palace of Schönbrunn on 22 July, the Legion was long gone from its vandalised palace at Mustapha. The organisation of its battalions on notionally 'national' lines – which did not stop most of the men in 6th Dutch-Belgian Battalion being German deserters who had entered France over the Belgian frontier – led to inter-battalion fighting so violent that the commanding general in Algiers, Duke René Savory of Rovigo[7], had to break them up into small detachments to avoid 'one drunken brawl touching off an insurrection'.[8]

With tribes constantly feuding outside the immediate areas of the few towns occupied by the French, when emissaries of the Sheikh of Biskra were killed by hereditary enemies while en route to treat with him, Rovigo ordered the massacre of every man, woman and child in the tribe responsible. Accustomed to European warfare, where such deliberate atrocities were no longer usual, the more thoughtful legionnaires must have asked themselves to what hell they had been consigned.

By the end of a year in North Africa, when it was honoured with the award of its first regimental banner, the Legion numbered 3,168 men, of whom the inspecting general opined on 1 December 1832 that the ninety-four Swiss, mostly from the disbanded Bourbon Guards regiments, were 'zealous'; the ninety-eight Belgians and Dutch were 'good soldiers', as were the nineteen Danes and Swedes and eighty-five Poles. The ten Englishmen had 'little known' about them; the 571 Italians were 'aloof and jealous', and he considered that the eighty-seven French had only joined for more rapid promotion than they could expect in a regular army unit. The root of the Legion's problem, he concluded, lay with the high number of German-speakers. These 2,196 men were, in his words, '… deserters or political refugees, medical students, lawyers or notaries *of a worrying imagination*. They must continually be watched'.[9]

They were presumably also better at sums than the general. But what was he complaining about? Apart from the Swiss and some of the Poles, most of the others had not chosen a military life. For political reasons they dared not return to their home countries. With France not having enough work for its own people, the Legion was the only employment they could find.

It was all very well for Rovigo to declare that the problem lay with 'a hundred or so bad characters, deserters from various armies, who require close watching'.[10] He believed that leaders 'who knew how to lead men could soon create an esprit de corps',[11] but what officers and NCOs could have produced first-class soldiers from such unsuitable material?

After his December 1833 inspection, Gen Voriol commented that 6th battalion at Annaba had regular uniforms but the others still had not. He castigated the French Legion officers for using 'insulting and disdainful expressions', which incited 'resistance and insubordination'. Regimental pride, he said, was non-existent, drunkenness endemic, the turnover of troops too great, with no one intending to re-enlist once his three years' service was completed.[12]

Many military units with poor reputations in peacetime first pull together and earn the approval of their critics when under enemy fire. The Legion could never build esprit de corps that way because it was constantly split up into small detachments, confined with other troops in a series of blockhouses built to warn of raiders approaching Algiers. What news from France reached them was of a country riven by widespread strikes threatening to bring down Louis-Philippe's tottering government. The Assembly was regularly split on many issues including the occupation of Algiers, while the French population in general cared not a jot for this travesty of an Empire that contributed nothing to their wellbeing. Had Algiers been worth having, they concluded, the English would probably have grabbed it in the first place, given their other interests in the Mediterranean.

On 1 April 1832 Col Michel Combe took command of this unhappy regiment. Less than a week passed before he found out the realities of war in Africa. Learning that many legionnaires had already deserted from at least one previous army, the El Ouffia tribe, in whose territory a blockhouse called Maison Carrée had been built, openly welcomed Legion deserters. On 6 April 1832 Sgt Muller of 3rd Battalion informed Maj de Musis that two Bedouin had offered him and a comrade asylum, presumably in return for their weapons. The three men pretended to take up the offer, but played a double game and led a large detachment to the tribe's camp, nearly losing their lives when the subterfuge was discovered just before the attack went in. In the resultant massacre the Legion killed sixty-eight members of El Ouffia. Two genuine deserters found in the camp also died. The loot, allegedly valued at 10,000 francs, was distributed according to rank in the normal way.[13]

The day after the massacre, a revenge attack was beaten off, but on 3 May near Maison Carrée twenty-seven legionnaires and twenty-five Chasseurs d'Afrique commanded by Maj de Musis were caught in an ambush. The Legion was not issued rifles until 1854 and the muzzle-loading muskets they had in 1832 were accurate at a maximum range of 100 metres, being viable only when used for disciplined volley firing by men who stood firm, with one rank aiming and firing at the mounted enemy armed with lances and camel-hide shields while the other reloaded.

This engagement began badly, with Musis abandoning his men and riding off with the cavalry, ostensibly to get reinforcements. Under the command of a young Swiss lieutenant named Cham, the legionnaires fired a single volley and then ran for the cover of a small wood some distance away. It was a fatal error that led to them being ridden down and speared from the saddle. The survivors taken prisoner were offered by their captors the choice of converting to Islam or death. All except one were killed, Cham earning the dubious distinction of becoming the first officer of the Legion to die in combat. The solitary convert to Islam, a Saxon called Wagner, found himself a slave in the enemy camp together with five deserters from the Legion, whose lot was so desperate that they attempted to escape and were killed in the attempt.

Wagner managed to get back to Algiers two weeks after his capture, whereupon Rovigo publicised his story that the Arabs forced deserters to write letters to their comrades saying that they would be rewarded with a horse, money and women, whereas most deserters not killed outright were used as slaves by their captors.[14] Musis' punishment was to be transferred to a penal infantry battalion, where he died two years later in an Arab ambush. Ironically, the Maison Carrée massacre happened only six weeks after the National Assembly passed a law declaring that no non-French person could serve in the armed forces.

On 9 November 1832 the Legion welcomed a new commander, Lt Col Joseph Bernelle. Two days later Abd el-Kader, who would be a thorn in the French side for years to come, arrived outside the gates of Oran at the head of 3,000 horsemen. Legionnaires of 4th Battalion were on the French left at the resulting battle on the slopes of Djebel Tafaraouini. In March 1833, 6th Battalion participated in the drive against the Ouled Yacub and Ouled Attia tribes near Algiers. In June, 4th and 5th Battalions took the port of Arzew before going on to capture the coastal city of Mostagenem, between Algiers and Oran.

Their losses in combat were insignificant compared with those from disease. Malaria and cholera were enemies more feared than the natives and dehydration from dysentery was the main cause of deaths. The Legion may have suffered more than the regular army units from being deliberately posted to unhealthy places like the penal battalions and units sent to Algeria for punishment, such as 66th Infantry Regiment, which had refused to open fire on striking workers during the November 1831 riots in Lyon. Of forty legionnaires posted to Maison Carrée in 1834 not one was still on his feet four weeks later, let alone in any condition to fight.

During the four years of the Legion's first posting to Algeria, approximately 3,200 men died from disease or were discharged as unfit for further duty: a casualty rate of one in four. Nor was hospitalisation a desirable option: conditions in the *lazaret* were so bad that gallows humour defined it as the place where legionnaires went to die. With no nursing or even proper bedding, the sick were so badly fed that they had to sell equipment and clothing to buy food. One dysentery sufferer was sentenced to two months in prison for selling his boots and gaiters in order to purchase the medicines without which he would have died.

Most of the time, the Legion was employed as a cheap labour force. The great tradition of road building, tunnelling and general civil engineering which is one of the proudest aspects of its colonial years obscures the fact that draining malarial marshes with pick and shovel was more dangerous than facing the enemy.

Despairing of bringing their elusive nomadic foes to battle, the French tried diplomacy. On 26 February 1834, Baron Louis Alexis Desmichels, governor of Oran, bought time in the struggle against Abd el-Kader by acknowledging him as the *amir* or commander of all the tribes of the Oranais region in return for Abd el-Kader's recognition of French sovereignty. Whilst neither side had any intention of abiding by the terms of the treaty, it was at least a more subtle approach than that of Gen Thomas Bugeaud in Paris. There, on 14 April he ordered the 35th Regiment of line to open fire on a demonstration organised by the Society for the Rights of Man, at the end of which twenty unarmed citizens lay dead.

A supporter of Napoleon during the Hundred Days, Bugeaud had bought his way back into favour under Louis-Philippe by accepting the unpopular role as commandant of the Vauban fortress at Blaye while that extraordinary woman the Duchess of Berry was confined there – as a plaque on her quarters bears witness today. Its portrait of her jailer shows a clean-shaven man with pock-marked cheeks and a strong nose and chin. Prematurely bald with a tonsure of white hair that earned him the soldiers' nickname of Le Père Bugeaud or 'Old Bugeaud', he wears an expression of world-weary disillusionment that belies his brutality, still echoed in Algeria each time an Arab mother warns her naughty son to be good by threatening, 'or else Bi-jo will get you'.

Mother of a grandson of Charles X known as the Miracle Child because he was born after the assassination of his father in 1820, the Duchess of Berry illicitly entered France twelve years later disguised as a washerwoman in the hope of claiming the throne for her son. Her short-lived rebellion in the Vendée ended after a few weeks with her arrest in Nantes, leading to her imprisonment at Blaye until she surprised Bugeaud and his political masters in Paris by giving birth to a daughter by an obscure Italian nobleman she had married before setting out for France. The scandal was considered by Louis-Philippe to render her claims to the throne on behalf of the Miracle Child so ridiculous that Bugeaud was ordered to escort her back to Palermo in Sicily, where he bade farewell and confessed to feeling as though a hundred-pound weight had been removed from his heart on being relieved of such a dishonourable duty.

During a debate the following year, a fellow-parliamentarian unwisely used Bugeaud's nickname, the Jailer, to his face. Immediately challenged to a duel, the offender was lying dead twenty-four hours later with Bugeaud's first shot lodged in his brains. And yet, the winner of that duel was to become one of the Legion's best-loved commanders!

In Algeria, Abd el-Kader was playing a waiting game, using the treaty with Desmichels to impose his authority on those tribes reluctant to acknowledge him. Inevitably the truce was broken, this time by the French. On 26 June 1835 at 0500hrs Gen Camille Trézel, hoping to avoid the worst of the midsummer heat, arranged his column of three battalions of infantry and a large supply convoy into a rough square formation screened by four squadrons of Chasseurs d'Afrique to cross the area of scrub called Muley-Ismaël near the city of Oran, 400km west of Algiers.

A Roman legionary of 3rd Augusta Legion in North Africa marched at the pace of around 30km a day. Trézel required at least the same of his men, despite their much less suitable thick woollen uniforms, knapsacks weighing over thirty-five kilos, each man carrying musket or rifle and bayonet, a pick or shovel, 300 rounds of ammunition[15] and wood for his cooking fire unless it was certain that wood was freely available at that night's camp.

In this engagement, Maj Ludwig Joseph Conrad's three companies of the Legion's Polish 4th Battalion were in the lead. Small, but broad, wearing a red skullcap instead of an officer's tricorne hat when in action, Conrad was a buccaneering soldier who had earned both decorations and several wounds in thirty years of derring-do since leaving the military academy of St Cyr.

The Italians of the 5th Battalion and two of the cavalry squadrons were on his left flank. While trapped in a narrow ravine, men of 4th Battalion came under fire from Arabs hiding in the undergrowth. Moving forward to engage in line formation, it was driven back. The 2nd Chasseurs d'Afrique then charged the concealed enemy, but when Col Oudinot at their head was shot his panicking bugler blew the retreat by mistake. In the resulting chaos, 5th Battalion moved forward on the left. Together with a battalion of the ill-fated 66th Infantry, they managed to drive the Arabs away from the baggage train. For seven hours a series of skirmishes raged until Trézel managed to disengage, leaving fifty-two dead and with 180 wounded to transport on the undamaged wagons that had been unloaded for use as ambulances.

The day after the nightmare of Muley-Ismaël he regrouped his forces beside the River Sig while attempting unsuccessfully to parley with Abd el-Kader. On the morning of 28 June, the French column set out, heading north for the comparative safety of the port of Arzew. Out of musket range, considerable numbers of mounted Arabs were visibly tracking the column's progress and biding their time to attack. At 1400hrs – the hottest time of day – they had the occasion that would have delighted any general. The French force was trapped between the edge of the Muley-Ismaël forest on their left and the Macta marshes on their right, both giving cover to their attackers, who fired the tinder-dry rushes to cause smoke and confusion, panicking the horses and harness mules of the baggage train.

The exposed Poles of 5th Battalion were ordered to keep the enemy at bay, but not allow themselves to become separated from the rest of the column. Conrad, however, impetuously disobeyed orders and led his men in a charge on the concealed enemy. It was a mistake. At the tree-line his men were driven back by a hail of fire, panicking also 66th Infantry Regiment and leaving the left flank of the column wide open. Trying to repair the breach, Conrad ordered the Italians from 4th Battalion to join him behind a hillock which gave them some temporary cover. Finding themselves unprotected, the muleteers cut the traces of the wagons, abandoning the wounded men in the hope of riding off to safety and adding to the confusion when swiftly bogged down in deep mud.

On riding up from the rearguard, Trézel found what remained of his column in disarray. Personally leading a charge of the two cavalry squadrons that had not fled, he managed to drive off Arabs who were killing the wounded, then deployed his small section of artillery with some Legion infantry and men from the penal Bataillons d'Afrique to cover him leading the rest of the column to safety at Arzew. The cost? Over 300 surviving wounded, sixty-two known dead and 280 missing in action, which almost certainly meant dead after mutilation and/or emasculation.

In the post-mortem, much blame was attached to the Legion under Conrad. Within the Legion itself recriminations bounced back and forward, the Poles accusing the Italians and vice versa. To try and avoid a repetition of this, and possibly also because the irregular arrivals of recruits made it impossible to keep nationally segregated battalions up to strength, Legion commander Bernelle took the radical step of deliberately mixing nationalities. It was at that moment that one could say the Legion as we know it had been born.

It was almost a still-birth. Even before the news of the débâcle in the Macta marshes put the Algerian adventure on hold, Louis-Philippe's government had been debating in Paris what to do with this ill-favoured child of the July Revolution.

Chapter 7

NO PAY, NO BULLETS, NO MERCY

Spain, 1835–1839

After the death of Spain's King Fernando VII, civil war broke out between his brother Don Carlos and the legitimate heir, Fernando's daughter the Infanta Isabella II, whose mother Queen Maria Cristina was acting as regent. Under the Four-Power Pact signed on 28 August 1834 France, England and Portugal promised interventionist forces to assist Isabella's liberal government – after which, France's first act was to transfer from Algeria to Spain 439 Spanish legionnaires in the Legion's 4th Battalion.

In Paris Adolphe Thiers, an ambitious journalist who had taken up politics in the July Revolution, was Minister of the Interior and would soon be Prime Minister. Eager to re-establish France as an international power after the humiliations of 1812 in Moscow and 1815 at Waterloo, Thiers was determined to at least equal the Portuguese and British interventionist forces south of the Pyrenees. When he now proposed committing *French* troops, Nicolas Soult's voice of reason warned from his personal experience of commanding Napoleon's army in the Peninsula War 1808–1813 that Spain was indeed a country where small armies were beaten and large armies starved. Better not to get involved, was the gist of his argument. However, Thiers' threat to resign if he did not get his own way persuaded Louis-Philippe to back him at a meeting of the Council of Ministers on 6 June 1835.

To avoid the possible embarrassment of French troops either being defeated in Spain or needing reinforcement, Soult decided to transfer the rest of the Legion from Algeria, so that France could be seen to be supportive without French nationals actually being involved. To ensure that the gesture did not even cost the overstretched French Exchequer any money, it was agreed that

Isabella's government in Madrid should be responsible for provisioning and paying the Legion, once on Spanish soil. A convention to this effect being signed in Paris, the Legion ceased to be part of France's armed forces on 29 June.

News of the Legion's transfer to the Spanish Crown infuriated its officers, who would have been prepared to fight for France in Spain, but not as Spanish soldiers. To calm the unrest, two spokesmen were sent from Paris to explain that whereas all legionnaires were obliged to go to Spain, French officers had the choice of resigning and transferring to other regiments, unless they had joined from civilian life, in which case they had to leave the army. Foreign officers who refused the transfer to Spain were back on the street. That was the stick. The carrot was an element of bribery, with promotions being offered to replace the resignations, which were so numerous that eighty-five junior officers took advantage of this.[1]

The military situation in Spain was that the Carlist forces in the northern provinces adjoining the Pyrenees had been very successful under the Basque Col Tomás Zumalacárregui until he was ordered by Don Carlos for strategic reasons to besiege the port of Bilbao. His irregulars being ill-equipped for this, the siege had to be abandoned, but not before inadequate treatment of a slight leg wound resulted in gangrene and cost Zumalacárregui's life.

On 28 July a Corsican separatist assassin narrowly missed killing Louis-Philippe in Paris, the multi-barrel gun he had invented for the purpose leaving forty of the king's escort dead. No one in the Legion would have mourned the monarch who had signed them away with a few strokes of his quill. And yet, when the now mixed battalions of the Legion landed at Tarragona on 17 August 1835 after being held in quarantine for cholera on Mallorca, the Germans and Italians were singing an especially composed hymn vaunting the role of the Legion in suppressing tyranny on behalf of freedom, as befitted grandsons of the Revolution of 1789. The welcome accorded the six battalions of legionnaires led by 123 officers was lukewarm, the population greeting the column of marching men led by Col Jean-Nicolas Bernelle on a horse, followed by his wife and her maid on mules, with some cries of '*Viva la libertad*!' and '*Viva la Francia*' but few monarchists daring to call out '*Viva la reína!*'

Those legionnaires who heaved a sigh of relief at being back on European soil and thought nothing could be worse than fighting guerrillas in Algeria were in for a rude awakening. In Catalunya, they fought at Artesa de Segre, Gerri and Pobla de Segur.

After marching 400km inland to Vitoria, the Legion found itself universally hated by a population of women, old men and children, whose men of military age were in the mountains with Don Carlos' irregulars while the Infanta's forces sat tight in the towns and cities. The hostility to men wearing French uniforms, so soon after Napoleon's armies had ravaged the peninsula, was exacerbated by Isabella's Prime Minister Juan Alvarez Mendizábal policy of selling off extensive Church properties to finance the war. Local priests told their congregations that the legionnaires were revolutionary atheists or worse.

The legionnaires in their blue jackets with red, yellow or green epaulettes and red trousers – and bright red shakos visible for miles[2] – had come from the intolerable heat of Algeria to the cold, bleached uplands of the Basque country as autumn was turning to winter, with the first snow silvering the peaks of the Pyrenees, beyond which lay the country that had given them away to a government in Madrid that had no resources to equip, feed or pay its own soldiers, let alone the foreigners in its service. Supply was so bad that operations had to be cancelled and engagements broken off because ammunition failed to arrive and many men sold their useless sabres for food.

Already occupying the best quarters in Vitoria when the Foreign Legion arrived was a British Legion commanded by George de Lacy Evans, who had fought brilliantly against the French at Vitoria in 1813. Favoured with the rank of lieutenant-general by Maria Cristina, he outranked his former enemy in the Peninsular War. Bernelle, given the courtesy title of Mariscal de Campo or Brigadier by the queen on 30 June 1835, found himself in an impossible situation. Whilst government forces were evenly matched numerically against the insurgents, far too many stayed safely in the garrisoned cities for them to have any hope of wiping out the elusive bands of guerrillas. Nor were Evans' men of the calibre to fight so uneven a war.

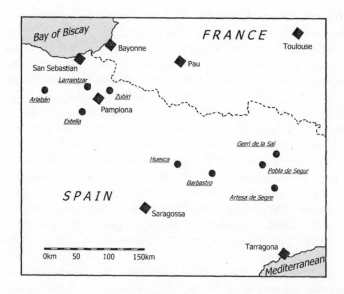

'The Spanish Intervention 1835–39 / Legion battles in italics

In England, the Duke of Wellington had opposed intervention for reasons similar to Soult's, and regular army officers had followed his lead. The 400 officers of the British Legion were therefore either second-rate mercenaries or restless amateurs with no previous military experience, who were simply out for an adventure. Nor were their 6,000-plus rank-and-file much better. Evans' force was a mirror of the Foreign Legion's beginnings in Algeria, whereas the officers and men Bernelle commanded had in the meantime been tried under fire and winnowed by desertion and discipline.

There were the usual internecine squabbles of military coalitions. Both the French and English accused their Spanish allies of talking, rather than fighting, and both suffered from irregular pay and inadequate provisioning. Prime Minister Mendizabal, in turn, called Evans 'a man of mighty pretensions and small performance'[3]. It was not a happy alliance.

Even after it relocated from Vitoria to the Navarrese capital Pamplona, casualties were high on both sides owing to the

Carlists' custom of killing wounded prisoners. The British Ambassador in Spain had managed to halt the practice and arrange exchanges of prisoners, but the Carlists claimed that the treaty they had signed did not cover foreign mercenaries like the legionnaires. After the Carlists captured 2nd Lt Durmoustier and thirty legionnaires, they were dragged from village to village blinded, naked and shackled, before eventually being shot. In retaliation, when Capt André-Camille Ferrary took a Carlist company prisoner, none survived. Ordered by the government in Paris to desist, Bernelle did so unilaterally – but resumed no-quarter warfare when the Carlists continued their atrocities.

Bernelle was the Legion commander with the worst job of all during its early years, disowned yet curbed by the government in Paris. He was a good-looking man with strong features that a moustache and neat goatee beard only served to emphasize. Aloof and autocratic, he was a strict disciplinarian even by the standards of the time when flogging was general in the British army and navy for petty offences. Discovering that caning was a normal punishment in the Spanish army, he introduced it in the Legion also. Whilst officers guilty of offences were usually placed under detention, his frequent resort to caning and the firing squad for rank-and-file caused widespread resentment.

On the plus side, his mixing of nationalities greatly improved esprit de corps and the addition of three squadrons of Polish lancers allegedly financed by the Spanish Minister in Paris, plus an ambulance section, a sapper unit and a battery of artillery under Capt Rousselet made the Legion a self-contained army at last. There is a mystery surrounding the money that paid for all this. The answer may lie in loot accumulated during the intervention and the allegations that the Legion occasionally took hostages for ransom.

There was nothing unusual for the time in the way Bernelle surrounded himself with a brilliantly uniformed cluster of staff officers, a number of whom were related to him. But it must have been hard for his officers and men, deprived of family life, to see his wife Tharsile not only living with him in quarters but riding around wearing the scarf of an aide-de-camp and issuing orders as though she was in command. This and her habit of ensuring favourable treatment for her toadies and punishment for anyone who crossed her earned her several nicknames from the legionnaires, the politest of which was 'Queen Isabella III'. On one occasion she gave a man fifteen days' imprisonment for the crime of seeing her informally dressed in her garden.[4]

The officers found their champion in Maj Conrad, who had been given the title *jefe de cuerpo* or colonel by the Spanish queen. He had the advantage not only of a more soldierly heartiness and up-and-at-'em attitude to war than his nominal superior, but also spoke fluent German, still the common language of the majority of legionnaires. In January 1836 Conrad started calling Madame Bernelle's bluff by promoting his own candidates to fill vacancies, which was his prerogative as acting colonel of the regiment. When Bernelle countered by obtaining from the War Minister in Paris confirmation of his wife's contrary decisions, Conrad resigned in fury, to the dismay of his supporters. This did more to shatter Legion morale than the Carlists could have hoped.

On 24 April, 4th and 5th Battalions won pyrrhic victories at Arlabán and Tirapegui in Navarre. The Legion's next success was snatched from the jaws of defeat by Rousselet's cannon at Zubiri on 1 August. In Paris, Thiers, whose ambition for France to be seen as an international power had caused the whole mess, was now Prime Minister. Despite Louis-Philippe's increasing distaste for the Spanish intervention, Thiers persuaded him to sign an ordinance of 16 December 1835 to raise a battalion of Spanish émigrés in Pau, literally in the shadow of the Pyrenees' northern flanks. Recruiting on 3 February 1836, this new 'legion' was supposedly for Algeria, but was sent to Spain that summer to make good the losses there. When Isabella's own army rebelled against the Infanta and her overpowering mother on 16 August 1836, and imposed a new and more liberal constitution, Thiers was outvoted in the Cabinet. He resigned on 25 August, and was replaced on 6 September by the haughty Count Louis-Mathieu Molé, a non-interventionist who despatched a second 'new' battalion of Spaniards from Pau to Algeria early in 1837 under Maj Alphonse Bedeau.[5]

Throughout the winter of 1835–36 and the following summer, Evans' legion of British volunteers was alternately idle in barracks or thrown into engagements it had no chance of winning, with the inevitable negative effect on morale. In contrast, Bernelle managed to gather his scattered battalions and commit them judiciously, so that the body count swung more and more in his favour. Perhaps as a consequence, desertion did not cause so many problems as it might have done with the French frontier so temptingly near.

By August 1836, a year after landing in Tarragona, the Legion's numbers were up, new recruits having more than compensated for the 117 killed in action and 380 dead from wounds and disease, executed by firing squad, taken prisoner or deserted. But the Legion was sick nonetheless. Six months after Conrad's departure Bernelle resigned in his turn, worn out with fighting against his own disgruntled officers and his political masters in Madrid. One of his chief complaints was that Paris did nothing to stop the Carlists' weapons and ammunition being smuggled into Spain across the Pyrenees. Louis-Philippe's representatives had been equally useless in bringing diplomatic pressure to bear on the Carlists to halt the continued murder of legionnaires taken prisoner.

Arriving in August, the new commander was an unlikely appointment. Waterloo veteran Col Jean-Louis Baux must have been desperate for a job after twenty years on half pay. Although personally courageous, he was a modest, withdrawn intellectual whose idea of a suitable uniform in which to arrive at his new command was a wide-brimmed hat, an old cape, ill-fitting breeches and awkward boots with very long spurs that hindered walking. Ironically nicknamed 'Le Beau' – a pun on his surname that needs no translation – Baux' appearance was hardly going to impress fashionable officers who judged a commander on his manners and dress as much as his military skills. Nor was an introvert likely to boost the morale of men whose pay was non-existent and many of whom were hospitalised as a result of eating the badly cured pork, unfit for human consumption, which was the only meat supplied.

Appalled at the French government's total lack of interest in the Legion's welfare, Madrid's inedible food and inadequate supplies of arms, and unable to control his own officers, Baux resigned after two months, following his first engagement with the Carlists at Estella, 30km southwest of Pamplona, which turned to disaster when the ammunition ran out.

His replacement was Joseph Conrad. Taking command on 10 November, he did more than any other colonel could have done to save the Legion's bacon, so to speak. Shortly after his arrival at the head of the last battalion of reinforcements to be sent to Spain, eight officers reported sick just so that they could have a meal in the hospital.[6] In a desperate measure to counter the shortage of rations while stationed at Zubiri, Conrad allowed the 300–400 men whose contract expired each month to leave and also released many who would otherwise have deserted and were prepared to walk the 25km that separated them from the French border. In December, when snow blocked the passes and made that option impossible, whole companies were threatening to go over to the Carlists. Many men did so, and this was to lead to one of the bloodiest confrontations in the Legion's history.

Even Conrad's natural authority and command of German could not stop the Legion's numbers dwindling to 3,841 by February 1837 from a peak strength of 6,134 men after the severe winter weather meant that sick legionnaires who could not keep up with the column froze to death by the wayside. Yet somehow the exhausted, starving, sick, repeatedly wounded men responded to the heroism of a few officers and NCOs – one of whom was a 44-year-old hard-drinking brawler from Württemberg.

At the battle of Larraintzar in the Pyrenees, Capt Johan Albrecht Hebig was cut off with his company on the exposed summit of a hill under enemy fire from two battalions of Carlists. For two hours, he stood in the open directing his men. When relieved, he had seven dead, but the enemy casualties all around the position were at least three times as high. Like all the Legion's battles in Spain, so much suffering for a hill without any importance was pointless, but Hebig's heroism would be repeated again and again – all the way to Dien Bien Phu.

After Larraintzar, desertion to the Carlists increased to the point where they were able to field a motley foreign legion of their own, composed of deserters from the French and English legions. To curb this, Col Conrad again resorted to the firing squad, but with the Legion reduced to two battalions, two light cavalry squadrons and a battery of light artillery, he had to sell his own horse to buy food after receiving no pay from Madrid for five months. By the end of March 1837 he was writing to his old comrade Gen Jean Harispe, commanding the garrison of Bayonne across the frontier, in uncharacteristically despairing tones: 'I really don't know how all this will end.'[7]

It ended near Huesca, an Aragonese city not far from the border of Catalunya. For weeks, the Legion had been harassing a Carlist force trying to break through from the war-ravaged Basque provinces to Catalunya on the Mediterranean coast, where they had strong support. At 1700hrs on 24 May Gen Iribarren, under whose orders Conrad was placed, ordered the Legion to attack the Carlists who had already stood down for the night, but had everything else in their favour. It was an order Conrad should have at least questioned. Instead, typically raring for a fight, he ordered his exhausted men forward. Cut off when the Spanish on their flanks held back and with Iribarren killed while personally leading a cavalry charge, Conrad ordered a fighting withdrawal, with many wounded men having to be carried by their comrades.

At 0100hrs next morning what remained of the Legion was licking its wounds in the village of Amudevar, after fighting their way clear and marching 20km through the night. Casualties totalled between 350 and 400 legionnaires and twenty-eight officers. Next day, a thousand of the survivors whose contracts were up, departed for Pamplona and demobilisation.

Then at last, any sane person might think Conrad would throw in the towel. Instead, the remnants of the Legion were still with their Spanish allies on 2 June, 50km to the east, when the Carlists halted for their midday meal in the town of Barbastro, preparatory to crossing the River Cinca, which was the last obstacle before the Catalunyan border. The new Spanish commander, Gen Marcelino Oraa, knew this was his last chance to bring them to battle before they linked up with Catalunyan reinforcements.

The Legion, on the right flank of the second line of attack, saw the Spaniards ahead of them break and run. Standing fast when the Carlists were upon them, they recognised in the other side's foreign legion many of their former comrades who had gone over to the enemy. As the battle raged around them, old friends greeted each other in French or their mother tongues, questions were asked and answered to catch up on what had happened since they last met ... and then the slaughter began.

A German officer serving with the Carlists, Baron Wilhelm von Rahden, wrote in his memoirs, 'The soldiers recognised each other during the combat. They approached each other as friends and then killed each other in cold blood.'[8]

Conrad was in the thick of the fray. To give a rallying point, he raised his red skull cap aloft on the end of his cane and shouted, 'Forward!' Whether anyone would have followed him after the nightmare of comrade killing comrade, no one will ever know because a musket ball shattered his head and he pitched to the ground, dead. Around him lay 715 of the Carlists' 875 foreigners.

The Legion's tradition of not abandoning dead bodies whenever possible was already in place. Present was François-Achille Bazaine, who had joined the Legion as a second lieutenant and would rise to become a Marshal of France. He wrote afterwards to Gen Harispe, '(Col Conrad) thought he could rally them. He advanced in front of the skirmish line, shouting, "Forward!" But the men ... continued to flee. His body almost fell into the hands of the enemy. With the help of an officer and four courageous (men), I got him onto my horse and across the battlefield. However, as we were outflanked on the left, it took me half an hour to get his body out of danger.'[9]

Conrad had informed Harispe weeks before that honour demanded he set an example to his demoralised and sorely tried men by constantly exposing himself to enemy fire. So was it suicide, as some of his men believed? Or a gesture of despair? Or simply sheer fatigue, combined with the necessity in the much depleted Legion to take abnormal risks? Even Louis-Philippe showed some guilt over this death out of all the thousands suffered in the Spanish intervention, personally giving a widow's pension to Conrad's wife while his son the duke of Orleans undertook to pay the fees of Conrad's two boys at a military school.

The decimated Carlist force was disbanded a few weeks later, but the war continued to be a running sore in the body of Spain for another fifteen months. Commanded by André-Camille Ferrary with the rank of lieutenant-colonel, what remained of the

Legion was reduced again and again until absorbed directly into the Constitutionalist army and finally disbanded in September 1838.

In January 1839 sixty-three officers and 159 NCOs and legionnaires with seventy-five mules rode and marched back into France, followed by an unknown number of wives and children, whose misery cannot be imagined – especially that of the orphans and widows, condemned to live on charity by begging unless the mothers were young enough to earn money through prostituting themselves. They cannot have looked much different from the last Carlists to flee across the frontier into France in May 1840, whose arrival in Perpignan was witnessed by Capt François Certain Canrobert: 'Some wore sandals. Others marched barefoot and even barelegged. Women, children and old people followed the soldiers, Lord knows in what rags and in what misery.'[10]

And that was the sorry end of the first French Foreign Legion: a testimony to the cynicism of politicians, who will always sacrifice the soldiers who serve them when self-interest so dictates – and to the heroism of men reduced to the level of beasts, yet who fought on like Greek Bronze Age heroes despite all the odds in the knowledge of almost certain death for a cause that was not theirs. It is worth asking why they did it because the Legion has done it again and again. The answer seems to be that, when betrayed by everyone else, the only reality for men in combat is the bond with comrades who share their hardships and risks. That is why they will risk their own lives trying to save a comrade's body. It also explains the viciousness of friends killing each other at Barbastro. In the final analysis, the greatest hatred is reserved for the man who betrays this sacred trust.

But politicians care little for either extreme of what former captain in the Royal Guard Alfred de Vigny called *servitude et grandeur militaires* in a book he published in 1835 while the Legion was en route between Algeria and Spain. As far as Paris was concerned, the tattered remains of the Legion that limped across the Pyrenean pass in January 1839 without any expectation of a hero's welcome were best disposed of by sending them back where they could be completely wiped out.

Chapter 8

BLOOD ON THE SAND

Algeria, 1835–1840

Marshal Bertrand Clauzel, the new Governor-General of Algeria, had been given the job largely because he presented to Louis-Philippe's government what sounded like the first intelligent plan for the country which looked beyond the immediate stage of military occupation. Having spent four years in exile in the United States to avoid prosecution after the Bourbon Restoration, Clauzel had seen what ruthless, hard-working European settlers could achieve after dispossessing the natives of an economically unexploited country. He envisaged driving all the peasantry off the fertile Mitidja Plain – the level coastal strip 100km long by 20km deep centred on Algiers – before draining its swamps and fortifying it with a chain of blockhouse forts, in whose arc of protection settlers from Europe could rapidly become self-sufficient and grow cash-crops for export, including cotton.

The beauty of Clauzel's plan was that, in the process, they would generate the taxation to pay the occupation forces. But first he had to 'dispossess the natives'. In December of 1835 Abd el-Kader was driven out of his home territory of Mouaskar, 80km southeast of Oran. However, with a flair for deploying his loosely federated tribes that would have done credit to Saladin, he took his revenge on 27 April 1836 by encircling and cutting off an important French camp on the Tafna estuary in western Algeria.

The man sent to relieve the siege was 'Jailer' Bugeaud, who began by telling his officers they were out of their minds to make war on an elusive and highly mobile enemy who knew the country by marching at the slow pace of heavy artillery limbers and an enormous supply train, as though for a set-piece battle against a European army.

Bugeaud had learned in the hard school of the Peninsular War against Wellington to cut supplies to what could be loaded on a mule and restrict artillery to light cannon that could likewise be dismantled and transported on mule-back. His officers thought him mad until his swift-moving columns outflanked the enemy near the Sikkak River, where Abd el-Kader had been expecting to ambush a ponderous Napoleonic army. Wrong-footing him by appearing from another direction, Bugeaud then altered the normal formation of column and square into a V-formation, using massed musket fire in place of the missing artillery to cut swathes in the enemy ranks as they tried to get to close quarters.

Among the dirty tricks Bugeaud introduced was an old one from his days against Wellington in Spain: loading muskets with one ball and then stuffing down the muzzle a second that had been cut nearly into four. The effect at close range was devastating, the deformed shrapnel-like projectiles tearing out huge lumps of flesh on impact. Sun Tsu said that killing one frightened a thousand. Bugeaud went further by ordering several hundred tribesmen thrown over a cliff to their deaths and then releasing a handful to spread the news.

Seeking a softer target than Abd el-Kader, Clauzel now turned his attention eastwards to the city of Constantine, still garrisoned by Turks commanded by the Bey Hajj Ahmed. It was as near as one can find to the non-existent 'impregnable fortress'. Isolated on a spur of rock, with steep precipices falling on three sides to the gorges of the River Rummel, the city could be approached only from the southwest, along a narrow ramp of land called Coudiat-Aty and an even narrower bridge.

In November 1836 Clauzel's force of 8,700 men was beaten back with heavy losses after shamefully abandoning to the enemy both their wounded and their artillery. Retreating through the winter storms in bad order for 65km to the town of Guelma, where Clauzel had founded a town and military camp on the ruins of the Byzantine walled city, they were savagely harassed all the way by the Turks and their Berber allies. After reaching the coast 60km further north at the port of Annaba, Clauzel could measure the scale of his defeat. In addition to the heavy casualties at Constantine and on the retreat, another thousand men died of various causes in hospital.

The first siege of Constantine was Clauzel's swansong. Post-Napoleonic France being rich in generals and marshals, he was replaced by Gen Charles Damrémont, who arrived full of confidence, little thinking that his death was imminent. Only three months after Conrad had left France with his final reinforcements for the Spanish intervention, the 'new' Legion in Algeria acquired eight companies of 'Hollanders', meaning men who had entered France from the Low Countries. They arrived on 15 December 1836 under the command of Maj Bedeau, who soon discovered that numbers meant little in the field. Allocated to 2nd Brigade charged with securing the coastal plain around Algiers, his Hollanders proved inapt for the task – which did not stop the continuing recruitment in France of men of the same indifferent quality.

On 30 May 1837 Thomas Bugeaud was showing another side of his personality by negotiating with Abd el-Kader the Treaty of the Tafna, under which a truce was bought in return for French confirmation of el-Kader as *amir* of two-thirds of Algeria. In this, Bugeaud was exceeding his political mandate from Paris in order to gain a short-term military respite, during which he could move forces from western and central Algeria eastwards in the effort to sort out the Turks in Constantine and avenge the shame of Clauzel's defeat.

The Turks had been invited into the country in the fourteenth century to drive out the Spanish. Reasoning that 'my enemy's enemy is my (temporary) ally', Abd el-Kader was happy to see Bugeaud's concentration of French forces in the east, which left him free to prepare for the next round in what would be a long war – ending only with the Evian Agreement in the summer of 1962 when the French were finally driven out of North Africa.

El-Kader was fighting a *jihad* against the infidel invaders, his tribes united by hatred of the French, but this did not prevent him hiring foreigners to provide the training and acquire the armaments he lacked. Of these, the two best known were the dubious Frenchman Léon Roches, who afterwards became a diplomat, and his compatriot Marius Garcin, who advised el-Kader's men on weapons training and obtained arms largely from France's traditional enemy, Britain.

With the help of other foreigners, el-Kader established a simple civil administration which moved several times between Mouaskar and Tagdempt. To ensure that his training bases and arsenals were out of French reach, he sited them in the interior at Saïda, Tiaret and even across the border of Morocco at Taza. There also, he stored the surplus produce that could be sold to buy weapons. All these measures would have come to nothing, had he not set a personal example of piety and austerity, living like the simplest of his people in a tent and eating the same food they ate.

In September 1837 another battalion of refugees had been recruited in France amid the total indifference of the French population and most of the government including Prime Minister Molé. Once shipped out to Algeria, the addition of this second battalion brought the new Legion up to the strength of a Napoleonic regiment, with two battalions in the field and another in quarters, recruiting and training new troops.

By October, Damrémont had made his preparations. On the first of the month, he rode out of his camp near Guelma with a force nearly three times the size of Clauzel's. To breach the walls of Constantine he had France's most famous artillery general, the universally respected Sylvain Charles Valée, nearing the end of his career at sixty-four years of age. Lt Gen Rohault de Fleury commanded the large battalion of sappers. The force of 20,000 soldiers included a Legion battalion of 500 men under Col Combe and Maj Bedeau. So large a force, with their mounts and baggage mules, made this a formidable logistical operation in a land both arid and hostile.

After a four-day march through enemy territory, they came in sight of what generals Valée and Fleury realised was going to be a formidable task, even if Damrémont was still feeling optimistic. Since driving off the French eleven months before, the Turks had not been idle. Hajj Ahmed had strengthened his own artillery with the abandoned French pieces, so that there were sixty-three cannon of varying age and accuracy served by experienced Turkish gunners massed on the walls opposite the Coudiat-Aty spur, across which the French had to advance.

Valée had a total of seventeen cannon and a battery of siege mortars. Before they could be positioned for use, Fleury's sappers had to construct siege-works about 400 metres from the city, whilst under enemy small arms fire. On 7 October the first sortie by the garrison was repulsed. On 9 October, the French bombardment began in foul weather, its priority being to silence the Turkish guns. On 11 October, as Valée started to pound away at a stretch of city wall in the hope of creating a breach, through which the attack could go in, several sorties from the city were beaten off with casualties on both sides. Even a slight wound could mean a lingering death from gangrene.

The wall was built of nearly two metres of dressed limestone with old buildings on the inside infilled with earth and debris, making it more shock-resistant than Valée had anticipated. This, and the need to sustain counter-battery fire to keep the Turkish gunners' heads down, were consuming the French ammunition at an alarming rate. With only 200 shot per cannon, things were getting tense for Valée.

That night, the sappers constructed emplacements for the shorter-range siege mortars much closer to the wall. In the bright moonlight, not only were they under musketry fire from the defenders, but could see many thousands of the Turks' Berber allies out of range, waiting on the surrounding hills. Early on 12 October, Damrémont was killed during a Turkish bombardment and Valée took overall command. The wall breached, the customary invitation was extended to the defenders to surrender and keep their lives. It was refused – but politely, which must have been a great relief to the native go-between who could have returned with his head in a basket.

Valée then took a gamble and expended much of the remaining shot to silence the Turkish guns and keep the musketeers off the walls while his siege mortars continued pounding away at the breach. In mid-afternoon, the Turks requested a truce, reasoning that if they could hold out for long enough the French would exhaust their provisions. In reply, Valée refused to treat until after the city had surrendered. By now, the forward French positions were within 100 metres of the breach. The noise of the bombardment was horrendous for the men waiting in the trenches to attack, while the Turks' return fire, both from cannon and small arms, kept their heads well down below the parapets.

The barrage lifting slightly, the first wave of the French assault went in, only to find itself trapped in the breach while the defenders poured upon them a murderous fire from all sides. The hundred legionnaires waiting in the trenches to go in with the second wave under Combe and Bedeau could see the problem: an inner wall that was still intact and barred access to the city. Desperate calls from the trapped survivors of the first wave for scaling equipment reached the trench in which the legionnaires crouched. Sappers ran forward under fire with ladders, ropes and explosives. Before they could set their charges, the inner wall erupted in a curtain of stones and fire, killing them and the survivors of the first wave except for a few wounded men in tattered uniforms, some on fire, who staggered back to the trenches screaming not to advance.

The Turks had made a fundamental error in destroying the inner wall. It was axiomatic of siege-craft to have another mine ready to blow when the French second wave entered the breach, but Combe and Bedeau led their hundred legionnaires forward. Once through the breach, they headed left through the maze of narrow streets, towards the nearest Turkish battery still in action. What happened next was described by Lt Achille de St-Arnaud – a man seeking glory to compensate for forty years of failure and setbacks that belied his fine military bearing, dashing moustache and goatee beard. After firing one ball, there was no time to reload muskets. Swords and bayonets plunged into living flesh. Disembowelled men screamed. 'The Turks,' St-Arnaud wrote in his memoirs, 'defended themselves with desperate courage. They fired (at us) and we killed them as they were reloading ... our bayonets left not a solitary one alive.'[1]

Sustained fire from a janissary barracks held up the attack only briefly. Advancing beside St-Arnaud, Combe took a bullet wound. He shrugged it off and carried on walking until mortally wounded shortly afterwards – which made him the second Legion commander to die in action. Once the barracks had been taken and all the inmates bayoneted to death, the remaining defenders begged to surrender. At that juncture the handful of French in the city were a mixture of legionnaires, men from the punishment battalions called 'Bataillons d'Afrique' and some other units.

Anyone not in French uniform was their target in a blood lust of kill-or-be-killed.

As the firing on both sides died away, the main body of the French poured into the town through the breach, looting and killing as they came. The sack of Constantine continued for three whole days before Valée could regain control of his men and set them to burying the enormous numbers of dead in a common grave outside the city. It is impossible to estimate the true value of the loot, but it must have been substantial since the inhabitants of Constantine, confident the French would be beaten off a second time, had not bothered to hide their valuables – out of which the ignorant looters were cheated for a few Turkish coins in an impromptu market set up by itinerant Jewish traders just outside the camp.

The scale of the casualties in the second-wave assault was clear from St-Arnaud's account: of fifty legionnaires in his immediate vicinity, ten died and eleven were wounded.[2] Their heroism at long last lifted the Legion from an 'asylum for misfortune' to a formation with battle honours. Bedeau was promoted to lieutenant-colonel and the following month Valée was promoted to marshal and appointed Governor-General of Algeria. As to St-Arnaud, his actions on 12 October restarted his military career that also ended with the baton of a marshal.

On 5 December in Paris Berlioz' massive *Requiem*, performed by 450 singers and musicians, was premiered in honour of the heroic dead at Constantine. Inspecting generals, however, continued to deplore the legionnaires' behaviour when not in action, listing always the same problems: desertion, insubordination, homosexuality, self-mutilation, brawling and getting money for booze by selling just about every item of equipment and uniform with the exception of their shakos, which no one in North Africa would buy.

The reaction of their officers was increasingly brutal punishment. Even Soult in faraway Paris was driven to protest about the 'insufficient food, hard and often unjust corporal punishments. Bread and water, the whip and the cane, are the means employed to correct insubordination. The result is a system of repression which is altogether alien to our French values.'[3]

Some courts martial were reluctant to convict Legion deserters because conditions in the punishment sections to which they would be sent were so inhumane. Maintaining discipline by harsh repression invited mutiny, a spectre only kept at bay by the policy of splitting up national groups. However, so many ex-Carlist refugees were recruited in 1839 and 1840 that entire battalions came to be composed of them. Three companies of these men, composing the 4th Battalion, arrived in Algiers in March 1840. Before the month was out, thirty of them attempted to desert to Abd el-Kader after murdering their officers. By luck or misjudgement, only one officer was wounded, but eight recaptured mutineers were shot as an example to their fellows.

By the middle of September an entire battalion of 600 ex-Carlists was training at Pau. Whether criminals as some of their French officers believed, or simply men brutalised by years of scorched-earth warfare, they were certainly guilty of rapes, thefts and murders there. Within days of their disembarkation in Algiers forty-four deserted with their weapons, which was always regarded as a capital crime. In the peak years of the Spanish recruitment, desertion rates ran as high as 11.9% and the lowest figure was 6.8%. These figures do not tell the full story because 'desertion' meant absence from one's unit for six days or more and many men returned, or were caught, earlier and thus technically had only been absent without leave.[4]

One instance of what they were fleeing from was the siege of Melyana. On 8 June 1840 a combined French force captured this strategic city fortified by Abd el-Kader as one of his centres of resistance in the Chélif valley. At 700 metres above sea level on the southern flanks of the Zaccar Gharbi, Melyana dominated the valley to the south and east. Hardly had it been captured by the French than it was besieged by a force of several thousand Arabs. The garrison, consisting of one Legion battalion, one from 3rd Tirailleurs and a handful of artillerymen and sappers, held them off throughout the scorching summer.

With no possibility of resupply in the heart of el-Kader's territory, bad water and severe food rationing that permitted only one meagre meal a day led to widespread sickness and deaths. On October 4 when the relief column finally fought its way through, half the original garrison men had died and the others were so emaciated that only 150 men were capable of holding a weapon. The condition of the others was so poor that only seventy survived of the original strength of 1,232.

During the siege twenty-five legionnaires had deserted. What became of them is not known, although el-Kader's adviser Marius Garcin recorded two battalions of European deserters, a squadron of cavalry and some trained artillerymen. Those deserters who could not stand the rigours of life in the Arab militia wandered hopelessly from tribe to tribe on the run from French retribution, earning a pitiful living by pretending a knowledge of European medicine, such as it then was, until they themselves died of disease or were murdered.

Chapter 9

A HEAD ON A SPEAR

Algeria, 1840–1849

The flow of refugees unwanted in France continued to boost numbers, so that in December 1840 the 'new' Legion was divided into two regiments, despite a shortage of experienced NCOs. The first regiment, of predominantly Nordic legionnaires, was stationed in Algiers initially, extending its range into the Oranais from 1843 inwards. The second, composed of Mediterraneans, was based in Constantine to cover the east of the country.

After his success against el-Kader in 1836, Bugeaud had returned to France making no secret of his revised opinion that the whole North African adventure was a ridiculous waste of lives and money because the Maghreb would never be satisfactorily subdued and, even if it was, the land was largely arid and therefore useless for colonisation. Since he had spent several years farming in France after his forced retirement in 1815, he was talking from personal experience, and had taken for his motto *ense et aratro* – meaning by sword and plough. However, every man has his price and Bugeaud's was the offer of the governor-generalship when Valée retired.

Returning to Algiers on 22 February 1841, Bugeaud found that el-Kader had drawn the correct conclusion from his defeat at the Sikkak River and was now extremely hard to bring to battle, even by lightly armed columns unencumbered with artillery or rations for a long period. Compelled by the ever-longer reach of the French to abandon a fixed capital for his state-within-a-state, he had reverted to the *smala*, a mobile encampment of 3,000 tents, from which he governed his people and organised the resistance to the French, moving its location every time the invaders got too near.

Bugeaud's way of beating el-Kader was to starve his people into submission. The *razzia*, from the Arabic *rhâzya*, was a punitive raid in tribal warfare. Bugeaud raised it to a science: 'Destroy the villages,' he said. 'Cut down the fruit trees, burn the harvest, empty the grain stores, search the ravines and caves to find the women, children and old people. That is the only way to defeat such proud mountain folk.'[1] Even date palms were cut down to blight an area for years until new palms could be brought in to production. Livestock was driven off and wells poisoned. This was total war.

A chain of fortified supply dumps extended the range of Bugeaud's flying columns. One of these at Sidi bel-Abbès, a place 100km south of Oran previously marked only by the grave of a holy man, was to become the Legion's home. A commission was set up by royal ordinance to design and build a complete town there, centred on a massive Legion barracks. Given that sort of protection, the initial population of 431 rose rapidly to 5,259 in 1859.

The attraction of *razzia* warfare for officers and men alike was that booty was divided among all ranks. The new policy was also used by recruiting officers to attract native infantry and horsemen. It was, however, heavily criticised in France and even by some officers in l'Armée d'Afrique. The tactics involved a rapid and stealthy approach. Once all escape had been blocked by native Spahi cavalry, every single man in the camp under attack was killed, along with many of the women and children.[2] Younger women who submitted were taken and used as 'free wives'. Some animals were slaughtered and eaten on the spot to give the first fresh meat tasted in months. Everything that could be of use was destroyed or stolen, underground silos emptied and the flocks – sometimes of thousands of animals – all driven off to the north for sale.

Whether for *razzias* or otherwise, Bugeaud thought little of the Legion, writing to Soult on 18 June 1842[3] that recruitment of foreign refugees should cease because the quality of soldiers it produced was so deplorable. Among other shortcomings he listed, they were no good at fighting and they were not fit enough to march in the heat of a North African summer. At the Sikkak River, he had had to send back to base two newly arrived regiments for this reason.[4] Once recruitment ceased, he argued, losses from disease and in combat would reduce the numbers of legionnaires until the last few could be absorbed into other units, the officers remustering or being retired.

His pleas were not heeded. Shipping off unwanted male immigrants to North Africa had become a part of French domestic policy and the vague idea that France had an empire in North Africa was to its rulers a compensation of sorts for the much reduced role they played in Europe. Other props to national pride that year were the return of Napoleon's body by the British, so that it could be accommodated in a sumptuous shrine at Les Invalides, and the erection of the column in the Place de la Bastille surmounted by a bronze statue of the spirit of Liberty, the base of the column being a mausoleum in which are conserved the remains of the 615 victims of the July Revolution.

In this jingoistic mood 'Old Bugeaud' could plead all he liked. He was stuck with the Legion and ironically became father-by-default to this bastard that no one wanted to own. Among the improvements he was to introduce was the slimming-down of the regulation European 40-kilo backpack – a cruel burden to men marching in the midsummer heat. More importantly, it was his introduction of *razzia* warfare that put an end to the often-fatal *cafard* in the blockhouses of the Mitidja Plain with their drunken brawls and the endless round of indiscipline and punishment. The new policy of marching light and living off the territory brought officer, NCO and common soldier closer, for they ate the same food and lived in the same conditions.

A mistake by any one of them could lose many lives, and when in territory where every native was an enemy, it was better to stay with the column even though debilitated with chronic diarrhoea, bleeding and blistered feet and footwear worn into holes than to lag behind at risk of an agonising death at the hands of men whose families had been killed by the French. Reporting sick was not advised. A Polish regimental surgeon by the name of Ridzeck bled to death seventeen legionnaires suffering from heatstroke, a condition rarely encountered in his home country. Angry at their failure to respond to his treatment, he conducted an autopsy by splitting the skull of one of his victims with an axe, to examine the brains. Thereafter, ether was used with better results.

In 1843 the arrival of Edme Patrice Maurice de MacMahon as colonel of 2nd Regiment did much to bring its men into line. One small change paid dividends: the ridiculous shakos were replaced by light képis with a neck-cloth to protect the back of the neck from sunburn. Desertion lessened and inspection reports improved to the point where the Legion began to attract officers who wanted to do some real soldiering with fast-track promotion, rather than rot away in a provincial garrison with its parades, drills, snobbery and promotion by seniority only, and gambling the only relief. While a cadet at the military academy of St Cyr, Charles-Nicolas Lacretelle expressed an ambition to join the dragoons, but a senior officer advised him that the cavalry was finished, whereas the infantry in Algeria had a lot to offer an ambitious young second-lieutenant. The best posting of all, Lacretelle was told, was the Foreign Legion, which was in the thick of every action. Lacretelle followed the advice, to the amazement of his fellow cadets, who had never heard of the Legion.[5]

In 1844, 2nd Regiment had thirteen captains, seven lieutenants and four second-lieutenants of foreign nationality. On 15 March Louis-Philippe's son the duke of Aumale personally led elements of the regiment in the successful assault on the fortified village of M'chouneche in the Aurès Mountains after several line regiments had failed to take it. The duke subsequently asked his father to honour the regiment with its own standard.

Little had been heard of el-Kader since his *smala* had been captured on 16 May 1843 minutes after he had fled. Pursued from refuge to refuge for six months, he was forced to seek asylum in Morocco that November. On 30 May 1844 he returned to Algeria at the head of the warriors of the *caïd* of Oujda, with a Moroccan army moving threateningly close to French territory in support. On 19 June, Bugeaud spiked their guns by occupying Oujda, a town just inside Moroccan territory. On 4 or 6 August De Joinville's fleet bombarded Tangiers as a hint to the sultan of Morocco not to meddle in Algeria. When that did not work, Bugeaud thrashed the Moroccan army at Isly near Oujda on 14 August. With Essaouira[6] taken the following day, the sultan bowed to the wind of change and signed a treaty with France on 10 September, under which he promised to intern or expel Abd el-Kader should he set foot again in Morocco.

Already some very unusual legionnaires were to be found in the ranks. Visiting a typical Legion fort at Khemis Miliana, some 90km southwest of Algiers, in 1844 military historian Count Pierre de Castellane found the garrison of 300 men including the son of a Privy Councillor to Austrian Emperor Francis II, a cardinal's nephew, a German banker's son and Lt Thomas Lansdown Parr Moore, a godson of Lord Byron who may have been the first Briton to serve in the Legion. Moore 'often took the portrait of a beautiful woman from his bosom and gazed earnestly upon it when he thought himself unobserved.'[7] Was he the first lovelorn legionnaire?

Typical of the Legion's bases in North Africa for the next century was the fort in which these men were shut up each night. Affording no more comfort to its occupants than the fortresses built by the Romans, often in the same places, it was a square of high walls pierced with firing slits at intervals, the crenellated parapet and watch-towers at each corner accessible by stairs shielded from missiles making it almost impossible to take by surprise. Built in this case of adobe bricks and elsewhere of local stone, they all had a single gateway high enough for a man on horseback to ride through and wide enough for a small cart. The men slept in hammocks slung in the dormitories, with three rooms reserved for the use of the officers. In the centre of the courtyard at Khemis was a sundial made from the base of a Roman column and a large tree, under which the officers enjoyed the cool of the evening with their glasses of absinthe. There was no other relief to the bare sun-baked earth and brick walls that drove men literally mad with boredom.[8]

In his 1844 inspection, Gen François de Barail found, not surprisingly, that the Spaniards of 2nd Regiment were the legionnaires best adapted to conditions in North Africa, having greater stamina and an ability to go for hours without water than the taller northerners of 1st Regiment. The Italians were judged the worst soldiers, followed by forty Britons who had deserted from Evans' expeditionary corps in Spain. One of their failings was that they could not exist on the basic rations, but needed twice the food of the Spaniards.

In the first example of British solidarity that became known in the Legion as 'the English Mafia', these men would all drop out together when one was exhausted on the march. MacMahon once sent a squadron of native cavalry pretending to be el-Kader's men to frighten them back onto the march by feigning an attack, firing into the air. The trick only worked once because the next time he tried it, the Britons formed a square and shot back at the Spahis.

On 18 March 1845 the treaty of Lalla-Marnia agreed for the first time a clearly defined frontier between Morocco and Algeria, which was placed under the Ministry of War and divided into three military regions based on Oran in the west, Algiers in the centre and Constantine in the east.

The year also saw in June one of the worst excesses of *razzia* warfare, Col Aimable Jean-Jacques Pélissier set fires in the entrances of some caves into which 500 members of the Ouled-Rhia tribe had fled for sanctuary, with the intention of asphyxiating them. There were protests in Paris when it was heard that his troops had entered the caves two days later to find every man, woman and child dead. In the infernal cycle of atrocity and retaliation, on 22 September a French column was massacred at Sidi-Brahim. Again, on 24 April 1846, el-Kader killed his many prisoners to speed up his retreat into Morocco. Repulsed by the sultan's forces, he was forced back into Algeria.

On 5 May 1847, after the government rejected his proposals for colonising Algeria with grants of land to veterans as the Romans had done, Bugeaud resigned, to be succeeded as Governor-General by the duke of Aumale. On 23 December, after a decade and a half of fighting the French, el-Kader finally surrendered to the ruthless Gen Lamoricière, who habitually cut the rations of his troops so that they were forced to loot Arab villages as part of his strategy of terror.[9] The captured Algerian leader was paraded through Paris as a curiosity, and then placed under house arrest in Toulon and Pau before being given the Château d'Amboise as a luxury prison. Ironically, one of his great-grandsons joined the Legion nearly a century later, serving in Vietnam and Algeria after the Second World War.

The following year, Bey Ahmed of Constantine also surrendered and was allowed to live with his harem and household in some luxury in Algiers. Ironically, as the Legion grew more respected, the government that had spawned it was failing. For the privileged middle classes Paris was still the capital of tolerance, where a poet like Charles Baudelaire and Prime Minister Adolphe Thiers could alike flaunt their mistresses – or three of them in the case of plump little Thiers, who kept a colleague's wife and her two daughters for his pleasure in addition to Madame Thiers.

However, the undercurrent of political unrest in France was becoming a flood. The year 1848 began with workers' parliaments springing up in every town. There, any man could voice his opinions and a few brave women also took the floor. Had any speaker reminded his listeners of the original liberal aspirations of the July monarchy, he would not have been believed. Strikes over the price of potatoes and bread, strikes over the cost of living generally, strikes over the wages paid to workers and over the unemployment problem were finally pulling Louis-Philippe down to where simply sacking yet another Prime Minister was not the remedy.

On 24 February 1848 he abdicated after yet another 'bloody affair', in which a crowd of workers had gathered outside the residence of François Guillaume Guizot, his last prime minister, who had resigned that day. To restore order, soldiers of 14th Regiment of line shot fifty-two of them dead. It was pointless for Louis-Philippe to place his crown on the head of his grandson the duke of Paris because the population wanted to see the back of the Bourbons. Queen Marie-Amélie was urging her husband to leave France before they took it into their heads to deal with her as they had with her namesake Marie-Antoinette only fifty-five years before.

The Chamber of Deputies' reaction to the succession of the duke of Paris was a hollow laugh. A provisional government was formed, but there was revolution in the air. As a show of force to impress the Parisians on 20 April, 400,000 soldiers from the National Guard and the army paraded on open ground to the west of the Arc de Triomphe and were there presented with new standards, after which they broke ranks and fraternised with the crowds. On 4 May the Second Republic was proclaimed, but those who breathed a sigh of relief that it had been accomplished without too much bloodshed had to think again eleven days later when a large and noisy crowd incited by the Society for the Rights of Man invaded the National Assembly waving tricolour flags under the pretext of reading a petition to send military support to suffering Poland. Accusation and counter-accusation flew on all sides. An alternative government was proclaimed. An hour later, its leaders were arrested.

The next month saw the archbishop of Paris assassinated in the street in broad daylight. On 21 June the Ministry of Public Works closed its Paris depot, which had been set up to guarantee work at reasonable rates to thousands of labourers in the reconstruction of the City of Light. Employees under twenty-five were ordered to join the army; those over that age were forbidden to stay in the capital unless they could prove at least six months' residence.

The workers' reply was swift. Barricades set up throughout the working-class quarters of eastern Paris were attacked with cannon- and musket-fire by the army after Gen Bréa crossed the lines to parley in the hope of avoiding more bloodshed and was slowly strangled by three workmen in full view of his troops. On 26 June as the debris was cleared away, his colleague Gen Louis-Eugéne Cavaignac proudly announced the victory of order over the anarchy provoked by his own brother Godefroi Cavaignac, President of the Society for the Rights of Man. Neither brother was destined to become the first president of the Second Republic. Living in exile at No 9 Berkeley Street in London was Prince Louis Napoleon Bonaparte, an opportunist nephew of the great emperor. Demonstrating his commitment to public order, he had served as a special constable in the suppression of the Chartist riots. Although forbidden as a member of the Bonaparte family to set foot in France, he had recently been elected deputy in absentio for the départements of Paris, Yonne, Charente-Inferièure and Corsica. Now, financed by two lady friends – Miss Elizabeth Harriet Howard loaned him over a quarter million dollars and his cousin Mathilde pawned her jewels for him – he installed himself in Paris as the compromise candidate for the presidency of the Second Republic.

When the results of the election were announced on December 20, Louis Napoleon Bonaparte was the clear victor with 5,434,226 votes against 1,448,107 votes for his nearest rival Gen Cavaignac. One of the first acts of the Second Republic's first president was to declare North Africa an integral part of France. He also introduced the system whereby any legionnaire who completed five years' service with good conduct was entitled to claim French citizenship. In addition, to show solidarity with the suffering Poles, all legionnaires of Polish nationality were allowed to resign. In 1st Regiment at what would become the Legion's 'home' in Sidi-bel-Abbès, south of Oran, twenty-three took advantage of this, but seventeen changed their minds within a month. The 2nd Regiment was harder hit, however when 618 of its Italian legionnaires decided to take advantage of a similar largesse to the Piedmontese ambassador to Paris.

In Algeria, the constant *razzias* in territory where life was already hard left ground where only hatred could grow. So when the first rumours of unrest in France were carried among the tribes by itinerant Jewish traders the officers of the Armée d'Afrique expected a countrywide uprising to kick them out of North Africa for good. That this did not occur was because most of the leaders who might have coordinated hostilities were dead or in exile. One action from this period does, however, deserve attention because it illustrates how differently the French conquest might have gone, had not most of its enemies been slowed down by the presence of their families and flocks of animals.

Based in the sub-Saharan frontier town of Biskra, Legion Maj Charles Haillard de St Germain was affected to the Arab Bureau – an organisation running spies among the tribes on the one hand and on the other collecting taxes and attempting to defuse tensions before they erupted into open hostilities. Supposedly as the eyes and ears of the army, St Germain was a disastrous appointment without any of the qualities for such a job. Deciding that the town needed a strong fortress, he used 2nd Regiment's 3rd Battalion as cheap labour and financed the purchase of materials by trebling the annual palm tree tax, which was levied on all trees, not only those bearing dates.

On 18 May 1849, Legion 2nd Lt Joseph Seroka entered the fortified village of Zaatcha to arrest its *caïd* Bouzian for fomenting the unrest at this new measure. After a scuffle with Bouzian's supporters, Seroka and his escort of Spahis withdrew. A back-up force of twenty Spahis and some *goumier* native infantry found the village gate locked against them.

Short of troops, St Germain attempted to get another tribe to do his work for him, but they simply used the excuse to settle old scores, which inspired the powerful Ouled-Sahnoun to attack an encampment of their hereditary enemies adjacent to St Germain's fort. After the Ouled-Sahnoun had threatened some of the legionnaires involved in the construction, a volley saw them off, but not before they had destroyed many of the irrigation channels vital for the township's food and water supply. This was a pointed reminder that by encouraging the locals to grow their own grain, St Germain had destroyed the market for the Ouled-Sahnoun's grain, traditionally traded for dates grown in and around Biskra.

About 100km to the northeast, Col Jean-Luc Carbuccia set out with St Germain, plus 600 legionnaires of the Italian-depleted 2nd Regiment, 400 men of the penal Bataillons d'Afrique and 250 mixed French and native cavalry. To travel into the arid Hodna Plain in mid-summer was inspired lunacy. Their camp surprised just before dawn on 9 July, the Ouled-Sahnoun were massacred, after which Carbuccia's men claimed as booty 2,000 camels and 12,000 sheep. High on his victory over the Ouled-Sahnoun, Carbuccia set off to teach the recalcitrant *caïd* a lesson.

The arrival of his column in the oasis on 16 July was enough to bring the headmen of the unfortified villages out in submission. Only Bouzian was missing, safe behind the stout walls of Zaatcha. A sortie from its single gate cost five French dead and twelve wounded. After softening up the walls with artillery, Carbuccia ordered St Germain to attack in the face of sustained fire from the slits in the walls. A few legionnaires almost reached the walls before being stopped by a moat of stagnant water, which reconnaissance would have revealed earlier. By nightfall, when St Germain withdrew, his legionnaires had suffered fourteen dead and seventy-one wounded.

Realising after three days of skirmishing that there was no future in besieging Zaatcha in midsummer, Carbuccia retreated to Biskra. His failure triggered off a series of actions that summer, in one of which St Germain was killed. Revenge began with the cooler weather on 7 October, when a force of 4,493 men under Col Herbillon arrived in the early morning outside Zaatcha after a forced march by night. About a quarter of the force was made up of legionnaires. The sapper colonel proposed a three-pronged attack, but Herbillon refused to divide his forces. Nor did he interdict use of Zaatcha's only gate, through which reinforcements and supplies reached the village every night.

The siege, with earthworks, barricades of palm trees, cannonry, assaults and sorties, destroyed the oasis, continuing until 8 November when a column of 1,200 Zouaves arrived as reinforcements under Gen Canrobert. The joy of the besiegers was short-lived when they realised that these men had brought with them the scourge of cholera. It was the Zouaves who finally broke into Zaatcha, massacring every inhabitant and presenting Canrobert with the head of Bouzian speared on a lance stuck into the ground outside his tent. Total French losses were confused by the enormous toll of disease, although the Legion appears to have lost 193 dead and 804 wounded – for what gain, is hard to say.

Chapter 10

CHAOS IN THE CRIMEA

1851–1855

Having, in his own eyes at least, successfully concluded his campaign against the Kabyles, St-Arnaud returned to Paris in June 1851. His reward was to be named Minister for War on 27 October in preparation for a coup d'état in which he would play a key part, mobilising 50,000 soldiers on the night of 1-2 December 1851 to seize key points in and around Paris. The National Assembly was dissolved, 240 deputies arrested and 380 protesting workers and liberal sympathisers manning the barricades were shot out of hand.[1]

In the next fortnight a total of 26,884 people judged hostile to the coup were arrested, with some 9,000 transported to Algeria in the same way that the British were transporting their undesirables to populate Australia and other colonies. The most unfortunate were 198 sent to fever-ridden Devil's Island in Cayenne, from which few ever returned. The working and peasant classes had paid a terrible price in lives for Napoleon I's ambition and had less desire to re-establish *la gloire de la France* under his nephew than to earn enough money from their wages in factories or be left with enough of the food they produced on the land to live decently. Throughout France, their widespread resistance to Louis Napoleon Bonaparte's coup was ruthlessly suppressed.

The date for the coup having been chosen as the anniversary of Napoleon's great victory at Austerlitz, exactly one year later on 2 December 1852 the Second Empire was proclaimed, with Louis Napoleon Bonaparte styling himself Emperor Napoleon III. Putting a spin on the truth, he adopted the slogan 'The Empire is for Peace', at the same time looking for an easily-won war to show the rest of Europe that France was again a powerful force to be reckoned with. France had neither the army nor the money to wage a full-scale war on its own, but with the sort of luck that sometimes happens to the wrong people, the Crimean campaign fell into his lap and solved the problem.

Ostensibly, this war was about religion. In the Ottoman province of Palestine the Church of the Nativity in Judean Bethlehem marked the site where the Roman Emperor Constantine's formidable mother St Helena had been persuaded that Christ was born. Russian Orthodox monks wanted to place a star on the roof, but were resisted by Roman Catholic monks in a struggle so violent that several died. In his capacity of 'protector of Orthodox believers in the Ottoman Empire', Russia's Tsar Nikolai I alleged that the local authorities had deliberately incited the murders and therefore declared war on Turkey to protect the Orthodox monks from further violence, while Catholic France naturally took the other side in the dispute.

The real causes of this war are rooted in the struggle of successive tsars to 'drive to the sea', expanding their territorial possessions from the tiny land-locked principality of Muscovy northwards to the White Sea, westwards to ice-free ports in the Baltic, eastwards to the Pacific and southwards to the Black Sea. In the process they created an empire stretching from St Petersburg right across northern Europe and Asia to Vladivostok. After Peter the Great travelled to Holland and Britain to study shipbuilding, they also had a steadily growing navy, its usefulness hampered by being split into four widely separated fleets.

The White Sea Fleet based in Archangel could only put to sea when the ice permitted. The Far Eastern Fleet was too distant from Europe to be of any use there and was essentially to guard the Asiatic seaboard from Japanese and American incursion. Deployment of the Baltic Fleet was dependent on whoever controlled the Danish straits, and the Black Sea Fleet could only emerge into the Mediterranean by permission of the Ottoman Empire, which controlled the Bosporus and Dardanelles.

That right was guaranteed by treaty, but Nikolai I saw unfettered control of the straits as the first step in Russia becoming a world power. In July 1853, he invoked his responsibility to the monks killed in Bethlehem as an excuse to invade the Danubian principalities to the west of the Black Sea in what is now Romania. The move was just the latest in a serious of earth tremors at the interface of the expanding Russian Empire and the collapsing Ottoman Empire which had been going on since 1676, and by which Russia had progressively shifted its European borders southward to the Black Sea, southwest to the Prut River, and south of the Caucasus Mountains in Asia.

France and Britain owed the Sublime Porte no favours but neither wanted to see the Russian Black Sea fleet freely coming and going into the Mediterranean. In a volte-face worthy of George Orwell's *1984*, France's on-again, off-again hostilities with Ottoman Turkey over Greek independence were called off and Napoleon III was granted by the Sublime Porte the status of 'protector of the holy places of Jerusalem'. England's motive was simpler: an abiding suspicion of Russia's covetous eye on India.

Louis-Philippe and the young Queen Victoria had paid state visits to each other's countries to mark the beginning of what eventually became known as the Entente Cordiale, and Napoleon III himself had spent happy years of exile north of the Channel. A joint war against distant Russia seemed to both countries a good chance of showing the potential of their young alliance to impress Austria, the great power of Europe, without disturbing the continental balance of power.

On 23 September 1853 the Royal Navy was ordered to Constantinople. Thus encouraged, the Turkish army under Omar Pasha attacked the Russian occupiers in the Danubian principalities on 4 October and won a victory at Oltenitza, the effect of which was more than cancelled out when the Russians destroyed the Turkish fleet shortly afterwards off Cape Sinop, 300km northeast of Ankara.

On 3 January 1854 both French and British warships engaged Russian vessels in the Black Sea to protect Turkish transports. Undeterred, on 20 March Russian troops drove south into Ottoman territory in what is modern Bulgaria. Seven days later, Britain and France declared war against Russia. Under the treaty of alliance dated 10 April, the first Anglo-French troops reached Varna in Bulgaria on 30 May, landing in the middle of a cholera epidemic.

Meanwhile, Austria was not idle, massing 50,000 men under arms in Galicia and Transylvania to counter the Russian threat in the Danubian principalities. That the war did not escalate and set all Europe in flames was largely due to a Prussian cavalry officer with an extraordinary talent for diplomacy. Edwin von Manteuffel was sent by King Friedrich Wilhelm IV of Prussia to St Petersburg, where he persuaded Tsar Nikolai I to withdraw the Russian troops from the Danubian principalities. Travelling immediately from there to Vienna, he next dissuaded Austria in return from joining the war against Russia. Despite this, the Tsar refused the settlements proposed by France, England, Austria and Prussia at the peace conference in Vienna on 8 August 1854, but at least von Manteuffel had the satisfaction of knowing a European war had been avoided.

At this point the western powers had shown their mettle and Russia had backed down with a bloody nose. Yet, despite the impossibility of conquering the country that had destroyed Napoleon's Grande Armée in 1812, Paris and London decided to send land forces to capture and destroy the main Russian naval base at Sevastopol on the Crimean peninsula as a way of putting the bear firmly back into his cage for a long time to come.

As French Minister of War, St-Arnaud feared the consequences of distracting the Armée d'Afrique from its mission of conquering and policing Algeria. However, it was now the only body of campaign-tested troops that France possessed. Accordingly, on 10 May Napoleon III decreed that Algeria should furnish contingents for the expeditionary force to compensate for the poor state of training in the regular regiments on French soil. For the Legion, this meant that each of the two regiments had to furnish two infantry battalions to a joint brigade for the Crimea. A fifth battalion, also drawn from the 1st Regiment, was to man the brigade depot stationed in the Turkish naval base at Gallipoli on the European side of the Dardanelles strait.

The reason for Bonaparte overriding his Minister for War in this way may lie in the advice he received from Corsican Bonapartist Gen Jean-Luc Carbuccia, who had lived down the shame of his defeat at Zaatcha by unquestioning devotion to the new emperor of France during and after the coup. Whatever the full story, the five Legion battalions were among the French and English troops that landed in Turkey that summer, to be cut to pieces by their old enemy cholera before ever seeing a Russian. Illness too, rather than protest at Napoleon III's decision, caused St-Arnaud to resign as Minister for War. He was dying of consumption and coughed blood into his handkerchief with embarrassing frequency. Accepting the position of commander-in-chief of the French expeditionary force seemed to guarantee him at least one last taste of glory before he died.

Gen Canrobert had, like Carbuccia, taken an active role in the coup of December 1851, and was rewarded with command of a division in the initially 37,000-strong French contingent with its 3,200 horses and mules. He made a point of reviewing the battalions of the 2nd Regiment, of which he had been colonel, and selected eight elite companies to form a *bataillon de marche* that would replace his heavy losses from cholera.

Although the way history is taught in British schools implies that Lord Raglan's British contingent were the main force in the Allied armies, after losses from cholera, dysentery and typhus they were actually the smallest contingent, being outnumbered two to one by the 22,000 Turks on the Allied side and eventually nine to one by French troops. London's limited interest in the campaign was obvious in the choice of Raglan as C-in-C of the British contingent. Having served as the Duke of Wellington's military secretary forty years before, the 67-year-old peer frequently referred to the Russian enemy as 'those Frenchies'. It was not an auspicious characteristic in the joint command shared with St-Arnaud.

This convoluted tale explains how 4,500 men who had joined the Legion to fight France's war in Africa came to land on the Crimean peninsula in September 1854 for the long investment of the fortress-port of Sevastopol, garrisoned by 135,000 Russian sailors, marines and army units.

On 14 September 120 troop transports and supply ships disembarked the first wave of the combined force on the shores of Kalamitsky Bay, 50km north of Sevastopol – the city of Caesar, as its Greek-speaking founders had baptised it. St-Arnaud's command included elements of line regiments, Zouaves, Algerian *tirailleurs*, Spahi cavalry, the Legion and the penal Bataillons d'Afrique. Also in the French contingent, to the mystification of the British, were *les cantinières* – women, usually wives of NCOs, who ran the canteens, provided extra rations in return for payment, toured the camps selling wine and spirits, sometimes serving as nursing orderlies.

Raglan's command numbered 27,000 officers and men at the time, drawn from the Grenadiers, 93rd Highlanders, Scots Fusiliers, Coldstream and Codrington's Brigade, five infantry divisions and a cavalry division. The supporting artillery had 26 field guns.

The Turkish general Ismail Pasha brought with him an even more heterogeneous collection. All able-bodied male subjects in the Ottoman Empire were liable for conscription on reaching twenty years of age, which gave a theoretical wartime army of 570,000 men, each recruit serving five years in active service and seven with the reserves. Ismail Pasha's command thus included troops from Egypt, Serbia, the Danubian principalities, Tunis and Tripoli. Cavalry were both irregular Polish units and Don Cossacks living in Ottoman territory. His infamous *bashi-bazouks* were regarded as the least reliable of all the troops, more prone to pillage and rape than standing firm and obeying orders.

Five days later, the combined force marched south in formation with the French in the centre, the English on the left flank and the Turks on the right. Before they reached the coast south of Balaklava, they had to cross five watercourses. The Bulganek River was forded without opposition, but the next river-crossing at the end of that day's march gave them a foretaste of what lay ahead. The Alma River, although fast-flowing, was shallow enough in places for men to wade across, but on the heights above its southern bank, the Russian positions manned by 37,000 men under Prince A. S. Menshikov were clearly visible.[2]

By 0700hrs next day, the French were drawn up in two lines facing south, brewing their ritual coffee while the English slowly took up their position on the right flank. The Turks were to the right of them and beyond the Turks, the sea. So confident of the outcome was Menshikov that he was entertaining thirty young ladies of the garrison to lunch – with the slaughter of the invaders to be viewed through spy-glasses as the intended entertainment.

At 1130hrs the Allies advanced, crossed the Alma and continued towards the Russian positions in full view of the enemy. Not having fought since Waterloo forty years before, the British contingent advanced in impeccable order with heavy European backpacks, suffering many casualties while the veterans of the Armée d'Afrique shed their backpacks at the river. The Legion was then ordered forward to occupy some high ground for two field artillery positions. At 300 metres' range – the limit for effective musketry – they began exchanging fire with the Russians on it. The rapidity of their reloading was due to the large leather cartridge pouches on their belts that earned them the nickname of 'leatherbellies'.

In Europe, manufacture of personal firearms was a cottage industry. Although the US military had already introduced production-line assembly of interchangeable parts, the great technological breakthrough was French. In 1849 Capt Claude-Etienne Minié made the round musket balls used until then obsolete by inventing longer, smaller-diameter bullets which retained velocity better, although their deformed projectiles were less accurate. The French army combined his ideas in the *carabine modèle 1846 à tige* and the *fusil d'infanterie 1848 à tige*.

In order to overcome the tendency of muzzle-loading rifled barrels to become increasingly difficult to load as powder residue collected in the grooves, Minié suggested a major simplification that enabled his new projectile to be loaded into dirty barrels with ease. Because it no longer deformed when being rammed home, it also had greater accuracy. William Russell, the London *Times* correspondent in the Crimea described how volleys of Minié balls clove through the Russian ranks 'like the hand of the Destroying Angel'.

However, although some of the British line infantry units had been issued with the new rifled musket on landing at Kalamitsky Bay, their lack of practice with the new weapon gave them no advantage at the Alma. Later in the war Russian infantry armed with smooth-bore muskets were no match for British soldiers firing P/51 rifled muskets, although many infantrymen in Raglan's force still had the old smooth-bore Brown Bess muskets their grandfathers had been issued to fight Napoleon.

At the Alma, after a series of skirmishes that lasted until 1730hrs, the Russians retreated. The Legion was then relieved, withdrew to the river, collected its backpacks and made camp, counting its casualties of five wounded officers and fifty-five other ranks wounded and dead. Expecting a trap, the divided Allied command did not pursue the retreating defenders, although it is possible that obeying Vegetius'[3] maxim that speed in warfare is even more important than numbers could have ended the campaign within days. Certainly, the Russians appreciated this respite, which permitted the Black Sea Fleet to scuttle a whole squadron of men o' war, blocking the entrance to Sevastopol harbour. Various subsequent delays also enabled Menshikov to improve his defences in many other ways.

On 26 September St-Arnaud, his tuberculosis exacerbated by severe cholera, was taken aboard the *Berthollet* for immediate repatriation to France, but died the same day, leaving Canrobert as C-in-C of the French contingent in the run-up to the next battle of the campaign over a month later on 25 October at Balaklava[4], overlooking the bay on the southern coast where the British were bringing in supplies, chosen by Raglan as a good anchorage for his richer officers' private yachts.

By then the *bataillon de marche* had been disbanded and the elite companies reintegrated in the Legion brigade that arrived in the second wave from Gallipoli under Achille Bazaine, that veteran of the first Legion now promoted to brigadier at the age of forty-three – a good two decades younger than many of his fellow commanders. With him came his young bride, Maria de la Soledad Tormo, the spirited and beautiful seventeen-year-old daughter of his former landlady in Tlemcen. Given their age difference, she would be an obvious target for other men's lust in a prolonged campaign.

Attractive and socially accomplished thanks to the education he had paid for, Maria had neglected none of her home comforts in accompanying her husband on this new adventure. The most cumbersome of them was her grand piano. Whether she played her part as the colonel's gracious lady by selflessly entertaining the sick and dying with her recitals, as was reported in Paris, she did entertain several of his fellow officers when Bazaine's duties took him away from home.

Russians regard the sheltered southeast coast of the Crimea as a winter riviera, but the Polish legionnaires must have shuddered at what winter would be like in their bleak and windswept tented encampment on the exposed plateau overlooking Strelitzka Bay. For men who had left Algeria in the heat of midsummer and survived the cholera and boredom of the depot, the approach of winter was firmly in Menshikov's favour.

On 5 November he launched 40,000 troops through the dawn mist against the weaker end of the line held by 8,000 English troops, many of whom died before even emerging from their tents. As reported in the *Times*, for two hours the balance of advantage in the battle of Inkerman swung to and fro until, around 1000hrs a French corps of 3,000 men including Chasseurs d'Afrique cavalrymen attacked the Russians on the flank at the same time as a further 8,000 Russians attacked the main French positions, including those of the Legion.[5] Not until after midday were the Russians driven off with casualties totalling 15,000, against 2,600 English and 900 French dead and wounded, among which the Legion counted three officers and forty-three legionnaires dead and many wounded.[6]

News of this victory and that of the Alma reached Paris and London within a day of the events via the new telegraph submarine cable laid under the Black Sea especially for the purpose. It may have sounded fine to Napoleon III and Queen Victoria, whose new poet laureate Alfred Tennyson immortalised in verse the English cavalrymen killed in the great blunder at Balaklava on 25 October, but Menshikov's ally General Winter attacked the Allies soon afterwards. On 14 November a violent storm heralded his arrival by flooding the trenches and blowing away many of the 12-man bell tents set up on the plateau above Sevastopol, leaving thousands of men with no shelter.

With all the firewood for miles around requisitioned for earthworks, men still wearing their summer uniforms died from exposure before the winter greatcoats were issued in December. Another consequence of the storm was shortages caused by many supply ships being driven aground after permission to enter the inadequate harbour in Cossack Bay was withheld by the Royal Navy harbourmaster. Among the drowned on HMS *Rip van*

Winkle were Richard Nicklin, the first official war photographer, and his two sapper darkroom assistants.

The appalling commissariat problems were caused largely by private contractors supplying substandard food and short measures, but great blame attaches also to Admiral Boxer, in charge of transport arrangement at Constantinople/Gallipoli. Ships arrived at Balaklava without prior notice and without manifests; some arrived at Constantinople and were sent back to Europe without being unloaded. In Cossack Bay the quayside was covered with rotting food, soaked boxes of ammunition and powder barrels, with the water of the harbour between the steam and sail-powered transport ships covered by a carpet of refuse and excrement. There was a lack of forage to feed the pack animals that might have moved supplies up to the plateau and cavalry horses were so starving that they ate each other's manes and tails in desperation. Only late in January 1855 was the situation partially rectified after British civilian navvies constructed a narrow-gauge railway line up to the heights.

News of this chaos reaching London in the highly critical despatches of William Russell, by February the groundswell of public criticism and complaint toppled the Aberdeen government, with Lord Palmerston replacing him as Prime Minister and Lord Panmure becoming Secretary for War. This resulted in some improvement in the organisation and administration of the British Army, and as spring approached the chaos was slowly cleared.

By March 1855 a Land Transport Corps was formed and in June 1855 a new-style medical corps was set up to provide hospital services on the peninsula, but by then hundreds of thousands had died unnecessarily. As a measure of that, in Üsküdar the death rate before Florence Nightingale's arrival had been 44%; six months later she had brought it down to 2.2% by imposing elementary hygiene and insisting on sound nursing practice – not that any legionnaires benefited from her attentions.

Chapter 11

THEIRS NOT TO REASON WHY

Crimea 1855–1856; Italy 1859

Once the ground froze up on the plateau above Sevastopol, it was almost impossible to dig trenches. From dawn to dusk protracted artillery duels between the Allied guns and the Russian batteries caused random casualties. Shattered by a Russian shell, frozen earth fragmented into ice shrapnel. And when the ground thawed, the trenches flooded again. Count Georges de Villebois-Mareuil described one anonymous legionnaire standing up in his trench when it would have been wiser not to. Perhaps the water-level in the trench was too high to squat. The count continued, 'The thoughtful face of an old soldier, hardened by firm resolution. One feels that (the legionnaire) is unaware of the intense cold, as he is of everything but the enemy and his single-minded goal (of) dying at his post. [1]

Having failed to attack Sevastopol after the initial landings, the Allies settled down to a long process of reducing by gunfire a city without a continuous defensive masonry wall. As evidenced by the unofficial photographs of Roger Fenton and James Robertson, superintendent of the Imperial Mint at Constantinople, the Sevastopol defences built by Menshikov's German sapper Gen Todleben were far more resilient and easily rebuilt earthworks reinforced with timber, brushwood and earth-filled cylindrical wicker baskets known as *gabions* – plus sandbags.

The main earthen rampart was protected by a palisade of sharpened stakes and a ditch and rifle pits, beyond which lay the forerunner of barbed wire – the *abattis* or tangle of earth and branches – and *fougasses*, which were pits filled with stones at the bottom of which lay an explosive charge. Incidental unpleasantness in wait for the unwary legionnaire included boot-piercing caltrops and concealed planks with sharp nails punched through, facing upwards. Beneath the ground, in an ugly rehearsal of Flanders 1914–18, both the Russian and Allied sappers mined and counter-mined, killing each other in the tunnels with sharpened shovels when they met.

The French positions were directed against the Flagstaff battery, the Central Bastion and the Quarantine Bastion, stretching on the right flank to the Malakov, the Little Redan and by the end of February 1855, the Mamelon strongpoint. If that sounds quite orderly, to call this a siege is a misnomer because the city could not be cordoned off altogether: vast stretches of countryside to north and east unoccupied by the Allies made it possible for the Russians to bring in supplies and reinforcements throughout the campaign.

The hellish daytime artillery bombardments ceased with the light, after which the night was taken up for both sides by patrolling in the no-man's-land between the lines and raiding parties suddenly erupting from the dark to murder all the men in a trench or rifle pit before disappearing as slyly as they had come.

For the Legion and most other Allied soldiers, issued clothing was so inadequate that wounded men of both sides were stripped of outer clothes, underwear and boots, long before their last breath. In the Crimean winter, this meant death by exposure for many who would have survived their wounds.

In Florence Nightingale's hospital at Üsküdar, across the Bosporus from Constantinople, the buildings had been infested with rats and fleas on her arrival and water was restricted to one pint per head per day for all purposes. Furniture, clothing, and bedding were either inadequate or totally lacking. The wards being grossly overcrowded, men lay in the corridors on straw palliasses in their own filth and everyone else's. At first refused entrance to the wards by the doctors, when finally admitted after the influx of wounded from the battle of Inkerman shortly after her arrival, the Lady with the Lamp requisitioned not medical supplies, but 200 scrubbing brushes and facilities for her patients' filthy and verminous clothes to be washed and disinfected outside the wards.

But she was dealing with men who had survived several days

before arriving at Üsküdar. If these were the conditions back at base, those in what passed for field hospitals just behind the lines on the other side of the Black Sea, and on board the transports bringing the wounded back, defy the modern imagination.

Wastage was so high that Napoleon III created another foreign legion by decree on 17 January 1855. During his years of exile, his own military education had been at officer school in Thun. Impressed by Swiss soldiery, he recruited in Switzerland – as the English were already doing to make good their losses – for what he had originally intended to call 'la Légion Suisse', until Col Johann Ulrich Ochsenbein, a Swiss professional soldier who was hired to command it, persuaded the Emperor that it would be a diplomatic faux pas. He was right: the recruiting competition between the English Swiss Legion of two regiments and the French Swiss Legion comprising two line regiments and a battalion of skirmishers led to federal legislation in 1859 forbidding Swiss citizens to serve in foreign armies.[2] Ochsenbein's new Legion was therefore officially referred to as 2nd Foreign Brigade, with 1st Brigade consisting of the Legion units already in the Crimea.

Promoted to general, Ochsenbein became the last foreigner to reach this rank in the French army. His legion never amounted to much except on paper, and he spent the rest of the Crimean campaign in Besançon near the Swiss border, trying to entice recruits to cross into France and sign up. Since the British were offering an enlistment bonus of 150 francs and he had only twenty francs per man to offer, recruitment was slow. A better source of reinforcements 'on the ground' was Sardinia-Piedmont, which joined the alliance against Russia in January 1855 and actually did sent 15,000 troops under Gen de la Marmora.

In the Crimea, the first Legion engagement of the New Year came on the night of 19–20 January when 2nd Battalion of the 2nd Regiment suffered a savage surprise attack. Similar Russian sorties in February and March left so many corpses littering the battlefield that truces were arranged for burial parties, with the officers in charge exchanging cigars, champagne and civilities with their opposite numbers in French, the second language of most of Menshikov's officers. There were few illicit perks for the burial squads; most of the bodies had by then already been plundered by men desperate enough to risk their lives for warmer clothing, a few coins in a purse strapped to the leg or the most coveted prize of all, a pair of *sapogi* or Russian boots.

On 3 February the overworked Tsar Nikolai I died of an ordinary cold that turned to pneumonia and was succeeded by his son Aleksandr II. At Sevastopol the change of Tsar made no difference. On 22 February and again on 22 March violent sorties from the garrison badly dented but did not destroy the siege lines, strengthened by the arrival of 13,500 Swiss, Germans and Poles and the contingent from Piedmont-Sardinia.

On 9 April the Allies began their second great bombardment of Sevastopol. 520 Allied guns poured 165,000 rounds into the complex of defences and were answered by 998 Russian guns firing about 90,000 rounds in reply. The two-way bombardment thundered on for ten days, directly causing 6,131 casualties to the defenders, 1,587 to the French and 263 in the much-reduced British line. Except to the dead and wounded, it made little difference because the Russians repaired the damage every night.

It was all very well for Raglan to hector Canrobert about launching a 'big push', but the main burden would have been on the French and Canrobert was under daily pressure via the telegraph cable to Varna from an Emperor with a magnificent new military moustache and a Hitler complex who always 'knew better' than his generals on the spot.

As winter became spring the British role in the siege was so severely handicapped by sickness that only 11,000 men were left fit to man the trenches, as against 90,000 French and 50,000 Turks facing 100,000 Russians. Raglan had anticipated that the campaign would be 'over by Christmas' and had to reduce rations so close to starvation level that the French took over responsibility for supplying both armies. In a major logistical effort during the eighteen months from July 1854 the French supply fleet delivered to the Crimean theatre 310,000 men, 42,000 horses, 1,676 artillery pieces and 600,000 tons of materiel.

Although hardly an impressionable child at the age of thirty-six, Tsar Aleksandr II had been educated by a Swiss republican tutor and was known to be liberal and pro-European in comparison with his overbearing father. In the hope that a major Allied victory would give Aleksandr reason to sue for peace, Napoleon III ordered a major French attack for 1 May. Its designated target was an important Russian bastion that was heavily mortaring the French lines. At 2030hrs that day six elite Legion companies spearheaded the attack with bayonets fixed. Driving off the Russian defenders, they were reinforced by the rest of 1st Regiment under Col Viénot. Repeated Russian counter-attacks were beaten off while legionnaires from 2nd Regiment dug and built desperately to link the French lines to the strongpoint with its eight captured mortars.

Cost of the operation? 480 French wounded and 118 dead, the latter including the third Legion commander to die in action, Col Viénot, whose name would be immortalised by calling the headquarters barracks at Sidi-bel-Abbès – and later in Aubagne – the Quartier Viénot.

Counter-attacks the following day were again beaten back, with 2nd Regiment and a battalion of 98th Infantry Regiment turning the enemy flank and holding their positions despite violent Russian counter-attacks. On 3 May another truce was called to bury the dead, already stinking in the hot sunshine, after which the Russians began the construction of a counter-fortification on high ground overlooking the French lines.

Finding it impossible to continue working with his sick and francophobic English opposite number and the interference of Napoleon III from Paris, Canrobert stepped down on 16 May to take command of the 4th Division under his successor Gen Pélissier. Although rejecting the more ridiculous orders from Paris – he even cut the telegraph line once – Pélissier was about to find that it was far easier to asphyxiate Algerian women and children than to kill armed Russian soldiers.

On 22 May legionnaires took part in the next 'big push'. At 2100hrs, two battalions of 2nd Regiment were among those who went over the top and took the first Russian trenches. Menshikov threw three battalions at them in an effort to retake the position, but when dawn came they were still there, looking out over a sea of corpses including five Legion officers and thirty-four men dead, with eight officers and 174 men wounded.[3]

Three other battalions of the Legion had not been so successful. During the next two days, the position changed hands no less than five times. Casualties included over 200 Legion dead and wounded. When another truce was arranged on 23 May to bury the dead, the job was made more repugnant than usual by bodies swollen with the heat coming apart at the joints.

Under pressure from Paris to end this embarrassingly protracted war of so little benefit to France, on 7 June Gen Pélissier launched an attack on the two key forts blocking the route to Sevastopol, known as the Redan and Malakov, whose positions on high ground at the southwestern edge of the walled city denied any cover to attackers. After occupying a nearby height called Green Hillock, the Zouaves and Algerian light infantry managed to penetrate the Malakov, but were driven out with heavy losses.

On 17 June a determined attack cost 3,000 Allied lives to no effect. On 28 June Lord Raglan died of dysentery, the body being shipped home to Bristol for a quiet burial at the family home. Raglan's deputy being too ill to stay in the Crimea, it was Gen Sir James Simpson who replaced him on 1 July. Pélissier had chosen the day of Raglan's death to expunge the disgraceful memory of Waterloo by another major attack on the Malakov, but the French, including a detachment of one hundred volunteer legionnaires serving as pioneers under Sgt Valliez, mistook an outburst of firing nearby as a signal to start ten minutes early. Alerted by the French move, the defenders of the Redan cut the English to pieces with grapeshot when their attack went in on time. Both attacks failed with a total of 6,000 casualties on the one day for no result whatsoever.

At the end of July, Aleksandr fired Menshikov and replaced him by Prince Gorchakov, whose first act was to launch an attack on 16 August with four infantry divisions and two artillery brigades across the Chornaya River. When it too failed, Gorchakov sent a dispatch to St Petersburg stating that there was no point in prolonging the defence of Sevastopol. Finally on 8 September, after a three-day Allied barrage by 800 cannon, legionnaires were in the forefront of a third assault, whose success was largely due to their construction under fire of a network of jumping-off trenches inching nearer and nearer to the Malakov each night and their movement of scaling ladders right up to the walls. The fort was taken by the Allies – at what total cost in lives on both sides no one was ever clear.

Three days later, the Russians blew up the remaining forts, burned or scuttled their ships in the harbour, and evacuated Sevastopol. In the sack of the town, the legionnaires defied all attempts to keep discipline, with so many getting drunk by looting the cellars of the wine merchants that 'as drunk as a legionnaire at Sevastopol' became a measure of inebriation for many years to come. Two drunken legionnaires poisoned the regimental mascot of 23rd Royal Welsh Fusiliers. Ceremonially interred with military honours, the goat was then dug up by its killers, skinned and made into a fur coat. A polite request from a fusilier major resulted in the legionnaire wearing it selling it back to the regiment for £20.[4]

Thanks to the telegraph cable under the Black Sea, Pélissier's reward was to learn four days later that he had been made a Marshal of France by his grateful emperor. Appointed ambassador to London, he was created Duc de Malakoff (sic) the following year, and left smog-bound Victorian London for the sunshine and clear skies of Algeria and the post of Governor-General that he held until his death in 1864.

A more immediate consolation for the loss of all the men whose deaths earned him these honours was his after sending Gen Bazaine with the Legion and a British brigade to reduce the Kinburn fortress in southern Ukraine. During his absence, the well-named Aimable Pélissier arrived at Madame Bazaine's house each afternoon, perhaps to listen to her piano-playing. Her husband can hardly have been unaware, since Pélissier came to visit in the only liveried coach of the whole Allied territory, formerly the property of a Russian nobleman.

Peace terms were not agreed until 1 February in Vienna, with ratification of the treaty in Paris on 2 March 1856, after a second winter spent by the surviving legionnaires in digging trenches and rebuilding some of the destroyed fortifications. On 13 April Pélissier was accompanied by Russian Gen Luders at a ceremony of remembrance in the French cemetery, where he announced that

Napoleon III was recognising the Legion's contribution to the war-effort by an offer of French nationality for all legionnaires who had taken part, with a transfer to a regular regiment if they so wished.

Russian losses in the campaign were put at 256,000 deaths, 128,700 in combat and the others from disease or exposure. For the Allies, the war marked the first time since the crusades that France and Britain had fought on the same side. The price of their victory was 252,600 lives, of which only 70,000 were lost in combat and almost three times as many died from cholera and/or dysentery as in battle.

In July 1856, two years after they had left Algeria, the survivors paraded in the Quartier Viénot at Sidi bel-Abbès to honour their fallen: twelve officers dead and sixty-six wounded in the war, with legionnaire casualties numbering 1,625. Of every three men who had set sail for the Crimea, fewer than two returned – a relatively low rate of casualties owing to the toughening-up they had received before shipping east.

The Legion's sacrifices were acknowledged by a decree signed by Jean-Baptiste Vaillant, the Minister for War, regularising the establishment of 1st and 2nd Régiments Etrangers or 'foreign regiments', as they would in future be officially known.[5] For convenience, the brigade returning from Crimea became 2nd Régiment Etranger and Ochsenbein's under-strength Swiss units formed the nub of 1st Régiment Etranger, which continued unofficially to be called 'the Swiss regiment'.

Under the peace treaty the Black Sea was declared a demilitarised zone, but fourteen years later Russia abrogated the treaty and built new bases and a new fleet. More importantly, the Allies had stabilised the disintegrating Ottoman Empire until it was dismantled by them after the First World War. Although the Legion veterans could not claim any Crimean victory as exclusively theirs and losses in combat and from disease had been no greater than during some equivalent periods in North Africa, they had fought as a unit on many occasions and built an *esprit de corps* and sense of regimental history that can be gained no other way.

More importantly for its status and the quality of its future officers, the Foreign Legion had also proven itself an integral part of France's military machine. Although a snobbish inspecting general deplored 'a regiment that is nothing more than an amalgamation of all the nations of Europe' in 1861[6], no officer in a line regiment could any longer accuse the men who returned from the Crimea of being just a band of convicts fighting infidel bandits on African soil or label the Legion a holding tank for misfortune, as Soult had done.

On 14 January 1858 an Italian anarchist attempted to assassinate Napoleon III on his way to the opera. There was nothing unusual in this – Louis-Philippe suffered one or more attempts on his life every year of his reign – but some said it was from that moment that the Emperor decided to get involved in Italian affairs despite the resistance of the Church and the business community, which feared new taxes to pay for another war.

The real reason for the Italian intervention was Napoleon III's determination to restore France's territorial integrity by repossessing Savoie and the county of Nice. In July 1858 he concluded a secret pact of mutual assistance with Camillo Cavour, the prime minister of Piedmont, with this restoration as the quid pro quo. So, when in April 1859 Austria was manoeuvred into declaring war on Piedmont-Sardinia, France honoured its side of the agreement by declaring war against Austria in support of Cavour on 3 May.

Ochsenbein was long gone, but 1st Regiment was already in Corsica, attempting unsuccessfully to recruit on the Italian mainland. Landing in Genoa on 11 May, it counted barely 600 men and was brigaded with 2nd Regiment of sixty officers and 1,400 men including the Crimean veterans who had arrived on 26 April directly from Algeria. Together they marched inland to confront the Austrian army at the small Lombard market-town of Magenta, 20km west of Milan.

The rest of the French army included the first military units to travel at least part of the way to the front by rail, but it was ill-equipped in terms of provisions, ammunition, horses, tents and even blankets. Having brought no siege artillery, about the only thing in its favour were sixty-eight new rifled cannon, superior to anything the Austrians possessed.

The brigade was part of Gen MacMahon's[7] army of 54,000 men facing 58,000 Austrian troops under Gen Franz Gyulai in a battle unlike the set-pieces of Napoleonic warfare because the countryside around Magenta was divided up into smallholdings, orchards and vineyards separated by dry-stone walls. In such a broken landscape cavalry could not manoeuvre and the lines of attacking French infantry soon became ragged and spread out.

Had not the Austrians been wearing white coats, they would have been hard to discern through the vines and the trees in the orchards. On 29 June, the first Legion officer to spot a flash of white through all the green, Capt Rembert of 1st Regiment ordered his men to charge, apparently on his own initiative. With the advantage of numbers in the immediate vicinity, the Austrians stood their ground. Seeing the position, Col Granet Lacrosse de Chabrière, commanding 2nd Regiment in the saddle of his white charger, brandished his sword above his head, ordered his men to down packs and cried, 'En avant!' They were his last words. Hardly had he issued the order than a bullet knocked him clean from the saddle, dead.

The joint attack of legionnaires and Zouaves pressed the Austrians back in a disciplined retreat until Chabrière's second-in-command Lt Col Antonio Martinez called a halt and prudently sent some grenadiers forward to draw fire and ascertain the enemy position. Shortly afterwards, they returned to report that the Austrians were marching out of Magenta in the opposite direction. Seizing the moment, Martinez ordered his legionnaires and the Zouaves to charge. 2nd Lt Charles-Jules Zédé, who had joined 2nd Regiment at Sidi-bel-Abbès straight from St Cyr in 1857, described in his Souvenirs what happened when the charge went in. 'The Austrians hardly resisted but surrendered en masse, and we were furious to see the officers ride away with their flags. Only one was captured ... by the Zouaves.'[8]

Writing a history of the Legion, one is often confronted with 'facts' that have become part of Legion lore, yet are pure invention. One that is true is of MacMahon riding past some Legion veterans he recognised from Sevastopol as they fixed their bayonets prior to the assault on the town. 'Voici la Légion,' he said to his aides, acknowledging the veterans' salutes. 'L'affaire est dans le sac!' – the Legion's here, so the affair is in the bag!

It is the sort of thing that senior officers say to boost morale at a critical moment, and was far from true. The main body of

Austrian troops had withdrawn, but Magenta was still defended by Croatians and some Tyrolean mountain troops in cover behind a railway embankment between the French and the town proper. As described by Zédé, what happened next was a scene from a Hollywood movie: 'Zouaves and legionnaires hurled themselves forward. Neither cannon-shot, nor the (musket) volleys of the Austrians could stop them and this torrent rolled towards Magenta, carrying all before it.'[9]

Wishful thinking. Two attacks were halted short of the embankment with heavy losses before the French broke through. Once in the streets, it was hand-to-hand fighting, or rather bayonet-to-bayonet. Given the mixture of nationalities fighting for both sides, the scene of carnage could have inspired Lenin's dictum that a bayonet is a weapon with a worker at both ends, whereas the more aristocratic sword usually had an officer at the blunt end.

Lt Col Martinez, blood streaming from an eye wound, yelled orders to break down doors from behind which the defenders were firing and set fire to houses with men inside given the choice of burning to death or coming out to be shot. Lit by the flames, the bloodshed continued until dawn next day. The few Austrians who had been taken alive were gathered in front of the church on the piazza. By this time it was proving impossible for the officers to regain control. An orgy fired by blood-lust turned into an orgy fired by alcohol. In the wine cellars some men got so drunk that they drowned where they lay in the wine gushing out of barrels whose taps nobody bothered to close. Those still sober could hardly walk through the town, so many bodies of dead and dying men and horses lay in the streets, the drunks mixed up among them.

Where the night had been hideous with screams and shots, the morning air was filled with the moans of men in agony, many of whom might have been saved, had there been any medical attention. Zédé recalled the scene as those men capable of standing up stripped the bodies of the fallen of their uniforms and equipment. Walking wounded hobbled and staggered about seeking help. There was none. One Polish legionnaire named Kamienski with an arm shattered by a musket ball found his own way to what passed for a dressing station in Magenta railway station, where the French doctors had no bandages, dressings or anaesthetics. All they could do was give the wounded some water to drink. Those who had surgical instruments saw no point in operating on men who would die in a few days from gangrene or blood poisoning, as happened to Kamienski.[10]

At Magenta, 2nd Regiment lost four officers killed and 250 men killed or wounded – which often came to the same thing. After burying the dead in huge common graves, the victorious French marched into Milan on 7 June with the Legion honoured by leading the parade. The population greeting them as liberators, in the euphoric mood of the moment local men signed up to enlist in the Legion, but few were there to answer to their names when the time came to re-embark for North Africa.

After another extremely bloody encounter of 300,000 men and 2,600 cannon on a front thirteen miles long south of Lake Garda at Solferino on 24 June, where the Legion was represented by 2nd Regiment, Napoleon III agreed peace terms with Austria on 8 July, to the distress of Cavour, who had hoped to free more territory south of the Alps from Austrian sovereignty before the withdrawal of his French allies. On 11 July the emperors of France and Austria signed the armistice treaty at Villafranca di Verona, but it was only in March 1860 that Cavour officially ceded to France the price of the intervention – Savoie and Nice.

For once, something good came out of the carnage. Present at Solferino was a Swiss humanitarian called Henri Dunant. Appalled by witnessing the senseless slaughter continuing for hours under a leaden sky with the wounded left untended in agony, he improvised emergency medical services for the casualties of both sides. It was this initiative that led to the foundation of the International Committee for the Relief of the Wounded in 1863, which became the International Committee of the Red Cross in 1876, and to the first Geneva Convention of 1864.

As for 2nd Regiment, having fought on European soil as an intrinsic part of the French army, it was rewarded with the honour of participating for the first time with the line regiments in MacMahon's victory parade on 14 August through a Paris being ravished by Baron Haussmann, the prefect of the Seine *département*, who was demolishing whole districts to create the elegant *grands boulevards* and spacious squares that made the French capital as we see it today.

After that brief moment of glory came the return to Algeria on 22 August. In October the Swiss-only regulation was rescinded, owing to lack of volunteers, after which anyone could join, with the uniform reverting to red trousers and blue tunics. The 1st Regiment returned to Algeria via Corsica in February 1860 and was amalgamated with 2nd Regiment to make a single foreign regiment once again, whose regimental colours were green and red, as they have remained ever since.

In Paris, one of Haussmann's new boulevards was named Magenta and a street was renamed Solferino in honour of the victory. MacMahon was ennobled as the duke of Magenta – and Soult's bastard, the Legion, was beyond any question legitimate at last.

Chapter 12

MYTH AND MADNESS IN MEXICO

1862-1863

Every historian of the Legion is impressed by the wealth of memoirs written by legionnaires of all ranks. Some are a mixture of fact and fantasy; others tell the unvarnished truth, but from the limited viewpoint of one man, whose eyes saw only what was within his personal horizons, narrowed by suffering or the heat of combat. Yet, all tell of actions that leave the reader marvelling at the courage, self-sacrifice and comradeship with which they fought for French interests against apparently unassailable odds as valiantly as Homer's heroes.

On 30 April each year, the Legion celebrates the anniversary, not of a victory, but of a defeat. On that day, wherever legionnaires or ex-legionnaires are gathered, in a ritual observed even by the men waiting to die at Dien Bien Phu in 1954, an officer or senior NCO reads aloud in French a story that all the others know by heart. In jerky military prose that has been rendered at some time or other with all the accents in the world, it goes like this:

The French army was besieging Puebla in Mexico. The Legion was ordered to patrol and make secure 20km of roads used by supply convoys. The Commanding Officer Col Jeanningros learned on 28 April 1863 that a large convoy of gold, siege materiel and munitions was heading for Puebla. His adjutant Capt Danjou persuaded him to send a company out ahead of the convoy. The third company was designated for the job but had no officers available to lead the patrol. Capt Danjou took command personally and second-lieutenants Maudet and Vilain, the standard-bearer and paymaster, volunteered to accompany him.

At 0100hrs on 30 April the three officers and sixty-two men of 3rd Company set out. After covering 20km they stopped at Palo Verde at 0700hrs to brew coffee. At this moment, the enemy came into sight and combat was immediately engaged. Capt Danjou ordered a defensive square to be formed, and victoriously (sic) fought off several cavalry charges, inflicting heavy losses on the enemy. On drawing level with the inn of Camerone, a large building comprising a courtyard surrounded by a three-metre-high wall, he decided to make a stand there in order to hold up the enemy and delay as long as possible the moment when they could attack the convoy.

While his men were hastily organising the defence of the inn, a Mexican officer called on Capt Danjou to surrender because he was heavily outnumbered. The reply was, 'We have cartridges and we won't surrender.' Then, raising his right hand, Danjou swore to fight to the death and made his men take the same oath. It was then 1000hrs.

Until 1800hrs these sixty men, who had neither eaten nor drunk since the previous day, held off 2,000 Mexicans - 800 cavalry and 1,200 foot-soldiers - despite the extreme heat and thirst. At noon Capt Danjou was killed by a bullet in his chest. At 1400hrs, 2nd Lt Vilain was killed by a bullet in the forehead. At this moment the Mexicans succeeded in setting fire to the inn.

Despite the heat and the smoke that added to their suffering, the legionnaires held on, but many had been hit. At 1700hrs, 2nd Lt Maudet had only twelve men still able to fight. At this moment the Mexican colonel assembled his men and told them they should be ashamed of themselves for not being able to defeat a handful of brave men. A Spanish-speaking legionnaire simultaneously translated his words for the other legionnaires.

Col Milán then called upon 2nd Lt Maudet to surrender, an offer which Maudet rejected with disdain. The Mexicans then made the final assault through breaches they had made in the walls. Soon only five men were left with Maudet: Cpl Maine, legionnaires Catteau, Wensel, Constantin and Léonard. With one cartridge left each, they fixed bayonets and faced the enemy in a corner of the courtyard with their backs to the wall. On a signal, they fired their rifles at point-blank range and bayonet-charged the enemy. 2nd Lt Maudet and two legionnaires fell dead.

Maine and his two comrades were about to be massacred when a Mexican officer threw himself in front of them and cried, 'Surrender!' They replied, 'We shall surrender if you promise to care for our wounded and if you permit us to keep our weapons.' Their bayonets were still dangerous. The officer replied, 'One can refuse nothing to men such as you.'

Capt Danjou's sixty men held on as they had sworn they would, fighting off 2,000 enemy for eleven hours. They killed 300 and wounded the same number. By their sacrifice in saving the convoy they carried out the mission that had been entrusted to them.

In addition to Napoleon III deciding that the name of Camerone should be inscribed on the flag of the Foreign Regiment and that the names of Danjou, Vilain and Maudet should be carved in gold on the walls of Les Invalides in Paris, a monument was erected in 1892 on the site of the battle. It bears the inscription:

Here, less than sixty men opposed a whole army.
Its numbers crushed them.
Life, but not courage, left these French soldiers
here on 30 April 1863.
The fatherland erected this monument to their memory.

That is the *récit officiel* - the official story. The truth is not quite as simple, but first - since more is known about these legendary soldiers than of most legionnaires, it is interesting to note that of the French officers Jean Danjou was thirty-five, Clément Maudet thirty-four and Jean Vilain twenty-seven. These were no dilettante younger sons of rich families, such as might have been found in a line regiment on garrison duty in France.

They were professional soldiers, and Danjou had more than medals to prove it. He wore a carved and articulated wooden hand, painted to resemble a leather glove, strapped to his left forearm in replacement of the one lost when his rifle burst during a mapping expedition in the Kabylia campaign. With no standard system of 'proving' barrels, this was a not uncommon accident of the times. He was also a veteran of the Italian intervention and had been awarded the Légion d'Honneur in the Crimea. Maudet and Vilain had served as NCOs before winning their commissions. Maudet, promoted only three months previously, was the most decorated officer in the battalion and therefore the flag-bearer. Acting paymaster Vilain had joined the Legion aged eighteen and had also been awarded the Légion d'Honneur for valour.

The 11 NCOs in the company had an average age of twenty-eight. Although three of the legionnaires were only eighteen, the forty-six of whom details are available had an average age of twenty-six. That this was on the young side in the 1860s, when it was generally between twenty-eight and thirty-two years old,[1] may be because the high rate of casualties during the month 3rd Company had spent in the fever belt had carried off the older men first. All of which bears out that the Legion was for the most part made up of veterans, not inexperienced youths 'avid for some great glory'. The most common previous profession declared on enlistment was *militaire* - a soldier in someone else's army.

That the policy of mixing men of many nationalities was in full force in 1863 is amply borne out by an analysis of the NCOs and men in 3rd Company that day whose nationality is recorded. It breaks down as follows: eighteen Germans, thirteen Belgians, eleven French who had enlisted as Belgian or Swiss to account for speaking the language, nine Swiss and one man each from Holland, Denmark, Spain, Austria and Italy, plus another Italian born in Algeria.

Read out on the Legion's 'birthday' each year, the official version of the battle of Camarón - to give the site of the battle its Mexican name - is a model of selfless heroism for other legionnaires to emulate. A civilian can find it difficult to credit that these men who had never met before joining the Legion regarded the oath they had sworn as more important than their own lives. They had no personal interest in the outcome of the battle either way, but were obeying orders for the benefit of a general who cold-bloodedly sent them to an area where many would die of tropical diseases and of an emperor in Paris who cared not a damn for them.

The first question to clear up is: what were French troops doing in Mexico? Notwithstanding its cost of 7,000 lives and 300 million francs[2], Napoleon III's 1862 intervention is now marked only by a few words in Mexican Spanish like *mariachi* - meaning originally the musicians who played at a mariage. The full story of Camerone begins two years before Danjou and all those men died - accepting for the moment that they did.

When Confederate artillery fired the first shots of the American Civil War at Fort Sumter guarding the entrance to the harbour of Charleston in South Carolina, the echoes reached all the way to Paris. An investment spree that might be labelled the Latin-American Bubble had enticed French and other European investors to buy bonds guaranteed by the Mexican government. President Ignacio Comonfort was replaced by Benito Pablo Juárez in a coup d'état in January 1861. After the civil war that had ravaged the country from 1857 to 1860, the Mexican economy was in such parlous state that Juárez was faced with an empty treasury. As a solution to this problem, he began nationalising and selling off Church property. In July of that year he announced that he was also suspending interest payment on all foreign debts for two years.

British, Spanish and French bond-holders demanded action from their governments. The fast-living illegitimate half-brother of Napoleon III, whom he would ennoble as Duc de Morny in 1862 and whose business interests included both a sugar empire and the fashionable spa and English gambling paradise at Deauville, was lobbying for his friends among them. Fed a tissue of lies by him, Napoleon III came to believe that the people of Mexico wanted to be rescued from Juárez and his Liberals by foreign intervention.

On 31 October 1861 Britain, France and Spain signed an agreement for a joint military expedition to safeguard these investments and protect their citizens in Mexico, many of whom had been killed during the civil war. Juárez agreed they might garrison Vera Cruz on the Gulf coast, plus Córdoba, Orizaba on the road from Vera Cruz to Mexico City and Tehuacan on condition that they did not interfere in 'the sovereignty, independence and territorial integrity of the Mexican Republic'.

This was in blatant defiance of the Monroe Doctrine enunciated by American President Monroe in December 1832. The Doctrine not only forbade US involvement in the affairs of the Old World; Article 4 stated quite specifically that any attempt by a European power to oppress or control any nation in the Western Hemisphere would be viewed as a hostile act against the United States. However, with the Confederate and Union states locked in bloody civil war, for the moment the European powers felt free to intervene south of the Rio Grande.

In December 1861 the expeditionary force of 7,000 Spaniards, 2,500 French, and 700 British Royal Marines landed and occupied Vera Cruz, from which the conquistadors' route known as the Camino Real or Royal Road ran through Soledad, Córdoba and Puebla to Mexico City, 300km inland. However, the mooted tripartite debt recovery by force of arms was still-born. After heavy losses from disease and hit-and-run guerrilla attacks, the British and Spanish withdrew what remained of their troops in April 1862, having realised that Napoleon III was using the tripartite intervention as cover for a far more ambitious plan of his own.

This was nothing less than an attempt to thwart Protestant Anglo-Saxon influence in the western hemisphere by creating a French-speaking area in Central and South America. The idea was not quite so crazy as it sounds. As place-names like Baton Rouge, Lafayette and New Orleans still testify in Louisiana - the state named for a French king - the western half of the Mississippi River basin had been French until 1803 when it was purchased by the

United States. At less than three cents per acre for 828,000 square miles it was the best bargain in US history. So, in a sense, Napoleon III was only trying to replace a colony his country had recently lost. Seen from Paris, the conquest of Mexico followed by placing a puppet king on its throne seemed logical steps in this plan.

The chosen puppet was the Archduke Ferdinand Maximilian Josef, brother of the Austrian Emperor - France's enemy of yesteryear. Maximilian was counselled both by Emperor Franz Joseph and British diplomats not to get involved in Napoleon III's scheme that took no account of either the political complexity of Mexican politics or the vastness of the country. From the northern border of Baja California to the eastern tip of the Yucatán peninsula is roughly the same distance as from Gibraltar to Moscow. However, representatives of the small number of immensely rich and conservative land-owning families in Mexico, thinking him an easily manipulated young man, persuaded the liberal-minded Maximilian that the people had elected him king. The lie was to cost his life and the sanity of his young Belgian wife Carlota.

Maximilian's main condition for becoming figure-head of the French adventure was that he be given a European army of 10,000 men to place him in power and keep him there, so the build-up of French troops in Mexico continued, with the Compagnie Générale Transatlantique purchasing the latest English propeller-driven steamships to inaugurate a regular service between French ports and Vera Cruz.

A month after the British and Spanish withdrawal, on 5 May came the first warning that the Mexican intervention was not going to be the push-over that Napoleon III and his Austrian protégé had hoped. Whatever the exact agreement with Juárez, it ended when French troops marched inland with the aim of occupying Mexico City. At Puebla the Mexicans not only resisted but defeated the French. Regrouping, the French commander-in-chief Gen Elie-Frédéric Forey settled down to take the city by siege. Reinforcements poured in across the Atlantic. In September, 28,000 men with fifty-six cannon disembarked at Vera Cruz for Forey's siege of Puebla, garrisoned by 22,000 Mexicans.

The 1st Régiment Etranger had actually been dissolved in 1861, with recruitment for the former 2nd RE suspended and legionnaires who had completed one year of their two-year engagements demobbed. This winding-down continued until 22 March 1864, when recruitment recommenced to make good the losses in Mexico. Long before then a number of junior Legion officers directly petitioned Napoleon III for a chance to join in what was dubbed *l'affaire Mexicana*. Unknown to them, their emperor was already considering leasing the Legion to Maximilian for ten years.

On 9 February 1863 two seven-company battalions of the Legion plus a headquarters and supply company totalling 2,000 men boarded the French naval vessels *St. Louis* and *Wagram* after loading their equipment and mules on the transport *Finistère* and left the 'great harbour' of Mers el-Kebir on the Gulf of Oran. The uncomfortable voyage through North Atlantic winter gales to Vera Cruz lasted until 28 March.

Instead of summoning the Legion up to the siege front where its combined experience from the Crimea and Italy would have been most useful, Forey gave it the job of securing the fever-ridden first 70km of the journey from Vera Cruz through the swamps and scrubland of the coastal plain where malaria was rife. So called 'Jesuits' powder' - the powdered bark of the cinchona tree - had first been used to treat the disease in Europe as long ago as 1642. England's Charles II and Louis XIV's son had both recovered thanks to it, but it was so expensive that nobody was going to waste it on mercenary soldiers. And since no one connected the mosquito's bite with the onset of the disease until a British army surgeon in India discovered the link in 1897, the legionnaires at Vera Cruz in 1863 never thought of taking precautions.

In addition, the area in which the Legion was stationed had just about every other affliction of the tropics, including a local variety of yellow fever called *vómito negro* which caused the sufferer to literally vomit up his own blood until he died after six or eight hours of agonising cramps. The chilling *Historique Sommaire* of the Legion has many laconic entries like, 'On 7 October Lt Barrera died of *vómito* at Córdoba'.[3] An officer who put his experiences down on paper, the impoverished Swiss aristocrat from Fribourg Capt Gabriel Diesbach de Torny, reckoned that the losses were far worse, with his company of 124 men reduced to twenty-five within the year.[4] Charles-Jules Zédé claimed that one-third of the Legion died of disease in 1863. His first sight of land on arrival at Vera Cruz was 'a muddy coast with no vegetation, littered with the hulks of wrecked ships. On our right, a small islet on which stood the derelict fortress of St Juan de Ulla. On the left, the arid Sacrifice Island, covered with a multitude of crosses marking the graves of sailors who had fallen victim to the unhealthy climate.'[5]

The legionnaires' first combat took place while they were still getting their bearings in early April. A large Mexican guerrilla band raided a railway work camp under Legion protection. The *guerilleros*, who alternated between being freedom fighters and simple banditry, had bitten off more than they could chew this time. Before they were driven off with heavy casualties, Lt Ernst Milson von Bolt killed the well-known guerrilla leader Antonio Diaz in hand-to-hand combat, an action for which he received the Légion d'Honneur.

All of which explains why 3rd Company was under-strength and short of officers on 29 April 1863 when a local woman arrived at its base camp on Mount Chiquihuite at siesta time and asked to speak with Col Pierre Jeanningros. Her father being a sergeant in the Mexican National Guard, Col Milán - the aristocratic, Spanish-looking military governor of Vera Cruz state - had come to dine in their home the previous evening. During the meal, the woman had overheard the two men discussing Milán's plan to ambush at Palo Verde a massive French convoy that had left Vera Cruz on 15 April. It consisted of sixty-four wagons and 150 pack mules carrying guns, ammunition and a pay chest of 14 million pesos in gold and silver coin to pay Forey's army plus all the local labourers, muleteers and camp followers outside Puebla. Her motive for bringing the information to Jeanningros was to save the life of her husband, a waggoner in the convoy who could well be killed in the ambush.

Jeanningros at once despatched a young Mexican with a message to Soledad for the officer commanding the convoy to halt there until its escort could be reinforced. In case the messenger fell into enemy hands, he decided also to send out 3rd Company as a back-up. However, the only officer of 3rd Company not ill or absent was the young acting paymaster, 2nd Lt Vilain.

Although his own engagement was completed and he was eligible for repatriation, Danjou had been infatuated with the Legion since he was fifteen, when a former employee of his father came to visit the family home in Languedoc while on leave from Algeria wearing the uniform of a second lieutenant in the Legion, and filled the boy's head with tales of daring and adventure. Despite his father wanting him in the family business, Danjou attended St Cyr and passed out in 1847 as a second-lieutenant. Bored stiff when posted to the 51st Line Regiment on garrison duty in France, he requested a transfer to the Legion, which he joined at Batna in Algeria on 24 September 1852. The Legion had been his whole life since then. Now it was to be his death also.

He volunteered to replace the absent captain of 3rd Company and Maudet volunteered to go along as second-in-command. By leaving at midnight, they could march eastwards towards the coast and reach Palo Verde at dawn, rest there until the following night and then reconnoitre the road to Soledad. If they saw the dust of the convoy heading their way, there might still be time to get a warning to it, for the heavily laden wagons' best speed rarely exceeded 2km an hour in those conditions. If there was no dust-cloud, that meant the messenger had got through.

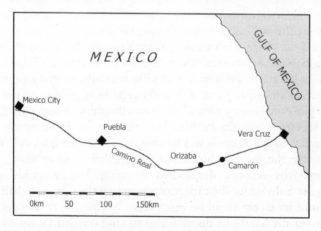

The Mexican Intervention 1862-63

Reduced by disease and deaths to sixty-two NCOs and men from its full strength of about 120, 3rd Company was roused at 2300hrs, given coffee and bread, setting off at 0100hrs as described in the official account, with the three officers mounted and the men on foot. Two mules were laden with rations and water for thirty-six hours and sixty cartridges per man. The distance from base to Palo Verde was 20km. By marching in the cool of the night, with spare ammunition and food carried on mules, it was possible to cover the distance before the heat of midday, even for men who had been ill for most of the thirty-four days since they landed in-country.

The climate in this part of Mexico is so hot and so humid that it is now the country's major sugar-growing area, boasting the world's largest refinery. At the time, the landscape through which the legionnaires had to march was mosquito-infested tropical scrub of bushes entangled with lianas that made progress off the road a matter of hacking every step of the way through it with the blade of a sabre. Despite its grand name the Royal Road was more of a track, badly in need of repair, with parapets washed away by the heavy rains and the muddy surface deeply rutted by the passage of supply wagons. Just before dawn the heavy downpour stopped and they were given breakfast of coffee and black bread at an outpost manned by an elite Legion grenadier company. Capt Gustave Saussier, in command of the post, offered Danjou some of his men, but Danjou turned down the offer, as instructed by Jeanningros. Odds of five or even ten to one were quite normal in Mexico and the Legion had little respect for the marksmanship of the *guerrilleros* who made up most of the forces in this region.[6]

Dawn at 0530hrs found the column heading downhill after cautiously negotiating the narrow ravine of Payo Ancho. Below them lay the Jalapa River. It was going to be a hot day. They passed through several ramshackle settlements from which the inhabitants had fled, this being a war zone. Normally the left-right rhythm of the march would have been given by the Italian drummer Casimiro Lai, but they were marching in silence, given the likely proximity of the enemy.

The village of Camarón was like all the others they passed, deserted and derelict from the war, with thatched roofs fallen in and the skeletal roof-timbers silhouetted against the lightening sky. To the left of the road stood a few abandoned hovels, with some more substantial dwellings 300 metres to the east. This was a property called Trinity Ranch, most of whose owners now lay in the cemetery at Palo Verde. On the left or north side of the Camino Real was its large main house with a dozen bedrooms. On the right or south side lay the single-storey stable block built around a courtyard with thin walls about three metres high broken only by two gateways wide and high enough for wagons to pass through. This too was derelict, the only signs of recent occupation being remains of campfires lit by *guerrilleros* camping there for the night.

After passing the ranch, Danjou split his troop into two sections, he following the road with one section and the two mules, while the other section marched parallel on the left flank, hacking its way through the scrub on the lookout for enemy activity. Finding nothing, it rejoined the rest of the column at Palo Verde about 0700hrs, where they unloaded the mules and took a rest break to brew coffee. As senior NCO, Sgt Maj Henri Tonel posted a ring of sentries.

The burning sun had already dried out the surface soil and was raising dust-devils everywhere. With the heat-haze, these made vision difficult, but before the hour was out the sentries discerned the tell-tale cloud of dust thrown up by an approaching party of riders. However, this was not the French convoy because it was coming from the wrong direction and was already quite close by the time Danjou's men could make out the riders' Mexican military caps and cowboy-type clothing.

The men sleeping in the shade of bushes were roused and those making coffee doused the fire by overturning the coffee onto it. Tonel ordered some men under Cpl Charles Magnin to catch the mules browsing nearby and reload the water containers on them. Within five minutes the company was formed up, weapons ready to give battle.

Chapter 13

DEATH IN THE AFTERNOON

Mexico 1863-1867

Danjou decided not to stay on the road, but to put the mounted Mexicans at a disadvantage by striking out cross-country in the direction of La Joya. Cutting their way through the bush with difficulty, his men seemed to have lost the enemy, but progress was so difficult that they turned back towards Camarón. As they approached the Trinity Ranch, a shot rang out from one of the windows. Surrounding the derelict buildings, they explored the interior but found no one there. Preparing to make a stand, Danjou hurriedly despatched some men with the now empty water containers to a gully that sometimes had pools of water in the bottom, but they returned empty-handed.

Despite the single shot aimed in their direction, there seemed to be no enemy nearby, so Danjou decided to set out for Chiquihuite. They had covered only 400 metres when the point man spotted several groups of Mexican horsemen about to charge. Calling on Lai to beat the signal *form a square!* Danjou got his men onto a small, bare hillock in defensive square formation. With Mexicans splitting into two squadrons to attack from both sides simultaneously and thus divide the Company's fire, the crisis of this first indecisive skirmish came when the noise and powder-smoke panicked the mules into running off, to be captured by the enemy.

The Mexicans withdrawing to a safe distance, Danjou ordered his men to hold their fire. Cavalry commander Jiménez boldly brought his men to within sixty metres before giving the order to charge again with lance and sabre.

Danjou yelled the order, 'Fire!'

The volley rang out, leaving men and horses on the ground with the untouched riders galloping out of range, pursued by fire at will. The open ground being ideal for cavalry charges, Danjou moved his men into the cover of a small wall and cactus hedge nearby, which would protect them from the horsemen at least on one side. Another, more cautious, Mexican charge was repulsed here. In the following lull, Danjou coolly decided to move his men by sections back to the nearest building, which was the stable block of the Trinity Ranch.

To gain the necessary respite he ordered the men to all shout at the top of their voices in unison, '*Vive l'Empereur!*' The ruse worked. Thinking that French reinforcements had arrived, the Mexicans held back just long enough to enable most of the legionnaires to reach the protecting walls of the ranch before any shots rang out. It was now about 0930hrs and Danjou had already lost sixteen men in his retreat to the ranch.

Taking stock of the situation, he realised that these were not the usual odds of five or ten to one, but vastly more. The sheer numbers had to mean that he was looking at the cavalry force with which Col Milán was intending to ambush the supply column. If he could keep them engaged at the ranch, he was ensuring the convoy's safety.

Built in traditional style with inward-facing rooms around a central courtyard protected by a 3-metre-high wall, the complex of buildings could be mistaken by French eyes for a wayside inn. It was designed to be easily defensible - but not against the odds Danjou was up against. The strength of 3rd Company at this point was three officers and forty-six NCOs and legionnaires. Setting them to make loopholes through the softer walls made of adobe and barricade the gateways with rubble and fallen timbers, he ordered Sgt Morzicki to the roof as lookout. From there, Morzicki cold see hundreds of horsemen and infantry in various military uniforms, supported by masses of guerrilla fighters in civilian clothes. All the regular troops were armed with the latest American carbines.

Nobody has explained why Milán kept all his troops at Trinity Ranch, instead of pinning Danjou's men down with a holding force and despatching the rest of his forces to ambush the convoy. It may be that Jeanningros' warning had reached the convoy commander, in which case Milán's assembled forces had nothing else to do.

Under sporadic fire from the attackers, Danjou calmly moved from point to point checking the defences. As the sun mounted in the sky, the heat in the courtyard built up. With the only drinkable liquid a bottle of wine from Danjou's saddle-bag, carefully looked after by his orderly Ulrich Konrad, Danjou ordered him to open it and give a few drops to each man.

From the roof, Morzicki warned of the approach of Lt Ramón Lainé, a young French-speaking Mexican officer with a white flag, who called out, 'We have more than 2,000 men and you are at the most sixty. Lay down your arms and surrender, to avoid a massacre.' Danjou's reply was, 'We have cartridges and shall not surrender.' Lainé withdrew and firing broke out on all sides, Danjou ordering his men to conserve ammunition by firing only at sure targets. With fire incoming over the tops of the walls and even from the roof, casualties began to mount. It was at this point that Danjou went the rounds making each man promise not to surrender, but fight on to the death.

At about 1100hrs almost all the ranch buildings were occupied by the enemy, with the legionnaires huddled behind barricades of corpses and rubble in the corners of the courtyard. Shot in the chest, Danjou fell, to die a few minutes later. Since the 3rd was Vilain's company, although he was the senior officer by promotion, Maudet courteously let him take command.

A bugle call was heard, signalling the arrival of more troops. The legionnaires' spirits rose in the hope that this might be Capt Saussier's grenadiers coming to their rescue or the advance guard of the convoy, but it turned out to be 1,000 more Mexican infantry arriving after a forced march. There were now so many uniforms: the grey with blue trimmings of Vera Cruz, the blue of Córdoba and the men from Jalapa with their blue coats, grey trousers and képis with neck cover. Some wore boots, some home-made peasant espadrilles. The officers were even more colourful, with red or blue stripes down their trousers, gold epaulettes, polished brass buttons and gleaming leather holsters on their belts. In contrast the blue coats and red trousers of the legionnaires were filthy and stained with the blood of the wearers and their comrades.

From his position on the roof, Morzicki could see that the position was hopeless. Seeing him up there, Lt Lainé approached again and repeated the offer of surrender. Without bothering to ask Vilain, Morzicki yelled back, '*Merde!*' Vilain's reply was the more correct: 'We shall not surrender!'

In addition to the fusillade that rang out from all sides, the legionnaires now heard the noise of picks and shovels as the Mexicans outside enlarged the loopholes into breaches in several places. Despite the heavy fire, Vilain kept doing the rounds of his men, who were calmly making every shot count. After one risk too many, he took a bullet through the forehead and died instantly about 1400hrs.

The wounded lay where they fell. Suffering the torment of thirst in the blazing sunshine, some were so desperate that they attempted to sip their own blood or urine. To the heat in the courtyard and the stifling powder-smoke the men could not avoid inhaling was added a new torture as the Mexicans set fire to the mouldering thatch of the roofs. Smoke billowed into the courtyard so thickly that the choking legionnaires with streaming eyes were reduced to firing at dim silhouettes creeping continually closer. When the fire died down after ninety minutes, the legionnaires had only a few metres separating them from the nearest enemy.

At 1700hrs a lull allowed Lt Maudet to take stock of his remaining men, spread out in the ruins of the stable block and courtyard, shortly after which they heard Milán haranguing his men to make the final attack. A third offer of surrender terms from outside was simply ignored by legionnaires with throats too parched to reply. By exploring their dead comrades' pockets for ammunition, from behind their parapets of corpses the eleven legionnaires still alive managed to slaughter so many adversaries in the new onslaught that the courtyard was carpeted with bloodstained bodies of dead and dying Mexicans.

One hour later, Maudet had only five men still able to fire a gun, with one cartridge apiece. Fixing bayonets, which gave them a small advantage at close quarters over the bayonet-less carbines of the Mexicans, they emerged from cover to make a suicide charge on the several hundred enemy confronting them. Seeing dozens of rifles immediately levelled at Maudet as the only officer, Belgian Legionnaire Victor Catteau threw himself forward to protect Maudet and died with nineteen bullets in his body. His sacrifice was vain: the lieutenant was also badly hit.

The remaining men on their feet had only seconds to live, had not Col Angel Lucio Cambas literally leaped between the desperate men, parried a blow aimed at him by Cpl Louis Maine and separated the two sides with the flat of his sword. Cambas had studied in France and spoke perfect French. '*Rendez-vous!*' he cried: Surrender!

Seeing that only he and two comrades were still on their feet, the dazed corporal answered with extraordinary presence of mind, 'We will if you promise to let us keep our weapons and equipment and to care for our wounded lieutenant.'

With a courtesy equally amazing at such a time and place, Cambas agreed: 'One can refuse nothing to men such as you.'

Giving orders for stretchers to be brought, Cambas led Maine and Legionnaire Godfied Wensel away through the crowd of excited and armed Mexicans - as they thought, to be put against a wall and shot. This very nearly was their fate, because a furious mounted *guerrillero* leaped from his horse with a revolver in both hands to kill them both. Without hesitation, Cambas drew his own revolver and shot the attacker dead. It was the last shot heard at Trinity Ranch that day, apart from *coups de grâce* for the injured horses.

The immaculate moustached Col Milán, who was the ranking Mexican officer present, was amazed that so few exhausted and wounded men had gone on fighting against such odds. Meeting the survivors shortly afterwards, he concluded, in the phrase that every legionnaire learns, '*Pero no son hombres, son demónios!*' They are not men, but devils!

Of the twenty legionnaires still alive, several were already dying. In Algeria, in Spain and even in Italy when fighting Franz Josef's Croatians, they would have had their throats slit there and then. With a compassion and chivalry rare in such a situation, the Mexicans loaded all those who could be transported onto improvised stretchers lashed two to a mule, and set off for the hospital at Huatusco.

With the heat and all the jerking and bumping, five more men died on the way. The survivors were nursed by the sisters of St

Vincent de Paul and an extraordinary widow, Doña Juana Marredo de Gómez, whom her patients called Mama Juana. Maudet was given even better treatment in the home of Col Francisco Maredo, whose daughter cared personally for the wounded man under Doña Gómez' instructions. Shortly before he died on 8 May, Maudet wrote for Mama Juana with great difficulty on a piece of paper, 'I left one mother in France and found another in Mexico.' He was buried with full military honours.

Back at Chiquihuite on the day of the battle, Col Jeanningros had no reason to suspect what had happened because it would have been quite normal for Danjou to rest his men during the day and return to base the following night. When they had not returned next morning, he ordered 1st Company out to search of them. As they neared Camarón, Danjou's drummer Casimiro Lai was found at the side of the road, miraculously still alive. His was the first eyewitness account to be recorded.

After receiving seven thrusts from cavalry lances and two bullet wounds, Lai had sheltered under a pile of corpses until nightfall enabled him to drag himself away from the site of the battle. Darkness brought the wounded man no rest. Coyotes attracted by the smell of blood would have attacked him, had he fallen asleep or fainted from loss of blood.

When Jeanningros reached the *hacienda*, the scale of the carnage was immediately apparent, even though the Mexicans had removed all the wounded of both sides and buried their dead. The naked bodies of some legionnaires, stripped of uniforms and boots, were found where they had been dumped in a ditch. Fearing that some of the 3,000 Mexicans were still in the neighbourhood, Jeanningros did not stay to bury them but retreated to his base, leaving the dead legionnaires unburied for another two days.

That same day Col Milán was awaiting the arrival of the convoy at La Joya, where he authorised Cpl Evariste Berg to write a letter to be delivered to Jeanningros, describing the end of 3rd Company. It began: 'In the enemy camp, 1 May 1863. Colonel, the 3rd of the 1st is dead, but it achieved so much that one can say it had some fine soldiers.' Never delivered to its addressee, the letter was published a few days later by several Mexican newspapers.

And that is as close to what actually happened at Camarón as one can get. Learning of the nearness of Milán's cavalry, the French convoy commander delayed his approach to the troubled area until his escort could be strengthened. When the reinforced convoy at last rendezvoused with Jeanningros' men at Palo Verde, the remains of the unburied legionnaires, scavenged by coyotes and vultures in the meantime, were laid to rest. The safe arrival of the convoy at Puebla was instrumental in the fall of the city on 17 May, by when Juárez had fled from Mexico City northwards to San Luis Potosí. So, in military terms, Danjou's no-surrender policy was the right one. In part posthumously, he had achieved far more than anyone could have asked.

Undetected by both sides' burial parties, an odd relic lay near Trinity Ranch. The carved wooden hand was eventually picked up by a local farmer of Anglo-French extraction named Langlais, and sold by him to Jeanningros two years later after much haggling over the price. Transported to the Quartier Viénot in Sidi-bel-Abbès, it travelled across the Mediterranean when the Legion left Algeria and today lies in a display case in the HQ museum at Aubagne.[1] Also to be seen on French soil are the railings from the common Legion grave at Camarón, now beside the war memorial outside the Legion village at Puyloubier near Aix-en-Provence.

There are three memorials now on the site of the battle: a Mexican one, a French one and one erected by the local authorities at what is now a weekend tourist venue for curious visitors from Mexico City. In timeless Latin, the French inscription is repeated as though to mark the death of Caesar's legionaries:

QVOS HIC NON PLVS LX
ADVERSI TOTIVS AGMINIS
MOLES CONSTRAVIT
VITA PRIAM QUAM VIRTVS
MILITES DESERVIT GALLICOS
DIE XXX MENSI APR. ANNI MDCCCLXIII

Here, less than sixty men confronted a whole army...

After a careful examination of all the evidence, the full story of Camarón is thus even more amazing than the terse us-and-them *récit officiel*. But how many did actually die at Trinity Ranch? The martyrology of the Legion implies that only Maudet, Cpl Maine and two, presumably wounded, legionnaires survived at the moment of surrender. But Lai also survived long enough to tell his story, although grievously wounded, and those nursed back to health in Huatusco were exchanged on 14 July in Coscomatepec for the captured Mexican Gen Manuel María Alba.

Brigadier Anthony Hunter-Choat, who began his distinguished military career as Legionnaire No 116798 and ended his five years' engagement as a sergeant in 1 REP, believes that as many as twenty-three men of 3rd Company were still alive at the time of the surrender.[2] This figure includes the sixteen taken prisoner during the retreat to the ranch. Given the odds against them and the length of the engagement, that so many survived even temporarily is astonishing. However, despite their amazing good fortune at Camarón, few of them ever returned to Europe. Apart from the ever-present risk of disease, violence was their way of life with duelling the most popular 'sport' for the officers. Cpl Berg was promoted after Camarón to lieutenant, but died the following year fighting a duel over a nebulous point of honour.

In September 1863, Napoleon III came up with the idea of dumping the Legion altogether by giving it lock, stock and barrel to Maximilian - as Louis-Philippe had done with the Infanta in Spain. Under the Convention of Miramar which they signed on 10 April 1864 the Régiment Etranger was to remain under French command until all other French forces were withdrawn, when it would become part of Maximilian's Mexican army. Wastage from disease and deaths in combat, plus repatriation of those lucky time-served legionnaires fit enough for repatriation, was to be offset by local recruitment in Mexico.

Like many politicians' plans for the military, this may have looked good on paper, but any Legion officer in Mexico could have told his emperor it would not work. Few 'white' Mexicans of any military experience, born to the saddle, wanted to enlist in a regiment that marched on foot even in the heat of midday. And when the sights were dropped to recruiting 'Indians' or peasants of mixed blood, they did not come running, either. An attempt to enlist American former Confederate soldiers seeking asylum in Mexico produced exactly one recruit, who was rejected after he insisted on a six-month probationary period before signing on. To remedy the poor recruitment figures, the initial engagement was upped from two to five years, where it still remains.

Crowned emperor on 10 June 1864, Maximilian declared his intention to rule as a benevolent dictator. In fairness to him, he did uphold Juárez' reforms of land tenure. This and his determination to abolish the peonage of the Indian peasants lost him the support of the landed families who had brought him to Mexico. He also forfeited Church support by refusing to restore its enormous properties confiscated by Juárez, having found so little in the treasury that he was obliged to dip into his own pocket for his and Carlota's daily expenses.

The French force initially 3,000 strong eventually swelled to 40,000 men commanded by Forey's successor Achille Bazaine. North of the Río Grande, with the victory of the Union over the Confederate armies in April 1865 both arms and volunteers for Juárez' Liberals began to flood across the border.

Since most of its enemies, whether regular forces or *guerrilleros*, were mounted, the Legion was severely handicapped by being an infantry formation. Some officers held that the American Civil War had demonstrated that the heyday of cavalry was past owing to increasingly effective artillery developed during that war, so that the need was for mounted infantry who could travel faster and dismount to fight on foot. In April 1864, 1st Battalion therefore formed a dragoon-type company called *la escadrón de le Legión*. [3]

After the fall of Oaxaca in February 1865 this nub was expanded by using the captured horses to mount German and Polish ex-cavalrymen. However, simply giving a man a spirited Indian-broken mustang with a Western saddle, when he neither knew how to ride nor how to care for his mount, was not the answer. Some European horses were sent out from France, but many broke their legs in storms and had to be shot en route. Since horses are unable to vomit and cannot be immobilised in stalls for more than a few days without becoming ill, numerous others simply died of seasickness or inactivity on the voyage.

At its peak in September 1866 the Legion's rapid-reaction force of 'cavalry' numbered only 240 riders, officers and men taken together. Bazaine wanted to introduce the light, fast-moving columns that had been so useful in Algeria, but the Legion's small numbers and the superior horsemanship of the Mexican regulars and *guerrilleros* meant that the mounted companies could not risk deploying far from infantry back-up. Their main effectiveness was in relieving the garrisons of beleaguered Legion posts.

By April 1865 the French army, supported by Belgian troops of Carlota's father King Leopold I of Belgium, had driven Juárez' Liberal forces northward almost to the border with Texas. But after the end of the American Civil War that month the United States demanded the withdrawal of French troops from Mexico because their presence conflicted with the Monroe Doctrine. Empress Carlota took ship for Europe, seeking to bring the Church over to Maximilian's side by lobbying Pope Pius IX. Since her husband had done nothing to restore confiscated Church lands, that failed.

Napoleon III now showing a total lack of further enthusiasm for his Mexican intervention, she suffered a nervous breakdown on realising that she and Maximilian had been pawns in a sordid commercial venture.

A formal protest from Washington at the presence of French troops on Mexican soil reached Paris on 6 November. On 12 February 1866 the reunited United States stepped up the diplomatic pressure by requiring the removal of all foreign troops. But the war dragged on. In March forty-three legionnaires brought to bay in a church north of Mexico City were rescued by their mounted comrades supported by infantry who force-marched the normally ten-day journey in half that time. In July of that year, 125 legionnaires were similarly trapped in a farm near Matehuala in the far north of San Luis Potosí state by a force of 500-plus for two days before they too were rescued by a mounted company. By then everybody knew the campaign was lost.

Viewed in any objective light, the Legion's activities in the sovereign federation of Mexico, against which Napoleon had not even bothered to declare war, amounted to brigandage. That their opponents were often bandits who raided convoys and lone stage coaches, killing and robbing the passengers, does not alter the fact that this was not war as it was understood in Europe. Yet even those legionnaires who escaped the hell of tropical illness, the inhuman pace of the forced marches, the tyranny of officers who had no private lives but lived only for 'honour', the adrenalin-rush of combat and the near-certainty of their own imminent deaths - even they came back for more.

Captured after the totally pointless massacre of 102 officers and men owing to a wrong command decision by Maj Paul-Aimable de Brian at a strategically unimportant and unreconnoitred Mexican position called Santa Isabella, a group of legionnaires was ordered by their captors to bury their fallen comrades in mass graves. Marched from there to a remote POW camp in desert country not far from the Río Grande, they overpowered their guards and hotfooted it into Texas, making their way to French-speaking New Orleans, where they took ship with God knows what funds for Vera Cruz. There, they reported for duty and re-entered the dreadful cycle all over again. The German sergeant who had organised the escape and held the group together received a medal for his service.

But few deserters returned voluntarily. This was not Algeria, with torture and death the likely fate of runaways, for the *guerrilleros* welcomed trained soldiers who turned their coats. To the individual legionnaire able to ride a horse, what difference did it make on whose side he fought in this messy war? Future Mexican President Porfirio Díaz even formed a corps of 300 French deserters to fight for Juárez, most of them ex-legionnaires.[4]

Logically enough, the rate of defection rose as the Legion moved into the states of Tamaulipas, Nuevo Leon and Coahuila that had a common border with Texas, causing the French vice-consul in Galveston to complain about the flood of deserters passing through. Desertions ran as high as eighty in one day when the Legion occupied Matamoros on the Mexico-Texas frontier in 1865. Although runaways were officially punished by the firing squad when recaptured - and many were shot *pour encourager les autres* - some officers regarded desertion as a natural wastage that rid a regiment of its less desirable members. Yet the Legion's desertion rate was not comparatively high. In the year after Camarón, it was 11.6%. In 1865 the figure was only 6% and in 1867 it was down to 5.8% - well below the figures for line regiments in Europe serving in far better conditions.

One alleged motive for enlisting to serve in Mexico was that men thought it would be easy to desert once there and make it into the United States, a land of milk and honey, but this hardly holds water, given the hundreds of thousands of impoverished Europeans who managed to emigrate to America even during the Civil War - so many that 500,000 soldiers in the Union armies had been born in Europe.

More to the point was that large numbers of male refugees arriving in France were given no option other than to enlist, and began causing trouble as soon as they reached the depot in Aix-en-Provence. Deprived of the civilian clothes in which they might run away - as *engagés volontaires* still are - they so frequently stole clothing from the local residents that Napoleon III was petitioned for the base to be moved. Repeating all the scandals of the Legion's first base at Langres and Bar-le-Duc under Baron Stoffel, 200 recruits went on the rampage in Aix-en-Provence after five trouble-makers were arrested. Echoing Stoffel's concern that his men would desert on the march to their port of embarkation, the recruits of 1865 were marched under escort to their port of embarkation like the convicts shipping out to Devil's Island, but so many men took any chance of escaping en route that the port of departure was changed from distant St Nazaire on the Atlantic coast to the much nearer Toulon on the Mediterranean coast.

By now, in France only Morny's business friends dreaming of Mexican gold wanted the war to continue. In Mexico, there can have been few people apart from Maximilian who did not give an inward cheer when Napoleon III ordered the repatriation of all French troops in December 1866. Leopold I made sure that all his troops left in January 1867.

Bazaine showed a similar concern to keep what remained of the Legion intact. In a remarkably co-ordinated eight-week operation, the fragmented force was withdrawn from all its isolated outposts and regrouped into six battalions in Mexico City and elsewhere before marching to Soledad. From there, a recently constructed railway whisked them through the fever belt, past uncounted marked and unmarked graves of their predecessors who had died of *vómito negro*, and down to the port of Vera Cruz where they shook the dust and mud of the New World off their boots and uniforms for ever.

As they had been since 1831, the vast majority of Legion officers in Mexico were unmarried. The tough and brutalising life they led, the duelling over dubious points of 'honour' and the raids that must have seemed to the local population no different from the predations of bands of outlaws, left them little time for a home life, even had women wanted to accompany them to such depressing and dangerous postings.

Passing through the town of Soledad on his way to Vera Cruz, Bazaine must have spared a thought for the eponymous wife he had left behind in Paris, where Madame Maria de la Soledad Bazaine had enjoyed her celebrity as the wife of a famous general without letting that handicap her numerous liaisons - until one lover too far resulted in the man's wife discovering Soledad's love letters. A spirited actress at the Comédie Française, she parcelled them up and posted them to Bazaine in Mexico, subsequently informing the 'other woman' what she had done. In desperation, Soledad went to Napoleon III for help, but he was powerless to halt the mail ship already on the high seas. Eight weeks after being posted, the embarrassing package arrived at Bazaine's HQ, where a loyal aide read the letters and destroyed them without informing his general. By that time, Soledad had committed suicide rather than face her husband's wrath.

Assuming her death to have been from cholera - that scourge of nineteenth-century France - Bazaine mourned for a respectable but brief period. He then repeated his script by courting and marrying another beautiful young girl - but this time from one of Mexico's richest families. He was fifty-four, with a marshal's baton as his reward for service to France; she was seventeen, the same age as Soledad when Bazaine married her and took her off to the Crimea.[5]

Before 1 March 1867 the last troopship had cleared the port of Vera Cruz and was navigating the outward passage between the grim offshore graveyard islands with its complement of legionnaires bound for Algeria. The Legion's casualties of the campaign included 1,918 officers and men dead, 83% of them from disease.

A few days later, Juárez and his army reoccupied Mexico City. Chased out of 'his' capital and duped by his conservative backers making him commander-in-chief of his dwindling army, Maximilian refused to abdicate from his specious throne. Brought to bay at Querétaro 200km to the northwest, the rump of it was surrounded, starved, and finally betrayed to Juárez's forces. Maximilian capitulated on 15 May 1867. Despite Giuseppe Garibaldi and many crowned heads of Europe and intellectuals like Victor Hugo petitioning Juárez to let him depart into exile, he was executed by firing squad just outside Querétaro on 19 June. When his Empress Carlota learned she was a widow is uncertain because she never recovered her sanity and spent the rest of her life in various institutions for the insane until her death in 1927 at the age of eighty-seven.

Chapter 14

WITH RIFLE-BUTT AND BAYONET

France, 1866-1870

Achille Bazaine's luck had enabled him to survive Algeria, the Crimea and Mexico - with each campaign moving him steadily up the ladder of promotion. Returning to Europe a full-blown marshal of France with his young bride, he had no reason to think that his next war would be his last, or that it would be sparked off by a telegram sent from the small spa town of Ems in Germany.

France had not withdrawn her forces from the Americas solely because of diplomatic pressure from Washington; there were more pressing concerns nearer home. On 3 July 1866 the decisive battle of the Seven Weeks' War between Prussia and Austria was fought near the East Bohemian town of Königgrätz[1] on the upper Elbe River, 100km east of Prague. This brief but violent spat between the fading power of the Austrian Empire and up-and-coming kingdom of Prussia put half a million men into uniform with orders to kill each other.

Some 241,000 Austrians equipped with muzzle-loading rifles, whose officers believed that the bayonet charge was the best use of infantry, were commanded by Gen Ludwig August von Benedek, who had accepted the post with reluctance because he knew neither the troops nor the terrain. Against them, 285,000 Prussians split into three armies were deployed in a long arc from the border of Saxony to Silesia. In command was the Chief of the Prussian Gen Staff Helmuth von Moltke, the first European commander to exploit railways to transport most of his troops rapidly to the front so that they arrived there fresh and not worn out by long route-marches. Decisively in this encounter, his infantry was armed with breech-loading 15.43mm Dreyse Zündnadelgewehr Modell 1862 needle guns that could fire six shots to the Austrians' one. The Prussians also cheated by lying prone to reduce their size as targets for return fire, instead of standing in Wellingtonian close-order to be mown down like ninepins without breaking ranks.

As a result, on 3 July at Königgrätz the Austrians lost three times as many men as von Moltke. This defeat of what had been the most powerful nation on the continent was enshrined in the Treaty of Prague, under which the balance of power in Europe was drastically changed. While letting Austria down gently, Prussia annexed the territory of Vienna's allies in Hannover, Nassau, Hesse-Kassel and Frankfurt, thus acquiring the lands that had separated the eastern and western parts of the Prussian state and enabling it to form the North German Federation. This set the scene for the Franco-Prussian War and both world wars, in all of which the Legion had its part to play.

Moltke's twin genius in this refashioning of Europe was the devious Prussian Prime Minister Otto von Bismarck, who had deliberately incited Austria to declare war by engineering a dispute over the administration of the counties of Schleswig and Holstein, which the two powers had controlled jointly since seizing them from Denmark in 1864. With the king of Hanover deposed and the ruling house of Hesse similarly divested of its powers, Prussia was now potentially the greatest power in Europe and Bismarck intended to realise that potential.

West of the Rhine, a few unheeded voices warned that the real loser at Königgrätz was *la belle France*, but in an uncanny pre-echo of Léon Blum's Popular Front policy in the 1930s, instead of preparing for the challenge from Prussia that was bound to come, the French government slimmed down the army. The Legion was reduced from six to four battalions on 4 April 1867, artillery and sapper units being the first to go as eighty-four specialist officers and 387 NCOs transferred to other regiments. Before the summer was out, further cutbacks reduced the rolls from 5,000 to 3,000 men by dint of transferring French-born legionnaires to regular regiments and prematurely sacking 1,000 foreigners.

For what was left of the Legion in a hundred postings throughout eastern Algeria, it was a grim life. Most of the time, legionnaires were employed as cheap labour on civil engineering projects. It was demoralising work for men who had joined up for death or glory. Gen Paul Adolphe Grisot wrote in his memoirs of the boredom and soul-shattering fatigue of the men labouring hard on reduced rations.[2] A poor harvest had pushed prices up to the level where a few home-grown vegetables or a stolen chicken would be the subject of talk for days in the mess. Many of the natives, too poor to pay for imported food, were dying of starvation even before a typhus epidemic broke out and cholera began claiming lives rapidly while the ever-present malaria continued to stalk its victims more slowly.

In the west of the province, beyond Oran and Sidi-bel-Abbès, typhus and cholera raged. Skirmishes with the elusive rebels based across the Moroccan frontier claimed lives, but the country was the main enemy. Algeria is not all date palms and sunshine. On the high plateau south of Oran the winter snow lingers. There, a Legion column returning to base at El Bayadh in April 1868 lost all its pack animals in foul weather and had to abandon most of its equipment after a company commander lost his bearings in a snowstorm and was tortured to death by Arab raiders from Morocco. No fewer than nineteen men committed suicide. In the same region another column policing the Moroccan frontier was lost in blizzards the following February and had the choice of aborting its mission after a total failure of resupply or starving to death, unless frostbite and hypothermia claimed them first.[3]

But nobody in Paris cared. In the last week of June 1870 gossip in the Ministries and the smart salons was of the candidacy for the Spanish throne of Prince Leopold of Hohenzollern-Sigmaringen, a cousin of the Prussian king Wilhelm I. At last the French government woke up to the true significance of Königgrätz and realised that this projected extension of Prussian influence into Spain was a pincer movement that would threaten France from both north and south.

On 6 July Foreign Minister Antoine Agénor de Gramont voiced French disapproval of the idea. Wilhelm I responded on 12 July by diplomatically confirming his cousin's renunciation of the Spanish throne, but Gramont was not satisfied. He ordered the French ambassador in Berlin, Count Victor Benedetti, to Ems, where Wilhelm I was taking the waters. Although the king politely confirmed the renunciation, Gramont ordered Benedetti to ask for assurances that no other Hohenzollern would ever again be a candidate for the Spanish throne. Politely but firmly, Wilhelm I replied through his aide-de-camp Prince Radziwill that he had nothing to add.

A full account of these exchanges was telegraphed by the king to his Prime Minister in Berlin, authorising him to publish it in whole or in part. Well knowing the sabre-rattling mood in Paris from his brief period spent there as Prussian ambassador to the court of Napoleon III - most of which time had been passed in dalliance with the beautiful wife of the Russian ambassador, Countess Katarina Orlova - Bismarck edited the telegram to give the impression that Benedetti had undiplomatically importuned King Wilhelm and been turned away by a lowly secretary. He also made sure his version was published in the *Norddeutsche Allgemeine Zeitung*, distributed free in Berlin the following day.[4] The date was crucial, 14 July being the anniversary of the storming of the Bastille and a national holiday when Gallic pride is at its zenith.

Why did Bismarck want a war with France? There is no evidence that he intended to occupy the country permanently. Even Hitler did not want to do that. What the devious Chancellor of Prussia wanted was to unite all Germany by sucking the southern German states into an alliance with the North German Federation for a patriotic war against the French - an alliance in which Prussia would be the dominant partner.

The government in Paris fell right into Bismarck's trap. On 15 July the necessary credits for a war were voted by the French parliament with less than ten dissenting voices. Adolphe Thiers was one of the few to plead for peace, arguing that France had sufficient internal problems without wasting money on a war. In January the funeral of Parisian journalist Victor Noir, assassinated by a cousin of the Emperor, had erupted in Republican demonstrations by a crowd of 100,000 protesters. In May a referendum had curbed the power of the Senate and divested Napoleon III of his functions as head of the Cabinet. Industrial unrest was rife, with troops frequently firing on and killing unarmed demonstrators in the streets outside mines and factories. Another revolution was simmering but the politicians did not want to know that every shot fired at demonstrators was a tick of the clock counting down the end of the Second Empire. For his pains, Thiers was shouted down and called a Prussian, among other things.

As part of the build-up, Bazaine was named commander of 3 Corps in the Army of the Rhine on 16 July, the day before French Prime Minister Emile Ollivier approved a declaration of war to avenge the alleged insult to France's ambassador. Those with a sense of history murmured that they were living through a repeat of 'the affair of the fly-whisk' when on 19 July the French chargé d'affaires in Berlin handed Bismarck the text of the declaration of war. In Paris, ministers including premier Ollivier talked of feeling light-hearted at the news. In the streets jubilant crowds were forgetting the unrest of yesterday and chanting bombastic slogans. 'To the Rhine!' was one of the more modest. 'Down with Bismarck!' was more common, while optimists chanted, 'Onwards to Berlin!' On 20 July War Minister Marshal Edmond Le Boeuf appointed himself Bazaine's superior as Général de Division of the Rhine army.

It has been said that Napoleon III's hurt pride stung him into declaring this war with all the irresponsibility of a headstrong young officer challenging another to a duel, but he no longer had the power to do that. Also, he was at the time so ill - perhaps psychosomatically after the curtailment of his powers as Emperor - that his family feared he would die. He was still visibly suffering when he departed for the front on 28 July, nominally taking supreme command at Metz in Alsace and leaving the Empress Eugénie as his constitutional regent.

As Bismarck had foreseen, the German-speaking states with the exception of Austria rallied to the Teutonic cause. Thanks to the draconian catch-all conscription laws the Iron Chancellor had introduced in Prussia, von Moltke could call on half a million trained men - twice the number of the immaculate French soldiers in their red trousers and blue coats marching along straight Napoleonic roads towards the long northeast frontier with Germany. With the telegraph providing instant communication, Moltke's logistics expert Count Albrecht von Roon soon had 1,183,000 Prussian reservists and regulars hurtling towards them on the steel rails that now knit virtually every major city in

Western Europe into one great network. On 2 August 1870 hostilities commenced at Saarbrücken.

Moltke was a very modern general, eager to exploit all the tools handed him by nineteenth-century technology. Unimpressed by the bravura of cavalry charges at the French army's annual manoeuvres, he intended employing Blitzkrieg - although the word had not then been coined - to reduce the cities that stood between him and Paris one after the other with the aid of Alfred Krupp's latest breech-loading cannon. Precision-manufactured in high-quality steel, they made the bronze muzzle-loading French cannon ranged against them in the fortress cities of northeast France look like museum pieces.

Le Boeuf bombastically announced to his Parliament that the country was 'so well prepared for war that, if it lasted a year, not a single soldier would be short of so much as a gaiter button,'[6] but smartness on parade was irrelevant in Bismarck's new-style warfare. True, margarine had just been invented by the winner of a competition to improve the rations in the French navy, but the only French invention liable to be of use in the coming confrontation was Antoine-Alphonse Chassepot's 11mm Fusil d'Infanterie Modèle 1866, which was more reliable and had a greater range and accuracy than the Dreyse. More than a million of them had been mass-produced by the start of the war, but new weapons on which troops have not trained do not always achieve their potential.

In contrast to Prussia, France had not rigidly enforced conscription since Waterloo. To support the under-strength French regular army, Le Boeuf now ordered the Armée d'Afrique to contribute units of the Chasseurs d'Afrique, the Zouaves and Algerian light infantry. Despite Bazaine's position in 3 Corps, the Legion was not wanted because recruiting to replace the losses in Mexico had raised the proportion of German-speaking legionnaires to 58% in 1866. Long before Rome invented the legion, commanders had been wary of committing foreign mercenary troops against their fellow-countrymen, so the Germans were out. The percentage of Belgians in the Legion was also high and Carlota's grieving father, after learning his lesson in Mexico, had made it plain to both sides that he wished his country and its citizens not to become involved in the coming war. So the Legion's Belgians were out, too.

In Algeria, legionnaires who had been hoping that the war would summon them to more soldierly duties north of the Mediterranean had their hopes crushed when two battalions were sent to replace the Europe-bound Zouaves at a post called locally El-Hasaiba - the Damned - because so many men posted there died there from malaria.

By 4 August Marshal MacMahon was in retreat with his Douay Division after being defeated by the Prussian Crown Prince Friedrich Wilhelm at Wissembourg in Alsace. Two days later, at Froeschwiller-Woerth, where the French 8th and 9th regiments of armoured cavalry were wiped out in heroic but pointless charges against Prussian artillery, Col Raphaël de Suzzoni told his men of 2nd Algerian *Tirailleurs* in Arabic that they would stand and die for France, but not give an inch. He died. They died. And 6,000 other French soldiers were taken prisoner. The inch was not given, but taken all the same.

The French retreat turned to a rout. On the same day at Forbach in neighbouring Lorraine Gen Charles-Auguste Frossard's troops were forced to retire when outflanked. The front was collapsing like a house of cards. All the courageous cavalry charges in Alsace were in vain. Modern warfare had arrived. Increasingly ill, on 10 or 12 August Napoleon III signed the order making Bazaine C-in-C of the Army of the Rhine.

Attempting to link up with MacMahon, Bazaine pushed towards Verdun and was wounded on 14 August at Borny. After indecisive battles at Mars-la-Tour and Gravelotte on 16 and 18 August, he fell back on the fortress-city of Metz with his army more or less intact.

By then MacMahon had been driven all the way back to Châlons-sur-Marne in Champagne. Three disastrous days later Bazaine and his army were surrounded in Metz. On 25 August MacMahon was ordered to break through and relieve Bazaine's encircled army. In vain.

In desperate need of reinforcements, Le Boeuf turned his eye to Tours in central France. Expecting a rush of foreign volunteers to die for France, he had sited there the depot of yet another foreign legion in the hope of attracting volunteers for the duration of hostilities. The rush had failed to materialise; recruits numbered less than a thousand men, half of them German. The Belgians who had joined up were shipped out of harm's way to Algeria in deference to King Leopold I's wishes, but the Germans were kept and the force was gazetted as 5th Battalion of the Régiment Etranger.

On 2 September thirty-nine French generals and 104,000 officers and men were captured at Sedan, where Hitler's troops would make their breakthrough on 13 May 1940. With them was their ailing emperor, who was driven in a calèche wearing general's uniform with four staff officers to meet the victorious king of Prussia. Ahead of him lay a brief imprisonment in Germany followed by exile in England.

Hearing the news, Empress Eugénie began packing, while her 14-year-old son the Crown Prince headed for asylum in Belgium. One of her last acts was to sign a decree transforming the battalion at Tours into 5th Foreign Regiment. On 4 September 1870 - just one month after the war had started - the Second Empire entered its death throes when the Paris mob invaded her former home the Palais Bourbon as she was setting up house safely across the Channel in Hastings. With emperor and empress gone, the Third Republic was born inauspiciously with Léon Gambetta and the military governor of Paris Gen Louis Jules Trochu - who had been an outspoken critic of French military unpreparedness - setting up a provisional Government of National Defence in Tours, where 5th Foreign Regiment had been forming up since 22 August. The Legion's hour - some say, its least honourable hour - was about to sound.

After its victory at Sedan, 2nd Prussian Army under Crown Prince Friedrich Wilhelm moved swiftly to besiege Paris. The railways converging on the capital from all directions were in their favour; it was far more difficult for the French to move their forces sideways between the several fronts. By 19 September Paris was besieged by two German armies totalling 400,000 trained soldiers. Whilst Trochu had over half a million men inside the siege lines for the defence of the capital, their quality was highly variable: seventeen line regiments with 200 cannon were supplemented by

15,000 sailors, 12,000 gendarmes and 465,000 men of the National Guard - 135,000 drawn from the provinces and 330,000 from Paris itself.

And yet Paris held, the citizens digging trenches to turn the city into a fortified camp that somehow managed to keep Moltke's investing armies at arms' length for four whole months. On 22 September the revolutionary Socialist Louis-Auguste Blanqui called openly for bloody revolution, inciting Karl Marx' rival, the Russian anarchist Mikhail Bakunin, to leave Switzerland for Lyon, where he single-handedly declared the abolition of the French state!

Peace feelers came to nothing. Toul fell. Strasbourg fell. With the telegraph lines into and out of Paris cut by the Germans, correspondence with the rest of the world was, as philatelists know, by 'pigeongrams' on paper or microfilm that were enlarged and copied down on arrival, by baskets of mail suspended beneath balloons and in waterproof metal spheres floated down the Seine from up-river for incoming mail and re-released to float downstream with outgoing letters. The Prussians used them for target practice. In desperation on 5 August Gambetta climbed into the wicker basket beneath a hot air balloon on the hill of Montmartre and floated over the siege lines to raise a new army in the provinces. He had intended to go south to Tours, but a fickle wind decided otherwise, carrying the balloon northwards and nearly landing him in Prussian territory.

Southwest of Paris, on 8 October 15,000 Bavarians under Gen von der Tann with 100 of Krupp's cannon laid siege to Orleans, defended by 10,000 men and a handful of bronze muzzle-loaders. Among them were 1,350 officers and men of the new 5th Foreign Regiment, about to be sorely tested, as well as some Zouaves and Algerian tirailleurs.

The battle of Tours began 20km north of the city at Artenay, where Maj Adolf von Heinleth's 4th Division was surprised to see crowds of townsfolk who had ridden or driven out in their coaches with picnic hampers to watch the fighting. At the first salvo of Krupp's cannon, they hastily fled - as did many of the French troops - causing widespread panic in the city. Bivouacking for the night after the battle, Heinleth prepared to take the outlying suburbs by storm the following day. Here, steel cannon were of limited use and he was counting on his Bavarian and Schwabian infantry to go in with rifle and bayonet at close quarters.

It gives some indication of the new Legion that among officers gazetted without scrutiny in this desperate hour was a lieutenant who defected to the Germans and a Spanish major who went over to the other side with all his arms and baggage. Among the men, one insane Turk spent more time fighting his comrades than the enemy and one of the hundred Irish volunteers spent most of his time writing newspaper despatches.

More serious than these few eccentrics was the general lack of training. The best NCOs had been siphoned away into regular regiments; those remaining hardly knew their men. And yet, the Legion fell back in reasonable order after being repeatedly outflanked as other units collapsed. By 1700hrs its commanding officer Maj Arago was dead, as were eighteen other officers and 580 men, with another 250 taken prisoner.[7]

In Heinleth's memoirs, he recorded: 'The Foreign Legion fought very stubbornly. In the burning and falling houses the gallant Schwabians fell on the brave international mercenaries with rifle-butts and bayonets... The French lost about 4,000 men killed, wounded or taken prisoner, among these the Foreign Legion contingent numbering 1,300 men lost ... nineteen officers and 900 rank-and-file.'[8]

Chapter 15

BLINDFOLDS AND BULLETS
ON THE BOULEVARDS

France 1870 - 1871

Wein, Weib, Gesang... It was indeed wine, women and song for the jubilant Germans that night, masters of the town where Joan the Maid had become the symbol of French national consciousness after being burned at the stake by the English in a different war. While the victors celebrated, the survivors of 5th Foreign Regiment sneaked out of the city in civilian clothes. Disguised as a dusty miller was a graduate of St Cyr who had enlisted as Sgt Kara, but would take his proper place in history after being crowned King Peter I of Serbia in 1903.

On 19 October two battalions of the old Legion totalling 2,000 men, but without their German legionnaires,[1] landed in France from Algeria and absorbed what remained of 5th Regiment. Gambetta, now Minister of War, allocated them to the 125,000-strong Army of the Loire tasked with retaking Orleans, but the people they had come to liberate gave the legionnaires a frigid welcome, foreshadowing the hostility of mayors in Flanders 1914-18, who refused shelter and forage to colonial troops and the Legion until forced to give it, sometimes at the point of an officer's sidearm. Living under canvas in the cold, wet weather of October 1870, the newly arrived legionnaires must have yearned for Algeria, sun, shovels and all.

What was Bazaine doing all this time? Cut off at Metz without hope of relief, he held out for fifty-four days until the end of October. Although later accused of traitorous inactivity, he was usefully tying up more than 200,000 Prussian troops who might otherwise have stormed Paris before its defences were ready. His unconditional capitulation on 27 October allowed 173,000 men,

1,570 cannon and fifty-three regimental flags to fall into Prussian hands. Living on much reduced rations, with their mounts and pack animals dying of starvation and then eaten as the only meat available in the treeless waste within the siege lines, they had rations left for only four days. Bazaine's capitulation was nevertheless treated as meriting the sentence of death.

By 2 November Gambetta's government had fled as far as Bordeaux, where it was attempting to raise and arm another half-million men. Paris was in ferment and starving. At the market in front of the Hôtel de Ville skinned rats were being sold at 50 to 75 centimes apiece, while a cat cost 8 francs - well outside the pocket of the workers. All the animals in the zoo at the Jardins d'Acclimation had been eaten long since, as had every horse within the siege lines. On 31 October, realising that the fall of Metz would release German forces to intensify the siege of Paris, the mob invaded the Hôtel de Ville. A battalion of the National Guard went over to the demonstrators' side and order was restored only with difficulty.

On 3 and 4 November Adolphe Thiers was at Versailles, trying to arrange peace terms with Bismarck. At Orleans, von der Tann was now outnumbered five to one by Gen Aurelle de Palladines' reinforced Army of the Loire. Seeking open ground to confront this threat, von der Tann moved his forces on 8 November out of the city to Coulmiers, 20km to the west. As the battle commenced the following morning, one of the German staff officers was Ernst Milson von Bolt, the ex-Legion lieutenant who had killed Antonio Diaz during the Mexican intervention and been awarded the Légion d'Honneur for it. Facing him in the Army of the Loire were many men he might have recognised through a telescope, had he the leisure to scan the thousands of faces marching towards the Prussian cannon.

One was that of Camarón survivor Félix Brunswick from Brussels, now promoted to sergeant. It may have been he who originated the legend that von Bolt ordered the German guns to cease firing on men with whom he had fought side by side in Mexico. The more likely truth is that firing ended when the Prussians disengaged to execute an orderly retreat northward. From Bordeaux a jubilant Gambetta ordered Palladines to convert

Orleans into an armed camp. Next day, batteries of artillery were already being moved in and trenches dug by the legionnaires.

To the government in Bordeaux, the symbolic recapture of Joan of Arc's hometown was seen as the first step in liberating Paris. To spur on the legionnaires digging-in in Orleans, Gambetta telegraphed de Palladines, 'Paris is hungry!' But dinner was not on the way. The 200,000 Prussians and allied forces released by the capitulation of Metz now sealed off the capital from the rest of the country even more effectively, to prepare for the final assault.

There was an unexploited army of 80,000 Bretons cooling its heels at Conlie, just north of Le Mans. In the last desperate days of November, Gambetta promised it arms, only to change his mind the next day lest they be used for a secessionist uprising, as had happened under the First Republic. Nor was von der Tann on the run yet. On 1 December he made a sudden stand and counter-attacked, pushing the Army of the Loire right back to Patay outside Orleans and retaking the city briefly on 4 December. With their backs to the Loire, the Legion and Zouaves were ordered to stand firm on the 'wrong' bank, covering the safe withdrawal of the rest of the army across the river.

It is a popular misconception that the French climate, apart from in the Alps and Pyrenees, is always milder than north of the Channel. Every few winters high pressure over Scandinavia brings Siberian weather as far south as the Dordogne. The leafless vines look like crosses in a white landscape. Mediterranean vegetation dies. Birds drop dead out of the sky from hypothermia. The mercury plunges to minus 25° Centigrade and lower. The winter of 1870-71 was like that. By 6 December the Legion was down to half-strength. The two battalions from Algeria had lost 210 men - some casualties, some prisoners and some killed by the severe cold as they slept in the open air. On 10 December, the sorry remnants were amalgamated as a single *bataillon de marche* ordered to strengthen the Eastern Army of Gen Charles Denis Nicolas Bourbaki, which was tasked with cutting German supply and communications lines in the Franche-Comté.

The legionnaires had been issued with two days' rations for a journey that should have taken thirty-six hours. In unheated open wagons officially labelled fit 'for 8 horses or 40 men', they froze for two weeks as their trains were snowed in, thawed out, shunted, coupled to engines and frozen up again. De-training at Ste Suzanne near Montbéliard in the Franche-Comté, they were immediately put into the line with their numbers swollen by 2,000 hastily armed but untrained Bretons whose numbers brought the regimental strength up to 3,000 *on paper*. Gen Grisot recounted how hard-pressed officers created new units by seeding these men with a mixture of inexperienced NCOs and veteran legionnaires.[2] Discipline was a major problem, with hungry men deserting their posts and using their weapons to hunt small game for the pot, cutting down fruit trees in the orchards for firewood and selling equipment for food and drink in the sub-zero weather.

The Prussians were more accustomed to, and better equipped for, the extremes of winter. On 5 January Krupp's cannon began a sustained artillery bombardment of Paris. Next day, revolutionary committees of the twenty *arrondissements* called for an end to Gambetta's Government of National Defence. The uprising had begun.

In Bismarck and von Moltke the Germans had a unified leadership that knew exactly what it wanted. On the French side all was confusion. In the east, where the Legion was, Gen Bourbaki - a fine-looking man with splendid moustaches and a chestful of medals - had a number of insurmountable problems: his provisional government was still in Bordeaux, his supplies were inadequate and the infrastructure of his country was falling to pieces around him.

In such circumstances it was hard for his troops, including the Legion, to maintain morale against so competent a commander as Edwin von Manteuffel, the man who had prevented the Crimean War from escalating and had distinguished himself during the previous year's invasion by winning the battles of Amiens and Rouen. In the war-within-a-war between these two ill-matched generals Bourbaki began well, with a minor victory over the Germans at Villersexel near Belfort on 9 January. His main problem was the government from which he took his orders, and which at one time ordered him to march southwest to Dijon and relieve the pressure on Garibaldi's Italian volunteers, who should have been supporting him in the rear! The new legionnaires' lack of training made them sitting ducks for the well-drilled enemy. On 19 January, not only was their paymaster killed in action and his pay-chest containing 4,341 francs captured by the Germans, but worse was to come during the night. No sentries having been posted by the inexperienced NCOs, a German patrol captured an entire company of shivering men warming themselves around their campfires. Yet, astonishingly, these ill-disciplined and largely untrained men marched into a German artillery barrage at Ste-Suzanne and briefly captured the enemy position before being driven off.

Unable to break through the enemy lines to relieve besieged Belfort, Bourbaki was finally too demoralised to command after being badly trounced at Héricourt, 10km short of the beleaguered city. Finding himself trapped between Manteuffel and the Swiss border with an exhausted army whose supplies were non-existent, he made the last of several unsuccessful attempts to kill himself on 22 January, and was replaced by Gen Justin Clinchant, a veteran of the Crimea and Mexico.

Scraping the bottom of the barrel, desperate for reinforcements, Gambetta ordered the Armée d'Afrique to ship to France the French-officered native cavalry still called Spahis from Ottoman days. However, the Spahis had no intention of dying for a France that was already beaten, and responded by murdering their officers and launching a stab-in-the-back campaign to get the French out of North Africa.

With tens of thousands near death from starvation in the capital, on 23 January Foreign Minister Jules Favre met secretly with the Prussians at Versailles to request terms. On 28 January a three-week armistice was granted by Bismarck to enable the election of a new legislature, with whom he could negotiate. The price for the armistice was the surrender of Paris and a fine of 2,000 million francs.

The Eastern Army was not included in the peace negotiations but left to fend for itself. Clinchant retreated, leaving two divisions including the Legion to hold Besançon, while Manteuffel chased him and the rest of his tattered army right into Switzerland. Crossing into the safety of neutral territory near Geneva, 87,847 weary men handed over to the Swiss an armoury including 285 cannon. Such was the confusion that no one ever knew exactly how many men died in combat, from ill-tended wounds or from frostbite and starvation. Clinchant himself was interned and released in March.

It was all over, bar the shouting. On 28 January the Ministry of the Interior had ordered all French units to lay down their arms. Deluding himself, or attempting to delude the voters about to go to the polls, Gambetta grandly declared that although Paris had been beaten, France itself was not defeated! In a general confusion that would be repeated in June 1940, the country's politicians were divided between those like him who wanted other people to go on dying for a lost cause and Adolphe Thiers, who could say in all honesty, 'I told you so. Stop the fighting.'

Thiers won, but inherited a country irrevocably divided and financially on the verge of ruin. One of the National Assembly's first acts was to stop the salaries of the National Guard and order them disarmed. On 6 March all Legion foreign volunteers and 415 conscripts enlisted for the duration were demobilised to save money. Although Belgian, Sgt Brunswick survived this purge to find himself a senior NCO commanding mostly Bretons in a rump Legion of sixty-six officers and 1,003 men.

By then, the Prussians had been in the western suburbs of Paris for three days. In the city centre on 18 March the National Guard occupied the Hôtel de Ville and ten people were killed when the forces of order tried to eject them. The army attempted to seize the artillery installed by the Communards on the hills of Montmartre and Belleville, but the National Guard's refusal to give way incited the soldiers to disobey orders and execute the two generals in command.

The flame of revolution spread like a forest fire before a strong wind. On 23 March the National Guard in Marseille stormed the Prefecture. On 24 March they proclaimed a Commune in Toulouse. On 27 March what remained of the Legion was ordered to join the Army of Versailles. By 29 March Paris was governed by the Communards,[3] who promulgated their own laws, abolishing conscription and imprisoning anyone suspected of loyalty to the Second Empire.

The red flag was flying on public buildings and all the churches were turned into debating clubs where restive audiences were harangued from the pulpit to support a workers' republic by men and women speakers, the latter demanding equal political rights and equal pay for equal work. While the many talked, a few extremists were already murdering hostages. Some were shot out of hand, others kept for show trials. In provincial cities such as Limoges, Communards stopped troops leaving for Versailles and Paris to suppress the rebellion. When the army suppressed the Commune in Marseille on 4 April, 150 Communards were shot and 900 arrested, to be transported at bayonet-point to the offshore prison-fortress of Château d'If in the Gulf of Lion. The rebels in Besançon failed to prevent the much-reduced Legion from leaving by train for Versailles, where it arrived on 1 April, with its dirtiest job ahead of it.

In Algeria another headache was brewing for Gambetta. On 8 April a *jihad* placed 3rd and 4th Battalions of the Legion - mostly stay-behind Germans - up against 150,000 armed Kabyles threatening to drive all French forces into the sea. By now hardly meriting the adjective 'foreign', the Legion in France was reinforced on 20 April by six officers and 370 conscripts from line regiments, bringing the strength up again to seventy-two officers and 1,373 men. Although almost all were French or Breton, the stigma of their next 'operation' has unfairly blighted the escutcheon of the Legion ever since and been the cause of both Communist and Socialist parties threatening to abolish it a century later.

On 2 May Paris trembled at the opening shots of the second bombardment that year, but this time the shells were French. On 10 May 1871 the peace treaty was signed in Frankfurt, with Bismarck refusing to evacuate the army of occupation before order had been restored in France. To that end, he agreed that the Versailles government might maintain an army outside Paris and ordered all the POWs held in Germany to be released so that they could strengthen it.

The bad news at the negotiating table for Thiers and Favre was that the indemnity imposed was raised to the figure of 5,000 million francs, with the Prussian armies to remain on French soil until it had been all paid! 'French soil' did not include the provinces of Alsace and Lorraine, now declared German territory.[4]

There was no choice. On 18 May the surrender terms were ratified by the National Assembly meeting in Versailles, after which, relying on the Prussians to prevent any insurgents from fleeing the capital to the north and east, the French army was ordered to suppress the rebellion. The anarchy of the Communards meant that orders given by their officers were habitually disobeyed, so that the massed artillery inside Paris was ill-commanded, with the gunners taking two hours off for lunch at midday and stopping when it was time for their evening *apéritif*. After dinner, it was sporadic at best. And yet by 19 May the Legion had lost three officers and fifteen legionnaires killed and nine officers and 102 men wounded - which often amounted to the same thing, given conditions in the field hospitals.

On 22 May the army discovered the city gate at St-Cloud unguarded and open. The Legion was among the units that immediately marched in and massacred 300 Communards in front of the Madeleine church to show that the government meant business. Atrocities multiplied on both sides, the immediate response of the people being to execute a group of six hostages that included the archbishop of Paris. Escalating the violence, the army shot 700 civilians in retaliation. This provoked a mob to break into the prison of La Grande Roquette and carry off forty-nine of the hostages locked up there, including priests and police, who were harried through the streets to cries of 'Kill the cops!' and 'Death to the Jesus-lovers!' They were pelted with filth, then shot and beaten to death in the rue Haxo.

By next morning the Tuileries and many of the government buildings and churches were aflame. In torrential rain and choking smoke, the Legion and other army units pursued the armed Communards into the Père Lachaise cemetery. There, they made a last-ditch stand among the tombs and family vaults until the ammunition ran out and they were finished off by bayonet and rifle-butt.

Such was the hatred this engendered among Parisians that legionnaires were warned not to loot liquor stores after a corporal died from drinking poisoned wine. On 26 May a Legion company shot prisoners after taking a barricade and ten cannon near the Porte de la Villette. The scale of massacres is unattested, but probably exceeded tenfold the victims in Robespierre's better-documented Terror of 1794. The Legion's regimental diary contains terse entries such as 'Numerous executions were carried out,' and 'The morning (of 30 May) was spent burying the bodies of (those shot on) 28 and 29 May.'

By the beginning of June the rebellion was over, but revenge continued. In retaliation for the murders under the Commune, both men and women were denounced and summarily shot as the government restored order. Long columns of prisoners were marched under escort through the Porte de la Muette, where Gen Gaston-Alexandre Galliffet conducted a personal *Selektion*, ordering individuals who caught his eye for no particular reason to be hauled out of the ranks and shot on the spot. The rest continued their doleful way under armed guard to prison camps at Satory, a military training area outside Versailles.

The politicians were also once again reshaping the Legion. To soak up the flood of refugees fleeing from annexed Alsace and Lorraine, it was allowed to recruit only men from these areas. Gen Alfred Chanzy, a future Governor-General of Algeria, who had seemingly forgotten how it had fought for him in the Army of the Loire, argued for the abolition of the Legion on the grounds that it was too dependent on its German NCOs. To redress the nationality imbalance, demobilised NCOs from regular regiments were offered the chance to remuster into the Legion. Those who did, found themselves deprived of their French pension rights and treated as foreigners by a bureaucratic sleight-of-hand. When the news got out, the flow dried up. As a result, Alsatians and Lorrainers became the backbone of the Legion until after the end of the First World War, constituting about 45% of NCOs even though from October 1881 French nationals were at last allowed to enlist.

The trial of the leading Communards began at Versailles on 17 August and ended on 22 September, with predictable results. By December the number of people shot was officially 30,000, with 40,000 more in prison, many facing transportation to New Caledonia and other prison colonies. Among victims of this purge were those Paris firemen who had stayed at their posts and fought fires during the siege after being ordered to abandon the city and join the army of Versailles. Because they were under military discipline[6], they were judged traitors and shot.

One of the last victims of the Franco-Prussian war was Achille Bazaine, sentenced on 10 December 1873 by a military court to be deprived of his rank and honours and be executed by firing squad for gross dereliction of duty in surrendering Metz. Marshal MacMahon, then president of the Third Republic, commuted the sentence to twenty years' imprisonment, making it obvious that Bazaine was a scapegoat to salve national honour.

Thanks to the enterprise of his young Mexican wife, Bazaine escaped on 9 August 1874 by shinning 150 metres down a smuggled rope from his cell in the supposedly escape-proof prison-fortress on the cliffs of the island of Ste-Marguerite off Cannes. At the bottom of the cliff, his wife waited in a skiff to ferry her 63-year-old, but presumably still very athletic, husband to a private yacht waiting off-shore. This took them to asylum in Spain, where at least she spoke the language. The other woman in Bazaine's life, Lady Luck had finally abandoned Bazaine. Unpardoned, he died in Madrid on 28 September 1888 after spending his last years there in illness and poverty.

It was a sad end for a man who had served the successive governments of France all his life. His retreat inside the walls of Metz had not only tied down 200,000 Prussians to give Paris a breathing space which would have made possible its relief, had the politicians stopped squabbling long enough. He had also kept his army intact and ready for redeployment against either the Prussian invaders or the Communard rebels, had the siege of Metz been lifted.

Those who had most to thank him for were the 140,000 soldiers in Metz, who would have starved to death if he had not agreed to surrender to the Prussians when he did. However much money Madame Bazaine may have obtained from her Mexican relatives to use as bribes, she could not have organised his escape from a military prison on her own. It would be nice to think that some of those officers and men who had walked alive out of the hell of Metz had a hand in ensuring that the disgraced commander to whom they owed their lives at least died in liberty, and not in a prison cell.

Chapter 16

TWEAKING THE DRAGON'S TAIL

Algeria 1871-1882;
Vietnam and Formosa 1883-1885

In July 1871 the French government decided that the battalions in France - 1st, 2nd and 5th with the *regiment de marche*, plus 6th Battalion forming up at Dunkirk and the detached company serving with the Army of the Loire - should be amalgamated with 3rd and 4th battalions in Algeria to make a total of four battalions in all. More often than most armies, the Legion has had to find a way round the *diktats* of its politicians. Public hostility towards Germany resulting in a ban on enlistment of Germans until 1880 meant little in practice since Germans continued to enlist by pretending to be Swiss-German or Alsatian.

With her continental army limited by Bismarck's curbs in the Treaty of Frankfurt, France decided that, since she could not expand in Europe, she would do what other European powers were doing at the time and grab her share of what came to be called the Third World. From 1882 onwards the expansion of French Algeria involved units of the Legion stationed there in a sustained programme of subduing the tribes deeper and deeper into the Sahara. France already controlled parts of West Africa, New Caledonia, the New Hebrides and Tahiti, which Gauguin would paint so compellingly. The following year she pushed the boundaries of her Indochinese possessions northwards into Tonkin or North Vietnam. Although the Church repeatedly brought pressure on French Catholic politicians to 'civilise the natives' by sending out missionaries, the prime motive - as with all nineteenth-century empires - was commercial: to acquire supplies of cheap raw materials from colonies obliged to buy in return relatively expensive manufactured goods.

Eugène Etienne, the long-serving Colonial Party *député* for Oran, put it succinctly, 'The only criterion to apply to any colonial enterprise is the balance of advantage and profit to be made for the mother country.'[1] In the eighteen years following the defeat of 1871, nineteen administrations succeeded one another in Paris without affecting the pace of colonial expansion. The resultant calls on the Legion tripled its size before the century was out, but initially the four battalions in Algeria were used mainly as cheap labour, digging ditches, hacking tunnels through mountains and draining swamps in an extraordinary programme of civil engineering that still benefits inhabitants of formerly French North Africa today.

All this changed when another charismatic commander arrived on the scene. Col François Oscar de Négrier, nephew of a Napoleonic general who had served in Africa, was a graduate of St Cyr who had distinguished himself by killing a classmate there in a duel. Typical of this dapper, short-tempered officer's concept of soldiering was his reaction to being hospitalised in besieged Metz during the Franco-Prussian war with leg wounds that should have kept him out of the saddle for some weeks. Discharging himself from the hospital, he had his horse saddled, was helped to mount it and then galloped through the lines, shooting dead two Uhlans who had the temerity to demand his papers. Reporting for further duty with the Northern Army, he was wounded twice more before the end of the war with Germany.

Having already served in Africa 1864-66, Négrier had his own ideas of how to get the Legion to down shovels and shoulder rifles. Given the vast distances to be covered and the necessity to surprise an enemy who knew the country intimately, he turned his hundred best marchers into semi-mounted infantry by requisitioning fifty mules from local Arabs on 8 December 1881. After loading their full packs, food, water and spare ammunition on a mule, two very fit legionnaires carrying only small packs and rifles could cover up to 60km in a ten-hour day, which was the maximum that could be forced out of a laden mule also doubling as the men's mount, one at a time to give their weary feet a rest.

Such a killing pace could not be kept up for long without exhausting man and mule, but done in short spurts it gained the vital element of surprise against an enemy who took it for granted that a French column would travel with a large and slow-moving supply train. An early success chalked up to this new modus operandi came when Négrier's semi-mounted infantry surprised the tribe of Sidi Slimane near the Moroccan border and forced them to abandon their tents, possessions and 4,000 sheep that were auctioned after return to base, providing each man with a bonus of 15 francs.

However, the last laugh this time was on the Legion. Slimane's master Bou-Amama determined to take revenge. On 28 April 1882 a survey party like the one on which Danjou had lost his hand was mapping the rugged territory around the Chott Tigri, a salt lake in the west of Algeria. The surveyors commanded by Capt de Castries were protected by two rifle companies and one of the new semi-mounted units under Lt Massone, making a total of around 300 officers and men, who marched right into a trap set by Bou-Amama. From declivities in the landscape a troop of 900 Arab horsemen and 1,600 tribesmen on foot swooped upon them without warning. The numbers of attackers - always exaggerated when they win - are to be taken with a pinch of the Chott's own salt, but it was certainly a large and dangerous party.

The drill for mounted infantry was to dismount immediately on contact, with designated men tethering the mules so they could not run off with the vital water and ammunition they carried, as had happened at Camarón. Meanwhile, their comrades formed a defensive square with the mules in the centre and returned the enemy fire. Even dragoons - who attacked in the saddle - had always dismounted in defence. However, in the heat of the moment and lacking practice in their new role, the legionnaires tried to counter-attack on mule-back against the mounted tribesmen.

It was a fatal error. For seven hours the legionnaires fought the tribesmen off in three separate square formations, unable to regroup and consolidate their position. By the time they had realised the error of that day's tactics, both officers and all the NCOs were dead. They were the lucky ones. Those captured by the Arabs were tortured to death within sight of their comrades out of rifle range so that no one could end their suffering with a well-aimed coup de grâce.

By the time Bou-Amama broke contact and headed west into the safety of Moroccan territory, the Legion had suffered 25% casualties: three officers and twenty-eight men were wounded, with forty-nine men dead in addition to the two officers of the mounted company. The survivors were limping back to the little fort of Gelloul, from which they had set out, when they met the relief column headed by Négrier, who was definitely not of the type of general to stay in base when there was some action in the offing.

Some officers argued that the mounted companies should have one mule per man; others maintained that this would merely encourage them to attempt cavalry manoeuvres with fatal results. The second argument won and the size of the companies was set at 215-230 men with half as many mules, plus horses for the officers.

Despite some initial setbacks, the overall success of Négrier's up-and-at-'em policy in Algeria earned him promotion to brigadier and a posting to Vietnam in September 1883.

Ten years earlier an unscrupulous French arms dealer called Jean Dupuis had hired a private army to capture the northern city of Hanoi so that he could monopolise the highly lucrative salt trade with the landlocked Chinese province of Yunnan by using a steamboat to tow laden junks up the Red River. An inglorious collusion of Catholic missionaries, crooks and French naval officers then pushed northwards from the Mekong delta 1,200km to the south, forcing a treaty on the mandarins of Hué in Central Vietnam, which in 1874 recognised the status quo and conceded to France certain rights in Hanoi and its seaport Haiphong. For the Vietnamese it was a choice of two evils: they were hoping that the French would drive out their Chinese occupiers, who regarded the north of the country as a buffer zone to protect their southwestern border.

On 8 November 1883, 1st Battalion disembarked at Haiphong to join Négrier, together with two battalions of Algerian *tirailleurs*. It was then he delivered his famous speech: 'You have become soldiers in order to die, and I am sending you where people die.' A six-hour journey between the sand-bars of the Cua Cam estuary in small boats after transhipping from their seagoing transports landed them at a bleak barracks in a fetid mosquito-infested swamp whose only neighbours were the customs house, an arsenal and a few other western buildings. None of the 600 legionnaires coming ashore that day with their commander Maj Marc-Edmond Dominé can have had any idea they were fighting a war in which their successors would still be dying for France seventy-one years later.

Travelling up-river by steamer to Hanoi - the Red River was a good 800 metres wide there - they passed through a plain where men and women under conical hats worked the vivid green rice fields that stretched as far as the eye could see with water buffaloes. The palm trees and villages whose thatched roofs peeped above the surrounding bamboo looked like paradise, compared with the aridity they had known in North Africa.

These peasants were not the enemy. The Legion's initial opponents were the 'Pavillon Noirs' or Black Flag mercenaries, conveniently deniable irregulars used by Beijing, who were named for the banners of that colour which they carried into battle. Two millennia after Sun Tzu had written *The Art of War*, their tactics were often primitive, for the most part 'human wave' attacks that cost enormous casualties, but their fort at Son Tay - only 60km from Hanoi - was a model of what could be done with local materials. With typical European arrogance, the round-eye newcomers created a mythical renegade military architect called 'Sir Collins' - possibly based on an arms dealer like Dupuis who had instructed his indigenous clients in the use of modern firearms - after deciding that only a European like themselves could have designed so sophisticated a fort.[2] Constructed by coolie labour of earth, bamboo and local bricks, the fortress was a complex of water-filled moats, dry ditches, palisades and ubiquitous punjee sticks to pierce the boot of an unwary attacker.

After Adm Amédée Courbet's gunboats steamed up the Red River to bombard the citadel on 16 December 1883, Legion sappers among his 5,000 troops wormed a hazardous way through the defences. 'Capt Mehl of the Foreign Legion fell with a mortal wound just as his men ... got onto the parapet. A legionnaire by name of Mammaert was the first to enter the fortress.'[3] The reduction of Son Tay after a fifteen-hour battle provoked a protest from Beijing's ambassador in Paris.

Négrier had a second Legion battalion arrive in February 1884. Meanwhile, Beijing had reinforced its garrison at Bac Ninh with a garrison of 15,000 Tonkinese under Chinese officers and NCOs, blocking the so-called Mandarin Road into China only 40km from Hanoi. On 12 March 1884 the two Legion battalions drove the garrison out. The giant Belgian Cpl Mammaert was again in the forefront of the fight, planting the French flag on the ramparts. An unpleasant surprise for his comrades, who were armed with the 1874 single-shot Gras rifle, came on discovering in the abandoned arsenal a substantial armoury of cutting-edge firearms including Martini-Henrys, Remingtons, Spencers and Winchester repeaters. They consoled themselves with the belief that no Chinese could shoot straight or stand fast when confronted with the point of a white man's bayonet.

Wanting to get back into the act from which it was being displaced by land forces, the French navy now carried the undeclared war with the Celestial Empire to Formosa - a diversion that was, even for nineteenth century imperialists, ill-considered arrogance. Adm Courbet began with a naval bombardment of the port and arsenal of the mainland city of Fu-zhou, which elicited a formal declaration of war from Beijing. Sailing across to Taiwan - then known by the Portuguese name of Formosa[4] - he landed his force of 1,800 marines, a penal battalion and 3rd and 4th Legion battalions near the north coast port of Chi-Lung. What he hoped to achieve is unknown since the only exploited resource of Taiwan was then a coalfield producing low-grade fuel.

Tan-Shui, 30km to the west, was the other port serving the capital Taipei. Attempting to capture it and interdict use of the estuary leading to Taipei, the French were repulsed and driven back with heavy losses to Chi-lung. The monsoon broke, turning the small port, dominated by high ground re-occupied by the enemy, into a swamp where malaria and cholera carried off their daily quota. As deaths reduced their numbers the defenders were so thinly spread that Chinese crept through the lines into the town at night, digging up corpses and cutting off heads to carry back as trophies for cash rewards.[5]

The garrison of legionnaires, marines and penal battalion soldiers was reduced to 600 men squatting in a wasteland of burned-out go-downs and hovels. Their appearance was euphemistically described by 19-year-old British legionnaire

Lionel Hart, who arrived there in January 1885 among Courbet's reinforcements, as 'pale and very tired'.[6] By the end of the month, the injection of new blood enabled the heights above Chi-lung to be retaken, but when a second column set out for Tan-Shui it was repulsed again, forcing even gung-ho Adm Courbet to acknowledge that the campaign was consuming lives for no point. The survivors were taken off and shipped to Vietnam.

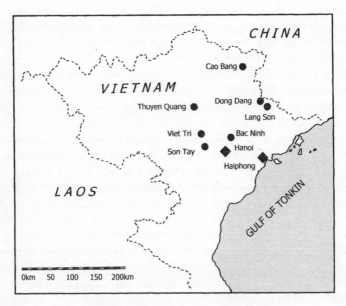

Tonkin / North Vietnam 1883-92

The previous summer, on 4 July France had presented to the United States surely the biggest birthday present ever: the Statue of Liberty. Around the same time, 20,000 regular Chinese soldiers and Black Flag irregulars had marched south from Yunnan Province into Vietnam and based themselves in and around the fortress of Thuyen Quang, on the Son Gam river[7] 165km northwest of Hanoi. Built of local brick with a perimeter wall of 1,200 metres, it stood in a clearing surrounded by thick jungle.

In the centre of the fort was a hillock crowned by a small pagoda that served as the officers' mess.

In open defiance of instructions from Paris to confine operations to the Red River delta around Hanoi and Haiphong, in mid-November 1884 Lt Col Charles Duchesne headed up-river with 700 legionnaires and marines supported by three gunboats, to winkle out the Black Flags. After fighting their way through one ambush, they succeeded in driving out the Chinese and installed their own garrison at Thuyen Quang. Commanding it was Maj Dominé with Legion captains Borelli and Moulinay each commanding a company. The combined strength was 319 men, plus 160 of the locally recruited but French-officered 8th Company of 1st Tonkinese light infantry under Capt Diaz. 'Odds and sods' included thirty-two gunners to serve the four - some say six - field artillery pieces that had been brought along as deck cargo, plus a small detachment of sappers.

Dominé was a classic nineteenth-century career soldier, who rose to colonel's rank after being wounded in Algeria and again fighting the Prussians in France. Forbidding the surgeon to amputate his arm on the second occasion, when his right elbow was shattered, he had opted to die rather than be unfit for further service, but survived against the odds with a stiff arm.

There were in all just over 600 men to hold the fort against the 20,000 or more Black Flags known to be in the vicinity. The only help on call was occasional fire-support from the thirteen-man crew of the gunboat *La Mitrailleuse*, commanded by Ensign Senes, that steamed at intervals up the nearby river. In the war of nerves following Duchesne's departure on 23 November with the other two gunboats, superstitious legionnaires found something uncanny in the fact that, like Danjou, Dominé had only one good arm.

Another Camarone legend was about to be born. Early in December 1884 a routine patrol from the fort briefly engaged a small force of armed men that melted away into the thick jungle. Sensing that this had been a probe for a much larger force, Maj Dominé ordered the infilled dry ditch protecting the outer perimeter wall to be dug out. Eight Legion sappers under Sgt Bobillot were sent to build a blockhouse on a rise 350 metres outside the perimeter, which had a clear view over the walls of the fort, and prevent the Chinese siting any heavy weapons there.

The sapper sergeant, a former journalist, used his imagination to excavate a partly subterranean command post, protected with ditches and mines. The work was still incomplete when several hundred Chinese regulars marched around the outpost without opening fire in an unnerving show of strength on 31 December. On New Year's Day the first human wave assault left the besieged legionnaires looking at 150 enemy dead and wounded lying around the camp, many victims of the cannon on *La Mitrailleuse*. With no Henri Dunant here to protect the wounded by appealing to Christian charity, they were routinely finished off in retaliation for the Chinese practice of displaying the severed heads of their prisoners or sending baskets of them back with insulting messages.[8]

On 16 January, legionnaires manning the walls observed Chinese coolies starting to dig trenches on all sides. By 20 January these had all linked up to cut Thuyen Quang off from the rest of the world. In the night of 26-27 January, the Black Flags fired the village 400 metres away from the fortress as a diversion and simultaneously attacked the fortress, only to be driven back with heavy casualties.

The enemy commander Liu Yung-fu[9] thereupon set his sappers to push their trenches closer and closer to the walls of the fort in the face of harassing fire from the cannon inside. They were also tunnelling under the obstacles Bobillot had placed around the blockhouse on the rise. Since staying there would have meant being blown up by a subterranean mine, the detachment was withdrawn under covering fire in the evening of 30 January and Bobillot's blockhouse destroyed by cannon fire.

Starting next morning, Liu Yung-fu had the perfect site on the mound from which to conduct day-long sniping of the main camp for the rest of the siege. This forced the French to keep their heads down in trenches and underground shelters, despite which precautions their casualties rose steadily, other ranks being communally buried with only a few officers given the dignity of a biscuit-box coffin. Having only twenty-nine shovels between them, the defenders had a choice of digging shelter for the living or graves for the dead, but the Chinese had plenty of digging tools and could be heard moving tons of earth each night as they tunnelled towards the perimeter wall. Lanterns were hung over it after dusk to discourage surprise attacks after the enemy saps came so near the walls that some legionnaires with an extraordinary sense of humour lassoed a black banner with a noose on a bamboo pole and hoisted it over the walls as a trophy.

On 3 February, a courageous Tonkinese 'coolie-tram' - as the local informants were called - volunteered to slip through the lines in peasant clothes. On the river bank, he made a crude flotation device of bamboo twigs, under which he floated past the Black Flag watchers while breathing through a tube with his head under water. No one held out much hope of him getting through. On 7 February Capt Diaz of the Tonkinese light infantry was hit in the forehead and killed. The other officers toasting his empty chair in the mess the following evening had to dive under the table when the first Chinese shell blew a hole in the roof of the pagoda above their heads. Their shock on realising that the enemy had managed to bring in artillery despite the mountainous nature of the area should have given Col Piroth food for thought at Dien Bien Phu.

Worse was shortly to come. On 11 February Legionnaire Vaury drove a pickaxe into a suspicious patch of earth well inside the walls, to find staring up at him a Chinese tunneller who shot him in the arm before retreating back underground. That very day at the French post of Viet Tri the coolie-tram delivered Dominé's message: 'Today I must inform you that, although our will to resist remains the same, our strength and health will soon be at an end. I think it most important that a column as strong as possible be sent to raise the siege of Thuyen Quang.'[10]

On the evening of the following day the Chinese breached the southwest wall with a black-powder mine but a rapid response by the defenders wiped out the first thirty or forty Black Flags through the gap and discouraged the rest from following them. Minutes later a second mine blew another breach. In the confused fighting the Legion suffered eleven casualties, which motivated them to make a sortie next morning and destroy the saps nearest the walls, while the breaches were repaired with bamboo buttressed by baskets of earth. In supervising work of this kind on 18 February Bobillot was shot in the neck, dying a lingering death in the sick bay four weeks later. By then, the Chinese had added heavy mortars to their armoury, so that any defender exposing himself for the needs of nature in daylight risked sniper bullets, cannonry and mortar shells.

At 0545hrs on 22 February the Black Flags set up the din of bugles and yelling that presaged a mass assault. The Legion immediately evacuated those stretches of the wall known to be mined - just before enormous explosions blew three more breaches in the walls totalling more than 60 metres in length. Through them, in a confusion of smoke, fumes and dust, a horde of Chinese beating gongs and screaming ran right onto a defensive mine planted in their path by Bobillot before he was shot. Driving back the survivors, the legionnaires patched up the gap with more bamboo and baskets of earth. The cost of the day to the Legion was Capt Moulinay and four men dead, with another officer, three NCOs and thirty-seven legionnaires wounded.

And so it went on: sleepless nights and days filled with sniping, mines, breaches, assaults with grenades and fizzing satchels of black powder hurled over the walls, ending in hand-to-hand mutual murder with knife and bayonet. When one huge explosion blew several legionnaires' bodies clean over the wall into the enemy trenches, in keeping with the Legion tradition of not leaving its dead behind Legionnaire Hinderschmidt hurled himself through the breach and retrieved several bodies to prevent their mutilation, carrying them back through a hail of fire in both directions until he too was hit in the throat.

'For nearly thirty minutes the fighting continued hand-to-hand in the breaches, the combatants separated only by the (improvised) bamboo palisades.'[11] Dominé's disciplined official account of one of the shorter attacks gives little idea of the horror - or perhaps by now the men were so numb with exhaustion and over-dosed with adrenalin from the weeks of fighting for their lives that it had come to seem normal to them. Spirits lifted briefly when good news from the outside world reached Thuyen Quang on 25 February, brought by the faithful coolie-tram.

Maj Dominé pinned up on a door for all to read the following notice: 'The (French) national flag was hoisted on 13 February at noon on the citadel of Lang Son. The Officer Commanding also informs the garrison that ... the entire 1st Brigade is marching up the (Son Gam) River to relieve Thuyen Quang.' There were by then approximately 200 men still able to bear arms in the fort, but only 180 working rifles between them, spread thinly along the 1,200-metre perimeter, 10% of which was mere bamboo palisade - and the situation was getting daily worse.

What was the point of all the suffering and the casualties? Did the Chinese need to tie up so many men and munitions taking a fort they could simply have walked around by following jungle trails, if their intention was to attack Hanoi from the northwest? It seems that Liu Yung-fu was playing a deeper game than he has been given credit for. Most urgently, as far as the defenders were concerned, where was the relief for which they yearned night and day?

Chapter 17

AS GOOD AS IT GETS

Vietnam 1885-1892

The appointment of a more aggressive Minister of War in Paris was all the encouragement C-in-C Vietnam Gen Brière de l'Isle needed to launch an ambitious push right along the Mandarin Road to Lang Son, the last garrison before the Chinese frontier, and there bar the route to further incursions. Included in his small army of twelve battalions of European and local forces that set out from the Red River delta on 3 February 1885 was Négrier - now a brigadier-general - with 1,800 legionnaires drawn from the two battalions freshly arrived from Formosa and an Algerian penal battalion, plus some artillery.

Once in the hills and jungle they were repeatedly held up by minor fortresses guarding the road. This campaign was hardly a shining example of sophisticated European tactics: assaulting a Chinese position frontally, one of Négrier's companies lost all its officers and a third of its men, when a simple flanking manoeuvre was subsequently found sufficient to panic the Chinese holding these positions into rapid withdrawal before their retreat was cut off. The weather was against the French and their Tonkinese troops; rain turned the so-called road into a river of mud, through which men and mules floundered for nine days until they drew in sight of Bac Viay, the last outpost before Lang Son, which was taken by an artillery barrage and an assault that cost 200 casualties. The way now lay open to their objective, a square walled city of some 400 metres on each side. To their surprise, the Chinese defenders melted away, allowing the French to march in. On 16 February, Brière de l'Isle handed over command to Négrier and marched back with a relief column commanded by Col Giovanelli to lift the siege of Thuyen Quang by a march of some 160km, much of it over mountain, swamp and jungle.

This was the moment Liu Yung-fu had planned for: the men dying in Thuyen Quang were the bait to draw a larger force into his trap. Attacked en route at Hoa Moc by the Black Flags, Giovanelli's column sustained casualties totalling approximately 500 men and twenty-seven officers, more than had been lost in the garrison they were coming to succour. The exact numbers are disputed, partly because so many men died of wounds before reaching any kind of medical treatment, and many succumbed to exhaustion from disease and the forced march.

Colonial domination was achieved by small numbers of European-led troops with modern arms maintaining what was effectively a rule of fear over millions of 'lesser peoples'. Liu Yung-Fu's double triumph showed that the *gwailo* foreign devils were not invincible. Having achieved his psychological purpose, his troops faded away into the jungle on 3 March, leaving only a small rearguard that held out to the last man against Legion bayonet charges.

Significantly, at Thuyen Quang, the same thing happened simultaneously after two and a half months of siege, with one company of Black Flags left behind as a blocking party. It was while the garrison was clearing this position to the last man with bullet and bayonet that Legionnaire Thiebald Streibler threw himself in front of Capt Borelli, as Legionnaire Catteau had done in attempting to save the life of Lt Maudet at Camarón. Streibler died instantly, riddled with bullets, but Borelli was saved from certain death.

When the relief party hove in sight of Thuyen Quang, they were confronted with a scene of arid desolation. Every tree, every stick of bamboo, had been cut for use in the 8km of trenches and parapets that zigzagged across the tortured earth, littered with rotting corpses, abandoned weapons and siege equipment. In the ruins of the fort fewer than 200 filthy, bearded ghosts drew themselves up on parade with Dominé at their head. Brière de l'Isle made the sort of speech generals make on such occasions. What did the twenty survivors crippled for life make of him telling them that they could hold their heads high to the end of their days when telling people they had been at Thuyen Quang?

Their sacrifice and that of their comrades who died there and at Hoa Moc is honoured in the Legion's marching song *Le Boudin*, which is chanted rather than sung at each meal in the mess. One verse goes,

> 'In Tonkin, the immortal Legion
> honoured our flag.
> Heroes of Camerone and model brothers
> sleep in peace in your graves.'

To honour the men who had died under his command at Thuyen Quang, especially Thiebald Streibler for saving his life, Capt Borelli wrote a poem twenty-seven verses long, entitled simply *To my men who are dead and in especial memory of Tirbald Steoberg (sic), who gave me his life on 3 March 1885 at the siege of Thuyen Quang*. Many critics have castigated Legion officers for spending their men's lives recklessly and neglecting their welfare, but the nineteenth-century upper classes from which officers were drawn were accustomed to use their servants harshly, whether in uniform or out. Even this short extract of Borelli's poem gives the lie to allegations that none of them cared.

> O my fellow-warriors, this is your
> officer of yesterday, come to talk with you -
> of what, I cannot tell for sure.
> But I salute my dead and say, thank you.
>
> Mercenaries, are you? You had to eat.
> Deserters? Well, you're not on trial now.
> So you're foreigners? Was the great
> Saxon marshal French, anyhow?
>
> They say you're without honour or faith,
> but what more could they have asked?
> Did you not fulfil unto death
> the sworn duty with which you were tasked?
>
> No guardsmen of pope or royal,
> no regiment in gold, scarlet and blue
> were ever as smart as you in uniforms all soiled
> or marched as prouder men than you.[1]

It is interesting that Borelli still felt it necessary, fifty years after Soult had formed the Legion, to rebut the accusations of the squabbling politicians back in Paris that legionnaires were riff-raff, turncoats, men without honour. Personally bringing back to the Legion chapel of the Quartier Viénot in Sidi-bel-Abbès two of the captured black flags, the grieving captain stipulated that they did not belong to France, and should the Legion ever be withdrawn to Europe, the flags must be burned first - as they duly were.

After the departure of Brière de l'Isle from Lang Son, things were quiet on the frontier for a while, although men at the outpost of Dong Dang, separated from the border by a plain of rice paddies, noted a strengthening of fortifications on the other side, behind which Chinese reinforcements flooded in until it was estimated an army of 40,000 men had built up.

On 22 March, the garrison at Dong Dang repulsed the first attack. History is unclear about what happened next. There were rumours at the time that Négrier had been urged by the pro-colonial Premier Jules Ferry to achieve a swift victory that would give him additional bargaining power at the negotiations with China in Paris. Négrier's bellicose temperament had earned him the Vietnamese nickname of 'Mau-Len' or Mr Quickly, so it is equally likely that he decided to bloody the Chinese nose once and for all in the belief that Beijing needed teaching a lesson, to put a stop to further incursions.

At the subsequent official enquiry, he contented himself with saying, 'Cavalry patrols and reconnaissance by officers reported from 15 March onwards a sustained build-up of Chinese forces. The Chinese tactics had recently consisted of constructing a fortified camp as close to (our lines) as possible and then moving against our lines of communication. The necessity to keep the enemy at a distance from the lines of communication made obligatory the occupation of Dong Dang. Given the small forces under our command, a passive defence obliging the defence of numerous posts was out of the question. It seemed preferable to combine all available forces in one massive push. The general decided immediately after the successful defence of Dong Dang (on 22 March) to take advantage of the enemy's demoralisation to attack (the nearest Chinese fort of) Bang-Bo with all his forces.'[2]

The terse military language obscures the political implications of cross-border warfare.

Immediately after crossing the frontier, the first wave of the French attack stalled on the steep slopes across the rice paddies from Dong Dang. With two French battalions and one of Tonkinese light infantry unable to advance, the Legion moved through them and drove the enemy back, enabling the main force to file through the pass called the Gates of China into Guangxi Province. When a second line of fortifications was also taken, a third was visible beyond it, and another beyond that. The Chinese had had three thousand years to construct their defences in depth.

After a large enemy force had tried to out-flank the French on the right, and been driven back by artillery, the Legion and other troops settled in for the night feeling optimistic after this early success. When the dawn mists cleared mid-morning on 24 March, they began the routine reduction of one enemy post after another. At mid-afternoon a massed Chinese counter-attack came in, which was their first indication that the enemy soldiers would fight far more tenaciously for their own country than when on foreign soil.

An estimated 25,000-30,000 well-led enemy troops rapidly fought their way to within arm's length of the French positions. Legionnaire Maury recalled later, 'Our ammunition was exhausted. I had only two bullets left and thought I should never escape alive from such a fight. Of ninety men, only twenty-seven were left.'[3] Another survivor, Legionnaire Bôn-Mat confessed later, 'Under fire from the front and both flanks, we took high casualties. The wounded and those too exhausted to keep up were abandoned, never to be seen again.'[4]

The reason why a third survivor wrote, 'My one aim at the time was to get clear. I had no wish to fall, wounded or not, into the hands of my pursuers,'[5] was apparent next morning. The disciplined Chinese having refrained from crossing the frontier, French scouting parties were sent back on the lookout for the missing and wounded. They were allowed to pass because the Chinese watching them from the heights wanted them to see what had happened to those they caught. In Bôn-Mat's own words, 'We brought back a dozen, but far more were found executed and horribly mutilated.'[6]

The regimental diary dryly records 2nd Battalion losing one captain and nine other ranks that day, with fifty-two wounded and two missing, but the total losses must have been high for Négrier to abandon Dong Dang and fall back on the positions around Lang Son, where the Legion gained a timely reinforcement with the arrival of 1,700 men from the rear.

At 0700hrs on 28 March, the Chinese launched wave after wave against the French positions, but were held off until dusk, when they retreated in impressively good order. The most controversial casualty of the day was Négrier, who took a chest wound around 1530hrs that obliged him to hand over command to Lt Col Paul Gustave Herbinger. Herbinger's until then brilliant army career was about to be blighted for ever.

Having been Professor of Military Tactics at the Ecole Supérieure de Guerre, he stunned his first orders meeting by informing the assembled officers that his professional appreciation of the situation was that Lang Son was untenable, given the forces massed against them and the problems of resupply, with many units already having run out of ammunition in combat. Having anticipated a Négrier-like order to hold at all costs, the officers were furious to learn that the fortress was to be abandoned that very night. One major of the Bataillons d'Afrique demanded the right to defend Lang Son single-handed, but Herbinger was adamant. Everything that could not be transported to the rear was to be destroyed.

Once the news passed down the chain of command, an orgy of looting and destruction began, with legionnaires helping themselves to officers' belongings and gorging on hoarded supplies before the quartermasters could destroy them. Inevitably they over-indulged on the unopened barrels of wine and *tafia*, a locally produced rum. The 2nd Battalion exceeded all others in this, according to Herbinger. However, Maj François George Diguet defended his men by pleading that *only twenty or so* were completely drunk - a capital offence on active service - and tried to shift blame to the quartermasters and sutlers for not breaking open the casks when destroying their other stores.

Legionnaire Maury recalled seeing 'several soldiers lying on the ground dead-drunk. We disarmed them and abandoned them.'[7] If dumping the artillery in the nearby river, despite the pleas of the gunners, was normal practice, it is a measure of the general panic that dumped likewise in the river was the pay-chest containing Mexican coinage to the value of 600,000 French francs, which had arrived only two days before. The retreat along the Mandarin Road to the delta was without major incident, although some Legion rearguards became separated from the main body and had to find their own way back on jungle trails, followed at a discreet distance by the Chinese, to make the point that their sting had not been drawn.

Herbinger was used as a scapegoat for the failure of Brière de l'Isle's policy and Négrier's impetuous incursion into China because he was the unpopular cold and clinical tactician who had admitted that the force of French arms was not absolute, while Négrier with his heroic wound had acted like the swashbuckling hero a good officer was supposed to be. To cover themselves for exceeding their mandate, generals Brière de l'Isle and Borgnis-Desbordes accused Herbinger of being an alcoholic and lied about the military situation to blacken his name still further.

Returning to France in June 1885, he demanded a court of enquiry to clear himself. The following February the court heard evidence from Maj Schaeffer commanding 3rd Battalion that the Chinese had been preparing a massive attack on the very day of the evacuation, but supporters of Brière de l'Isle and Négrier insisted that supplies had been adequate to hold out.

In fact the garrison had been on half-rations for several days, artillery ammunition was all but exhausted and bullets were down to seventeen rounds per man. Although cleared, Herbinger died three months later at the age of forty-seven, a broken man. In fact, his appreciation of the situation had been accurate. With Chinese regular and Black Flag forces building up all along the frontier, there had been no chance of holding Lang Son without colossal loss of life and equally no chance of evacuating the 3,700-man garrison once it was surrounded by the enormous forces the Chinese had brought into the field.

As it was, the arrival in Paris of news of the costly defeats in Vietnam brought down Jules Ferry's government - the longest-lasting of the Third Republic. However, that is not our affair. The Legion does not make policy; it only carries it out as far as human courage can, and no one could accuse it of failing in that respect during the conquest of Vietnam. A complex of internal problems and foreign threats elsewhere obliged the Chinese to sign a cease-fire agreement on 4 April. This led to the Treaty of Tientsin in June 1885, whereby they abandoned their claims on Tonkin. That, in turn, sparked a palace revolution in Hué, with the fourteen-year-old king fleeing to the mountains to organise resistance to the French. They simply replaced him with a puppet and divided the country, like Algeria, into three military-administrative areas: Tonkin, Annam and Cochinchina in the south.

Thereafter, Vietnam became the Legion's posting of choice. Between 1887 and 1909 statistics show surprisingly few legionnaires in the theatre dying in combat: only 271 against exactly ten times that many deaths from disease,[8] for Vietnam was known as the land where 'dysentery is queen and malaria king'.[9] In one particularly bad period before cheap modern prophylaxis for malaria arrived, Legion Sgt Ernest Bolis arrived in-country with a company of 116 men and noted that only sixteen were fit enough to be returned to Sidi-bel-Abbès by the end of their tour. The others had all died or become unfit for further soldiering.[10]

But there were good reasons for wanting to go east. One year in Vietnam counted as two for pension purposes, whereas service in Algeria was considered a home posting. In addition there was a colonial allowance that did not apply in North Africa. Whereas other French units in Indochina lived like kings, with native servants to wash their clothes, clean their weapons and even carry them on patrol, the Legion was tougher, forbidding the handling of weapons by servants, who nevertheless washed the legionnaire's underwear and cleaned his uniform and other equipment - a luxury unheard of in North Africa.

For those who did not mind seeing betel-blackened teeth in the mouth of their bed-mate, the *congai* hired long-term for a few piastres a week was not only a nightly solace. It was quite normal for the wives of Tonkinese light infantrymen to march along at the end of a column with their cooking utensils and much of their husbands' kit balanced on a bamboo pole over their shoulders.

Sometimes they did more than that. As Herbinger knew all too well, on the march to Lang Son and the subsequent campaign on the Chinese frontier, the issued rations were way below starvation level. Some 8,000 coolies and 800 Chinese ponies, able to stand the climate and terrain better than mules, had been impressed to carry the dismantled artillery pieces, food and ammunition for the Lang Son expedition. But the impressed labour melted away at the first unguarded moment, terrified by the Chinese practice of killing all coolies taken prisoner. It was the enterprising *congais* like that of Legionnaire Bôn-Mat who saved the day by travelling back and forth to the delta buying supplementary food for their 'husbands' and their comrades.

Alcohol was everywhere the legionnaire's release. In Vietnam *tafia* and *choum-choum* were cheap. But opium at two piastres for a pipe was the great relaxation for officer and man alike. Initially frowned on by Paris and the Church, it came to be the social drug of the colonial scene in the early twentieth century, so much so that by 1914 it was a government monopoly, producing a third of all the tax levied in Indochina.[11] In the Legion, providing a man did not become so addicted that it affected discipline and military usefulness, the officers turned a blind eye.

In 1891 the new Governor-General Antoine de Lanessan divided the frontier with China into four sectors, placing a colonel in charge of each with instructions to 'pacify' his area by his own methods. It was hard and dirty work. Legion and other patrols travelled light on jungle trails. East of Suez, legionnaires wore white uniforms and exchanged their képis for pith helmets, which were believed to prevent sunstroke. Since the Chinese used the white helmets to single out European targets, the Legion often wore non-standard headgear.

One account explained the procedure when there were no facilities to evacuate the wounded: 'If we left a chap, we would find him butchered by the pirates who … stuck a (bamboo stake) up his arse until it came out of his shoulder. So when there was one who was on his last legs, we gave him a drink of *tafia* and then we said, "Now it's your last mouthful." We would stick the barrel in his mouth and pull the trigger. Then we could go off with a clear conscience.'[12]

In August 1892 a patrol from Cao Bang, ambushed by an armed band near the border, took refuge in the Chinese frontier post of

Bo Cup, where the commander's embarrassed acquiescence to their request was explained when a large patrol of his soldiers returned to base obviously having been in a fire-fight, and some came up to congratulate the Legion lieutenant on the skill with which he had extricated his men from their ambush.

Soldiers keep a sense of humour when civilians might not. Marshal Joseph Galliéni recalled his days as a colonel commanding 2nd Military District, in which Lang Son lay. After a number of incursions in the summer of 1896 he protested to his Chinese opposite number Marshal Sou, who apologised but said he could not control his troops. However, he had no objection to them being shot out of hand if caught in *flagrante delicto*. Galliéni's remedy was to play Sou's own game and replace his regular troops on that stretch of the border with legionnaires, who also indulged in cross-border raids for pillage and food. When Sou protested, Galliéni replied that the legionnaires were foreigners, over whom he had no control, but if Sou wished to shoot them, that was fine by him. The Chinese raids stopped.

Most colonial soldiering in Indochina after the initial conquests consisted not of great battles and prolonged sieges. It was a slow routine of patrols, garrison boredom and R and R where opium, women and alcohol fostered the dream of the exotic east that had made them volunteer. Volunteer they did, despite the health risks that awaited them. The Legion always had more men wanting to ship east than were required there, although a fair number of these volunteers changed their mind on the long and uncomfortable sea voyage, jumping ship in the Suez Canal, opened in 1869, or in a port of call where they risked the bullets of the sentries on the gangway for an uncertain future, penniless in a strange land.

Yet those who did come surrendered something of themselves to this strange and fertile country which had been at war for a thousand years and would be so for another century. Even today, recalling the landscape, the Vietnamese people and the way of life, old legionnaires who served there sigh, *'Qu'elle était belle, la vie là-bas!'* For the European settlers, it was a beautiful life. For a legionnaire, it was as good as it gets.

Chapter 18

WAR ON THE BELLY OF DAN

Dahomey 1892-1894

The Legion's elevation to the status of a brigade in December 1884 made little difference to the units in Vietnam. In Algeria, 1st Regiment, abbreviated to 1 RE - the letters standing for *régiment étranger* - was based at Sidi-bel-Abbès with 2 RE in Saïda, 90km to the southeast. In July 1892 each of the regiments was ordered to furnish 400 men for a *régiment de marche* to be sent to Dahomey, now Benin in West Africa.[1]

There were both pros and cons to this system of temporary units. Its advocates argued that they permitted the best men to be taken for a specific mission without bringing along the dross. Its opponents argued that the effect on morale was bad because it divided legionnaires into two classes - those who always got the plum jobs and those who became despondent lead-swingers. Better, they said, to take a company that had trained together, get the slackers up to scratch and use volunteers to replace those physically unfit for the mission.

Invalided back from Vietnam with black-water fever, but now cured, Sgt Frederic Martyn could not wait to get abroad again. Dining in town to escape the monotony of canteen food, he learned of this opportunity to escape the boredom of depot life on seeing a copy of the *Echo d'Oran* newspaper. Reading that the Minister of War had placed at the disposal of the navy a battalion of the Foreign Legion that would be leaving on 4 August for Dahomey, Martyn and fellow-sergeant Ivan Petrovski rushed back to barracks to put their names down as volunteers. Well down the list, they pinned their hopes on knowing the nominated battalion commander Maj Marius-Paul Faurax, under whom they had served in Tonkin.[2]

Rumours that King Behanzin of Dahomey kept a bodyguard of female warriors may have helped fuel their enthusiasm. The Amazons, as they were dubbed, were originally all captives trained as warriors and forbidden on pain of death to have sex with any male apart from the king. Since he had a large harem, this condemned them to lifelong virginity, of which the main compensation was to live in the royal household and eat its food. Such was the status this conferred that important families donated daughters to the royal guard, much as medieval Europeans donated boys to the Church as oblates.

Sir Richard Burton, visiting West Africa in 1861 had described them as less than seductive: '… with a development of adipose tissue, which suggested anything but ancient virginity. I saw old, ugly and square-built frows *(Frauen)* trudging grumpily along with the face of Cook after being much nagged by the Missus.' He divided them into five categories: the blunderbuss women, each followed by her ammunition porter; the elephant huntresses, said to be the bravest; the razor women, who looked like scarecrows; the infantry, whom he found 'rather mild in appearance;' and the elite archeresses. After pointing out that the object of Dahomeyan warfare was capturing slaves, he concluded that the women were certainly as brave as, if not braver than, their male counterparts.[3]

Whether out of uninformed lust for these female warrior or not, so many legionnaires volunteered at bel-Abbès that the colonel of 1 RE simply appointed Faurax's senior captain, lieutenant and second-lieutenant, leaving those officers to select the NCOs and men they wanted. The tall German-born Capt Paul Brundsaux, whose Vietnamese nickname 'Loum-Loum' referred to his rampant beard, and whose obsession with obedience had once put his daughter in the cells at bel-Abbès, was an obvious choice for the *régiment de marche*. It was thanks to his daughter that he was serving in the Legion at all, having resigned from the regular army in Bizerta when refused permission to marry her mother, who was pregnant with his child. Although a graduate of St Cyr, he had lost three years' seniority by resigning in order to get married and re-enlist in the Legion afterwards. He had also been rewarded for his integrity with a 'foreign' commission, only valid for service in the colonies, which prevented him ever transferring back to a regular regiment.

The seventeen-day voyage from Oran to Cotonou on the Slave Coast in the transports *Ville de St-Louis* and *Mytho* was without incident. On 23 August 1892 legionnaires on deck sighted the palm trees and sandy beaches of the coast, the ships' captains moored off-shore and the men prepared to disembark into lighters and pirogues that would take them through the surf to the shore.

Their first sight of the country was as disappointing as the arrival at Haiphong. Cotonou then consisted of a handful of dilapidated native huts with a long wharf reaching out to sea, a rudimentary factory processing almonds and palm oil, the resident's house, a small sick bay and a crudely built blockhouse with a small French garrison to protect this disputed trading post. A journey of 30km inland in pirogues towed behind French gunboats brought them to the former Portuguese slaving port of Porto Novo on the shores of the Nokoué lagoon, where the King of Tofa was waiting to welcome them wearing a French naval officer's cap, an embroidered frock coat and nothing underneath. Regally impervious to their laughter at his appearance, the king could afford to smile indulgently at these foreigners, bound up-country to die from disease or wounds in a war to keep him on his squalid throne.

His capital was a sprawling, fever-ridden village of mud huts with thatched roofs in a marsh beside the lagoon. The 'barracks' in which the legionnaires exchanged their uniforms for light tropical clothing and pith helmets was merely a collection of open-sided sheds with palm-leaf roofs. The local custom of burying the dead beneath the family home permeated everything with the smell of putrefaction, so no one was sorry on 1 September when the arrival of locally impressed porters to carry their equipment meant they could march north to join the rest of the 4,000-strong expeditionary force commanded by Col Alfred-Amédée Dodds, an extraordinary mulatto graduate of St Cyr who came from Senegal.

The name Dahomey was derived from Dan-ho-me, meaning 'on the belly of Dan' because King Behanzin's 'palace' was built on the grave of a murdered predecessor. Dodds planned to follow the Ouémé River northwards and come at Behanzin's capital from the southeast. This doubled the mileage from the coast but had the advantage of avoiding extensive fever-marshes that lay in the direct course. The crime for which Behanzin was to be punished was that of invading his former vassal kingdom of Tofa, now under French protection, after German arms traders wanting a war to shift their stocks had told him that Germany had 'finished off' France in 1871.

As any modern map shows, West Africa was literally carved up by the European colonial powers, all grabbing slices of the cake. The 1892 Dahomey campaign resulted from French claims based on 'treaties' forged by unscrupulous traders that the coastal strip from Cotonou to the former British and French slaving port of Ouidah[4] had been ceded to France. Needing Ouidah to ship the palm oil that was his kingdom's only export now that the slave trade had been abolished, Behanzin had used German-supplied weapons to attack Porto Novo in 1890 and regain control of Ouidah. The subsequent uneasy truce was broken in 1892 when some of his soldiers fired on a French gunboat on the River Ouémé, giving Eugene Etienne, now Minister for the Colonies, the pretext for mounting Dodds' expedition.

Moving off from Porto Novo, progress along the eastern bank of the Ouémé River was slow, averaging about 8km a day through difficult country. A few lucky units were able to ride regally on the river in pirogues towed by French gunboats, but for most it was a painful progress. Martyn recalled how, 'One hour we would be struggling through a mangrove swamp, and the next forcing our way through tall grasses that reached well above our heads and chopping our way through thick bush. We carried nothing except our arms and 150 rounds of ammunition per man and even this light load was as much as we could struggle along with.'[5] Other men remembered chiefly the suffocating, cloying heat. For those who had been careless enough to walk around barefoot after marching all day in boots, the agony of jiggers penetrating under their toenails, whence they had to be removed by a native using a hot needle, simply compounded the discomfort.

On 11 September the advance guard reached the town of Dogba, where the sappers were to erect a bridge to get everyone across to the western bank, after which there was only one more river crossing before Abomey. Dodds prudently decided to call a halt at Dogba until stragglers and the Legion reinforcements caught up with the main body. On arrival there, the Legion built a Roman-type marching camp of ditch and rampart on three sides, with the river securing their backs.

Just before first light on 19 September the marine pickets outside the perimeter heard movements in the nearby jungle. Assuming that the black shapes between the trees were the native porters relieving themselves, they were taken by surprise when hundreds of Dahomeyan warriors erupted from the surrounding darkness and hurled themselves forward screaming and ululating. However, this was no undisciplined tribal assault. The Dahomeyan army was well drilled in volley firing and simple manoeuvres. It numbered around 4,500 regular warriors, of whom 800 were the Amazons, plus the same number of 'reservists', all commanded by full-time war chiefs.

The pickets' first shots as they ran back inside the camp woke their restive comrades, sleeping with weapons stacked outside each tent. The Legion's bugle-calls, Loum-Loum's bellowed orders and the high-pitched battle screams of the attackers combined into the din of battle. Luckily, although the Dahomeyans had purchased from the German arms dealers 2,000 modern Mauser and vintage Chassepot rifles, Winchester repeaters, five clapped-out French machine guns and even six Krupp cannon, their firearms were rarely cleaned and were usually discharged with the eyes shut in the belief that small arms were self-aiming. Most of Behanzin's warriors were anyway still armed with ancient blunderbusses, bows and arrows and swords and spears whose long, thin hand-forged blades served both for slashing and stabbing.

'(My legionnaires) were already running towards me rifle in hand, some in their undershorts, some in their shirts,' wrote Lt Jacquot of that morning. 'No matter, they were there, and by the time Maj Faurax arrived two minutes later we had already commenced firing on the large numbers of enemy fortunately entangled in the *abattis* barrier of cut (thorn) trees with their branches facing outwards between the jungle and this side of the camp.'[6]

Martyn described firing as fast as he could load, with each shot knocking over a black shadow in the grey pre-dawn light. When Henri-Paul Lelièvre reached the firing line, he found the Dahomeyans no more than 10 metres distant, some coolly returning the legionnaires' fire seated on small stools they had brought with them for the purpose. Jacquot again: 'The infantry fired salvoes. The artillery shot canister (shrapnel) at a range of less than 100 metres. The gunboat *Opale* peppered the woods with shells from her Hotchkiss gun[7] which whistled past above our heads.'[8]

Maj Faurax, who insisted on mounting his horse to oversee the mêlée and be visible to his men, caught a bullet and died shortly afterwards. He was probably a victim of one of the small number of snipers hidden in the trees, who did take careful aim before firing. According to Legion legend, his last words to Dodds were, 'Were you satisfied with my men?'[9] Be that as it may, it was the legionnaires' bayonet counter-attack that broke the first wave of Behanzin's warriors.

Four more mass attacks after dawn were reminiscent of the Chinese human waves in Vietnam. Martyn takes up the story when the legionnaires ended the battle by making a bayonet charge at the wall of bodies in front of them: 'We were ramming our bayonets into their bodies until the hilt came up against the flesh with a sickening thud, and then throwing them off to make room for another, like a farm labourer forking hay, until we had to clamber over dead and dying men piled two or three high to get at the living... . They couldn't run away, for the great mass behind was pushing them onto our bayonets. It was a terrible slaughter.'[10]

By 0900hrs the attackers who could still walk had melted away into the jungle. The wounded were finished off with bayonets. A few prisoners taken unhurt were shot immediately afterwards, including two of Behanzin's Amazons, wearing blue, knee-length cotton kilts held up by leather cartridge belts and with their oiled bodies naked from the waist up. The sexually curious legionnaires noted that some of the dead Amazons were barely nubile, while others were much older, with flaccid pendulous breasts. Both male and female bodies were disposed of the same way - some to the crocodiles in the river and some on a huge funeral pyre that smouldered on nauseatingly for days. At the price of five dead and sixty wounded, Dodd's column claimed a body-count of 832 enemy dead.

A spokesman for Benhanzin was conducted into Dodds' presence to sue for peace and at the same time warn that his master was 'the shark that eats the French'. He was told to return with the message that Dodds was 'the whale that eats the shark'.[11]

Progress, once across the Ouémé, was slow with frequent ambushes. Reinforced nightly guard duty and dawn stand-tos added to the misery. On 28 September the gunboats were ambushed while reconnoitring up-river. After dark on 30 September, the French camp was bombarded by artillery from the opposite bank, but without casualties because ranging was so poor that the shells landed in the jungle well beyond the camp.

On 4 October as the Senegalese advance guard neared the village of Poguessa, the Sudanese native cavalry and a company of Hausa infantry in the lead bore the brunt of an ambush, under which they broke and ran for the rear. Snipers in the trees killed three officers, but once again the Dahomeyans' artillery shells passed harmlessly overhead. When the French ceased fire on command, the enemy assumed they must be out of ammunition and attacked again.

A company of the Legion was ordered to outflank them on the left, while the gunboats bombarded the enemy reserves, forming up in clearings visible from the river. Among the bodies counted on the battlefield strewn with fetishes that were supposed to deflect French bullets lay more than thirty Amazons, whom Martyn reckoned had fought at least as courageously as the men alongside them. A French marine who grabbed one female survivor with sexual intent was rewarded by her biting his nose so hard that an officer had to run her through with his sabre before she would let go. Among the unwounded prisoners tied up outside Dodd's tent for interrogation was another Amazon who appeared to be about fifteen years old. Smiling prettily at her captors, she pleaded for her life, but was shot with the others because there were neither provisions for feeding prisoners nor spare men to guard them.

Ambushes, skirmishes, bombardments, hacking a way through jungle and scrub to avoid being ambushed even more often when staying on the main trails … the French were now suffering from thirst as the retreating Dahomeyans had poisoned or filled in all the wells. Torrential rain was welcomed as a source of water, all too soon exhausted. The advance ground to a halt. On 16 October Dodds was compelled to retreat in order to give his sick and wounded a chance of recovery. Lips blackened, tongues swollen,

The price of glory: General Rollet's Monument aux Morts (*above*) at Legion HQ in Aubagne commemorates 35,000 dead legionnaires, including this one who died in 1950 in Vietnam (*below*). *(1. ALE / 2. Author's collection)*

3.-5. Marshal Soult (*left*) fathered a bastard for King Louis-Philippe (*centre*), who wanted an empire without spilling French blood.(*3. & 4. Author's collection / 5. MLE*)

6.-8. In Spain, Col Bernelle (*left*) caned starving legionnaires, but Madame Bernelle (*centre*) thought she was the commanding officer. Their enemy Maj Conrad (*right*) died at Barbastro fighting renegade legionnaires. (*6. 7. 8. all MLE*)

9.-11. Col Chabrière (*left*) died a hero's death at Magenta. All that remained of Col Danjou (*centre*) in Mexico was his wooden hand. Col Jeanningros (*right*) sent him and his men to their deaths. (*9. MLE / 10. Author's collection / 11. MLE*)

12.-14. Gen Bazaine (*left*) came home with a rich wife and a marshal's baton to disgrace. Alan Seeger had a rendezvous with death as Harvard poet (*centre*) and Legion corporal (*right*). (*12 & 13. both Author's collection / 14. MLE*)

15.-17. Jazz composer Cole Porter (*left*) sang 'Who wants to be a legionnaire? I do'. Capt Maire (*centre*) marched his men into a friendly barrage. Gen Rollet (*right*) became the father of Soult's bastard. (*15. Author's collection / 16. MLE / 17. Author's collection*)

18.-20. Hero in the Western Desert, Col Amilakvari (*left*) loved the mistress of Gen Koenig (*centre*). Col Jeanpierre (*right*) loved his men, but took one risk too many in Algeria. (*18. MLE / 19. Author's collection / 20. MLE*)

21. The scarecrows of Algiers get their first real uniforms in 1840. *(MLE)*

22. The death of Col Chabrière at Magenta, 1859. *(MLE)*

23. Two of the heroes of Camarón. But how many really died at Trinity Ranch in April 1863? *(MLE)*

24. The toughest of the tough (*above*). A mounted company crossing a *wadi* during the brutal 1912 Moroccan campaign. *(Author's collection)*

25. Beating up the German consul, legionnaires like these (*below*) with their Lebel 1896 rifles provoked an international incident at Agadir in 1911. *(ALE)*

26. '*I joined for the glory.*' Alan Seeger wrote. Foreign volunteers march off to the front, a short bus-ride away from Paris in Autumn 1914. *(ALE)*

27. General Rollet's shrine (*above*), the other house of the Legion at Sidi bel-Abbès. *(author's collection)*

28. Waiting for the enemy (*below*) somewhere in Algeria *c.*1935. *(author's collection)*

29. Off to the front (*left*): a Legion NCO bids farewell to his Vietnamese wife and child in Sidi bel-Abbès, March 1940 *(ALE)*

30. Waiting for the Wehrmacht (*below*): a Legion machine-gunner somewhere in France, May 1940 *(ALE)*

Opposite:

31. Legion volunteers (*above*) at Gare de Lyon in Paris, marching off to defeat and death, May 1940 *(ALE)*

32. Western Desert, July 1942 (*below*). Gen Montgomery did *not* love Gen Koenig's heroes of Bir Hakeim *(ALE)*

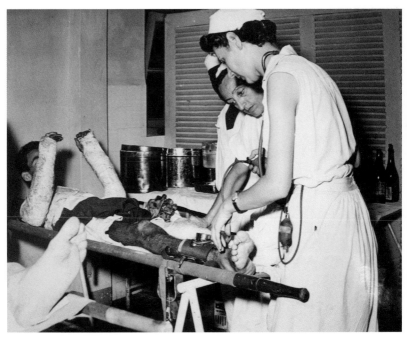

33. It will be a while before this unlucky legionnaire in a Saigon hospital (*above*) feels like chatting up his nurses, Vietnam 1950 *(ALE)*

34. Typical Legion camp in Vietnam (*below*). Note the sharpened bamboo stakes instead of barbed wire. *(ALE)*

35. Is this my lucky day? The last man of this Legion patrol in the Delta (*above*) seems to be having second thoughts, Northern Vietnam *c.*1950 *(ALE)*

36. Mortar crew of 1 BEP at Dien Bien Phu on 22 March 1954. Only one man in four came home alive. *(ALE)*

37. Rollet's mules long forgotten, an AMX tank of 1 REC (*left*) patrols on the Tunisian border, summer 1958 *(ALE)*

38. 1 REC back at base (*above*) after chasing the *fells* through the Aurès Mountains of Algeria in 1957 *(ALE)*

39. Taking the war to an elusive enemy (*below right*). Col Jeanpierre's paras of 1 REP exit a Shawnee H-21 Flying Banana in the Aurès, 1959 *(ALE)*

40. Today's mechanised, hi-tech legionnaires (*above*) still have to march, but mostly on parade. *(author's collection)*

41. Only one recruit in six makes it through six months of hell to win a white *kepi*. Legionnaires from three continents (*below*) relaxing after passing-out parade at 4 RE's HQ, Quartier Danjou, Castelnaudary. *(Author's collection)*

men were dehydrating at an alarming rate, especially those suffering from dysentery - which Martyn estimated as high as one in five of the Europeans. Burying their dead as they went, the Legion trekked back the way they had come, carrying the wounded with them.

On 17 October, after a convoy of 200 sick was despatched back to the coast, protected by two companies of native troops, the slimmed-down column numbered fifty-three officers, 1,533 other ranks and 2,000 porters. It was badly in need of two Senegalese infantry companies that arrived as reinforcements, enabling Dodds to create four ad hoc battalions of one 'light' Legion company and two native companies in each.

The outcome was still in the balance, but fortuitous help was on the way in the shape of an epidemic of smallpox among the Dahomeyans and an uprising by the Yoruba slaves who cultivated their crops, thousands of whom took advantage of their masters' preoccupation with the French invasion to go on the rampage, causing damage to property and loss of life that distracted Behanzin's chiefs at just the right moment for Dodds.

On 26 October, together with reinforcements bringing artillery up from the coast, he turned back once again towards Behanzin's capital. Taking the town of Kana on the way, even Martyn and the other legionnaires who had seen horrific 'honour guards' of rows of impaled enemy heads at bandit camps in Vietnam were aghast at the Dahomeyans' furniture made from human bones and the skulls used as plates and drinking vessels. The sight of so many human body parts displayed as grotesque artefacts made the Senegalese infantrymen fear that juju would claim their souls in this macabre place.

Three weeks later, after fruitless peace negotiations with Behanzin, who had neither the ready cash nor the control over his chiefs at this stage to comply with the harsh and unconditional terms imposed by Dodds - now elevated to general's rank to give him the status to deal with a king - the French column entered Abomey on 16 November, to find even more gruesome sights, including the king's throne constructed of human bones. Of Behanzin himself there was no sign, so Dodds appointed one of the absent king's brothers as puppet monarch.

Statistics are notoriously misleading. The government in Paris could claim a victory for the reasonable price of eleven officers and seventy men dead and twenty-five officers and 411 men wounded, but those figures do not include the losses five times as high from disease, heat-stroke or simple dehydration - nor the men who were repatriated with health broken for the rest of their lives. Of the original 800 legionnaires from 1 RE and 2 RE who had landed at Cotonou on 23 August only 450 could reply, *'Présent!'* at the end of the expedition, but the Legion's 35% attrition from sickness was far less than the toll on the French marines, whose numbers were so reduced by disease that they had ceased to exist as a fighting force.

Whether the difference was because of all the toughening-up legionnaires had gone through in Algeria, or simply because they were older men in their prime whereas the marine recruits were young, fresh out of Europe and not physically fully developed, was a debate never settled. It remained true of other wars, however, that legionnaires suffered fewer losses from disease than other European forces. Yet, of 219 legionnaires evacuated from Cotonou on 25 December 1892, only 150 could walk down the gangway on docking at Oran; the others were stretcher cases. Among their souvenirs was Behanzin's white parasol edged with fifty human lower jaws.

The little war on the belly of Dan ground to a halt by fits and starts as Behanzin was harried from village to village in the bush. When, on 26 January 1894 the deposed king was finally brought to bay, his European captors stared with surprise at this captive whose reign of cannibalism and terror they had ended. He was a quiet, rather studious-looking young man of indeterminate age, who was to spend the rest of his natural life in relatively comfortable exile with four wives and four of their children, a Dahomeyan prince and his wife, plus an interpreter, on the Caribbean island of Martinique and later in Algeria, a hostage for the good behaviour of his people.

Chapter 19

THE CUT-PRICE CAMPAIGN

Madagascar, 1895

Dahomey was far from being the Legion's only commitment south of the Sahara during the last years of the nineteenth century. It was a period when tearaway officers from many European nations carved off chunks of Africa or Asia for their political masters in London, Madrid, Lisbon, Berlin and Rome - with the satisfaction of naming after themselves or their monarchs features of landscape hitherto unseen by European eyes.

Among the Legion's mounted companies thus occupied while Dodd's column was pursuing Behanzin through the bush was a party of four officers and 120 emaciated legionnaires who staggered back into the French post at Kayes on the Mali-Senegal border on 3 May 1893 after covering nearly 3,000km in eight months of exploration and fighting in the uncharted areas of what is now up-country Ivory Coast, Mali and Guinea. Invalided back to bel-Abbès after enduring appalling privations, they vanished from history.

The French aim in this scatter-shot approach was to gain control over the Dark Continent from the West African coast right across to the Red Sea. At the eastern end, this collided with the British imperial imperative of controlling Egypt and the Suez Canal - Red Sea imperial route to India and also constructing a railroad from Cairo all the way south to the Cape of Good Hope.

Clashes were inevitable, the most famous being in July 1896 when Capt Jean-Baptiste Marchand with a column of Senegalese infantry reached Fashoda[1] in southern Sudan after an epic 3,000km safari that began in Libreville on the West Coast. When the future Lord Kitchener also arrived in Fashoda on 18 September after fighting his way south from Egypt via

Omdurman and Khartoum, Marchand refused to give up the fort. Combat was narrowly avoided only by him agreeing to fly British and Egyptian flags alongside the tricolour on its tower.

On this occasion, the French withdrew with ill grace after Foreign Secretary Lord Salisbury promised political support against the growing strength of the German Empire. On other occasions the clashes of geopolitical interest were avoided by European powers exchanging one area of influence for another, as when Britain swapped dominion over the island of Heligoland for Germany's interests in Zanzibar and the adjacent African mainland[2] at the same time as ceding to France the fourth largest island in the world in return for her trading privileges in Zanzibar. After thus acquiring Madagascar, Paris was faced four years later with an anti-colonial uprising on the island which resulted in the Armée d'Afrique being required to contribute a Legion battalion of twenty-two officers and 818 other ranks to a punitive expedition of 30,000 men under Jacques-Charles Duchesne, who had retaken Thuyen Quang as a Legion lieutenant-colonel and was now a general.

Madagascar was then dominated by the Merina tribe, itself ruled by the Hova caste headed by Queen Ranavalona III, who had been converted to the Church of England in 1868 by Anglican missionaries. In fact, the real power was vested in the hands of her husband and Prime Minister, Rainilaiarivony. European arms dealers had equipped the Merina royal guard with modern Remington rifles, but the rest of Queen Ranavalona's army of 40,000 men was armed with muzzle-loading muskets, spears and bows and arrows.

Although trained by two British soldiers of fortune, Col Charles Shervington and Gen Digby Willoughby, the Hova officer corps was concerned mainly with the grandeur of its uniforms: gold braid on cap, belt and the frog of the scabbard of an enormous sabre trailing on the ground, red stripes on trousers and huge gold epaulettes. A lieutenant had five gold stripes on his sleeve, a general eleven and a field marshal seventeen! The Antananarivo correspondent of the *Daily Telegraph*, himself a relic of the British presence on the island, commented that this was an army with 'no commissariat, no pay (and) no outfit except a rifle, a few rounds of ball cartridge and a bit of calico.'[3] Apart from much marching in parades, training was non-existent owing to a shortage of ammunition that prevented them firing their weapons.

Such an army could hardly have opposed a landing in force at Taomasina[4], the east coast port nearest the capital Antananarivo.[5] There, after a bombardment that drove out the local inhabitants, the French navy had established a base of sorts in December 1894. There was also a French naval base at Diego Suarez in the very north of the island. So it remains a mystery why Duchesne opted to land on the side of the world's fourth largest island *opposite* to the capital. The probable explanation lies in that perennial bugbear of the armed forces: inter-service rivalry, the War Ministry in Paris having undercut by 30 million francs the budget demanded by the French navy to conquer Madagascar using marines landed on the east coast.

The climate of Madagascar being decidedly tropical, Duchesne planned for his soldiers to march light, with all their equipment and heavy weapons transported on 5,000 of the infamous Lefèbre carts, extremely heavy two-wheeled barrows designed to army specifications and transported in kit form, to be assembled once ashore and then dragged or pushed through 300 miles of tropical rainforest over mountains rising to 800 metres-plus above sea level.

The best laid plans of generals 'gang oft agley'. The invasion went aglay on Day One when the disembarkation at Mahajanga[6] on the northwest coast had to be completely rethought because the pioneers building a wharf, at which Duchesne's flotilla of eleven ships led by the *Primaguet* were to unload and disembark their troops, discovered by soundings that access to it by shipping was impossible owing to a coral reef which presumably was shown on naval charts, but had not been disclosed to them. In addition, although the great inlet called the Bay of Mahajanga looked on a map in the War Ministry in Paris like a splendid way of shuttling the whole force 50km inland using small river boats that had been transported dismantled in the fleets' holds, it was found to have so violent a tidal swell that each boat launched was soon swamped - as the navy must have known when presenting its alternative plan.

Compounding all these problems, there were no roads along which to push the carts! While disembarkation continued from

January to April, Duchesne's solution to this last problem was to launch a recruiting drive for porters to haul the carts while his men constructed the roads. The call for 2,000 coolies from Vietnam brought no response. All he could recruit was a force of 1,000-plus Somalis from the East African mainland. Then Algeria came up trumps with 3,500 Kabyles, who cannot have known the work that was going to be demanded of them, nor that they would be ill-fed even on the voyage out and later turned away from aid posts when in need of medical treatment on the island.[7]

Another 2,000 men of mixed races and doubtful physique were raised from the slums of the towns and cities of the Maghreb. With the addition of some locally recruited natives of the Sakalave tribe, hereditary enemies of the dominant Merinas, Duchesne eventually had a force of 7,715 porters to transport the equipment of his 658 officers and 14,773 men. The term 'equipment' did not include the men's packs, which they had to carry themselves.

To make the tracks on which the barrows could travel along a route following the right bank of the Betsiboka and Ikopa rivers, once again the legionnaires' cutting edges were more often pickaxes and spades than bayonets. With gallows humour, these tools were collectively nicknamed 'the 1895 model' as though they had been rifles. So many men died of heat-stroke while wielding them in tropical temperatures that the working day was reduced to between dawn and 1000hrs with a second session from 1730hrs until the evening meal.

Off-duty, there was little to do apart from getting drunk and running amok. If native women were nearby, the results were predictable. When Paul Rollet landed as a young lieutenant on Madagascar in the occupation forces seven years later, he discovered that nine of his legionnaires had typically run amok in a native village recently, raping all the women.[8] The 150 Legion reinforcements who arrived in Mahajanga in 1895 had no black marks against them, but a company of conscripts for 200th Infantry Regiment arriving with them disappeared into the village of Makoas on their very first evening ashore to kidnap all the women at gunpoint.[9]

After seven weeks' agonised work, bridging rivers and hacking a road of sorts through fever-ridden lowland jungle and scrub, only a quarter of the route had been covered and resupply was already so poor that the legionnaires were for the most part living off the land, slaughtering any livestock they came across. Compared with road-building, the fighting was easy. On 2 May at Marovoay on the mouth of the Betsiboka River, the Merina defenders ran away so fast that the pursuing legionnaires were unable to keep up with them. On 9 June at Maevatanana on the Ikopa River 100km inland, they watched the same thing happen again.

Duchesne did not let the deaths from heat-stroke and fever deter him from pushing the column on until it reached the town of Andriba on the healthier high plateau after seventeen nightmare weeks of hacking a way through the mountains and jungles. Long before then, the aid stations and field hospitals had been revealed as grossly inadequate because the army's budget had been trimmed by cutting back on such 'luxuries' as these.

Although quinine was available in theory on this campaign - it had not been issued at all in Dahomey - the supplies were intermittent because it had been so loaded in the holds that it was the last item to be brought ashore. Even when it was issued, men often did not bother to take it. The connection between the insect and the disease had been discovered only the previous year by a British army doctor working in India, so no one yet thought of taking any precautions against mosquitoes.

At Andriba on 21 August after a three-hour cannonade by the French artillery, so painfully dragged up from the coast by Gen Emile Voyron's 2nd Brigade, put the Malagasy defenders to flight, Duchesne decided to crowd the pace by leaving the most exhausted behind and picking a flying column of the 5,000 fittest men to force-march the rest of the way with 3,000 mules for transport, leaving Voyron to follow on with the slower movers. Of the Legion's original landed strength of 840, the medics - whose standards were pretty low, given that most men were suffering from malaria anyway - were able to pass as fit for this operation only nineteen officers and 330 men. From these, the fittest 150 were selected for the final stage of the war.

Frederic Martyn, now a lieutenant, was among the reinforcements who caught up at this time, as did Capt Brundsaux, to find they were joining an army of fever-racked, emaciated scarecrows. Watching them being reviewed by Duchesne on 12 September, Lt Gustave Langlois wrote that the men were 'so downcast, depressed and pale, they seemed more dead than alive. Their clothes were rags. Their boots had disintegrated. Their helmets were too large for their skull-like heads and concealing almost entirely the yellow faces with eyes the colour of fever. They seemed so pathetic, so poor and so miserable that tears sprang to my eyes.'[10]

Two days later, this ghost of a flying column set out on the last lap, along what passed for a road to the capital, 160km to the southeast. In the force of 4,013 other ranks under 237 officers, the Régiment d'Afrique was composed of two battalions of Algerian *tirailleurs* and a 'battalion' of the Legion only 150 strong. Before the day was out, they ran into the first of a series of defensive positions. Next morning, the legionnaires' role was to advance through a marsh towards the Merina artillery, most of whose shells failed to explode. The gunners and supporting infantry ran away when the Legion fired their first volley at 2,000 metres - well out of accurate range.

Langlois again: 'One of the defenders ran off with no self-respect. Two or three other men stood up, looked around and also legged it. As one man, they suddenly erupted out of their trench and disappeared fast down the ravines, throwing away their arms, the faster to get away. We greeted their grotesque flight with yelled insults.'[11]

After the adrenalin of this push-over attack, fatigue set in. There was no pursuit because so few could still run. A night march on 18 September left a great tail of stragglers who could not keep up in the climb to the next line of fortifications on the Ambohimenas Mountains, where it was so cold at night that men who collapsed from exhaustion on the way were stiffened corpses before sun-up. Langlois recalled reluctantly beating his laggards with a club to keep them moving, for their own good.

At dawn, the Régiment d'Afrique, such as it was, was tasked with the frontal assault. The Merina artillery, as usual, was ineffective. When the legionnaires were still more than 1,000 metres distant, the line of white-clad figures on the fortifications started to thin out. With the appearance of some marines and armed Sakalave tribesmen on a ridge line flanking the fortifications, the defenders' panic was such that the first legionnaires reached the impressively designed line of defences to find it unoccupied.

An English officer in the Malagasy army told the British vice-consul how 300 men died falling down a precipice in the rout, while others had bribed their officers to desert, which gave them the excuse to run away. They hardly needed an excuse: given only fifteen cartridges per man, all they had to do was fire them off at the first sight of the French and then retire. In desperation the Merinas were sending chain-gangs of prisoners up to the front, to replace the panickers.

Beyond the victorious French now lay a landscape of small villages surrounded by rice paddies, but what should have been a joyous advance on the capital became a grim test of endurance. Here in the uplands, fever was not the main enemy. Sheer fatigue was claiming lives. Even legionnaires toughened by years of campaigning in Algeria had used the last of their strength climbing up to the fortifications in the mountains. Suicides of those who could not face another day's marching became more frequent as morale plummeted to a new low with supplies running out. The daily ration of sixteen hardtack biscuits was reduced to eight, then four, with the sick paying for favours by handing theirs to fitter men. Men who dropped out singly were set upon by the natives and hacked to death, but Merinas taken prisoner were not killed because they were too useful as porters, to carry their captors' packs.

On the morning of 26 September, the head of the long-drawn-out column reached the last pass and looked down on Antananarivo, 20km distant. For forty-eight hours, the men were allowed to rest before the final assault, which cost the Legion six wounded, but was for the most part unopposed as Queen Ranavalona's army - whom its British advisers were unable to control - went through a mock defence and melted away at the first contact.

On the morning of 30 September the French occupied the final ridge, 4km from Antananarivo. From this vantage point, the artillery began to soften up the town by a bombardment that soon had the inhabitants fleeing into the countryside for safety. Just before the Legion was due to move off, spearheading the final assault, artillery damage to the roof of the queen's palace was rewarded by the display of a white flag. Langlois was angry that his legionnaires were ordered to stay with the guns and thus denied the honour of being first into the captured capital.

Prime Minister Rainilaiarivony was forced to accept humiliating surrender terms. Ahead of him lay exile in Algeria, but this did not guarantee peace on the Island he had left. Less than twelve months later a fresh uprising by the Menalambos party had to be put down by Gen Josef-Simon Galliéni, who exiled Queen Ranavalona to La Réunion and abolished the monarchy.

So Duchesne's costly victory was a case of taking a sledgehammer to crush a nut and nearly destroying the sledgehammer before realising that the nut was a grape. To the end, like the generals of the First World War dining and dancing in their chateaux behind the lines, he appears to have lived in a world of his own. On one occasion, noticing three officers and ten men from a pioneer unit returning from a work-site, he called out, 'That's a lot of officers for so few men!' apparently unaware that he was addressing all that remained of a pioneer company, reduced by disease and the privations of building bridges and laying causeways over swamps.[12]

All the weeks of agony, exhaustion and disease for the expeditionary force had cost 4,613 European lives, a quarter as many African troops and 1,143 Kabyles. Since battle casualties had been comparatively negligible, the blame lay squarely on Duchesne for organising his private war so appallingly.

The Legion had once again endured more than any other European troops. At roll call on 1 September, 450 legionnaires were still able to stand and answer to their names, which is not to say that they could all have held a rifle and assaulted an enemy position. But other units, of which 200th Infantry Regiment is an example, had ceased to have a separate existence because the numbers of fit men were so small they had to be reformed into *régiments mixtes*. Only twenty of 150 Chasseurs d'Afrique were still able to mount a horse. Even the Chasseurs à Pied, recruited largely from the fittest French Alpine troops, had only 350 men out of 800 still able to shoulder a rifle.[13] The 13th Marine Regiment was down to 1,500 men from its original strength of 2,400 after being in-country only three months. Of the sick, crammed into the holds of the transports for the return voyage, 554 died before reaching France and a further 348 afterwards.

In the sordid annals of inter-service rivalry, there are few worse examples than Gen Duchesne's cut-price campaign in Madagascar.

Chapter 20:

MIRACLE AND MASSACRE AT TAGHIT

Morocco and Algeria, 1901-1903

The paranoid mistrust of France's nineteenth-century leaders for their army, which could by force of arms so easily topple them from their precarious positions of power, appeared to be justified when a Jewish captain working in the War Office was sentenced to life imprisonment on Devil's Island in 1894 for allegedly passing intelligence to the German military attaché in Paris. Five years passed before Capt Alfred Dreyfus was brought back to France, to be court-martialled again and 'pardoned' for a crime he had not committed. Not until July 1906 was his name cleared and he reinstated with appropriate seniority after it had been ascertained that the true perpetrator of the crime was his colleague Ferdinand Walter Esterhazy, who had served as a Legion officer in the Franco-Prussian War.

Forgetting that many civilians had shared the anti-Semitic sentiments of Dreyfus' enemies in uniform, loudly trumpeted by the scandal sheet *La Libre Parole*, the public was encouraged to take the whole sordid business as yet another proof of the untrustworthiness of a military caste that was capable of leaking secrets to the enemy and unjustly sending one of its own to Devil's Island.

Accordingly, on becoming Minister of War in 1901, Gen Louis André established a system of secret files recording each officer's political and religious beliefs, promotion being reserved for those whose opinions, or lack of them, made them 'safe' appointees. When a nationalist *député* revealed this pre-Gestapo snooping in October 1904[1], André was forced to resign, bringing down the government of Emile Combes a month later.

However, the damage had been done. With the army now run by a clique of unimaginative time-servers, the manhood of France was to pay dearly the next time the Germans invaded in 1914. In the Pay Corps, for example, 31.9% of all officers rose to brigadier rank or beyond, while in line regiments only a miserable 1.5% of captains ever reached the rank of major.[2] So it was not surprising that ambitious and well-connected young officers went for the rapid progress only possible in administrative branches, while outspoken officers in the fighting arms stagnated with consequent effect on morale - nowhere more so than in the Legion, where outstanding leaders of men like Paul 'Loum-Loum' Brundsaux might have ended his career as a captain, had not the First World War swept him upwards to brigadier's rank.

By 1900 the European powers had staked their claims to most of the Dark Continent with the exception of Morocco, whose successive sultans and their advisers had managed to pursue an independent course between the minefields of colonial diplomacy. Although their country measures 1,328km north to south and 765km east to west, outside the coastal farmlands much of it is arid mountain and desert. Two things made it desirable to European colonisers: mineral deposits and its strategic position.

Because the northern tip of the country lies only 13km from the Spanish coast, the area around Ceuta and Melilla had been Spanish territory for centuries. In 1859 a dispute over the boundaries of Ceuta ended with the Spaniards expanding the enclave the following year, capturing Tétouan and staking out for themselves a larger Spanish zone that included the iron ore mines in the Rif Mountains. To buy its way out of the dispute cost Morocco an indemnity of $20 million, the acceptance of Ceuta's expanded frontiers, and the promise to cede to Spain another enclave at Ifni.

Other European powers with designs on Morocco included Germany and Russia, but Britain and France had specific reasons to get involved. The English, who had held Gibraltar with its harbour and naval dockyard since 1704, required at the very least Morocco's benevolent neutrality because of its position overlooking the straits through which thousands of their merchant and naval vessels travelled to India and the Far East each year since the opening of the Suez Canal. The French argued that Morocco had to be under their control to ensure that Algerian 'rebels' could not find asylum across the unguarded frontier between the two countries. In the event, to ward off a French invasion, the Moroccans defied their religious duty to protect fellow-Muslim Abd el-Kader and chased him back into Algeria for Gen Lamoricière to arrest.

Upon the death of Morocco's Sultan Sidi Muhammad in 1873, his son Moulay Hassan I continued the struggle to preserve his country's independence. After he died in 1894 while leading an expeditionary force that failed to subjugate the Atlas tribesmen who pillaged the trans-Saharan caravans, his *vizier* Ba Ahmed ruled as regent until 1901 in the name of the boy sultan Abd al-Aziz - an Anglophile lover of hi-tech, who scandalised the more religious of his subjects by riding a bicycle and installing an elevator in his palace.

For many reasons, the French in Algeria watched events in Morocco like a fox watching the chicken coop. The pipe-dream of a trans-Saharan railroad cost the life of Col Paul Flatters of the Bureau Arabe at the hands of the Tuareg across whose sands he was surveying its course. His companions were saved by an influential Tuareg woman named Tarichat, who took them into her tent and refused access to their would-be killers.[3] An even crazier plan than Flatters' - in fact, one unequalled until Soviet planners dried up the Aral Sea by diverting the waters of the Syr Darya and Amu Darya rivers - was the idea of diverting the River Niger to turn the Sahara into an inland sea. More realistic were the ambitions of twelve petroleum exploration companies after huge reserves of oil were discovered in the Sahara just when the future importance of motor transport was becoming obvious.

To encourage settlers to emigrate to Algeria, the French government offered free passages across the Mediterranean, but many were so disillusioned by the realities of life in Algeria that they caught the next ship back to Toulon or Marseilles. The 1902 census revealed that the only increase in the country's European population was the arrival in-country of 40,000 troops. If life was hard for European settlers, for the Muslim natives it was worse. In Paris, *Le Temps* newspaper wrote, 'Taxes, injustice and insults are all the natives have.'[4] Across the Channel the eponymous London *Times*, had this to say: 'The natives pay the majority of the taxes and receive little enough in exchange. They are placed in a situation where they must choose between resignation to utter misery and revolt.'[5]

The inevitable uprising started on 2 July 1900 with the decapitation of five Italian legionnaires in the Tuat area of the Sahara. In 1901 the British market for esparto grass, used to manufacture ropes, sandals, baskets and mats, collapsed and caused widespread unemployment in the highlands where it had been the main cash crop, forcing the dispossessed peasants into banditry. On 29 April 1901 the European village of Marguerite, only 80km from Algiers, was raided by 400 tribesmen, who sacked the place, killing almost all the 200 inhabitants. Repeated outrages of this nature drove many European farmers off the land that had been given to them and into the cities like Algiers and Oran where life at least resembled what they had known in Europe.

French forces based in Algeria crossed repeatedly into Moroccan territory with impunity. In 1845 the military government of Algeria had told its western neighbour that there was no point in defining a formal frontier south of a point roughly 300km inland from the coast between Aïn Sefra in Algeria and Figuig in Morocco, since it was an impoverished semi-desert region merging gradually into the Sahara, inhabited only by nomads who acknowledged no other authority than their own leaders.

The Moroccans took this to mean that, if a frontier were one day drawn further inland, it should be a line roughly north-south from this point. As can be seen from any map, France took advantage of this ambiguity to push the undefined border further and further west. In one incident, Col Bertrand commanding 1 RE had the nerve to lead 2,000 men across the desert with a supply train of 4,500 camels to occupy the Moroccan oasis of Igli, which lay well to the west of the undefined frontier. Once again, the men on the spot were exceeding their brief. Premier Georges Clemenceau, chiefly remembered today for the harsh revenge he took on Germany in the 1919 Versailles Treaty, announced that Morocco was '... a wasps' nest. We might certainly take possession of it, but at what cost in blood and money?'[6]

To list all the Legion's engagements in the disputed area during the last decade of the nineteenth century and the first decade of the twentieth would be onerous both to write and to read. To the men who were there, living the life of Beau Geste before he had been created by P.C. Wren - and who could recount every blood-chilling moment of their skirmishes and *razzias* in the mountains and deserts of North Africa - each awful ordeal, each gruelling march to the limits of human endurance and beyond, is the stuff of legend. To those who never heard the blood pounding in their ears as they raced to form a defensive square under fire from tribesmen who emasculated their captives, a few examples serve to give the tenor of legionary life during these years.

For endurance? After the capture of the important oasis of Timimoun in the Sahara on 7 May 1900, Maj Let led nine officers and 400 men of 2 RE back to base not by the vulture-flying route of 500km, but in a great odyssey that covered a distance three times as great in midsummer temperatures reaching 50° Centigrade in the shade, had there been any shade apart from the shadows thrown by their camels. After a march like that, over sand too hot to touch and long stretches of sharp, cutting stones, they arrived back at base with uniforms and boots torn to pieces.

For sheer nerve? In another raid like that of Bertrand, barely two weeks after the return of those men, Maj Bichemin with a battalion of Algerian *tirailleurs* was deploying a mounted company of 2 RE ahead of the main column at the end of a *razzia* in which they had carried off 4,000 camels. The mind boggles at the sheer length of a train of so many camels roped one behind the other, plodding through the dunes and across the stony wastes.

When it became obvious that the desperate owners intended to repossess the beasts which were both their wealth and their source of meat, a section of the mounted company was detailed off to escort the camels out of immediate danger, while the main body of troops engaged the desperate tribesmen. They, however, were not more stupid than their oppressors, and refused to take the bait, using the broken landscape to keep out of sight until the camels and their guards were beyond immediate help from the main column, when 300 horsemen and 600 tribesmen on foot launched an all-out attack. Such was its speed that, before the legionnaires could tether their mules, eight men were dead and another eight wounded. With desperate courage and impeccable fire discipline, they formed a square and fired only to kill. Somehow they managed to hold on long enough for a squadron of Spahis, alerted by the firing, to ride back and put their attackers to flight.

It is to be borne in mind that when small numbers of Europeans, as here, held off large forces of Saharan tribesmen, they had the advantage not only of training and discipline, but also weaponry, for many of the tribesmen were still armed with sword, lance and a small shield of hide carried on the left arm - of scant use against firearms.

On 1 June 1903 the newly appointed governor of Algeria, Célestin Jonnart, was ambushed near Figuig, at the very point inland where the French had begun pushing back the Moroccan frontier westwards. Had anyone asked them, the men of 2 RE included in the punitive column sent out to avenge this outrage two weeks later in the waterless wasteland between Wadi Gur and Wadi Zisfana might well have wondered what such an important civilian was doing in the disputed area. But nobody did ask.

And so it went on, the relentless pushing outwards of the industrialised Europeans and the hopeless resistance of the desert tribes with no more concept of *owning* the land in between this well and that oasis to which they had hereditary rights than had the Manhattan Indians who sold hunting rights on the island that bears their name in 1626 for trinkets and cloth valued at 60 guilders - and were then informed by Peter Minuit, Director General of New Netherland Province, that they had 'signed' a deed of land ownership and no longer had any right to be there.

Eccentric Europeans have always been attracted to the emptiness of arid lands. One such was a former officer of 4th Hussars named Charles de Foucauld. As a young blade, his reputation for extravagant womanising that culminated in shipping his mistress to Algeria in a packing case was known throughout the army - as was the lavishness of his table. When younger, his gluttony at family meals had terrified younger relatives, whose food he ate in addition to his own.

Posted to the Chasseurs d'Afrique, this self-indulgent playboy grew bored and resigned his commission, later to return to Algiers and apprentice himself to Oscar MacCarthy, the greatest authority on North Africa and its cultures, who was the custodian of the Moustafa Pasha library of 25,000 volumes. Living native-style in MacCarthy's house, Foucauld studied Arabic, mastering the language and script well enough to travel, disguised as an itinerant Jewish trader but at risk of his life if his imposture was discovered, to the forbidden city of Fez.

Learning enough of the Koran and Hebrew prayers for the purpose triggered a passionate conversion to Christianity, which led him next on pilgrimage to Rome. Becoming a Trappist monk, he accused his brothers in the Order of not living the 'life of Nazareth' in poverty, danger and discomfort sufficient for his excessive temperament. After his return to Algeria in 1901, he founded his own Order named the Little Brothers of the Sacred Heart of Jesus, whose Rule imposed such rigour and discomfort that he was its only member.

For his 'mother house', after several trials he chose a squalid and uncomfortable self-built two-metre square hermitage near the most desolate French base in Algeria, at Ben-Abbès on the Wadi Souara. The brand-new fort there looked out over the pink dunes of the Western Erg to the north and east. To the west a rocky wasteland stretched away into Morocco and to the south lay an unmeasured expanse of black rock and shale. Aïn Sefra, the nearest railhead and resupply point, lay 400km distant.

Whatever his former fellow-officers felt about his back-to-Nazareth religion, Foucauld's personal courage and indifference to illness, malnutrition and danger excited their admiration to the point that he seemed to them sainthood incarnate. The army and Legion officers in the 800-strong garrison at Ben-Abbès gave him ample provisions which he passed on to anyone who asked, be they slaves or free, while punishing himself by a near-starvation diet of gruel, figs and bread made from home-ground barley. His logic was that since the White Fathers and other missionary orders had failed at the cost of their lives to impose the Gospel on the natives, he would do it by his example of chosen poverty and humility. It entirely escaped his imagination that desert-dwellers, being eternally poor and close to starvation, saw no virtue in that condition.

Nevertheless, it seemed that God was on the French side when one of Foucauld's ex-slave converts was reported to have whispered to him in the hermitage confessional that Sherif Moulay-Moustafa had assembled an army of somewhere between

4,000 and 9,000 men - the impossibility of accurate head-counting was partly due to the tendency for tribes to withdraw from any joint enterprise when their hereditary enemies joined it. The intention was to administer a sharp lesson to the garrison of the remote post at Taghit, who had forced the surrounding tribes to pay tribute taxes.

The Col de Taghit was a naturally flat passage so narrow that only three camels could pass abreast between the huge dunes of the Grand Erg and an expanse of uncrossable, bare windswept rock. The approach to the col was barred by the *ksar*, or fortified village, of Taghit.[7]

Foucauld passed the alert on to the threatened garrison. At Taghit in the heat of midsummer, from 17 to 20 August 1903, Capt Susbielle with 470 men in an assortment of French uniforms and just two 80mm field howitzers as their sole artillery held Moulay-Moustafa's army at bay. The last reinforcements to arrive before the tribesmen surrounded the post were a platoon from a penal battalion and 1st platoon of 22nd Mounted Company of 2 RE under Lt Pointurier, who force-marched them 60km overnight to get there in time.

By the end of the brief siege when the tribesmen withdrew, nine defenders were dead and twenty-one wounded. Enemy casualties were estimated at 1,200. The crusader saint of Beni-Abbès wrote in his diary, 'This is the finest feat of arms in Algeria for forty years.'[8] As news of it travelled rapidly through the army network, it was regarded as a miracle that Foucauld's charity in 'giving the Gospel' to a humble slave-woman should have enabled the forewarned garrison to hold out and lose so few men against such odds.

Like many such legends, this one was false. Foucauld had nothing to do with warning Susbielle at Taghit because at the time he had been haggling with the Vatican for permission to celebrate Mass on a year-long tour of the Saharan oases with one donkey for him to ride on and one servant - a freed slave - walking behind. Hearing of the attack, he hurried to Taghit to fulfil his mission by ministering to the wounded. Arriving on 6 September, he cared for the injured and blessed the dead. The real miracle of Taghit was that none of the wounded died after his arrival, owing to Foucauld's selfless nursing.[9]

Even before he arrived, a mixed column of Spahis and legionnaires had been ambushed on 2 September by 300 tribesmen from Moulay-Moustafa's army at the bleak, featureless nearby caravan halt of El Mounghar, described by a legionnaire who was there as 'nowhere, nothing, a hypothetical point on a map'.[10] Choosing their moment when the legionnaires were preparing coffee at 0930hrs after an all-night march, the tribesmen stampeded the camels and the legionnaires' mules, together with their water and spare ammunition.

Divided into two groups on neighbouring hillocks - one commanded by Danish aristocrat Christian Selchauhansen and the other by Capt Vauchez - the legionnaires and some dismounted Spahis fought desperately. After the tall, blond Dane was mortally wounded, two of his men attempted to rescue him, but were killed in the attempt.[11] Command now passed to a corporal named Tisserand, who ordered the men to shoot only at certain targets. Thinking this meant they were out of ammunition, the tribesmen moved in too close, enabling Tisserand to lead a desperate bayonet charge that drove them off for the moment.

On the other hillock, Capt Vauchez was also among the early casualties. Command passed to Sgt Maj Tissier, killed shortly afterwards. The desperate survivors held their attackers at bay until 1620hrs, when Capt Susbielle returned with the Spahis who had been sent to get help and a group of volunteers, plus Capt Bonnelet of 1 RE at the head of his mounted company. By the time the tribesmen had been driven off, thirty-six men lay dead, forty-nine were wounded and only twenty legionnaires were still able to stand on their feet.

The subsequent enquiry placed the blame squarely on Capt Vauchez, while Tisserand's heroism was recognised by posthumous promotion to second-lieutenant. Since officers promoted from the ranks were customarily transferred to another regiment to avoid disciplinary problems with former comrades, 2nd Lt Tisserand (deceased) was gazetted to 1 RE.

Chapter 21

IN THE KINGDOM OF THE WEST

North Africa 1901-1914

To establish a political alibi, French accounts of cross-border incursions always stressed that the attackers - as at Taghit and El Mounghar - were 'Moroccan rebels'.[1] This conveniently overlooked the fact that the tribesmen concerned did not consider themselves subject to the sultan or anyone else and had no concept of lines drawn on a piece of paper, never having seen a map. Inside Morocco, or 'the kingdom of the West' to translate its Arabic title[2], events were moving in favour of one or other of the colonial powers. After coming of age in 1901 the young sultan Abd el-Aziz surrounded himself with European companions and adopted their customs, which scandalised the more religious of his subjects. Popular discontent was so widespread that the pretender Bu Hmara established a rival court for a while near Melilla.

Col Louis Hubert Gonzalve Lyautey believed deeply in the nineteenth-century vision of European colonial conquest as a civilising force in the world, having soldiered under Gen Galliéni in Vietnam and Madagascar. A cavalryman despite a childhood spinal injury, Lyautey returned to France in 1902 to command 14th Hussars at Alençon. It was apparently Governor-General Jonnart who recommended he be given command at Aïn Sefra, from where the disputed frontier with Morocco was policed.

Whatever Paris thought, Lyautey had no intention of fighting a defensive war. In his book, it was better to take the war to the enemy by laying waste his ground. To show the pacified tribes in Algeria that France could and would protect them from their enemies, wherever they came from, he planned three large bases 150km inside Moroccan territory, spaced approximately 150km apart, from which Legion mounted companies could move out to head off any threatening move into French-occupied Algeria.

These were not to be mere mud-brick blockhouses, but substantial citadels with high walls and gate towers - effectively townships founded for an exclusively military purpose. Although the immense five-storey barrack blocks in bel-Abbès and Saïda were built like barracks in any southern French city, these new bases of Lyautey's reflected his love of the exotic in their Moorish arches and windows shaded by louvered shutters like a modern tourist hotel. Since the only maps of the disputed area were made by the colonial army, he simply invented place-names for his new bases to obscure their actual locations inside Moroccan territory so that no interfering politician or diplomat would know exactly what he was up to.

He was greatly helped when Great Britain and France signed the Entente Cordiale on 8 April 1904 as a way of offsetting conflicting colonial interests and warning an increasingly bellicose Germany to keep its distance. Among other provisions, the Entente granted freedom of action to Great Britain for her colonial plans in Egypt and to France similarly in Morocco, with a proviso that reasonable allowance be made for Spain's interests there. Other clauses redefined the frontier of Nigeria in France's favour, and gave her control of the upper Gambia valley. The eastern parts of Thailand, adjacent to French Indochina, also became a French zone.

A secret clause of the Entente that was not made public for seven years was a provision that Britain would turn a blind eye to France annexing the whole of Morocco apart from the Spanish zone, should the sultan prove incapable of exercising authority over his own subjects. Since no sultan had ever been able to control either the desert tribes in the south who conducted most of the armed raids into Algeria or the fiercely independent Berbers in the Rif Mountains, this was London's green light to Lyautey.

Furious at the rapprochement of Britain and France - two traditional enemies Germany had been counting on dealing with separately - Kaiser Wilhelm II visited Tangier on 31 March 1905 and declared his support for Moroccan independence. Thus encouraged, the young sultan revoked his treaties with France. The resultant diplomatic panic was resolved at the Algeciras Conference that lasted from January to April 1906, where the trading rights of German and other nations in Morocco were upheld in principle, but the policing of the country was entrusted to France, with the north of the country being declared a sphere of Spanish influence. Italy's non-interference in this plan was bought by support for Rome's claims to Libya. Once these conflicts of colonial interest had been resolved, the European powers concerned met with Moroccan representatives at Algeciras to discuss the country's future, using the sultan's European debts as a lever to impose French and Spanish Customs collectors in Moroccan ports.

German pressure over Morocco thus achieved the reverse of what Wilhelm II had hoped. For the first time since the Crimean campaign the growing menace of German militarism forced the British and French general staffs to talk to each other. Reflecting their growing concern over the build-up of the Kaiser's navy, the support of the Royal Navy was promised to France during the amicable discussions, should her coastline and ports ever be menaced by the German Fleet.

Despite Moroccan protests to Paris about his encroachments across the border from Algeria, Lyautey took no notice and was rewarded in 1906 by being appointed commandant of the Oranais military district. What life was like for legionnaires caught up in his manoeuvring comes over quite well in one of the unpublished memoirs in the archives at Aubagne. Sgt Lefèvre's eyewitness account[3] goes into some detail about an operation commanded by Gen Vigy beginning in April 1908 when three French columns marched and rode across the ambiguous frontier to head off and destroy a *harka* - a coalition of Moroccan tribes threatening Lyautey's base at Bechar.

On 14 April the advance column consisting of 24th Mounted Company of 1 RE and a unit of Algerian Spahis encamped in the oasis of El-Menabha on the Wadi Guir. The legionnaires immediately started building defensive walls with the stones lying around, so that there was a semblance of a camp when the main party of Legion infantry, Algerian tirailleurs, some Zouaves and a battery of 80mm howitzers, all supported by a baggage train of 800 camels, arrived at 1700hrs. The *harka* was only 10km or so distant, its scouts well aware of the French moves. At 0510hrs the following morning shots from high ground overlooking the oasis killed men asleep in their white canvas tents while others grabbed their rifles from the stacks and took shelter behind the perimeter wall on the side nearest the firing in preparation for the onslaught.

It came from behind them. The camp was suddenly full of white-robed figures firing at anyone in French uniform and slashing holes in the tents, through which to shoot those still inside. Forty-seven legionnaires of 2 RE holding a section of the wall were forced to retreat back into the camp in the uncertain light, as were the tirailleurs on their flank. The battery was now firing at the hill where the main enemy force was concentrated. Under cover of this impromptu barrage, seventy-five legionnaires from the mounted company assaulted the hill and dislodged the main Moroccan force, losing ten killed and seventeen wounded in the process.

Luckily for the French, the raiders were more interested in grabbing loot than winning the battle. This enabled the defenders to gain the upper hand, more often with bayonet than bullet. As the blood-red sun came up over the arid landscape, they pursued the last interlopers for up to 2km from the oasis, shooting them down like cardboard targets on the firing range before retiring to count their losses. On the way back, they bayoneted or shot all the wounded Arabs before sitting down amidst the corpses in the ruin of their camp to have breakfast.[4] Since French losses were lower than the enemy's by a ratio of approximately two to one, Gen Vigy claimed the engagement as a victory - which it was not, since the tribes could afford to lose ten times more men than he could.

Northwest of Bechar in the palm groves at Beni Ouzien the *harka* reformed in early May. Approaching them along the valley of the Wadi Guir, Sgt Lefèvre had time to notice the comparative fertility of the land: fields of wheat and barley demarcated by low dry-stone walls, groves of palm trees and vegetable patches nestling like children in the protection of a mud-walled *ksar*. The intrepid photographer Jules Imbert photographed one of them shortly afterwards, in November or December 1908. His glass-negative pictures show the 8m-high walls of Bou Denib pocked with loopholes and firing slits, making it an ugly place to assault by a force without artillery.[5] Inside the walls were, not a few mud huts, but substantial lime-washed houses and a mosque whose white minaret rises high over the township.

After the monotonous dun-coloured desert through which they had marched, greenery was a relief for the legionnaires' eyes, but whatever poetic thoughts the sight of vegetation evoked were soon swept away in preparation for the business which had brought them there. After the artillery had softened up the target, 24th Mounted Company went in on foot. Once among the date palms of the oasis, they picked their way through the bodies, shooting and bayoneting everyone in their path. Lacking any communications, they could not call in the artillery, which had to cease firing or risk wiping them out. The 24th lost fifteen dead including the officer commanding, while enemy losses could not be estimated because the legionnaires had to withdraw with the coming of dusk. From the plantations, lamentations could be heard as families mourned their dead warriors.

Using the 24th as shock troops in this way cost Gen Vigy a reprimand on the grounds that he should have committed the infantry held in reserve. Gen Bailloud, commanding 19 Corps, also disapproved of the lack of any real battle plan which had placed the legionnaires of the 24th at a disadvantage in the palm groves without artillery support. In his opinion, Vigy had been obsessed with the idea of using a mounted company as elite troops, perhaps carried away by the dead officer commanding 24th Mounted Company pleading we-can-do-it. Whatever the reason, their reward after this mauling was to be held in reserve next day when the *ksar* of Bou Denib was taken by storm. They did, however, join in the looting after the 500 men and 300 women found there were driven out and held prisoner in open ground outside the walls. Lefèvre records the legionnaires loading their mules with dates, flour, clothes and weapons stolen from the houses.

Official accounts of battles are so clinical that one forgets the misery of warfare. On this occasion, a small chink in the official jargon of times, units involved and body counts allows a brief glimpse of suffering humanity: a desperate mother pleaded with Sgt Lefèvre to help find her child, from whom she had been separated during the fighting. When he did so, she gave him the only possession left to her: a glass necklace from the Sudan.

The *harka* that had drawn the French to Bou Denib disappeared into thin air, but reappeared to attack the *ksar* in August, by which time it was garrisoned by 24th Mounted Company with another unit of legionnaires in an outlying blockhouse. Successive assaults were broken by the artillery installed on the walls until a large relief column hove into sight, enabling a French attack on the *harka* by approximately 5,000 men and eighteen guns about dawn on 7 September.

So great was the slaughter that Lefèvre recorded attacking Moroccans being mown down by the artillery, which was then turned on the enormous tented camp of the *harka* spreading across the Plain of Djorf. Those who could, grabbed whatever belongings had not been destroyed in the bombardment and ran or rode away, each man for himself. Pursuing them, 24th Mounted Company found injured and dead Moroccans everywhere, still encountering what Lefèvre called, 'human debris at 10km from the battlefield'. The inhabitants of Bou Denib forced to bury the dead did the job in a hurry and not very well. 'Feet, hands and heads were to be seen everywhere sticking out. The foul stench (of putrefaction) was everywhere.'[6]

Vigy was not the only general impressed with the potential of the mounted companies, some officers arguing that the entire Legion should be reorganised on their model. Yet the price paid by legionnaires serving in them for earning twice normal pay was high: rest periods were few and men deserted from sheer exhaustion. Such was the turnover of trained men in mounted companies that when Gen Bailloud sought out the 24th in 1910 to congratulate the men who had fought at El-Menabha and Bou Denib, not one was still serving in the company.[7] In July 1910, eighteen legionnaires deserted from 3rd Mounted Company of 1 RE in Algeria. Despite the investigation laying the blame on the stress of constant campaigning, the cause appears to have been the murder of one of their sick comrades by Arabs after he had been denied his turns on muleback by a bullying NCO and could no longer keep up with the company on foot.

While the French were bludgeoning their way into Morocco across the desert, things were deteriorating rapidly inside the country. Within months of the Algeciras Conference, British and

French officials and civilians were being assassinated. When a number of French labourers rebuilding the port of Casablanca were killed in July 1907, the warship *Galilée* bombarded the city's native quarter before landing a force of marines to protect foreigners sheltering in the French Consulate from riots aimed at driving out the increasing number of European incomers. This was followed up by an expeditionary force of 3,000 men, including a Legion contingent, which grew in six months to an army of occupation totalling 14,000 men under Gen Albert D'Amade, who imposed martial law for 75km around Casablanca.

Although some Legion units coming from the desert, where there were no witnesses left alive to tell tales, did introduce bayoneting or shooting of wounded captives and looting of 'enemy' property, one would think that the German residents of Morocco would nevertheless prefer to have their personal safety from the Muslim rioters guaranteed by troops controlled by another European power. Yet, the Legion in particular was out of favour with them. In the ten years preceding the First World War, recruiting of Germans dropped by half, from 34% to around 16% of the intake.[8]

Part of the reason was that Germany's colonial wars gave young men seeking adventure in exotic places the chance to do so in the Kaiser's uniforms. Secondly, the increasing professionalism of the German army discouraged traditional NCO bullying that had previously driven conscripts to desertion and suicide. Thirdly, sensational books by ex-legionnaires like Erwin Rosen recounted details of punishments such as *le silo*, a conical hole dug in the ground, in which a defaulter was confined in his own filth for days and nights one end, unable to lie down or sit, so that when he was taken out, he was unable to stand. According to Rosen, Gen Négrier found fifteen *silos* occupied during an inspection of the barracks at Saïda and immediately abolished the punishment.[9]

Since punishment time did not count for pay or towards demobilisation, Rosen stated that a five-year engagement could easily last eight years or longer because of time spent confined to barracks or undergoing other punishment. With legionnaires' pay calculated at 5 centimes per day for the first three years and 10 centimes for the fourth and fifth years, he reckoned that the total pay for the five years was 127 francs and 75 centimes![10]

This sort of negative publicity fed the fires of anti-French feeling, creating a number of organisations such as the Völkerrechtsbund zür Bekämpfung der Fremdenlegion - or Protection League against the Foreign Legion - that dissuaded young Germans from enlisting in the service of foreign powers, especially France. The shortfall in recruits from east of the Rhine was to some extent made good by French marines and men from regular and colonial regiments with bad disciplinary records joining the Legion as a way of completing the fifteen years' service necessary to qualify for pension rights. Compounding the problem, foreign legionnaires with a record of good conduct who acquired French nationality after five years' service frequently opted to join regular regiments with better pay, conditions of service and prospect of promotion.

Alcohol was always a problem in the Legion, with inspecting Gen Herson, who decorated the flag of 1 RE at bel-Abbès on 27 April 1906, singling out for especial criticism in his report the huge upsurge in the selling of equipment to buy booze and consequent drink-fuelled destruction of equipment and barrack fixtures and fittings.[11] On a similar wavelength is the complaint of Col Désorthès commanding 2 RE that he had signed 1,482 sentences of thirty to sixty days' imprisonment in 1905, during which year there had also been 334 courts martial in the regiment. All this was in addition to the traditional physical punishments regularly handed out by NCOs and junior officers, such as *le tombeau* when a defaulter was made to dig his grave and sleep in it, no matter what the weather and *la crapaudine*, meaning roughly 'trussed like a turkey', for which a defaulter had his wrists pinioned behind his back, his ankles shackled and drawn tightly up to the wrists, resulting in agonising cramps with no marks of violence shown on the body afterwards.

Discipline might have been less harsh, had the Legion a sufficient complement of officers and NCOs. A line infantry company had three officers, six sergeants and eleven corporals for a nominal roll of 148 men, but which was often closer to 120. Legion companies usually numbered 200 or more, but had the same number of officers and NCOs without any supernumeraries.

The shortage was compounded by the policy of detaching legionnaires to postings spread out in Indochina, Madagascar, Algeria and Morocco. Also, the six-month convalescent leave to which cadres were entitled after serving two years east of Suez meant that a battalion often counted only five or six officers, with each company having only one or two sergeants.

It was easy under these conditions for German expats in Morocco, under the guise of offering hospitality to lonely men far from their homes and families, to entice several hundred discontented legionnaires to travel on a clandestine 'underground railway' back to Europe. In August 1908 Gen D'Amade signalled his ambassador in Tangiers regarding a German newspaper report that had come to his attention, which boasted how a German merchant vessel, the *Riga*, had landed fifteen German deserters from the Legion at Tangiers on 16 August.

On paper, desertion from the Legion at this time was no worse than from most French army regiments. In 1907, 36% of reservists in mainland France failed to report for training and between 1906 and 1911 the number of courts martial in the regular army doubled, which was unusual in time of peace. In the month preceding the general's signal, eighteen Germans had deserted from the Legion and the total for that calendar year included twenty-nine other Germans. The route they travelled was revealed in September 1908 by a neat piece of military detective work. A Russian, a Swiss, an Austrian and three German legionnaires in civilian clothing and waving a laisser-passer issued by the German consul in Casablanca attempted to board the mail steamer *Cintra* while it was moored in the harbour on its regular call.

A Legion NCO posted on the quayside for the purpose recognised some of the deserters and alerted the French harbour officer on duty, who informed the French consulate. Whether the boatman panicked on being ordered to return to the quay or, as some said, because the deserters were drunk from premature celebration of their escape, the dinghy in which they were being rowed out to the *Cintra* overturned, spilling them all into the water. Hauled soaking onto the dockside, the whole party now found themselves arrested by the military police waiting there.

MPs not being known for using kid gloves when apprehending deserters, the ripples on the diplomatic pond spread fast after the German consul and a Moroccan army guard from the consulate were also struck in the resulting fracas. In Berlin, Chancellor Bernhard von Bülow summoned the French ambassador to demand the release of the three Germans illegally arrested on non-French territory and an apology and damages for the maltreatment of consulate staff.

In Berlin Crown Prince Wilhelm, known to his British relatives for some intimate reason as 'Little Willy' - and who compensated by a predilection for wearing immensely long ceremonial swords that had to be held out in front of him to avoid tripping up anyone walking behind - immediately started threatening to unleash his favourite Pomeranian grenadiers west of the Rhine to avenge this dastardly insult to German sovereignty. Even more curiously, his father gave an interview to the eccentric Col Montagu-Stuart-Wortley, whose house in England he had rented for the summer. Stuart-Wortly sent it to Berlin for approval, where Bülow was apparently too busy to read it himself and passed it to a subordinate, who thought he was merely to correct the grammar, not edit the content.

A recipe for disaster.[12] Published in the *Daily Telegraph* on 28 October, the interview with the Kaiser stressed that he personally liked the British, whereas most of his subjects did not. It also included the immortal lines, spoken at a Guildhall dinner in the City: 'You English are as mad, mad, mad as March hares, (and) there is nothing in Germany's recent action with regard to Morocco which runs contrary to the explicit declaration of my love of peace'. On being briefed on this by the Foreign Office, the private response of King Edward VII - who had never much liked his cousin the Kaiser or Little Willy - was succinctly reduced to six words: 'Trust French Government will remain firm, E.R.'[13]

On 7 November the British and Russian ambassadors in Paris informed the Quai d'Orsay that London and Moscow supported the position taken by Paris vis-à-vis Berlin. This growing tension over a handful of Legion deserters could have been the spark that ignited the First World War, had not von Bülow advised the Kaiser that it would be some years before Germany was ready for war against an alliance of Britain, France and Russia. Instead he found a way out without loss of face when his Austrian counterpart advised going to arbitration at the International Tribunal at The Hague.

On 24 November the German submission to the Court was that treaty rights conceded by the sultan placed German citizens in Morocco under the exclusive jurisdiction of the German consul in Casablanca, that the arrest was therefore a violation of consular immunity and that the German deserters should be handed over to him. The French position was that Germany had no rights in Morocco over persons not of German nationality and no authority to protect Germans in the service of a foreign power, especially since the incident occurred in an area under military law.

Meantime, fifty German legionnaires of 2 RE were arrested after commandeering a train at gunpoint between Aïn Sefra and Saïda in the hope of reaching the distant coast and taking ship for Europe. The ringleader was a Bavarian named Pal, who had previously deserted from 1 RE, in which he had served under another name. A charismatic fantasist, he had convinced his companions that he was on a secret mission from Berlin to rescue them. His sentence was twenty years' hard labour.

Desertion was a game of chance. Those picked up within six days were simply dealt with as AWOL cases and men who deserted when drunk were often treated leniently. On one occasion a Legion sergeant attacked the NCO of a penal battalion who had forced a deserter to march back without boots.[14] Those returned by native troops, however, had often been maltreated and even dragged behind galloping horses. At the far end of the scale, men who deserted with their weapons and were tracked down by native soldiers were often killed by them because it was easier to bring back a head for the reward than a live man. Those caught by the enemy in the aftermath of a *razzia* had the worst fate, being used as slaves or slowly tortured to death.

None of this bothered the judges at The Hague. After deliberating from 1-19 May 1909, the five learned lawyers handed down a political compromise, rather than a judgement. It censured Germany for 'a grave and manifest fault' in aiding non-Germans to desert, and found it had no right to protect the German deserters either. France was diplomatically rebuked for using excessive force and lacking respect for consular staff. The real feeling of the Court, however, is evident from its failure to recommend return of any of the deserting legionnaires to German custody.[15]

Oil was poured on the troubled Rhine by the French confirming German trading rights in Morocco - probably because, with the country falling apart at the seams, they were not worth much anyway. Paul Revoil, a future governor-general of Algeria, bribed the young sultan with a loan of 7.5 million francs from the Banque de Paris et des Pays-Bas to finance his dream of modernising the system of land tenure in Morocco. The project failed miserably owing to a lack of European-educated surveyors and the general hostility to social change. Abd al-Aziz finally had to pay the price for what his subjects saw as excessive collaboration with the Europeans, being deposed by his brother Moulay Abd al-Hafid. Civil disorder increased until he in turn was forced three years later to beg the French to rescue him while besieged by tribesmen in Fez. The French relief column that raised the siege had a high Legion component.

With the country in turmoil outside the heavily occupied areas, Berlin despatched the gunboat *Panther* to Agadir on 1 July 1911, ostensibly to protect German interests during a local uprising, but in reality to show the French an iron fist in a very thin glove. Known as 'the Agadir Incident', this show of force was yet another of what Winston Churchill called footsteps on the road to Armageddon. That autumn the Cabinet in London was discussing contingency plans for eventual war, but the crisis was defused by a Franco-German convention of 4 November, which acknowledged the French protectorate of Morocco in return for strips of territory in the Congo basin being ceded to Germany. Spanish objections were overcome by a Franco-Spanish treaty of 27 November revising the previous Franco-Spanish boundaries in Morocco in favour of Madrid and the creation of the international zone around Tangiers.

Abd al-Hafid's rescue by the French came with a price tag. Forced to sign the Treaty of Fez on 30 March 1912, under which he acknowledged the French protectorate in return for the promise of support for his claim to be sultan, he was left with a hollow semblance of authority. Lyautey had been recalled to

France in 1910 to command an army corps at Rennes. Returning now as first Resident-General of the Protectorate of Morocco, one of his first acts was to replace Abd al-Hafid by his more malleable younger brother Moulay Jussef, who was required to 'govern' his country through a new administration staffed by French officials.

Country districts were administered by French contrôleurs civils; in important areas such as Fez officers of general rank supervised the administration. In the south a number of Berber chiefs or *caïds* were allowed to remain semi-independent. The impotence of Moroccans in government is exemplified by Muhammad al-Moqri, who was grand vizier when the protectorate was inaugurated and still held the same post when Morocco recovered its independence forty-four years later. He was then more than 100 years old.

While administratively Lyautey showed a tolerance and respect for local customs that impressed all races with his personal dignity and his competence, when campaigning he was ruthless. The pacification proceeded by fits and starts, with the forces pushing in from Algeria finally meeting those pushing east from the Atlantic coast at Taza only three months before the outbreak of the First World War in August 1914. It was a link-up more symbolic than real: Morocco was far from being subdued, for the nineteen tribes of the Rif continued to fight against both the Spanish in the north of their territory and the French in the south for many years to come.

A major asset of colonies was the reservoir of manpower they represented. When war loomed in 1914 the Legion was hard put to fulfil its quota. In 1913 Gen Antoine Drude, commanding Oran military district, had complained that 2 RE in Saïda was 500 men under strength and 1 RE in bel-Abbès 1,000 men short.[16] Ordered to send the equivalent of forty battalions to France, Lyautey fulfilled his quota with Zouaves, Spahis, the penal Bataillons d'Afrique and some newly raised Moroccan units. The only European troops left to him were two battalions of German and Austrian legionnaires, who had exercised their right not to be sent to fight against their countrymen. On their unlikely shoulders for the next four years rested the burden of maintaining French rule in Morocco.

Chapter 22

CHAOS AND CONFUSION

France, 1914

In November 1913 the hot topic on the terraces of smart boulevard cafes in Paris had been Marcel Proust's inability to find a publisher for his novel *Swann's Way*.[1] At Nouvelle Revue Française, editor André Gide would not touch it with a barge-pole. After the publishing houses Mercure de France and Fasquelle had also turned it down, Bernard Grasset did agree to publish Proust's novel, but with so little expectation of success that the author had to meet all the production costs out of his own pocket.

The population of the capital was still deep in denial during the first months of 1914. Although the state visit in April of Britain's King George V and his German queen, Princess Mary of Teck, was a show of solidarity for Berlin's benefit, everyone pretended officially that it was in celebration of the tenth anniversary of the Entente. Across the Rhine, the pace of German preparations for a massive offensive on land and sea was such that the question occupying the French general staff was not whether there would be war, but when and on what pretext Germany would launch the offensive so long planned by the great warlord Count Alfred von Schlieffen. The answer came when terrorist Gavrilo Princip assassinated Archduke Francis Ferdinand and his consort Sophie von Hohenberg on 28 June in Sarajevo.

In Paris, the first move of the general staff was sartorial. On 2 July the trousers of French soldiers, traditionally made of red cloth to conceal bloodstains on the battlefield, were changed to a grey-blue marginally less visible. On 15 July the long-resisted law introducing income tax was finally passed, and everyone knew why the government needed the money. In the last days of the month the army began requisitioning the wheat harvest. Before many weeks, it would be requisitioning also bridles, harness, reins and saddles, fodder - and horses of all breeds and sizes by the hundred thousand for remounts and to haul artillery and supplies to the front, where the few motor vehicles would become bogged down off-road.

On 1 August the country moved onto a war footing with the proclamation of a general mobilisation order, greeted by Swiss author Blaise Cendrars[2] and a group of fellow intellectuals in Paris calling on 'every man worthy of the name' who loved France to become actively involved in 'the most formidable conflagration in history'.[3] Equally enthusiastic for the French cause, titled Russian émigrés and Italian artisans living in Paris banded together with their fellows to try and find some military unit in which to enlist.

Members of the British colony received a formally worded circular *Object: The Formation of a British Volunteer Corps, to offer its services to the French War Minister.* Addressed to all men with military experience, it ended with the exhortation: 'God save the King! *Vive la France!*' British volunteers spent a few days drilling in the Magic City amusement park, while émigré Russians hired a cinema with a flat floor for the purpose, clearing the seats away to make themselves a drill hall. The Americans learned to march in the gardens of the Palais Royal after their mettle was aroused by the Committee of the Friends of France evoked the shared revolutionary past of France and the US. That appeal ended, *'Vive la France immortelle! Vive la colonie americaine!'*[4] Jewish immigrants issued a multilingual call to arms: '... even if we are not yet French by right, we are French in our hearts and souls and our most sacred duty is to place ourselves at the disposal of this great and noble nation in order to take part in its defence. Foreign Jews, do your duty and *Vive la France!*'[5]

On 3 August Germany formally declared war and made its point by the first air raid on civilian targets. The town of Lunéville suffered three bombs dropped by hand from the nacelle of a dirigible airship. War in the air had begun spectacularly, but this was to be the railway war par excellence: 4,278 trains were commandeered to move reservists from all over France to the front. In Britain eighty trains a day ran men and supplies to

Southampton docks for Gen Sir John French's initial expeditionary force of one cavalry and six infantry divisions.

The mobilisation order signed by President Poincaré did not directly affect the Legion, but since no foreigner was legally permitted to serve in the French army, it was to the Legion's recruiting offices that foreign volunteers were directed. A year earlier the total strength of 1 RE and 2 RE had been around 10,521 men. In the first eight months of the war 32,296 foreign volunteers flocked to the colours of France[6], many of them euphorically casting themselves as St George tilting at the barbaric German dragon to save the virgin of French literature, art and civilisation. Before the war ended with the Armistice of 11 November 1918, another 11,000 volunteers would join the Legion. Of these, a total of 31,000 were wounded, dead or missing in action by the time the last shot was fired.

Not all the men included in the statistics were true volunteers because many legionnaires from belligerent countries whose contract expired during the war chose re-enlistment in preference to internment as enemy aliens. In 1 RE, 70% of NCOs in 2nd Mounted Company were German. They and others risked a firing squad if taken prisoner by compatriots on the western front. For this reason many German- and Austrian-born legionnaires volunteering for Europe changed their names officially to French ones. Others opted to remain with the garrison forces in North Africa and Indo-China or to serve in theatres of war where they would not be confronting compatriots across No Man's Land. In the reverse direction, colonial troops from Vietnam, from North Africa and Senegal took ship for Europe, Algeria alone providing at its peak 170,000 men - who arrived in France in organised military units with their own officers and were often thrown into the worst sectors of the line without any preparation. In contrast, the flood of foreigners volunteering their services inside France produced chaos and confusion, had more been needed. The urgent requirement was for tough and disciplined veterans, not enthusiastic amateurs who would be more liability than asset.

On 8 August the *Journal Officiel* finally announced that foreign civilians in France might enlist for the duration of hostilities, but only in the Foreign Legion. Not all of them stayed. Those whose homelands became allies of France, transferred to serve with their compatriots. Thus British legionnaires later transferred to the BEF, Italians served under their own flag when Rome declared for the Allies and Americans left to become 'doughboys' with all the advantage of combat experience after the US entered the war in 1917.

In his autobiographical *La Main Coupée*, Blaise Cendrars wrongly averred that, 'it had taken a whole month of talks with the Minister of War before he ... would accept into the recruiting offices this army of foreign volunteers'.[7] Cendrars signed up on 3 September, by which time the German guns were audible throughout Paris, but he was not among the first volunteers. Two weeks earlier, on 25 August after enlisting at the Hôtel des Invalides across the Champs de Mars from the Eiffel Tower, the Harvard poet Alan Seeger led fifty fellow Americans through the streets waving the stars and stripes, cheered by crowds all the way to the Gare St-Lazare, where they entrained for Toulouse with no idea of the hell they had signed up for. Just before he was killed two years later, Seeger wrote in his diary, speaking for so many of the eager volunteers in August 1914: 'It was for the glory alone that I engaged.'[8]

On 12 August 1 RE and 2 RE each had one *bataillon de marche* in Morocco and formed four further half-battalions for service in Europe, excluding legionnaires from future enemy nations, who were to stay in Africa. On 28 August the men from 1 RE entrained at bel-Abbès and headed north once in France, absorbing Italian and other volunteers at the recruiting depot in Avignon on the way. There, Swiss recruit Jean Reybaz recorded his horror at the way in which the veteran legionnaires stole everything from the middle-class volunteers.[9]

The men from 2 RE followed a different route after leaving Saïda, stopping in Toulouse to absorb into the 2nd/2nd those US and other volunteers who had been training at the Quartier Pérignon. American Henry Farnsworth considered the Legion NCOs' military competence mighty comforting after all the pointless marching up and down he had put in under drill sergeants from the Paris fire brigade. If the reaction of the hardened NCOs of 2 RE to these soft civilians they had rapidly to convert into soldiers can be imagined, many volunteers were equally horrified to find themselves sleeping in dormitories with men who habitually stole comrades' equipment rather than clean their own, and occasionally sold it for drink. The politically conscious East European refugees were also aghast to find that their NCOs gave not a damn for politics and did not care for whom or against whom they were fighting.[10]

The friction when lesser-educated long-service professionals and better-educated short-service amateurs are thrown together in uniform - as during the US draft for Vietnam and the years of National Service in Britain - was far more acute in 1914 when the class/education gap was so wide. Seeger wrote, 'Discontent has more than the usual to feed upon, where a majority of men who engaged voluntarily were thrown into a regiment made up almost entirely of the dregs of society, refugees from justice and roughs, commanded by NCOs who treated us all without distinction in the same manner they were habituated to treat their unruly brood in Africa'.[11]

The Legion was more than ever 'run by its sergeants' because many serving Legion officers seeking promotion had transferred to line regiments during the summer of 1914 in the erroneous belief that the government would respect the prohibition on serving in France embodied in the Legion's original constitution. The shortfall was made up by outsiders who came to serve with Legion units, but stayed only long enough to gain a citation and maybe the Croix de Guerre, awarded to all members of a trench raid that brought back prisoners for interrogation. Their swift arrival and departure did nothing to build up the essential trust between officers and men. One of the reservist sergeants of 2nd/1st, whose most important duty was distributing the mail, was Edouard Daladier, the future French Prime Minister.

The French general staff has rightly been much criticised for wasting lives to no purpose, as have British generals like Haig, who took over command from Gen French on 17 December 1915. The *idée fixe* in Paris on the outbreak of war was to throw everything into an all-out attempt to regain the so-called lost *départements* of Alsace and Lorraine, seized by Prussia after the war of 1870-71. This obsession blinded the French General Staff to the main thrust of the German armies under Count Alfred von Schlieffen's plan, modified by his successor Helmuth von Moltke.

Schlieffen had planned to cope with a war on two fronts - against France and Russia bound by treaty to support each other - by leaving only a holding force on the eastern front where the enemy needed six weeks to mobilise its huge but ill-equipped army[12] and use this crucial time-lag to knock out France by holding the southern part of the western front with eight divisions while fifty-four divisions on the right flank of the German advance,[13] where it would avoid the extensive French frontier fortifications by rolling through neutral Belgium, bypassing the fortresses at Liège and Namur - which were sited to protect the approach to Brussels, and not Paris - before entering France near Lille. The Plan was then to divide forces, one half wheeling southwards to sweep around Paris while the other swept eastwards to sever the French line of retreat from the frontier. With the French armies in the north encircled and Paris surrounded, France would be forced into a humiliating surrender. Only after a lightning victory in France did Schlieffen intend to ship the major part of his armies eastwards rapidly by rail to deal with the Russian bear, slowly awakening from his winter sleep.

But Schlieffen retired in 1905. His successor Gen Helmuth von Moltke the Younger - son of the victor of 1871 - was too cautious to put so many eggs in the flanking basket and thus threw away the chance of rapid victory while the French were too obsessed with Alsace and Lorraine to stop him. The result was an early success as his troops pushed through 'poor little Belgium' where Austrian Skoda 305mm howitzers and Krupp's 420mm Big Bertha cannon - the largest and most powerful artillery pieces ever produced until then - fired delayed-action shells that exploded inside the fortresses after penetrating their reinforced-concrete walls.

Moltke nearly made it to Paris before being held, but final victory eluded him because, although his artillery easily outranged the French 75mm guns, one cannot occupy terrain with guns, and his watering-down of Schlieffen's plan meant that he had too few troops available at the sharp end to encircle the capital or cut off the French retreat. So, when he had to wheel east while still to the north of Paris, Gen Galliéni as military commandant of the city heaved a sigh of relief, knowing that Moltke must lack the men and resources to encircle the city as his father had done in 1871.

By then, President Poincaré and the government were safely removed to Bordeaux, about as far from the advancing Germans as they could get. In the French army's final desperate stand before Paris that now ensued, sleep was hard to come by as the guns thundered just over the horizon and whatever troops could be thrown together were trucked to the front an hour or so away in commandeered taxis and open-top omnibuses. The Battle of the Frontiers, as this stage of the war came to be known, was the largest armed conflict history had seen, with more than 2 million men involved. From 14 August to the start of the first battle of the Marne on 6 September, it cost France one in ten of her officers and 300,000 other ranks. In the fighting on the Marne during the next twelve days the much decorated Moroccan Division alone lost forty-six of its 103 officers and 4,300 of their 5,000 men.

On 18 October, the 2nd/1st and 2nd/2nd Régiments de Marche (conventionally referred to for convenience as 'RM') marched out of their camp at Mailly in Champagne to relieve the Senegalese light infantry who had been holding the line at Verzy, a scant 4km distant. Immediately, with one of those strokes of the admin pen that bewilder simple soldiers, they were split up, with 2nd/2nd despatched to the Aisne front and 2nd/1st sent a few kilometres north to the front at Prunay, where the forward trench was within 700 metres of the enemy. It was in this 'relatively quiet' sector of the front that they and two other RM would remain, brigaded with 4th RM of Algerian tirailleurs until April 1915.

'Relatively quiet' covered minor adjustments of the line that cost lives and included not only the hazards to which the veterans had been accustomed in North Africa, but also the impossibility of ever getting warm and dry in the cold and mud of the trenches, plus new terrors like the *Minenwerfer* mortars that hurled unwieldy bombs short distances and the risk of being literally under-mined and blown sky-high without warning. Among the wounded was Maxim Gorky's adopted son Legionnaire Zinovi Pechkoff, who gained the Médaille Militaire for losing an arm, but went on to be a captain and command a battalion in Morocco and Algeria until 1939 after inventing an original method of mounting

The Legion in France 1914-18

Actions featured in text: 1. Verzy; 2. Prunay; 3. Clermont-en-Argonne; 4. Neuve Chapelle; 5. Ypres; 6. Hill 140; 7. Souain/Navarin Farm; 8. Cumières; 9. Assevilliers/Belloy-en-Santerre; 10. Aubérive; 11. Hangard; 12. Château-Salins

his horse by seizing the reins between his teeth and using his single arm to vault into the saddle. Everyone was worn down by the impossibility of a normal sleep-rhythm. With the cookhouses situated three hours' march to the rear, there was no way of reheating whatever food did arrive.

Almost 5,000 Italians enrolled in 4th/1st RM of the Legion[14] commanded by Lt Col Ricciotti Garibaldi, son of the Italian revolutionary leader. First dubbed 'the Italian Legion', it became known as the Garibaldi Legion because it still numbered among its officers four members of the illustrious Italian family after Capt Bruno Garibaldi died in its first action in Champagne.

On 26 December 1914 at 0300hrs those who had managed to sleep in the sub-zero temperature were awakened. After an issue of eau-de-vie they moved up into the front line about 500 metres from the enemy. The barrage supposedly cutting the German wire directly ahead of them was so deafening that few men could hear the shouted orders and the buglers playing the Charge. Despite this, the Italian sappers, who had been cutting passages through the French wire in the night, arrived at the German entanglements to find them still intact. Hacking away with their wire-cutters, they were mown down by machine guns from the German lines and the eventual way through the wire was provided by the weight of dead men pulling it down for their comrades to scramble over.

The objective only partially attained, they crouched in the German trenches or a few metres short of them among the bodies of comrades and those defenders who had been too slow to run for the rear. Then the German artillery began, pre-ranged on the captured trenches. After an hour of steady if unspectacular losses, the Italians were ordered to retreat back to the start line, in the course of which they endured more casualties.

On 5 January, the 1st and 3rd Battalions were again in action. After eight huge mines laid by sappers beneath the German positions opposite them were detonated, they seized three lines of trench, taking more than 100 prisoners and two machine guns, temporarily advancing the line by 500 metres. On 7, 8 and 9 January they were again in combat against the Silesian dragoons and Hessian Landwehr, losing 429 including another grandson of Giuseppi Garibaldi[15] to no obvious effect before being reformed on 10 January at Clermont-en-Argonne.

On 5 March 1915 their high losses and the certainty of Italy's coming declaration[16] on the Allied side - in order to exact revenge on Austro-Hungary for its long occupation of the peninsula that had been ended with French help - entailed the disbandment of 4th/1st RM. The majority of the Italian legionnaires headed for home and only 127 volunteered to stay in France with the 1st Brigade of the Legion, commanded by Col Théodore Pein.

Chapter 23

GUNS AND GAS IN THE TRENCHES

France, 1915

Pein was an interesting man of action, who could not have been more different from the blasé French staff officers in their châteaux behind the lines. A first-generation *pied noir*, to whom the desert and mountains of North Africa were home, he had once defied Lyautey to prove that the Sahara could be crossed on a motorcycle. When it broke down after a few days' crashing along desert camel-tracks, he and his batman almost died of thirst, but his spirit was unscathed.

His men included American journalist Henry Weston Farnsworth of Groton and Harvard, who noted in his barrack room a grizzled Alsatian who had done fourteen years with the Legion in the Far East, a black Fijian student from Oxford and former brigadier Moussorgsky, a cousin of the composer. Fellow scribe Blaise Cendrars listed in his intake of volunteers 'tailors, furriers, upholsterers, goldsmiths and concierges, night-club musicians, racing cyclists, pimps and pickpockets … also a few sons of the nobility like the Polish knight Przybyszewski and Bengoechea, the son of the richest banker in Lima, Peru, plus a few intellectuals from Montparnasse who, like me, were enchanted by the obscene argot of these exhilarating companions.'[1]

The reference to cyclists was presumably to François Faber, the Luxemburger who had won the Tour de France in 1909. Promoted corporal, he was swiftly killed in combat. Had Cendrars wanted further alliteration beginning with the letter *p*, he could have mentioned a painter and a prince and future king. Moïse Kisling, whose fellow-artists Modigliani, Cocteau and Max Jacob frequented his studio in Montparnasse, enlisted in August 1914 for the duration, as did Prince Louis II of Monaco.

Veterans the Legion NCOs certainly were, but desert-warfare tricks like sleeping with rifle tied to one's wrist to prevent Arab intruders stealing it were useless in the war just beginning - as were the rifles for most of the time. The French army standard-issue Lebel rifle - with its twisting bolt action that jammed with mud or sand far too easily and a long barrel that impeded movement in the confines of the trenches, gave away movements by sticking up above the parapet and, with bayonet attached, was fatally unwieldy at close quarters - was of so little use against machine guns, mortars and artillery that popular humour alleged it had been invented to keep rear-echelon NCOs busy with drill and weapon cleaning. The well-honed blade of an entrenching shovel was of far more use to these biped trench rats, both for digging the holes that saved their lives from air-bursts and for slashing an enemy's face or cleaving his head when taking a trench.

Cendrars described the sordid reality of moving up to the line, so different from the glory of battle he had imagined. To avoid being seen by a German spotter plane that brought down a 'stonk' which could wipe them all out before they ever reached the front line, they moved at night, groping their way without even a candle through knee-deep mud where the duckboards had been destroyed by shelling, tripping over spilled sandbags and painfully colliding with wattle splinter barriers placed across the trench.

The new arrivals' noses picked up the strange cloying stink of unburied bodies and the lingering acrid chemical bite of explosives as well as more familiar smells that told them the clinging mud through which they were walking and into which they fell from time to time was compounded as much of excrement and urine, for there was no sanitation except the trench itself. Sleep tempted no one on the first night, ears straining to distinguish the scrabbling of rats foraging for human flesh from the rustle of a raiding party about to kill them with stick grenades, clubs and bayonets. When dawn came, the landscape in front of them and behind was a tortured treeless wasteland, viewable only through a crude cardboard periscope, except by those intent on suicide.

The days were spent huddled on wet straw mattresses in man-made caves, with Balaklava helmets pulled down over their faces, muffled in as many layers of clothing as possible - all of them damp.

For companions, there were the rats and lice. At dusk, weary men emerged to repair the stretches of trench destroyed during the daylight bombardments, to risk their lives in the communication trenches fetching water and food that was rarely hot by the time they got it back to their comrades, to stand sentry in the darkness full of menace and movement, to slither out into No Man's Land with a wiring party and repair the entanglements damaged that day at risk of bumping into a German patrol or, worst of all, being despatched to raid a trench and bring back a shivering, terrified Bavarian or Saxon for interrogation by men who had killed his comrades.

Bumping into the enemy in the dark of No Man's Land, they were always at a disadvantage, for the Germans were better fed and clothed, better trained and far better equipped. Cendrars and Seeger both agreed how the *poilus*[2] coveted German grenades, Luger automatic pistols, electric torches and flares that were the most prized booty. The disparity was general: even the French artillery was outranged by the German batteries, safely out of reach of counter-battery fire. The commonest piece on the French side was the famous 75mm gun designed in 1897, which lacked the elevation necessary to hit a target concealed behind a fold in the terrain, and often had not the range to roll a barrage ahead of an advance. While the guns were being moved forward to a new position, the advancing men had no cover at all and would often be at the limit of the new range, to find themselves taking friendly fire as soon as their own guns opened up anew.

It was nine-tenths boredom interrupted by one-tenth terror, someone said. Seeger described in a letter to his father dated 11 January 1915, which was hardly calculated to reassure an anxious parent, how he and Kiffin Rockwell, a fellow Harvard man who would become famous as one of the Lafayette Squadron pilots later in the war, were manning an observation point in a ruined chateau identified only as 'C …' to get through the censorship. A German grenade landed at their feet. By reflex, Rockwell bent and threw it away just in time. Seeger ran to tell their corporal that the enemy were very close. He yelled, '*Aux armes!*' as another grenade landed inches away. Throwing themselves flat, they lifted their heads after the explosion to see the door kicked in as the first

Germans poured into the room. As the trio fled for their lives, the corporal was shot and battered to death with rifle butts.[3]

The western front was not the only campaign where the Legion was in action. From St Petersburg, Grand Duke Nikolai had been begging for any intervention to draw Central Powers' forces away from the eastern front and give the Russians a breathing space. So, when Turkey declared war against the Allies early in November 1914 the French and British general staffs re-examined a plan to seize by force the 50km-long Dardanelles channel and occupy Constantinople. The difficulties were immense, but on 2 January 1915 the Allies agreed to mount a combined naval and military operation. On January 28 the Dardanelles committee decided on naval action alone, using obsolete warships too old and slow for the main battle fleet. On 16 February this decision also was modified, since the navy could not force a passage as long as the well-sited coastal batteries remained in Turkish hands.

With a large Franco-British ground-force assembled in Egypt, the Royal Navy bombardment of land targets began on 16 February but was halted by bad weather and not resumed until the end of the month. Some demolition parties of marines landed almost unopposed, but bad weather again intervened. On 18 March the bombardment continued, but the loss of three battleships sunk and three others damaged confirmed naval opinion that success required large-scale landings. These began in the early hours of 25 April - the British at Cape Hellas with Australian and New Zealand forces on the Gallipoli peninsula while the French force of four battalions of Tunisian *Zouaves* and one Legion battalion - rather grandly designated the Régiment de Marche d'Afrique and commanded by Gen Maurice Sarrail - was landed opposite on the Anatolian shore near Kumkale.

The legionnaires fared no better than the British and Anzac forces on the other shore. By the end of the first week of May only one captain survived to command the RMA, under him a few hundred men who included one Legion NCO and a handful of legionnaires. Their agony was not yet over. Regrouped into a multi-national force under Sarrail, ahead of them lay the long slog from Salonika through parts of Macedonia, their only real success the capture of Monastir from the Bulgarians. Despite Sarrail hailing this as a victory, so few of his 'army' were still alive that it was dissolved shortly before the end of the war and the survivors shipped back to France.

Meanwhile, in France by April 1915 the volunteers had modified the protocol of what they regarded as useless confrontations that led only to reprisal raids. In a forerunner of the 'fragging' of over-zealous NCOs and officers in Vietnam, Cendrars recounts his squad ambushing an officious lieutenant, to discourage him from paying further visits to the front line.[4]

When a hidebound NCO wanted to put Cendrars on a charge for fraternising with the enemy, he explained that both sides needed fuel from a slag-heap between the lines in this coal-mining area. Rather than kill each other for something of which there was plenty for everyone, they took turns - the Germans one night and the legionnaires the next. Was that fraternising? And if the odd present of beer or food or cigarettes or newspapers was left where the other side would find it the following night, that had nothing to do with winning or losing the war, so far as the volunteers were concerned.[5]

As the weather improved, a new hazard was introduced. The Germans had been using gas since January in Poland, where the air had been too cold for it to vaporise with full effect. On the western front, the French had shot tear gas grenades into German trenches as early as August 1914. At Neuve Chapelle in October that year German shells containing a chemical irritant that produced violent sneezing fits had landed in the French lines. Just after 1700hrs on 22 April 1915 French sentries in the Ypres salient watched uncomprehendingly as a ground-clinging yellow-green mist floated towards them from the German lines.

The problem with releasing gas from canisters was that a change in wind direction could blow it back on the chemical squads. Once the technical problems of compressing it into shells had been solved, the gas could be delivered accurately on target. To all the other horrors of the trenches was added that of being blinded and having the lining of the lungs so burned that men drowned in their own secretions. The banging of an improvised gong and the cry of 'Gas!' had everyone fumbling for his unwieldy mask, wearing which he had to sleep, to dig in and even to climb over the parapet and run through mud, wire and machine gun fire. Horses and the dogs used for carrying messages between the front and reserve trenches to coordinate artillery barrages also had to be accustomed to wearing helmets like huge feed-bags strapped over their eyes, nostrils and mouths. The first protection the legionnaires had was home-made. By urinating on a sock and holding it as a pad against the nostrils, the naturally present ammonia had some neutralising effect on chlorine gas, but worse was to come when mustard gas was introduced by the Germans in 1917, causing burns on the slightest skin contact that erupted into huge blisters.

The next major action in which the Legion took part was on altogether another scale. On 9 May 1915 the Moroccan Division including four battalions of 2nd/1st RMLE was tasked with taking a spur of the Vimy ridge 10km north of Arras and designated Hill 140 on their officers' maps. Before dawn a five-hour 'softening-up' barrage kept the Germans down in their deep dugouts on Hill 140 and was supposedly cutting the barbed wire entanglements between the lines. At 0958hrs the guns were silenced. The stillness is there yet, echoing in visitors' ears nine decades later. Still there too are the holes and hummocks sculpted from cold earth and warm bodies by the barrages, now softened by time but still oddly unnatural. Green with grass it is again, but this is not a pleasant land.

On that fatal morning, the silence was broken at 1000hrs by whistles in the other regiments and bugle calls in the Legion trenches, followed by shouted commands as temporarily deafened officers and men clambered up the scaling ladders and over the parapets to walk, weighted down with weapons and equipment, towards the wire which, as so often, was not cut. Emerging unscathed from their dugouts, so deep and well-constructed that they made the Allies' trench accommodation look like the scrapings of animals, the Germans manned their machine guns before the legionnaires with wire-cutters had made the first snip on the intact wire. At 600 rounds per minute they scythed down the men queuing up to pass through the narrow gaps before they had time to work out that this assault was not going to be the promised 'walk-over'.

Seeger described it thus:

> ... on those furthest rims of hallowed ground
> where the forlorn, the gallant charge expires
> when the slain bugler has long ceased to sound,
> and on tangled wires
> the last wild rally staggers, crumbles, stops,
> withered beneath the shrapnel's iron showers ... [6]

From behind the German lines, artillery pre-ranged on the wire began blowing into shreds living and dead bodies. But still the survivors pressed on to the next wire and then to the trenches beyond. Finding them largely deserted, they cleared out the remaining defenders with grenade and bayonet. No time to feel victorious: before they could take shelter in the recently vacated dugouts, some veteran who knew what to expect yelled at the novices that a fresh barrage was incoming. Whether ill-timed 'friendly' shells or German ones ranged on the lost trenches, what did it matter? Each was as deadly as the other.

Where were the reinforcements, they asked each other. The 156th Infantry Regiment was supposed to be keeping up with the Legion on its right flank, but became bogged down in the outskirts of the well-fortified road junction of Neuville-St-Vaast. The legionnaires had moved too fast. Now they paid the penalty. With snipers and machine guns in their rear, they were exposed in a salient impossible to hold. But hold they did. All three battalion commanders dead, Col Pein unwisely but typically left his command post to go forward with the second wave, and took a sniper's bullet through the lungs while reconnoitring between the first and second German lines in expectation of a counter-attack. Rescued by two legionnaires from the shell-hole into which he had dragged himself, he was carried back to the French lines, but died shortly afterwards and was buried in the nearby village of Acq.

A counter-attack by an Alsatian unit around 1500hrs drove the legionnaires - there were few officers still alive by then - from the crest of Hill 140, but they clung to the lower slopes, waiting for the reinforcements that did not come, with only field rations and water they had carried with them, plus what could be looted from abandoned German stores and dead bodies. Nor was there any sign of activity on their flanks, with the exception of the Algerians in the Moroccan Division to the left. By nightfall casualties mounted to 1,889 dead - nearly half the men who had climbed out of their trenches twelve hours before.

Exactly a week later, 2km northwards along the line, the survivors of Hill 140 were in the second wave of an attack on Hill 119, behind the Zouaves who bore the brunt of the attack. Under heavy machine gun fire they crossed the ravine below the hill and took the position with heavy losses. One mistake they did not make this time was to leave any Germans alive behind them. The main hazard was ill-coordinated friendly fire. Reinforcements failed to arrive so that the Legion and the Moroccan Division had to hold the position all night after a heavy counter-attack at around 2000hrs had them at a disadvantage in trenches that had not been 'turned around' and therefore had the parapets facing the wrong way.

All the valour was in vain. On the morning of 17 June began a German barrage so heavy that the order was given to retreat, back across the ravine once again swept by machine gun fire, where casualties included one of the replacement battalion commanders. To the men involved it had been a bloodier 'do' than 9 May, although officially out of an attacking force of sixty-seven officers and 2,509 men there were only forty-five dead and 320 wounded. Missing in action were another 263 men who would never again answer *'Présent!'* at roll call.

In their innocence the volunteers had thought that selfless courage would force a breakthrough to end the war swiftly. For the first time in their privileged lives they had known terror and discomfort and seen the friends with whom they enlisted die, while their officers came and went in the hunt for career prospects and the martinet NCOs from the Paris fire department departed for more congenial duties. Lacking the regular soldier's conviction that thinking was someone else's job, they voiced their opinions that the Allied war effort was not being managed well enough to merit their sacrifices.

To some extent the Legion tradition of mixing nationalities muted this protest, but units where many men shared a common language made their discontent heard. On 16 June 1915 the Greek Battalion refused to advance, telling their colonel that they had enlisted to fight Turks, not Germans. Whether because he promised them a transfer to the Dardanelles, or because the Algerian light infantry behind them were fixing bayonets, they agreed to go forward. But words are not action. In vain Swiss-born Lt Marolf yelled in Greek, 'Forward!' but his men had disappeared in the other direction.

Running desperately after them, he found them cowering in shell holes and trenches. On 19 June the colonel had again to intervene - after which the Greeks were sent out of the line 'for training'. The subsequent court martial acquitted Marolf and the battalion was disbanded, its Greek legionnaires being despatched to the Turkish campaign, where those who continued the fight earned no recorded distinctions. More or less simultaneously, men from Alsace and Lorraine who had not declared a wish to serve on the western front were reassigned to North Africa and other theatres. Losses in action, plus these departures, brought Legion strength in France from four battalions at the beginning of May down to two - with plummeting morale.

The Greeks, perhaps because they were the first to mutiny, got away with it. The Russian volunteers were less lucky.[7] They included many second-generation Jewish immigrants from Eastern Europe living in Paris, who had joined up to avoid incarceration as enemy aliens. Between seven and eleven were court-martialled for refusing to obey orders and shot.[8] After this, recruitment of foreign Jews declined precipitately. Whether there was an element of anti-Semitism is unknown: reliable sources put the number of executions in French army units in 1915 as high as 442, nearly as many as the 528 men who were shot after the great mutinies of 1917.[9]

Some say that this purge of dissidents is the reason why Legion morale climbed back up from its 1915 low, but it is equally possible that the numbing effect of trench warfare simply sapped the energy to do anything except go on fighting with the expectation of dying - not for France or *for* anything. The Tommies' song said it all: 'We're here because we're, because we're here, because we're here...'

Taken out of the line to regroup in July, the remnants of 3rd/1st and 4th/1st were amalgamated into 2nd/1st and 2nd/2nd RM attached on paper to the Moroccan Division. By now they were wearing the new horizon-blue uniform and distinctive 'Adrian' steel helmet, with little to distinguish them from other *poilus*.

It was about this time that Alan Seeger wrote in a letter home: 'If it must be, let it come in the heat of action. Why flinch? It is by far the noblest form in which death can come. It is in a sense almost a privilege… .' To modern eyes, that reads so high-flown. But that was Alan Seeger. T. S. Eliot, a classmate of his at Harvard wrote when reviewing Seeger's book *Poems*, '… as one who knew him can attest, (he) lived his whole life on this plane, with impeccable poetic dignity; everything about him was in keeping.' Dignity? Yes, but there is also a deep despair in Alan Seeger's best-known poem. *Rendevzous with Death* was written shortly before his death:

> God knows 'twere better to be deep
> pillowed in silk and scented down,
> where love throbs out in blissful sleep,
> pulse nigh to pulse, and breath to breath,
> where hushed awakenings are dear …
> …but I've a rendezvous with Death
> at midnight in some flaming town,
> when Spring trips north again this year,
> and I to my pledged word am true.
> I shall not fail that rendezvous.

Seeger's poem expresses the fatalism of many volunteers when the Legion was thrown into Marshal Joffre's autumn offensive in Champagne, which began on 22 September with a softening-up bombardment that lasted three days and nights. In a trial run of new technology, it was intended that observers in spotter planes should direct the artillery. Squares of white cloth were issued, to be sewn onto the backs of the men's capes. Large enough to see from the air, they were supposed to enable the aviators to 'creep' the barrage just ahead of their advance. The idea was beaten by the weather on 25 September, when a thick ground fog and heavy rain prevented the spotter planes taking off. Nor could the observers have seen men on the ground, had they done so.

At 0915hrs, 2nd/2nd RM nevertheless jumped off to relieve the colonial marines who had taken a German battery on the heavily defended Butte de Souain. They then held it while following waves passed through the position. 'Passed through the position' is perhaps a euphemism. According to the regimental diary, men of 171st Infantry Regiment broke and started to run until rallied by the legionnaires. 'Rallied', may have meant, as on other occasions, that they took their chances with the Germans rather than be shot by the Legion, whose increasing professionalism is borne out by their success that day - at least partly owing to the lessons that had learned on Hills 140 and 119 in the Artois sector.

The 2nd/2nd now advanced until disaster struck at 1030hrs as they were attacking the German second line near the ruins of Navarin Farm. Rounds from the French heavy batteries were falling short of the farm, right onto the legionnaires, clinging to the open ground for dear life. The artillery liaison officers desperately fired signal rockets to lengthen the range but, in the smoke and fog, these could not be seen at the batteries. As the surviving liaison officers fought their way back through the communications trenches through the second wave moving forward, men at the point were also taking incoming fire from the German batteries behind the line, some of these being gas shells.[10]

Writing about his experiences at Navarin Farm three days later US legionnaire Edward Morlae recorded that, immediately the legionnaires had driven the Saxons out of the second-line trench, they turned it around. 'In what seemed half a minute we had formed a continuous parapet 12-14in in height. Between each pair of comrades there remained a partition wall of dust (sic) 10-15 in thick, the usefulness of which was demonstrated by a shell which fell into Blondino's niche, blowing him to pieces without injuring either of his neighbours to right or left.[11] Morlae also describes what it was like to be under a barrage. The terrifying noise, of course, but also, 'out of the blackness fell a trickling rain of pieces of metal, lumps of earth, knapsacks, rifles, cartridges and lumps of human flesh.'[12]

Unable to write ever again, fellow American Henry Weston Farnsworth of Groton and Harvard lay dead. Among the many other Legion casualties at Navarin Farm was a former British officer. John Ford Elkington won the Médaille Militaire and was the first British recipient of the Croix de Guerre. On 28 September, he lost a leg while attacking enemy trenches. Fifty years old, he had joined the Legion after being court-martialled and cashiered for cowardice after his battalion had been nearly wiped out at Mons. To persuade the mayor of nearby St Quentin to help the survivors, Elkington had signed a piece of paper saying that he would surrender to the Germans, should they reach the town. The mayor wanted to prevent fighting that would destroy his village, but Elkington's signature caused him to be found unfit to hold the King's commission. His legionary anonymity being broken by the publication of the French awards for bravery, King George V had the following notice published in the *London Gazette:* 'The King has been graciously pleased to approve the re-instatement of John Ford Elkington in the rank of lieutenant-colonel of the Royal Warwickshire Regiment with his previous seniority.' Elkington was also awarded the DSO.[13]

One of the 602 other casualties who paid the price for Navarin Farm was Cpl Cendrars, whose badly mutilated arm was amputated the following day, in compensation for which he too received the Médaille Militaire. The 30% attrition rate caused Lt Col Cot to break off the action and request the withdrawal of 2nd/2nd to the rear.

On 20 and 21 August, RMLE won a notable victory at Cumières, capturing 680 prisoners and fifteen guns for the cost of fifty-three dead and 271 wounded or missing in action. These were considered negligible losses for achieving a unit's objectives. By the end of 1915 the Legion in France had no spare fat. On 11 November the 3,316 remaining men were re-grouped to become the single Régiment de Marche de la Légion Etrangère, commanded by Lt Col Cot. By then, the surviving volunteer poets and pimps, grocers and graduates had been forged by the fire of battle into an elite fighting machine.

RMLE was one of only five regiments to be awarded the Médaille Militaire in the war and was the second most decorated regiment in the French armies, surpassed only by the Régiment d'Infanterie Coloniale du Maroc.[14] Today's legionnaires of 3 RE who sport the double shoulder lanyard combining the colours of the Legion of Honour and the Croix de Guerre 1914-18 have to thank their predecessors of RMLE who earned the honour with their spilled blood, torn bodies and shattered minds.

Chapter 24

RENDEZVOUS WITH DEATH

France 1916-1918

The strategic purpose of the First Battle of the Somme was to draw German forces away from the hard-pressed French line at Verdun. It began with an unrelenting bombardment along a 60km front from 24 June to 1 July 1916, when 60,000 British and 40,000 French troops went over the top in the first wave, having been assured yet again that the German fortifications and wire had been destroyed.

Not only had the long preparation forewarned the Germans exactly where to expect the attack, its halting was their signal to emerge from two- and three-level dugouts with reinforced concrete roofs, in time to slaughter the attackers. With British losses standing at 57,450 on the first day, the impetus had been lost at the outset. Before the long drawn-out nightmare ended, it had claimed 704,000 Allied dead against 237,159 German casualties.[1] To the east at the same time, the French lost about 400,000 in the fighting around Verdun, as against German casualties of 350,000 in round figures, so the diversion had been more costly than the main 'show'.

On 1 July RMLE was in reserve and moved up to what had been the sleepy little Picardy village of Assevilliers[2] after it had been taken by colonial infantry troops. After digging in, they waited three days for orders. Across the line, only 2km away from Assevilliers lay the heavily fortified village of Belloy-en-Santerre, honeycombed with German defences above and below ground, where Seeger had his rendezvous.

He and his fellow volunteers filed up to their jumping-off points about a kilometre from the German forward positions at dawn on 5 July. A Legion bugler sounded *Le Boudin* and the Charge. The heavily laden legionnaires had no chance of charging anywhere, but heaved themselves over the parapets and walked in open order across the sloping ground leading up to the shall-battered village in an unnerving calm broken only by an occasional shout and a few distant explosions.

The defenders watched them coming, waiting in disciplined silence until the first men were a mere 300 metres distant before opening up with machine guns. Two minutes later, hardly a man was still standing in 11th Company on the right flank. Those still able to move were rallied by a Swiss, Capt Tscharner, under whose command they seized the open sewer just south of the village, in which odiferous but life-saving cover they watched the second wave going down under the horizontal hail of machine gun fire. Among the casualties spun round and knocked to the ground was the Harvard poet who had joined up 'for the glory'.

Foreseeing his death 'when Spring comes back with rustling shade', Alan Seeger had got the season wrong but been right about the location being 'on some scarred slope of battered hill'. He lay gut-shot and writhing in agony in a shell-hole within sight of the sewer, alternately screaming for water and crying for his mother until he died. The terse, sanitised citation beside his Médaille Militaire in the Legion museum at Aubagne reads, '(This) young legionnaire, an enthusiastic, energetic and passionate lover of France (was a) volunteer enlisted at the beginning of hostilities (who gave) proof of admirable courage and spirit (and) fell gloriously before Belloy-en-Santerre on 11 July 1916. At Bel-Abbès, 24 July 1924, Colonel Boulet-Desbareau, Commandant 4th Foreign Regiment.'[3]

Seeger's comrades had to leave him where he lay. Climbing out of the sewage ditch, they found themselves in a two-hour house-to-house killing match to drive the Germans out of Belloy with grenades and bayonets. Nightfall found them trying desperately to refortify the ruined village in certain expectation of German counter-attacks. In one day RMLE had lost twenty-five officers and 844 men, representing one third of its strength. When it was relieved next morning, the legionnaires took to the rear with them 750 prisoners - a tally that would have been higher, had not many Germans feared surrendering to the Legion after all the horror stories spread about it in Germany before the war.

In their next engagement on the night of 7 July another 400 men were badly wounded or killed. During one week on the Somme, half the *régiment de marche* had accompanied Seeger to his rendezvous.

In December 1916 Gen Robert George Nivelle replaced Joffre as C-in-C. In May he had succeeded Gen Philippe Pétain as commander of 2nd Army at Verdun, where his use of creeping artillery barrages in two highly successful counter-attacks enabled the French to retake nearly all the ground gained by the Germans over the previous six months. He was promoted for the second time in seven months - over the heads of many senior generals - because his well-argued philosophy of frontal attacks in coordination with massive artillery bombardments impressed the politicians, including Britain's Prime Minister David Lloyd George. His subordinates, however, were waiting for him to fall flat on his face - which he did metaphorically with the Aisne offensive, in company with 120,000 French casualties.

As so often with replacement generals who have been impatiently waiting their turn, Nivelle was convinced that he knew what to do. The key to unlocking the stalemate on the western front, he said, was to stop Joffre's 'nibbling away' at the enemy line, and make one colossal attack. As would Navarre's plan in 1954, this sounded good to his friends in high political places.

To its misfortune, the Moroccan Division including RMLE was a flange on Nivelle's key, which started to turn in the German lock on 16 April with 800,000 men walking across No Man's Land on an 80km front stretching from near Soissons in the west to east of Reims. Everything had been pre-planned: the exact tonnage of ammunition in each calibre calculated, as was the number of meals, the timing of the barrage and the rhythm of the advance.

The objective allocated to RMLE next day was a crucial strongpoint defended by interlocking machine-gun nests, on a spur called Le Golfe near Holy Name Hill. Below it a flat killing ground, over which they had to advance, wheel left and encircle of the village of Aubérive, cutting the Germans there off from resupply. However, so complex was the network of trenches, tunnels and dug-outs that the Germans named it *das Labyrinth*. Impregnable to a frontal attack, it was to be taken by 1st Battalion under Maj de Sampigny attacking northwards and 3rd Battalion under Maj Deville bearing east to overwhelm the Golfe spur, with 2nd Battalion under Maj Wadell held in reserve.

Unless the machine guns on Le Golfe were knocked out first by artillery, it was a suicide mission, but in order not to forewarn the Germans, there was to be no heavy barrage. Instead, trench mortars and 37mm cannon were to be used tactically with local commanders able to call down fire from 75s and 105s situated further back, as and when necessary. Liaison was to be by signal flares and runners. Two things in favour of the attackers were the issue to the Division of less give-away khaki uniforms and the weather, which looked set on fair the previous evening.

Just after 0100hrs the 1st Battalion started moving up along the communications trenches to the front line, followed by 3rd battalion. The weather broke, with the chalky mud in the flooded trenches smearing white streaks on their khaki trousers. Ordered over the top in strong wind and pouring rain at 0445hrs on 17 April - the peculiar timing meant that the German artillery only began its barrage, prepared for a start on the hour, ten or fifteen minutes into the action - 1st Battalion slid and slipped through the icy mud in the darkness, followed by the men of 3rd Battalion. Gaps in the French wire had been made in the night by wiring parties, but passages through the German entanglements still had to be cut by sappers with wire-cutters - all this in driving wind and rain and under fire from machine guns and German artillery.

About 0700hrs, Lt Col Duriez, the rather overweight colonel of RMLE, was mortally wounded and passed command to Maj Deville. The defenders' heavy fire swept the flat ground below them, by which time the advance had splintered into small groups of men belly-crawling through the mud, clinging to what little cover they could find under the harsh light of magnesium flares while they reconnoitred ways between the enemy strong-points. Reaching Birch Wood, 3rd Battalion cleared it with bayonet and grenade at point-blank range, often recognising friend from enemy by voice alone in a downpour of sleet turning to snow.

Unable to hold the first line, the Germans withdrew to the second with the legionnaires in close pursuit to avoid the barrage bound to hit the lost trench. The nearer to Aubérive they got, in the Byzance, Dardanelles and Prinz Eitel trenches, the more desperate the resistance of the Germans opposing them with machine guns, stick grenades and flame-throwers - used for the first time against British troops at Hooge on 30 July 1915. By dusk, sixteen hours after jumping off, they had taken the south side of the salient in close-quarter fighting, during which each man used up ten or more grenades.

By dawn on 19 April the Aubérive strongpoint had been so pummelled by the French artillery that the Germans had withdrawn, leaving clothing, ammunition and even a canteen of hot coffee, eagerly swallowed by men who had had no clean drinking water for three days and nights. One of the company commanders, Capt Fernand Victor-Marie Maire, himself the son of a former legionnaire, decided that in such a situation one extra risk made no difference to one's personal chances of survival, but might make all the difference between swift success and slow attrition. Instead of waiting for the softening-up barrage to cease, he led his men across the open ground between their position and the German trenches before the 'friendly' shells had ceased falling, with the result that they were in the German first line before the defenders had emerged from their deep dug-outs.

With bayonet and grenade - consumption stayed at ten per man per day throughout this action - the position was taken before the flanking companies had reached their objectives. In return for heavy losses including Duriez and captains Germann and Manurien, RMLE secured a 2km-square dent in the German salient. But Maire had been right to take the risk: elsewhere in one action the dawn complement of 275 men stood at 19 by nightfall. Maire was another Legion legend in the making. One night he reluctantly agreed to make a fourth at bridge in a dugout with some other officers waiting to go over the top at dawn. After the last game they shook hands and went to their units. By 0600hrs Maire was lying on the ground with a bullet in his left thigh, but before the stretcher-bearers had carried him to the aid post, the other three bridge-players were already dead.[4]

On 21 April the 6th Company was 'resting' in a captured German trench on the spur designated Trench 67 on French maps. Unable to sleep in the near-zero damp and filth, German-born Sgt Maj Max-Emmanuel Mader decided that it would be prudent to reconnoitre further along the well-constructed trench towards the enemy. Taking with him a young sentry, 18-year-old Legionnaire Bangerter, he rounded a corner in the trench to find a clear view over a valley along which a French lieutenant was leading a patrol marching with rifles slung, seemingly unaware that they were in sight of a German emplacement whose machine gunners were waiting for their prey to come into range.

Bangerter wanted to fire a warning flare to warn off the patrol, but Mader had a better idea. Waking ten of his men, he led them in a low crouch along a fold in the terrain to short-cut the bend of the trench and bring them out above the nest. The Germans in it were too concentrated on the patrol below to hear the approach of the men behind them until a score of grenades landed among them, killing and injuring most. The survivors were taken prisoner. At that point, no one could have criticised Mader for leaving the forewarned patrol to extricate itself. Instead, he ordered his men to secure the emplacement against counter-attack and ran down into the valley - a sweating, unkempt, bearded figure in a muddy uniform neither recognisably French nor German, yelling at the bewildered lieutenant and patrol to follow him.

He then interrogated the surviving machine-gunners in fluent German, learning the exact location of a nearby camouflaged battery. With his legionnaires and a company of light infantry he located and captured the battery after a five-hour battle with a company of the Imperial Guard. For this, he was awarded the Legion of Honour and became the most-decorated NCO in France.

RMLE's remarkable record in capturing 7km of trenches and the battery at the Aubérive salient had cost sixteen officers and 777 men. Many of these lives could have been saved, had the supply of munitions been adequate. The regimental diary recorded how, 'Men could be seen crying with rage. Only the lack of grenades stopped them.'[5]

But there was nothing about that in 4th Army's General Order No. 809 of 7 May 1917. It read: (The RMLE is a) marvellous regiment which incites the hatred of the enemy and (inspires) the highest level of sacrifice. On 17 April under the orders of Lt Col Duriez (it) attacked an enemy forewarned and heavily entrenched, capturing his first lines. Halted by machine gun fire and despite the loss of its mortally wounded commanding officer, (RMLE) continued the operation under the orders of battalion commander Deville and by unceasing close-quarters combat for the next five days and nights until the objective was secured, deprived the enemy of 2km square of terrain, forcing by its sustained attacks the evacuation of a heavily defended village that had resisted all our attacks for two whole years. (signed) Anthoine, Commanding General'

Duriez' replacement, Lt Col Paul Rollet was a soldier's soldier who had passed out 311th in his *promotion* of 587 cadets at St-Cyr. Four years later, in December 1899, this short, slightly built but ferociously bearded officer who would become known as 'the father of the Legion' applied for a transfer from the boredom of garrison duty in the Ardennes to join the Legion, earning the respect of his men in Algeria, Madagascar and Morocco by courage and physical toughness. On every *razzia* he made a point of walking twice as far as his men, who took turns to ride on the mules while he stayed on foot the whole time, wearing out the rope soles of his non-issue footwear so fast that he received the nickname 'Captain Espadrilles'.

In France, he insisted on wearing a képi instead of a steel helmet and carried a rolled umbrella instead of a sidearm in combat - not because the weight of a revolver in its holster spoiled the hang of his uniform as some officers felt, but because he believed that having a weapon distracted a commander's thoughts from his primary business of commanding his men. Their affection was gained by his strict fairness and a willingness to fight for them against higher authority - a characteristic no more appreciated by French generals than in other armies. Typical of this up-and-at-'em officer was Rollet's decision to transfer from the Legion to a regular regiment in 1914 for fear of being left out of the coming war.

The arrival of this new commander with a reputation among the long-service NCOs for having *baraka*, or luck, came just at the right moment, when the costly failure of Nivelle's failed Aisne offensive broke whatever will to continue the war still existed in many French regiments, resulting in widespread mutinies. RMLE does not appear to have been affected, possibly because so many of the men had volunteered, whereas most soldiers in regular regiments were conscripts enrolled against their will.

A second black mark against the Legion - the first was for the executions in Paris after the Commune - was earned by the way legionnaires now acted as military police, of whom there were nowhere near enough to prevent whole units leaving their positions and heading to the rear. Morale in the much-abused French army slowly climbed back up after the sacking of Nivelle and his replacement by Gen Philippe Pétain on 15 May 1917. While agreeing with Nivelle about coordinating artillery to reduce the horrific infantry losses, Pétain saw clearly that incentive must be mixed with punishment because the stick without the carrot was killing the donkey.

On personal tours of canteens and cookhouses he horrified his aides-de-camp by insisting on eating the *poilus'* food and tasting their wine, to test the quality with his own taste buds, and had no hesitation in castigating cooks and commissariat officers for failing to do their duty and ensure the fighting men were properly and regularly fed. Among other incentives he introduced were leave for men who had not been home in years - and the award to RMLE of the yellow and green shoulder lanyard of the Médaille Militaire. To a civilian it seems nothing in return for all the suffering, but all the small authorised variations to uniform are expressions of regimental pride and there are moments when nothing else is left to motivate exhausted and disorientated men in action.

In January 1918 RMLE was taken out of the line in Lorraine to reinforce troops endeavouring to hold the German 'bulge' near Soissons and Compiègne, only 60km northeast of Paris. With the gradual collapse of the eastern front as the Bolshevik revolution incited more and more Russian soldiers to shoot their officers, throw away their weapons and walk home, Berlin had started moving fifty divisions from its eastern armies to the western front. Signature of the treaties of Brest-Litovsk on 3 March 1918 finally released the manpower for Berlin to launch another huge 'push' by 2nd and 17th German armies between Arras and St Quentin while 18th Army protected their left flank.

Known by the Allies as the Second Battle of the Somme, it was preceded by a bombardment from 6,000 guns. On 26 April RMLE was among mainly British troops defending the strategic communications centre of Amiens. Ordered to occupy a wooded hillock at Hangard, 15km south-east of the town, where the price of touching a shattered tree or the ground was immediate blistering from the mustard gas lingering everywhere, the legionnaires advancing behind British tanks found themselves in a very different situation from the static war of the trenches.

In the absence of radio communications, a rolling barrage only worked when a strict timetable was adhered to. With the front pushed forward in one place and lagging behind in another, that was impossible. Taking advantage of the partly wooded landscape and a thick fog, small parties of German machine-gunners managed to lie low as 'stay-behinds' and take the legionnaires from the rear, so that their maximum advance was less than a kilometre. Driven back, they counter-attacked and managed to hang on to the wood until relieved on 6 May, but in conditions of sustained artillery bombardments and ground attacks so horrific that 1st Battalion was down to one officer and 187 men. Command of one company eventually fell on the shoulders of the longest-serving legionnaire, a Luxemburger named Kemmlet, after every officer had been killed.

RMLE's well-merited rest from the line was cut short by Gen Erich von Ludendorff finally launching Operation Blücher on 27 May. On a front extending from north of Soissons, eastward toward Reims, fifteen German divisions attacked the seven French and British divisions opposite them, and swarmed over the ridge of the Chemin des Dames[6] and across the Aisne River. By 30 May they were back on the Marne, between Château-Thierry and Dormans.

With the rest of the Moroccan Division, RMLE was transported in buses to the west of Soissons, there to hold the wavering line - which they did at a cost of forty-two killed and 289 wounded or missing in action and despite a desperate shortage of ammunition. Added to the stress of combat was the impossibility of restful sleep, repeated gas attacks during the next few days necessitating continuous wearing of the cumbersome masks. Praise for their courage must have rung hollowly in the ears of the survivors: the losses since Hangard stood at 1,250 men, with no replacements at all.

On 14 July Rollet marched at the head of an RMLE colour party in the Bastille Day parade, where the regiment was awarded the Médaille Militaire, officially for valour, but off-the-record for standing firm during the mutinies. Four days later, it was business as usual when the Moroccan Division formed part of Gen Ferdinand Foch's attempt to nip off the German salient south of Soissons. RMLE, seriously under-strength, attacked at 0445hrs behind a screen of Renault light tanks, not much helped by an ill-coordinated barrage. In two hours, they took 450 prisoners. Three times on 20 July the Germans counter-attacked, but the Legion held - at a cost of 780 men.

One of the few personal stories with a happy outcome is of Sgt Maj Mader, who had his right arm and most of his shoulder blown away. In the Boer War, largely fought over dry virgin terrain, most gunshot wounds had healed naturally, but in the richly manured farmland of northern France and Flanders the heavy dose of bacteria injected by projectiles into even relatively superficial wounds, plus the presence of chlorine, and/or mustard gas molecules and other chemical residue from exploded munitions in the soil, led all too often to gas gangrene, amputation and death.

The French word *triage* - meaning originally 'division into three lots' - came to be used in military English because the field surgeons in aid posts had to divide casualties into those who could be moved to base without attention, those who needed immediate surgery if they were to survive and those on whom surgery would be a waste of time. The last category was simply left to die. By any reckoning, Mader was in the third group. What he said on regaining consciousness to find a padre giving him the last rites, has sadly not been recorded, but incredibly his indomitable will and iron constitution pulled him through to sport the button of the Legion of Honour on his lapel for a normal span of life.

Massing an unheard-of concentration of artillery for the preliminary softening-up of the German line, Pétain ordered a limited offensive near Verdun in August, in which RMLE suffered losses of only fifty-three dead and 271 wounded/missing in action for a booty that included sixteen heavy guns and 680 prisoners. This resulted in its regimental flag being decorated with the Legion of Honour, and a second shoulder lanyard in red, to commemorate on each legionnaire's uniform the honour to the flag.

On 1 September RMLE succeeded in taking two villages near Soissons that had resisted American attacks and found itself fighting the new war of movement and infiltration, with some companies down to their last fifty men. With the rest of the Moroccan Division they reached the Hindenburg Line of concrete pillboxes and extensively wired trench systems, where they distinguished themselves by capturing twice their own number of prisoners. Ordered by Gen Mangin to take the Vauxaillon railway tunnel, Rollet marched into it at the head of his exhausted men, together with a drummer and bugler playing *Le Boudin*. Harassed by friendly and hostile fire, by the time the survivors reached the far end of the tunnel, they were down to 50% of strength at the outset of the battle. In recognition of the loss of 1,433 officers and men, a new lanyard was created for the survivors, combining the colours of the Legion of Honour and the Croix de Guerre.

In the final months of the war leading up to the Armistice that stilled the guns on the stroke of the eleventh hour of the eleventh day of the eleventh month of 1918, RMLE was a skeleton. Despite Rollet's personal belief in the Legion, the *régiment de marche* had found it impossible to recruit and make good its losses. The young men of Europe had had enough of war and the colonial battalions had no spare flesh.

Col Bouchez, commanding 1st Moroccan Brigade, sent a pessimistic report to the commanding general of 1st Moroccan Division (to which the Legion nominally belonged). Entitled *Reconstitution of the Regiment of the Foreign Legion*, it read in part: 'Since the entry into the war of Belgium, Italy, America, Greece and the setting up of the Czech and Armenian armies, the Legion has seen its sources of recruitment dry up. Only the Swiss and Spanish continue to enlist - in numbers insufficient to remedy the situation. Thereby, the existence of the Legion is threatened, and yet a regiment that has such traditions and such a past must not die. If the Legion does die, it will be impossible to reconstitute in peacetime. We must remember the hostile publicity in the foreign press.'[7]

By the time the Czech army was formed in 1918, Rollet had lost 1,020 men to the various armies of the later belligerent powers, although he believed that they transferred more in fear of the shame of not being seen to fight for their own country than because they wanted to leave the Legion.[8] The Russians in France were legally citizens of a neutral state since Brest-Litovsk, and therefore recruitable, but the three Tsarist battalions sent to fight on the western front by Grand Duke Nikolai had mutinied at La Courtine in 1917 in sympathy with the Bolshevik Revolution. In 1918, after 265 men in one unit of 694 declared no further interest in the war, 375 Russians were drafted in June and July, but refused to risk death in combat for a cause that was not theirs.

On 6 November 1918 Rollet had an interview in Paris with the White Russian Gen Ignatiev, whose condition for enrolling what remained of his army was that his officers be allowed to retain their rank. Rollet retorted that he already had four Russian officers and needed no more, thank you. So that came to nothing.

Rather late in the war, an American fan of the Legion named Frank S. Butterworth attempted to recruit an American regiment for the Foreign Legion on US territory until informed by the US Secretary for War that this was unconstitutional.[9] In any case the famous Lafayette Squadron of American flyers had quietly been legitimised as 103rd Pursuit Squadron of the US Air Service in January 1918.[10] There was, of course, the possibility of drawing on the African colonial regiments to fill the gaps in RMLE, but at a time when the British and US armies segregated black and white troops, this option did not occur to Rollet. His alternative suggestion that each regular regiment should donate a few men to the Legion fell on deaf ears although the largest national group left in RMLE at the end of the war were 905 French legionnaires.

Complicating Rollet's problem was a tendency on the part of army recruiters to get around the prohibition of foreigners serving in the French army by placing foreigners in the Legion for a token period of days only and then transferring them to French regiments. Julian Green, a volunteer US ambulance driver in France who sought to enlist in the Legion, rather than be returned to the States for basic training and then being shipped back to Europe, found 'this difficulty was neatly got round by first having me sign up in the Foreign Legion (in which I remained for the space of an hour), and then transferring me from the Legion into the regular army.'[11] Similarly, millionaire's son and gay jazz composer Cole Porter enlisted on 20 April 1918, but was immediately posted to 3rd Artillery Regiment at the artillery school in Fontainebleau[12] in keeping with Pétain's preference for gunners rather than more cannon-fodder. Serving with his battery from 20 September to 23 January 1919, he was then detached to the staff of the US military attaché and formally demobbed on 17 April.

RMLE ended the war in Château-Salins - a town in Lorraine that had been German since 1870, with Berlin its capital, not Paris. Giving not a damn for that, Rollet intended to honour the dead legionnaires while the guns were still ringing in the survivors' ears. He marched his men through the town in a victory parade all of their own, preceded by drummers, buglers and the regimental flag, than which only that of the Colonial Infantry Regiment of Morocco was more decorated.

At the victory parade in Paris the following year for once Rollet obeyed orders to wear a helmet. On seeing the flame of the Tomb of the Unknown Soldier beneath the Arc de Triomphe, he was perhaps feeling what Legionnaire Pascal Bonetti put into words in 1920:

> Four years he suffered and bled in that hell
> before the evening when he, too, fell.
> Is the Unknown Soldier whose tomb enhances
> all the epic pomp and glory of the past
> perhaps a foreigner who became a son of France
> not by blood received, but by blood shed at last?[13]

There is every chance of it, despite a rumour difficult to verify, that the first randomly chosen Unknown turned out to be an African colonial soldier and was hastily replaced. According to the *Livre d'Or des Légionnaires Morts pour le France au cours de le Grande Guerre 1914-1918*, 14,512 Italians, 455 Russians and 578 Swiss died in Legion uniform, as against sixty-nine Americans and two Britons on the eastern front and eighteen on the western front - these low figures being due to British enlistment in the BEF from the start of the war.

Chapter 25

IDENTITY CRISIS

North Africa 1918-1940

The scale of French casualties relative to the total adult male population in the First World War was far higher than for Britain and would have brought down the administration in Washington, had it been equalled in the US forces. As the war memorial in any small French village still testifies, one in three young Frenchmen became a casualty during the four years of carnage. The masculine depopulation was such that glancing through the telephone directory of any commune in the south of the country today can reveal more Italian and Spanish surnames than French ones. To replace the dead Frenchmen hundreds of thousands of landless men from Leon and Lombardy and Cantabria and Calabria walked across the Alps and the Pyrenees into southern France, where they laboured in the fields, looked after the animals and pruned the vines of the dead *poilus*. The local girls, inheritors of the property their brothers, fiancés and husbands had died to defend, married the immigrants as the only men available to father the next generation.

Within the Legion there was no longer a French-born majority in the ranks. In some battalions, the percentage of French recruits fell as low as 7%, giving them swift promotion, in many cases to sergeant within a year of signing on. In 1920, 72% of legionnaires originated from what had been enemy nations in the Great War. Fourteen years later that figure was down to 44% and although only 16% were French-born, they made 35% of NCOs.[1] This was not necessarily due to chauvinism, but because the language of command was French and many foreign legionnaires never mastered it sufficiently to make themselves clearly understood - a potentially fatal situation in combat.

Throughout these years Rollet clung obstinately to his vision for a bigger, better Legion of the future. Realising that the citations and honours showered on men from fifty-one nations in RMLE throughout the war counted for little with the top brass and politicians, he managed to persuade them that the Legion would make an excellent training school for the best young officers emerging from St Cyr, who could afterwards be implanted in regular regiments to imbue them with energy and valour. His most powerful political ally was Gen Jean Mordacq, *chef de cabinet* to Prime Minister George 'Tiger' Clemenceau. Mordacq had served with the Legion before the war and was convinced that now more than ever before France needed foreign soldiers in the colonies, to avoid spilling any more French blood. He accordingly drew up a blueprint in 1919 for several foreign divisions comprising regiments of infantry, cavalry, artillery and engineers.[2]

Another powerful ally was Lyautey, who had not obeyed orders to retreat for the duration of the war into a few international enclaves on the coast where foreigners could be kept safe. However, his *effectif* had been so whittled down by deaths in combat and desertion that he had resorted to compulsory transfers from other corps to keep up even a semblance of normal strength in the five battalions in Morocco, largely composed of Germans and Austrians. They were divided into two irreconcilable camps: those who had wanted, but not been able, to return to Europe at the outbreak of war and those volunteers who had been sent to North Africa to avoid fighting their compatriots in Europe.

Recruitment was so bad by June 1918 that Lyautey proposed offering a re-enlistment bonus of 500 francs to anyone who would remuster and sending the rest to the POW camps on Corsica, where they could cause little harm.[3]

His postwar plans for completing the colonisation of Morocco envisaged stationing there permanently 30,000 European troops, including a large share of Mordacq's expanded Legion. However, Mordacq's plan was thrown out by a Parliament where many *députés* feared a predominantly German mercenary force in French uniform at a time when the regular army was mainly composed of short-term conscripts. Although few civilians imagined that it would be only two decades before Germany invaded France for the third time in seventy years, a significant proportion of her politicians guessed that their neighbours across the Rhine would wriggle out of their Versailles Treaty obligations and menace France again before too many years had passed. To their way of thinking, with some Legion battalions composed mainly of *schleus*[4], who could trust such an army? Never again would it set foot on French soil, they swore.

However, nobody objected to the beasts from the east being used to expand and keep the peace in French overseas possessions, although a limit had to be set to the heights to which non-French officers could rise. And so was born the rule that foreigners could serve up to captain's rank, above which ceiling only French nationals were eligible. That too caused problems, for finding French-born officers was difficult in the years immediately after the war, when professional soldiers were regarded so askance in France that few would go out in public wearing uniform, if they could avoid it. The result was that some of the Legion's new officers were a rather wild lot, who would not have been commissioned into regular units because they were bound to cause trouble.

Other officers were too meek and mild, rotated into the Legion under a training programme called 'Théatre des Opérations Extérieures' to widen the experience of cadres from administrative posts in regular regiments. They found themselves thwarted at every turn by experienced NCOs who took a delight in undermining their authority. Humiliated every time a swaggering long-service legionnaire did not salute them off-duty, the TOE officers took refuge in dreams of a more congenial next posting.

Whatever Paris thought about them, the international reputation for valour of France's two most decorated regiments - RMLE and the Régiment d'Infanterie Coloniale du Maroc - was such that in October 1919 the Spanish government sent Maj José Millan Astray y Terreros, one of its most experienced colonial soldiers, into French Morocco to study first-hand the organisation and methods of Lyautey's military government and decide how they might be applied in the Spanish enclaves. Millan Astray returned to Madrid with his own ideas for a differently organised Spanish Foreign Legion for deployment in North Africa.

In January 1920 a royal decree created his new army as 3rd Extranjeros and he was promoted to lieutenant-colonel as its first commander. *La Bandera*, as it came to be known, never acquired the glamour of its older French brother.

It is not surprising that Millan Astray was unimpressed by Lyautey's Legion of enemy alien stay-behinds and veterans from the trenches who intended to live long enough to collect their pensions, plus refugee career soldiers from armies that no longer existed after the Russian Revolution and the general upheaval in eastern Europe. For these last to return home would have meant a firing squad, if they were lucky. Homeless, their families dead, their property destroyed or sequestrated, where else could they go, but the Legion? With no hope of regaining their former ranks, they signed on as ordinary legionnaires.

Col Rollet, inspecting new recruits: 'What did you do before joining the Legion?' Recruit: 'I was a general, Colonel.'

If many similar anecdotes relished by legionnaires are apocryphal, the above exchange may well have taken place while Rollet was inspecting a new intake arriving at Sidi bel-Abbès in 1920. The recruit in question would have been White Russian Gen Boris Krechatisky, who went to the bottom of the military ladder and volunteered as an ordinary legionnaire because soldiering was the only trade he knew and nobody else would give him a job.[5]

Rollet blamed many of the Legion's problems of discipline and morale on what he considered the contaminating influence of European civilians in Algeria. Given the chance, he would have moved it wholesale into the interior of Morocco, where there were no settlers. In the event, 1 RE remained based in bel-Abbès, while 2 RE moved from Saïda to Meknès in Morocco. The rump of RMLE became 3 RE, based in Fez, Morocco, and commanded by Rollet from its inception in January 1920 until March 1925 when he married an attractive and much younger wife, Clémentine Hébert. To provide the couple with a semblance of normal European life, he was given command of 1 RE in Sidi bel-Abbès.

In this post-war expansion of the Legion, 4 RE was created in Meknès in December 1920 and then moved to Marrakesh in central Morocco. Two years later the Régiment Etranger de Cavalerie was set up 1,500km to the east, in Sousse, Tunisia. REC was largely recruited from Cossacks, Poles and Russians from the White armies with a few of the Kaiser's Uhlans for good measure, officered by French cavalrymen from the Spahis and Chasseurs d'Afrique. One outstanding legionnaire, a former Tsarist hussar colonel calling himself Odintsoff reduced his age by more than a decade in order to enlist. So many of his fellow émigrés were sons of the nobility that the regiment was dubbed 'Le Royal Etranger' even though the war they were to fight would be far from the glittering cavalry parades and exhilarating charges across the plains of central and eastern Europe, to which they were accustomed.

Of the thousands of Tsarist officers and NCOs who found themselves starving in Constantinople after escaping the Red Army at the end of the Russian Civil War, several hundred accepted free passage on French ships bringing them directly to

North Africa, where their nothing-left-to-lose-but-my-life temperament introduced into the panoply of Legion horseplay the lunatic Russian roulette called *Cuckoo*.[6] A more sober applicant to join the Legion was Finland's greatest soldier Gen Mannerheim. A prophet in his own country, he applied in 1925 to serve with the Legion in Morocco but was politely informed that there was no post suitable for a cavalry officer aged fifty-nine.

Four years later, the Legion's strength on paper totalled eighteen battalions of infantry, six cavalry squadrons, five mounted companies and four engineering companies. One year later the three battalions stationed in Indo-China became 5 RE. This was probably the high point in real Legion strength, with 33,000 men in all. Just before the outbreak of the Second World War three battalions from 1 RE and one from 2 RE became 6 RE in Syria and 2 REC was created in July 1939, to earn the distinction of being the most often disbanded and reconstituted unit in the Legion! The infantry regiments became designated REI, meaning Régiment Etranger d'Infanterie, to distinguish them from the other arms.

After the flood of recruits whose lives had been shattered by the war and the Russian Revolution came a new crop with the Depression, when workless men enlisted from all walks of life, one quarter of them under twenty years old and 64% under twenty-five. Of them, 73% had been labourers or skilled manual workers, and 7% had worked on the land. It was the 13% of white-collar recruits who gave a problem in what was a physically very demanding world. As to exactly how unfit they were, opinions differ. Some inter-war memoirs infer that the medical examination given to recruits was a mere formality; others, that it paid rigorous attention to eyesight and good teeth. Many problems stemmed from childhood malnutrition in men who had grown up during the war, when the British Isles had been blockaded by U-boats and Germany had also been cut off from many of her traditional food suppliers. Even men who had grown up in the country and eaten well as children could also be very unfit after being unemployed during the Depression and having eaten poorly and irregularly for months before joining up.

The new recruits' mental attitudes also gave problems, the regimental diarist of 2 REI complaining in 1921 that the new legionnaires had not 'come to the Legion in search of adventure and ... the desire to live peacefully while waiting for better times seems to be (their) main motivating force. The present legionnaires are ... more malleable, less drunken but also softer. The rather large numbers of letters that they write and receive shows that they have not broken with their old countries.'[7] It was also an indication that they were better educated than the hard men of the old Legion.

Whilst less prone to drink-related indiscipline than their predecessors, such men were hardly ideal material to turn into brutal and licentious soldiery, but Rollet could have done with more, all the same. One battalion commander even went so far in 1923 as to suggest that the now traditional five-year engagement be shortened to three years in order to attract recruits who wanted a brief adventure, but not a military career. The introduction of a enlistment cash bonus and another cash bonus on completion of basic training - two incentives the old lags had never known - was resisted by some officers on the grounds that they furnished unhappy young recruits with the very money needed to finance desertion.

Before the war, when the majority of legionnaires had been French, desertion en masse was rare because if they went 'home' they would be caught, but if the post-war foreign recruits could make it home or to some neutral country, they were safe. So they did desert more often and in larger numbers. Those caught after an absence of longer than six days, or who had taken their weapons with them, purged their crime in the Legion's penal battalion in Bechar, 400km south of bel-Abbès. There, an average day might be spent making by hand a quota of 1,000 adobe bricks per man. Any offence against the draconian regulations was punished by *le peleton* - drilling for hours at the double in temperatures in the high forties, wearing full parade uniform and with backpack stuffed with rocks and shoulder straps replaced with wire that cut into the shoulders.

What *could* a recruit do with the cash burning a hole in his pocket in a garrison town like bel-Abbès? There were at the time only three pleasures on sale: alcohol, a good meal and sex. Until the Legion's own medically supervised brothels were established to reduce the incidence of venereal disease[8], three *maisons de tolérance* in the native town were in-bounds for Legion personnel, of which Le Chat Noir and Au Palmier were legendary for their hordes of naked and semi-naked girls who swarmed over every man entering. A slightly better tone was to be found at Le Moulin Rouge, where the 'meat' stood or sat quietly at one end of the room. After a customer had made his selection and paid the madam, she called the girl over and sent them both upstairs with a clean towel.

Smashing up a brothel or a bar in a drunken brawl was so common that it was punished locally with a spell in the cells. The Danish Prince Aage had been director of a bank that went bust in 1922. Promoted lieutenant, he was a popular officer, and once had some defaulting legionnaires from Denmark released from the cells to be interviewed over dinner by a woman journalist from Copenhagen. In a Tailhook Scandal preview, the dinner ended with her weeping and semi-naked, but no one got punished for that.

Aage thought that there was a woman behind every legionnaire and told a story of a lieutenant and one of his men both killed in the same engagement, who were both found to be carrying in their pockets a photograph of the same woman. The idea made a good joke in the 1931 Laurel and Hardy film spoof of Beau Geste entitled *Beau Hunks*, in which both men join up because they have been jilted by the same girl - only to find that all the other men in the company also carry her photograph next to their hearts, as does a local bandit chief killed on patrol! *Plus ça change* ... In 1999 the author asked a Legion jungle warfare instructor why most men join up today. His answer was the same as that of Prince Aage more than half a century before. '*Histoire de nana, le plus souvent,*' he replied: girl trouble, usually.

Although Rollet and the other Legion colonels resented the many films, novels and autobiographical accounts of the inter-war period that sensationalised the legionnaire's life, they were really his best advertisements even before synchronised soundtracks became possible with Al Jolson's *The Jazz Singer* in 1927. No young man yearning for the Old West of cowboy films could put the clock back to that age when men were men and did what men had to do, leaving a beautiful woman crying softly in the background, but he could join the Legion.

Film producers loved the desert because it was a cheap location around Hollywood. Matinee idol Rudolph Valentino's box office successes included *The Sheik* (1921), *Blood and Sand* (1922) and *Son of the Sheik* (1926). At least one recruit saw a film glamorising the Legion in London and walked straight from the cinema to volunteer at the French consulate on Brompton Road.[9] Any man coming out of the smoke-filled darkness of the local cinema, where the flickering shafts of light from the projection booth painted his longings in black and white on the silver screen, could fantasise on the way back to his lonely digs or Salvation Army dormitory about walking into a Legion recruiting office and signing on to test just how tough he was among strangers who would become his best buddies and appreciate his true worth. To lonely men who felt undervalued in civilian life, to men who had no special skills or education, to men who had been *rejected*, whether by society or a woman, it was a dream that could come true. Rollet's genius was to package the dream, by doing which he became truly the Father of the Legion.

After 1918 an all-army commission recommended the same uniform for all French soldiers. The regular regiments then wore the horizon-blue uniform introduced in 1914, the colonial formations wore khaki and the legion in Syria had to be fitted out in US Army surplus clothing left behind by their erstwhile allies. Tourists passing through North Africa between the wars were amazed to see legionnaires going off on patrol wearing sandals and items of Arab clothing. They were often unshaven and did not bother to salute officers. The only invariable item of kit was the képi with its flap of cloth hanging down at the rear to protect the neck from sunburn.

During the war, the képi had been replaced by a forage cap or a steel helmet in the trenches. Epaulettes too disappeared in 1915. But in 1922 a stock of old khaki képis was dug up from some stores and distributed to legionnaires serving in Morocco. The pre-war cap covers of long-service men had been nearly white from repeated washings and the action of the sun, so the new recruits bleached theirs artificially to make it look as though they had 'got some time in'.

Throughout 1924 and 1925 Rollet was firing memoranda at the

War Ministry in Paris arguing for official permission to replace the regulation white pith helmet and the forage cap by the képi for all Legion units. On 18 June 1926 permission was at last granted - not for a white képi, but a red one. Individual commanders took the law into their own hands and soon most képis were white, with only 1 RE and 4 RE still in the red ones.

There was a masochistic bravado in the obsession with wearing white képis, which made wonderful targets for the concealed enemy in mountain and desert warfare. The high incidence of head wounds caused the powers-that-be to consider issuing tin helmets of the type worn in the trenches until someone pointed out that they would fry the brains of the wearers during summer in the Sahara. The new compromise was to let the Legion wear khaki képis.

Legionnaire Jean Martin recorded the confusion that resulted. Ordered to dye their bleached képis, the men produced a rainbow of hues, with the machine gunners flaunting caps of a pale mauve despite orders to the contrary and punishments.[10] The colour competition was not resolved until Bastille Day 1939, when for the first time the Legion contingent in the 14 July parade marched down the Champs Elysées in immaculate *white* képis. Today, the *engagé volontaire* receives his white képi at the end of his six-month basic training in a quasi-religious ceremony, followed by a collective booze-up.

Another traditional piece of Legion uniform that saw the light of day again under Rollet was the blue sash wound around the waist. Although men get attached to distinguishing items of uniform, nobody much cared for the waist sash, for to drop one's pants necessitated undoing all two metres' length of it and finding either a comrade to hold one end or a door to jam it in, in order to spin round three times to wind it tight again afterwards. Which is why the legionnaires being shipped to the war in Europe in 1939 jettisoned their sashes overboard as soon as they were out of sight of land, only to have some Colonel Blimp in the stores find a new supply that caught up with them while training for the Narvik intervention - for which they were particularly inappropriate. Three years later in the heat of the Libyan Desert they were again ordered to wear them - over British army short-sleeved shirts and baggy shorts!

But those are details. Rollet unveiled his new product in all its glory on the Legion's centenary in 1931. He could have chosen the Legion's real birthday, commemorating Louis-Philippe's decree in 1831; instead, he chose the battle of Camarón, seizing on it, rather than the story of one of the Legion's many victories because it epitomised the legionnaire's duty of unflinching obedience unto death. There had been some improvised Fêtes de Camerone celebrated in 1913 and 1914, but on 30 April 1931 Rollet outshone them all by producing a spectacular parade for visiting dignitaries and twenty-seven delegations of former legionnaires - *les anciens de la Légion*.

Every cult needs a shrine. Had Camarón been on French territory, Rollet would have built it there. Sidi bel-Abbès was the next best place. For a Bible, he commissioned the respected military historian Jean Brunon to research and compile a hagiographical history of the Legion, called appropriately *Le Livre d'Or*, or Golden Book, in which bel-Abbès is referred to as 'the mother house' - as though the Legion were a latter-day Order of the Templars.[11]

Leading that first Camerone Day parade in bel-Abbès was a corps of bearded pioneers to 'open the road' in the Hohenlohe slow march of eighty-eight paces to the minute. The pioneers wearing cowhide aprons and carrying at the slope huge tree-felling axes instead of rifles are now traditional at the head of Legion parades. The beards were originally, under the Second Empire, to make a sapper immediately identifiable among clean-shaven comrades in the confusion of battle. Rollet revived them for theatrical effect.

The climax of the celebration in 1931 was the ceremonial consecration of the Monument aux Morts, a huge terrestrial bronze globe cast by Legion engineers with Camarón indicated by a gold star and all the countries where the Legion has fought outlined in gold. At each corner of the square marble base, for whose construction Maj Maire was responsible, stands a life-size bronze statue of a legionnaire with rifle reversed in mourning for his dead comrades. One of them is recognisably the immortal Loum-Loum. The monument cost the equivalent of £8,000 - a considerable amount at the time - and was paid for on the basis of one day's pay each by 30,000 legionnaires and officers, whose names are enshrined in the base.

Marching songs, except ribald ones, are not as important in the British forces as in most European armies. The Legion has many, of which the one chanted at every meal time is 'Black Pudding'. *Le Boudin* is as near a national anthem as the Legion gets. Rollet elevated it to the status of classical music, with a band of 180 musicians to play it at his parade, repeated every week thereafter as *la revue des categories* and held, not inside the Quartier Viénot barracks at bel-Abbès but in the Sacred Way leading from the barracks into the centre of town.

All his new Legion lacked was a code of honour. The old Legion had many times abandoned men who could not keep up with the hard pace of a column marching in the dry heat of the Sahara or in the dripping jungles of Madagascar. In the Vietnamese intervention too, those who could not keep up were not just abandoned to the Chinese or local bandits, but given a coup de grâce to save them from an agonising death. As late as the war in the Rif, legionnaires attested to having left dying men behind because they were already burdened with carrying the wounded with a chance of survival.[12]

There is something sacrificial in the idea of living men risking their own lives in order to recover a dead comrade's body, as required by the Code of Honour invented in the 1980s, since when it has been chanted on parade as a mystic pledge to the unseen faceless god whose device is the flaming grenade with the slogan *Legio patria nostra*. Some legionnaires do not even understand all the words for the first months of their training, but then how many Christians or Muslims or Buddhists *really* believe the words of the prayers they utter as an affirmation of belonging to a congregation or a community? In the same way the chanting of the Legion songs and the Code of Honour is a statement of belonging to a family or brotherhood.

Rollet was as shrewd a psychologist as he was a gifted leader - perhaps the first is part of the second - and in creating a ready-made identity for the legionnaire, he was baiting a hook. Many men and women don uniform as soldiers, sailors, airmen, doctors, nurses, priests and nuns because it gives them an identity. Rollet's genius was to make this identity of legionnaire available for men from all educational and social classes anywhere in the world by not defining too closely the image, except in ideals they could all reach out for.

A number of psychologists and psychiatrists have tried to analyse the Legion's mystique. If one believes the psychobabble, all legionnaires are emotionally inadequate and enlist to find an identity or a family they can belong to. But that does not explain why royals like Peter of Serbia, Louis II of Monaco, Sisowath Monireth of Thailand, Aage of Denmark and Amilakvari from Georgia and all the former and future generals, writers and government ministers joined as ordinary legionnaires? Didn't they have an identity already? The truth is that there are many reasons for a man to become a legionnaire and Rollet's branding still allows young men not even born in his lifetime to live the dream in fulfilment of an inner need so deep that in return they will give their lives when called upon to do so.

Chapter 26

AT BOTH ENDS OF THE MED

North Africa, 1918-1933;
Syria/Lebanon 1918-1927

During the First World War, Lyautey managed to hold on to most of France's gains in Morocco. As his forces slowly built up again after the cessation of hostilities, the annual rhythm was to send fighting columns each spring further and further into unsubdued territory and there build ugly but functional blockhouse forts, in which a garrison was abandoned for months, well stocked with food and ammunition. Once the main force had left the area, every sortie for water, to effect repairs to the outside of the walls or whatever, laid them open to ambush. A posting to these forts in featureless desert and bleak mountain scenery with no contact with the local population, nor even the sight of living animals for months on end, where one saw only the same few faces day after day - and came to hate them - drove men into depression. They blamed it on the bite of the *cafard* cockroach, but it was really sensory deprivation, for which the only remedy was to numb oneself with alcohol.

The feeling of being relentlessly watched by invisible eyes and the ever-present danger of being killed by a hidden marksman preyed on the nerves of men living on a knife-edge. With masochistic glee they told each other horror stories, like the one about the night at Tadlount in Morocco in 1923 when Lt Christian Aage despatched a four-man guard to an outlying tower, where they were to spend the night after drawing up the ladder which was the only access. When they did not return to the fort in the morning, he took six men to investigate. They found the ladder lying in the desert. At the top of the tower the German corporal was lying with his throat cut from ear to ear, while a

Russian legionnaire crouched in a corner, out of his mind but physically unharmed. The other two legionnaires were never found. Stories like this soon went the rounds.

It was all very well for officers like Prince Aage to talk of bayonet assaults as beautiful work. The everyday reality of Moroccan warfare was hardship, torture and mutilation, which made excellent material for sensationalised legionnaires' memoirs such as *Hell Hounds of France* and *Legion of the Lost* by 'ex-légionnaire 1384'.[1]

The man of the moment who arose to exploit the vulnerability and the poor morale of the French and Spanish colonial forces in Morocco was an exceptional Berber warlord of the Banu Uriaghel tribe. Abd el-Krim was educated in the Spanish enclave at Tetouan by European teachers and also attended Islamic school in Fez before entering the Bureau of Native Affairs. Elected *qadi al-qudat* or chief Muslim judge in Melilla, he was the editor of the Arabic supplement of the Spanish-language newspaper *El Telegrama del Rif*. Imprisoned in 1917 for writing anti-colonialist articles, he was released the following year but came to fear for his safety when the Spanish authorities started cracking down on dissidents and even handing back refugees from French territory, which had not formerly been the custom.

Taking to the mountains of the Rif with his brother as chief-of-staff, he achieved the difficult feat of raising a temporary confederation of tribes to fight the Spanish, killing somewhere around 13,000 of their soldiers including Gen Manuel Silvestre, the most senior officer in Spanish North Africa. In the second half of his campaign, Abd el-Krim also routed La Bandera and narrowly missed killing Col Francisco Franco, who reached safety in Tetouan on 13 December 1924 leaving several thousand more men dead behind him. The weapons abandoned in their headlong flight were carefully collected and carted off for future use. Thus came about the nightmare of colonial warfare, the ideal situation in which was summed up in Hilaire Belloc's couplet:

> Whatever happens, we have got
> the Maxim gun and they have not.

Abd el-Krim not only had machine guns; he also had a favourable Press, with British and American journalists apparently thinking that he intended to introduce Western-style democracy.[2] Most importantly, he had Franco's artillery. Unwilling to wait until the guns were pointed at him, Lyautey decided to strike first by establishing a blocking line of sixty-six forts garrisoned with Senegalese and Algerian troops, stretching from Fez to Kifan in territory claimed, but not occupied, by Spain.

In all this the Legion had little part because fear of their men deserting to Spanish territory made their commanders keep them well away from the border. When even the threat of being sent to Bechar if caught was not enough to dissuade 106 of his men from deserting into Spanish Morocco by the simple expedient of walking there, Fernand Maire introduced a bounty system, offering the local Berber tribesmen 20 francs for returning a deserter alive or 100 francs for bringing back just the man's head.

This contrasted with Abd el-Krim's enlightened approach. He forbade his men to torture and kill Legion deserters and instead hired them as instructors to pass on to his tribesmen their expertise with captured weapons. To encourage more legionnaires to turn their coats, he printed leaflets in German, which they could bring with them as safe-conducts, and which promised better pay than in the Legion and/or repatriation through Tangiers. After his capture, he admitted to a French journalist that he had never trusted the men who came to offer him their services after deserting from La Bandera or the Legion, and allowed them into action only under close surveillance.

During the period when French military attachés and consuls abroad were actively recruiting to fill the post-war gap, they arranged the transportation of men who in many cases signed up on a whim, or from hunger, but who would have changed their minds if left to find their own way to France. It is for this reason that the Legion now offers no travel assistance to would-be legionnaires. If they do not have the initiative and determination to get to a recruiting office in France under their own steam, they are the wrong type.[3]

Joseph Klems was a pretty good example of this. A German from Düsseldorf, he joined the Legion in 1920 and served in the mounted company of 2 REI, winning his sergeant's stripes two years later. For reasons that had something to do with excessive violence to subordinates, he was broken. In many armies, NCOs are promoted, busted and promoted again. Certainly, this was normal form in the old Legion where drink caused many men to lose their stripes. But in Klems' case, once no longer protected by his rank, he was put through the mill by men who had suffered under him while he was a sergeant.

Instead of taking his punishment and learning to behave better when next promoted, he deserted with his rifle in 1923 and passed himself off among the Berbers of the Middle Atlas as *hadji-aliman* - a German convert to Islam who had been on the *hadj* to Mecca. The penalty for failing in this ruse would have been surgical. To carry it off successfully implies some mastery of the Koran, or perhaps the mentality of a con-man. Whichever, Abd el-Krim saw in Klems the man he had been waiting for, and put him in charge of the artillery and machine guns captured from Gen Silvestre, which were by then sadly in need of tender loving care.

Until Lyautey drew his line in the sand too close for Abd el-Krim's comfort, the Berber warlord had no overt quarrel with the French, but since the new line of blockhouses cut his Riffians off from their food sources in the Ouerrha valley, he unleashed 4,000 warriors against them on 13 April 1925. Thanks to Klems training the Berber tribesmen in modern infantry tactics instead of indulging in the traditional *fantasia* of deliberately exposing themselves to French bullets as a demonstration of their trust in Allah to protect them, half of Lyautey's blockhouse forts were neutralised in weeks, thirty being evacuated as impossible to defend and nine captured by el-Krim and Klems, with the defenders slaughtered.

Although certainly sensationalised, this account by an anonymous British legionnaire described what it was like to be at the receiving end of such an attack:

'I woke with a start to hear a shrill cry like a child screaming in pain, then a volley of rifle shots rent the air, followed by the well-known shout of, *'Illah, illah allah akbar!'* I leaped to my feet as I heard the *sous-officier* crying, *'Aux armes! Aux armes! Prenez la garde, légionnaires!'* Men were crying out as they fell, pierced by knife or bullet. My friend Dell (a Canadian), the one man in the Legion I cared for, had been cut up right from the chest, and his eyes were staring with a pitiful look of surprise in his deadly white face. One hand was on his rifle, but the other had been shot away.

'Seeing the dark faces of the Arabs in front of me and knowing it was they who had knifed my pal, I went berserk and fought like a madman. From another part of the fort we could hear the sharp rat-tat of the machine guns, but where we were they could not be used as the enemy were right in the middle of us. (The Captain) seemed madder than ever, and now and again he roared with laughter. He emptied his revolver into the thick of the fight, standing on the edge of the wall and suddenly with one last cry of *Vive la Légion!* I saw him topple over backwards and disappear.'[4]

In the fort at Beni Derkul Lt Pol Lapeyre held out with his Senegalese garrison for seven weeks. With no chance of relief, he laid demolition charges and blew the entire fort up with himself and his men inside as the doors were at last forced with a battering ram and the tribesmen poured through. To relieve another besieged fort where ammunition was almost down to the last bullet husbanded to blow out one's own brains, two officers and forty legionnaires of 6th Battalion of 1 REI volunteered to infiltrate the siege lines at night and rescue the garrison.

A lieutenant and ten men made it as far as the blockhouse, where the noise of their arrival prompted the defenders to prime the fuses set to blow the whole place up. This obliged the rescuers to attempt an immediate return journey through the lines of now thoroughly aroused besiegers in company with the remnants of the garrison. Three legionnaires only made it back to base, earning a mention in despatches.[5]

Given the rapid development of aerial warfare in the First World War, it would have been surprising if the French command had not used aircraft to support ground troops working in such difficult mountainous terrain. US ex-legionnaire Charles Sweeney was hired to organise on a shoe-string budget a group of daredevil American pilots in the Escadrille Chérifienne, or Cherif Squadron, who flew 470 missions in the Rif war before being disbanded under diplomatic pressure from Washington in November 1925. Anticipating the Luftwaffe's last flights over Gen Paulus' forces marooned at Stalingrad to drop cargoes of Iron

Crosses, the future C-in-C Vietnam Jean-Marie de Lattre de Tassigny tried to get Sweeney's pilots to airdrop into forts surrounded by Abd el-Krim's forces small bundles of ice cubes and medals. It was not a success. Bombing tribal villages was easy with no anti-aircraft defences to worry about, but precision airdrops into the interior courtyard of surrounded blockhouses proved impossible.

Lyautey appealed to Paris for reinforcements, but his political masters turned a deaf ear. The only concession was the authorisation to form horse-mounted Legion cavalry units to compensate for the disbanding of the Algerian Spahis, suspected of nationalist tendencies. Not every Legion officer was in favour of mounting legionnaires on horses, one to a man. Gen Niessel, commanding 19 Army Corps in Algiers, reckoned that it would simply enable them to desert too fast to be caught! Even Rollet thought cavalry unnecessary, seeing the Legion as an infantry arm. He also agitated against Legion artillery because gunnery officers were cool and calculating mathematicians, who would ruin the gung-ho ambience of Legion messes.[6] Nevertheless, four companies of sappers were formed and several battalions given their own field batteries.

In the Rif war, Klems shrewdly decided which posts to attack and which to surround by a small besieging force while the main Moroccan Liberation Army continued on its victorious progress. Each victory of the tribal confederation brought more men to Abd el-Krim's banner, frightening Madrid and Paris into making peace overtures that he turned down in the hope of forcing out of them an autonomous Republic of the Rif.

In Paris, the politicians blamed Lyautey for the situation he had foreseen, with the result that in June 1925 the man who had ruled Morocco single-handed for so many years was consigned to oblivion in France. Marshal Philippe Pétain had retired from military and political life to raise chickens on a farm in Provence with his new wife. In July, he crossed the Mediterranean to take command of what was now considered a full-blown war, arriving in Morocco with all the advantages Lyautey had begged for and not been given.

To restore French prestige, fifty battalions were extracted from the French army of occupation in the Rhineland and sent to Morocco. With 160,000 French and 200,000 Spanish troops against him, Abd el-Krim's forces melted away, weakened by poor harvests and an epidemic of typhus sweeping through their mountain villages. Aware that the fragmented campaign against a mobile enemy which Lyautey had been fighting was a very different war from what he had known in Europe, Pétain was too shrewd an old soldier to rush into battle. One lesson he had learned at St-Cyr was that time spent in preparation is seldom wasted. So he took his time, refusing to be drawn into premature rescues of isolated Legion outposts, reasoning that they could be re-established when he had taken out Abd el-Krim and that the men in them were not his responsibility.

Each afternoon, he wrote to his wife, giving her detailed instructions of which chickens to keep and which to kill off when their laying fell behind his quota for them, but that domestic image contrasts ill with the business of his mornings when Vegetius'[7] maxim *First lay waste the enemy's land* could have been the motto on the wall of his office. In mid-September he launched his offensive with modern equipment, artillery, motorised divisions and reconnaissance aircraft as well as huge columns of mules, camels and men including Moroccan mercenaries - all meticulously organised down to the placing of the Bordel Mobile de Campagne in the safest place on the march, its dozen or more Moroccan girls aged between fifteen and eighteen being visited between fixed hours by scores of men each evening.[8]

Relentlessly, Pétain's columns burned crops and destroyed homes to leave the surviving tribesmen and their families starving and homeless in the cruel sub-zero winter of the Rif. On 8 May 1926, Spanish and French forces moved in for the kill and slaughtered so many of el-Krim's army that two weeks later on 23 May its leader was brought to bay. Surrounded, luckily for him by French forces, Abd el-Krim signed the surrender treaty on 26 May, all his dreams of independence shattered. To the incomprehension of his Spanish allies, who wanted to shoot the captive Berber leader, Pétain exiled Abd el-Krim to a comfortable estate on the remote island of La Réunion in the Indian Ocean with a generous pension of 100,000 francs per annum.

In 1947, as a gesture of clemency, the first president of the Fourth Republic Vincent Auriol commuted this to a more pleasant exile on the French Riviera. When the ship transporting Abd el-Krim and forty-two members of his household was passing through the Suez Canal, the 65-year-old warrior managed to slip ashore at Port Said and go to ground among his co-religionists. He lived in Cairo preaching the liberation of the Maghreb until shortly before it began under the FLN in 1954.

Pétain's defeat of the confederation did not stop the tribesmen of the Rif from returning home to rebuild their ruined villages and defy the French from inaccessible mountain fastnesses, much as the Pathan tribesmen had defied the soldiers of the Raj on the Northwest Frontier. Not until the summer of 1933 did the last Riffians surrender.

It has been claimed that Abd el-Krim's initial successes against Spanish and French troops inspired other colonial uprisings, in particular the Druze Revolt in Syria of 1925, but all they have in common is the cause: the high-handed arrogance of the European colonial administrators, insensitive to local and religious customs. Although the native peoples were not supposed to know about it, the Middle East was carved up as early as 9 May 1916 by an agreement signed by Sir Mark Sykes for Britain and Georges Picot for France and kept secret until 'blown' after the Revolution by the Soviet government. The main provisions were that France should get Syria, Lebanon and some other territory after the war, while Britain grabbed oil-rich Iraq and the Palestinian ports of Haifa and Acre, to which it was intended to build a pipeline. The mission of archaeologist-turned-soldier T. E. Lawrence starting in October of that year was a scam and his promise to Sharif Hussein ibn-Ali of Mecca that he would have a country of his own to rule after the war in return for raising the tribes of the Hejaz against the Ottoman Empire, was thus completely deceitful. Seldom has more misery come out of one set of lies.

As a token of Franco-British solidarity, Paris sent a *régiment de marche* to fight in Gen Allenby's army. More of a mixed bag than most of its kind, this comprised both French and Algerian infantry, a squadron of aircraft and one of African cavalry, plus some officers to command a hotchpotch of locally recruited Syrian and Armenian ex-soldiers. The last element was known as La Légion d'Orient, and claimed some remarkable successes against the Turks.

When the French took over Syria and Lebanon with the approval of the League of Nations after the First World War, one of their first acts was to expel Sharif Hussein from Damascus, after which the embarrassed British created a consolation prize for him in the form of a puppet-king's throne in Baghdad. Among the cocktail of religions and races he thus left behind in Syria/Lebanon was the religious minority of 100,000 Druzes or *muwahhidun*, who had broken away from the rest of Islam in the eleventh century and permitted neither conversion nor intermarriage with their neighbours.

With all its commitments in North Africa and the post-war recruiting problems, the Legion had little manpower to spare, but to establish French control in Syria, two battalions of 4 REI and a squadron of 1 REC were shipped there, as well as some Saharan camel corps riders under French officers and colonial troops from Senegal and Madagascar. The war of 'pacification' that ensued was very like the one going on in the Rif, with atrocities on both sides, but needed no inspiration by Abd el-Krim or anyone else because the ingredients were local.

Things were relatively peaceful by 1923 when a certain Capt Carbillet was appointed governor of the area of Jabal al-Duruz, where most of the Druzes lived. Carbillet seems to have been the best kind of French colonial administrator, squeezing out of the taxes he collected the necessary funds to build schools and roads and provide clean water supplies, and in other ways improving the lot of the local population. In 1925 he stepped down, or was sacked, and five Druze leaders sought an interview with France's High Commissioner for Syria to reassure themselves about his successor.

The current High Commissioner was Gen Maurice Sarrail, whom we last met leading the surviving legionnaires from the Dardanelles to Salonika in the Great War. The appointment of one of France's least diplomatic soldiers to such a post was an appalling choice. Typically, instead of listening to the worries of the Druzes, he clapped all five in prison for their brazen effrontery. It was the spark in a powder keg. Starting in July 1925 Druze guerrilla fighters led by Sultan al-Atrash raided towns and held up trains, defeating various French military units throughout August, including detachments of 4 REI. The Druzes were joined in September by Syrian nationalists calling for a countrywide uprising. With Damascus in ferment, the French bombed the city, causing a thousand casualties[9] and fanning the flames of revolt throughout Syria and Lebanon.

The reaction of the government in Paris to the defeat of a mixed force of 3,000 Malagasy and Syrian troops in French uniform was to order Sidi bel-Abbès to despatch a battalion of legionnaires to Syria to sort out the mess. US legionnaire Bennett Doty from Demopolis in Alabama was in 8th Battalion of 1 REI and wrote a book about his experiences, *Legion of the Damned*. It could have been entitled *Legion of the Drunk*, for, according to him the sea voyage to Beirut was one long alcoholic binge from start to finish.

That accords with the story of unemployed Welsh miner John Harvey, who joined up and found himself grooming the mounts of the aristocratic White Russian riders of 4 Squadron 1 REC in Sousse, Tunisia. Drafted to Syria with 165 horses and fifteen pack mules, Harvey was locked up in his lieutenant's cabin when the transport *Porthos* called at the British-controlled ports of Alexandria, Port Said and Jaffa, in case he jumped ship. His garbled story of the fighting in Syria is interesting because it illustrates how many soldiers have fought - like the Tommies in France 1914-18, who thought that Germany was just over the horizon - with no clear idea of where they were or what they were fighting for. Nor did he have much understanding of the Legion's structure beyond that of his own unit and officers.

Harvey's Levantine geography is likewise vague, but his account of travelling inland from the port of Beirut on a train attacked by Druzes is graphic enough, with the attackers riding alongside like Indians in a Western film and the legionnaires firing back through slats in the carriage sides. The odds were radically changed against the Druzes when the machine gun company of 4 REI opened up on them, but before arrival in Damascus, four of Harvey's comrades were wounded and three civilian passengers were dead.

He was lucky the machine gunners had come along for the ride. In a recent attack on the same line, casualties had numbered over seventy, with the train out of control for several kilometres after the engine-driver was shot dead. Eventually a passenger managed to clamber onto the footplate and avert disaster by closing the wide-open throttle.[10]

On 10 September 1925 Doty, Harvey and the Cossacks and ex-hussars of 1 REC rendezvoused with 5th battalion of 4 REI at the village of Musseifré, clearing a landing strip and building six strong-points around the village while 1 REC threw out a screen of mounted skirmishers to give them cover from the Druzes known to be in the surrounding countryside. In the late summer heat, with only combat rations and brackish local well-water that had to be boiled before it could be drunk, Doty's alcohol-deprived comrades were near mutiny at the end of three days' labouring.

When scouts heliographed a warning on 16 September that a large party of Druzes was approaching, no one apparently took much notice. At 0300hrs next morning the first shots roused the defenders to send up flares that revealed hundreds of white-robed men crawling towards the inadequate wire defences. Infiltrators killed the men guarding the legionnaires' horses and slaughtered some of them on the spot, riding the others out of town through gaps between the strong-points. The Legion marksmen treated this as sport, shooting the horses first and then using the riders scrambling for safety as target practice.

When the main attack came in, the numbers were so great that the defenders' machine guns jammed from the heat of continuous firing. Shooting through loopholes, Doty saw the mass of attackers reach within a few metres of the walls several times. Under plunging fire also from infiltrators who had climbed onto the roofs of the houses and a holy man's tomb behind them, the drunken slobs whose behaviour had so appalled him on board ship now revealed their true colours as highly trained and disciplined soldiers with nerves of steel. A 37mm machine-gun crew took care of the infiltrators on the roofs, but only after several officers and NCOs had been shot.

Towards dawn commanding officer Capt Landriau was hoping for French aircraft to bomb the Druzes after daylight. Ammunition was running out and each man was warned to keep the last bullet for himself, but the Druzes melted away with the daylight, taking their wounded with them. Out of 165 men, 1 REC had lost twenty-five dead, with twenty-four wounded. Relief came in the form of a battalion of 16th Algerian *tirailleurs*, who charged into the village and cleaned out the few remaining Druzes.

On 19 November the same men under Capt Landriau were in a crumbling hill fort built by the Turks at Rachaya on the flanks of Mount Hermon, together with a squadron of Tunisian Spahis. A patrol under Lt Gardy was ambushed nearby, which was the first indication that a force of 4,000 Druzes, well provided with arms and ammunition from looted Turkish magazines had surrounded the fort. The only outgoing communication being by carrier pigeon, the garrison's last message was, *Send a battalion*. Again, ammunition became so scarce that bayonet charges were the only way to force the attackers back and gain some breathing space. It was a Hollywood script in reverse, with the cavalry dying on its feet until rescued by a column of Algerian infantry from the Bekaa valley.

At the far end of the Mediterranean, the war in the Rif continued. At Djihani in 1929 an inexperienced Italian lieutenant allowed himself to be tricked into a battle in open country with the result that forty-one legionnaires died. Such a loss was nothing compared with the Great War, but French public opinion was outraged and moves were made at last to update the Legion's equipment. In March 1930 the first motorised company was created at Meknès by equipping Lt Gambiez and his men of the mounted company of 2nd Battalion of 2 REI with four Berliet armoured cars to replace their mules. Motor transport requiring roads, roads were built using the civil engineering experience of the Legion. A 140km highway from Marrakesh to Ouarzazarte was constructed, in the process a 700-metre tunnel having to be hacked with picks through a mountain that stood in the way.

And still the war of skirmishes and *razzias* went on fanning the flames of bitterness that flared up on 23 May 1930, when a Legion mounted company was surrounded in the Wadi Guir by 750 tribesmen and only rescued from complete annihilation by their comrades of 3rd Mounted Company of 2 REI and a squadron of

Spahis. On 29 August, 1st Mounted Company of 2 REI lost twenty-one dead at Tadighoust.

One enemy stronghold held out for three months against the Legion. At Jebel Baddou in the Atlas Mountains 3,000 tribesmen and their families, supported by several hundred refugees from elsewhere with flocks of 15,000 sheep, were eventually driven out of their homes and took refuge in the extensive caves of the area, emerging only for water from nearby springs. Bombed from the air and mercilessly machine-gunned from the ground, they finally surrendered to slake their and their children's thirst, but not before many of the men had thrown themselves over a precipice for the pleasure of taking one of the assaulting legionnaires with them at the end of his long climb. After the 'rebels' had handed over their weapons, salt was metaphorically rubbed in their wounds by the sight of a French victory parade on the spot, the participants in which then feasted on a *méchoui* of the tribesmen's sheep, cooked whole on spits over the embers in a huge fire-pit. The scene could have been from one of those desert films that caught the imagination of would-be legionnaires between the wars.

One of history's lesser secrets is whether any legionnaire was similarly motivated by seeing the operetta *Desert Song*, written by Sigmund Romberg with lyrics by Oscar Hammerstein. The plot corresponded loosely with Klems' story. Finally brought to bay in a cave after being betrayed to the French by one of his unwilling Berber wives, he was expected to make a heroic last stand and then 'do the decent thing' and shoot himself, rather than be taken.

Not Klems. He surrendered, was court-martialled and sentenced to death early in 1927. However, political instability in Paris and pressure from German diplomats had the sentence commuted to life imprisonment on Devil's Island. After seven half-starved years in the misery of *le bagne* there, he was released in 1934, following representations to Paris by Hitler's new National Socialist government in Berlin. Repatriated to Germany, Klems committed suicide while held in jail for some minor offence, shortly before Hitler invaded Poland on 1 September 1939.

Chapter 27

VETERANS AND VOLUNTEERS:
CONFUSION AND COURAGE

France, 1939-1940; Norway 1940

The version of the 1940 French defeat and capitulation usually accepted in Anglo-Saxon countries was created when stand-alone Britain boosted its morale by accusing its continental allies of having 'let us down'. This simplification is as true - and as misleading - as for a Frenchman to say that the British had fought to the last drop of French blood before unilaterally renouncing their obligations at Dunkirk.

By vilifying the French army for having no fighting spirit, Britons could pat themselves on the back and say, 'It would never happen here,' ignoring the fact that Britain was as ill prepared for war as France, despite the dire warnings of Churchill and his 'war party' during the 1930s. The only reason why it 'never happened here' was that Britain had twenty nautical miles or more between her shores and the Wehrmacht, which was well equipped and trained for continental river crossings, but not for an invasion of Britain, because that was not on Hitler's original agenda.

The French general staff's monumental error was to regard the immense investment in the subterranean citadels and immovable artillery of the Maginot Line as an English Channel. Incredibly, they forgot the modified Schlieffen plan that had brought the Germans to the outskirts of Paris so swiftly in 1914 and shut their eyes to geography: at the western end of the Line, Holland and Belgium provided the perfect terrain for Guderian's Panzers to outflank it - as his tankers' fathers in the Kaiser's uniforms had done twenty-five years before.

The *Anschluss* with Austria and the invasion of Czechoslovakia in 1938 and the end of the Spanish Civil War in May 1939 all produced influxes of volunteers to the Legion. As war crept nearer in the summer of that year the French War Ministry could not make up its mind about the foreigners volunteering to fight for France. The vacillation continued until 16 September in the second week of war. Among those kept waiting for an answer was the American flier Charles Sweeney, who again offered to form a squadron of fellow Americans to fly French planes. He was still waiting in May 1940, by which time his offer had been overtaken by events.

Some foreigners resident in France volunteered to enlist from political conviction and some for love for the country and way of life, which was considerably more tolerant of black people, drink, drugs and sexual nonconformity than 1930s Britain or America. Others were political exiles from Germany and Eastern European countries who thought a French uniform would provide an insurance policy against the day the Gestapo came looking for them.

As in 1914, the French government decided that foreigners could serve only in Legion uniform. The first Legion regiment to reach France was 11 REI commanded by the much-wounded veteran Col Fernand Maire, comprising 2,500 long-service legionnaires and 500 Legion reservists with an armoured element from 7th North African Division and 97th Divisional Reconnaissance Group. To distinguish the new volunteer units from this 'old' Legion, they were formed into Régiments de Marche de Volontaires Etrangers (RMVE) with a number in the 20 series. In 1939, 21 RMVE and 22 RMVE recruited more or less any foreigner willing to put on a French uniform and were allocated a sprinkling of Legion officers and NCOs, making up the cadres with recalled Legion reservists. In May 1940, 23 RMVE was formed.

Apart from 3,000 battle-experienced Spanish anti-fascist refugees who had fled Franco at the end of the Spanish civil war and since been held in concentration camps in southern France, many of the RMVE volunteers were unfit white-collar men. They tended to cause friction once in uniform by clinging together in linguistic groupings, and the argumentative nature of the Jewish East Europeans irritated veteran NCOs when they responded to orders with the word, 'Why?' Nor were reservist NCOs very happy to be back in Legion uniform; having acquired wives and children, they found it hard to return to the bachelor life of boozing and brawling.

Each of the RMVEs and 12 REI, after being brought up to strength with volunteers, had around 300 Jewish recruits, with 400 more being trained in North Africa. In Col Maire's 11 REI at La Valbonne near Lyon there were another 1,800. The high proportion began to alarm not only Legion officers trying to convert these over-educated civilians into blindly obedient soldiers, but also the general staff. On 14 February 1940, when one might think that any soldier was better than none, it issued an instruction that in future foreign Jewish volunteers for the Legion were to be turned away under various pretexts without making it obvious that 'special measures' were being taken against them.[1]

Apart from the Legion policy of avoiding concentrations of any nationality, there was a second reason to be wary of the Spaniards and the East Europeans: both groups included many Communists. Since the signature of the German-Soviet Non-Aggression Pact, the Communist International, which controlled the non-Soviet Communist parties, was pro-German - changing sides after 20 months of war when Hitler invaded the USSR in June 1941. Any foreign Communist was therefore suspect at the outbreak of war, when the French Communist party was outlawed and its members driven underground.

Whatever their political or racial background, the volunteers were issued out-of-date equipment, or none at all by a commissariat in chaos. Things were so bad in 12 REI that Lt Georges Masselot had to write his own training manuals for the largely obsolete weapons issued, many of which were lacking parts and therefore useless. Masselot's volunteers had so little webbing that they were driven to tying their equipment onto themselves with string.[2]

A mobile foreign reconnaissance unit designated 97 GERD was created from 2nd squadron of 1 REC with officers from 2 REC, formed in July 1939 and disbanded after the Armistice of June 1940. Of all the Legion formations in France, only 13 DBLE was armed with the current infantry rifle, model MAS 36 - and that was for their mission to Narvik. The others all had the detested First World War Lebel. Given the role of Panzers in spearheading any German attack, it was deplorable that the Legion was never issued any anti-tank weapons. However, since the RMVE were held in training camps until May 1940, it seems that there was no real intention to allow them into combat until the situation was so desperate that they were flung into the front on a sink-or-swim basis.

Ordered into action straight from the training camp at La Valbonne on 11 May 12 REI, on whose strength were 600 Polish Jews and 900 Spanish refugees[3], was ordered to defend Soissons in Picardy. Attacked by Stukas and Panzers, by 6 June the regiment was shattered after fighting its way out of encirclement. Its commander Col Besson commented afterwards that the German NCOs who had been excellent in training camp were less than bold in combat, almost certainly because they knew what would happen to them if taken prisoner. One of his junior officers, Lt Albert Brothier did appreciate that his Spanish and East European recruits were highly motivated - never mind that they ignored Legion traditions and were slovenly on parade.[4]

An incident during the retreat from Soissons illustrates another problem of the 'political' volunteers. One of the ex-Communist Poles, who had left the Party in disgust after the German-Soviet Non-Aggression Pact of 23 August 1939 divided his homeland between the two signatories, recounted how on being wounded he called out to comrades running past to help him. They, however, were 'loyal' Party members and deliberately left him to die. He owed his life to a long-service Legion NCO who risked his life to come back for the wounded man.[5]

By the Armistice of 22 June 1940, 12 REI had made its way in the flood of refugees to Limoges in central France, but numbered only 300 out of the 2,800 men who had finished training. Losses in Maire's 11 REI on the Somme front reached 50% between 9 and 22 June - and eventually around 75%. The regimental flag was burned to save it falling into enemy hands close to the church of Crézilles, near Nancy. There too, according to Legionnaire Georges Manue two deserters were shot a few hours before the Armistice,[6] after which the long-service men somehow managed to make their way through a country in total chaos back to the Mediterranean and across to North Africa.

Of the volunteer units, 21 RMVE was moved from the Maginot Line to the Verdun front, where it was shattered by the German attacks of the night of 8-9 June and ceased to exist except on paper. Disarmed after the Armistice at Nancy, the survivors were herded initially into 'cages' and then permanent POW camps. On 13 June 24 RMVE broke and ran on the Marne front, but since all around them was in confusion, that is hardly an indictment. For two nightmare days and nights 23 RMVE survived Panzer attacks supported by Stuka strafing missions before disengaging on 17 June, when Marshal Pétain broadcast an ambiguous order that was widely taken to mean laying down one's arms.

The record of 22 RMVE was as good as any regular regiment. Transported straight from its training camp to the front in Alsace, lacking much essential equipment, it had been re-assigned immediately and sent by train, truck and finally by a six-day march through the confusion of the main attack to Marchelépot on the Somme. There it withstood heavy German attacks from 22 May until 6 June, when the supply of ammunition was exhausted. A number of the volunteers used their last cartridge to blow their brains out, rather than be captured by the Germans; others, of German origin, were shot immediately after being taken prisoner, despite their French uniforms and papers. Of the remainder, many both from Poland and Spain were to die not in POW camps treated according to the rules of war, but in German concentration and death camps.

Thus the record of the volunteers was no worse than that of regular units, overwhelmed and out-generalled all along the front. Considering that many of the civilian volunteers knew the French uniform they wore would not be respected under the Geneva Convention on capture, their courage is incredible.

After the Allied invasion of North Africa the Legion regiments there fought for De Gaulle's Free French, but one legendary unit was Gaullist throughout the war, and represented half of his entire army in 1940. Formed in Algeria like a *régiment de marche*, but smaller, 13th Demi-Brigade de la Légion Etrangère - abbreviated to 13 DBLE - was posted to northern Syria but shipped instead to

France and set to practise arctic warfare techniques. At this point, the legionnaires guessed they were going to be sent north - although one can never be certain of such things in any army.

Three months after the alliance with Germany in August 1939, the USSR invaded its western neighbour Finland. The vastly smaller Finnish army fought a series of brilliant rearguard actions against the enormous Red Army throughout that winter, inflicting huge casualties on the Russian soldiers whose best generals were either rotting in Gulag camps or had been shot in Stalin's purges. Since the USSR had allied itself with Nazi Germany, Britain and France prepared to intervene on the side of the Finns in Operation Petsamo. Owing to differences of opinion between London, which wanted to concentrate on the main threat on the Franco-German frontier, and the French General Staff toying with a number of interventions elsewhere in the hope that they would delay the German invasion,[7] nothing was done before the Finns surrendered on 13 March 1940.

On 8 April Royal Navy vessels mined Norwegian waters against German invasion. The government in Oslo protested, but the following day Hitler invaded anyway. At last the British and French decided to act and destroy the strategic port of Narvik, through which high-grade Swedish iron ore was exported to Germany. Under Lt Col Raoul-Charles Magrin-Vernerey, 13 DBLE was integrated into a mixed Franco-British-Norwegian-Polish force that included two Norwegian brigades, a Polish contingent and three battalions of 24 Brigade of Guards. The French contingent was commanded by Gen Marie-Emile Antoine Bethouart. They left Brest aboard the Canadian Pacific liner *Monarch of Bermuda*, supported by seven Royal Navy vessels, and disembarked on 13 May against heavy German ground and air attack in the fishing ports of Bjerkvik and Meby, about 10km north of Narvik at the head of Herjangs Fjord. Simultaneously, to the south of Narvik a British force was landed at Ankenes, the idea being to use the two bridgeheads as a pincer between which to squeeze the 4,500 German and Austrian forces[8] occupying Narvik itself.

Bethouart had graduated from St Cyr in the same promotion as De Gaulle. He and Magrin-Vernerey were the sort of officer who could have stemmed the German advance, had they been given the men and equipment. Magrin-Vernerey had actually run away from home to join the Legion at the age of fifteen, but been rejected as obviously under-age. By the end of the First World War he was a captain in 60th Infantry, had been wounded seven times and made Chevalier de la Légion d'Honneur. His entitlement to a 90% disability pension did not stop him serving between the wars with the Legion in North Africa, the Middle East and Vietnam. He and Bethouart were now about to win the only French victory of 1939-40.

From the moment 1st battalion of 13 DBLE waded ashore from their improvised invasion fleet of wooden whalers towed by MTBs, time was against them. So was the weather. The snow, bloodstained in many places by the shattered bodies of the local inhabitants blown to pieces by the naval guns, was still knee-high. Yet, despite the pessimistic predictions of the regulars, Capt Pierre-Olivier Lapie was impressed to see his hitherto sullen Spaniards show their toughness in combat while the East Europeans - whose wealth of academic qualifications had earned 13 DBLE the mocking sobriquet *la troupe des intellectuals* - showed their true worth once they had a German uniform in their sights.[9]

Knowing it could only be a matter of days before Gen Gerd von Rundstedt's forty-five Wehrmacht divisions started to move into France, Bethouart and Magrin-Vernerey were determined to do their job against the clock. However, by the time they had put several German units to flight, abandoning equipment and prisoners as they retreated, the phoney war was over and Guderian's Panzers were blitzkrieging their way through Holland and Belgium.

Accordingly the British troops in the Norwegian 'sideshow' were ordered to withdraw on 24 May, and prepared to do so, but Bethouart and Magrin-Vernerey ignored their instructions from Paris to do likewise. Although lacking the forces to hold Narvik against German counter-attack, they decided to continue the mission as a way of salving national pride in the throes of defeat. The 2nd Battalion of 13 DBLE moved in from the south and 1st Battalion re-embarked to land just north of Narvik on the night of 27-28 May. Against all the odds, it fought its way through a series of heavily defended railway tunnels into the city, demolishing many harbour installations and destroying several Luftwaffe aircraft on the ground at the local airfield. For his part in the grim battle of the tunnel, British legionnaire James Williamson won both the Croix de Guerre with star and Norwegian bar.

A company of 2nd Battalion under Lt Szabo pushed on along the railway lines, over which the iron ore had to travel, nearly to the Swedish frontier. Spearheaded by the motorcycle unit of Jacques 'Toto' Lefort, they managed briefly to cut off all the German forces to the north of them before being forced to withdraw undefeated or risk being stranded by the ebbing tide of war. After two captured German aircrew shot two British guards with a concealed Luger pistol, the legionnaires executed them both.[10]

Having liberated forty Allied prisoners, capturing 400 German soldiers and blowing up a great deal of military equipment, 13 DBLE was evacuated on 7 June. Its numbers were reduced by seven officers, five NCOs and fifty-five legionnaires - two of whom, according to long-service legionnaire Charles Favrel were shot for desertion after a field court martial, despite claiming to have been left behind when they fell asleep from exhaustion.[11] According to him also another Spanish legionnaire was shot for looting, but these things are still impossible to verify officially.

Chapter 28

WHOSE SIDE ARE WE ON, SERGEANT?

France - North Africa - Syria - Britain, 1940

If the story of the Legion in the Second World War reads confusingly, it was far worse for the men involved. In Syria, John Harvey was typical of British and other legionnaires who were unclear where they were or for what political purpose they were fighting, but most combatants at least know which side of a conflict they are on. During this war many legionnaires and other French servicemen asked their superiors this question, only to learn that they were not sure, either. 'Fighting for France' could mean loyalty to the legal government in Vichy, or it could mean fighting against that government with De Gaulle.

When 13 DBLE returned to France via Glasgow on 14 June, it disembarked to find the home front in such chaos that there were no orders for it. The frustration of Bethouart and a fire-eater like Magrin-Vernery can be imagined. Discipline was hard to maintain. *Pour encourager les autres,* two brothers who attempted to desert were executed[1] and Magrin-Vernery is reputed to have personally shot dead a young infantry lieutenant who told him that continuing resistance would only cause trouble for everyone.[2]

On 18 June Col Charles De Gaulle - a protégé of Pétain, who had protected him from the many enemies he made by his outspoken criticism of French strategy and generalship in the 1930s - made his famous appeal to French men and women to continue the fight. Those who were free to do so were invited to join his Free French forces which, at the time, existed only in his own imagination. De Gaulle's lone voice crying in the wilderness of defeat touched a chord in Magrin-Vernerey's indomitable soul, but the renegade colonel in London was technically a traitor, betraying his government - which had fled from Paris to Bordeaux.

It was one thing to commit treason himself, but no French officer could order his men to betray their government, whatever they thought of its policies. Magrin-Vernerey therefore gave his veterans of Narvik the choice of surrendering in France or joining De Gaulle. Those who wanted to accompany him to Britain stayed with, or were transferred to, 1st Battalion. The others, on the roll of 2nd Battalion, opted to remain in France and make their way back to North Africa under Maj Boyer-Resses.

German tanks were on the outskirts of the port-city of Brest as Magrin-Vernerey embarked 500 men on the next ship leaving for Southampton. Maj Pierre Koenig and Lt Dmitri Amilakvari literally missed the boat while reconnoitring near Rennes. They solved that problem by commandeering a fishing boat to make the crossing, and caught up with the others at De Gaulle's Free French forces camp in Trentham Park near Stoke-on-Trent. Sleeping in the open on the first night and in tents thereafter, they found 13 DBLE the only organised formation among a collection of men from the French army, navy and air force who had been evacuated from Dunkirk. With local stores unable to cope for four days, food was scarce until deer roaming the park were slaughtered, butchered and cooked in washing boilers.

Magrin-Vernerey was promoted by De Gaulle to full colonel in recognition of the success of the Narvik raid and, happily for chroniclers, changed his name for the simpler *nom de guerre* Monclar - this in the hope of avoiding trouble for his family in France. His men, however, were far from happy with what they had got themselves into by following him to Britain. On the very day that the Armistice took effect in France, twenty-nine Republican Spaniards who believed that the Legion was to be disbanded and they would be handed over to Franco, mutinied and were escorted to prison by British police, no cells having been constructed in Trentham Park.

The sorry story escalated, with many other Spaniards striking in sympathy.[3] They too were handed over to the police. Given an ultimatum offering either 'repatriation' to Legion units in North Africa or staying in Britain with the Free French, the Spaniards demonstrated the depth of their despair at a choice between two alternatives, neither of which corresponded with their needs, by voting instead to stay in the cells. Some French officers and NCOs were anglophobic, for the same vague reasons that many insular Britons dislike the French. They argued that sending the Spaniards to British prisons was not the way to treat fellow-legionnaires, however troublesome.

De Gaulle's haughty 'State visit' to the camp on 30 June did nothing to heal the rift. Many legionnaires boycotted the visit with no effect since De Gaulle had no intention of talking to other ranks - which his mentor Pétain would have done in the circumstances, to let them vent their grievances.

Although having no great reason to love the British, Monclar decided that since they were the only allies offering a chance of redressing the shame of defeat, it was best to conceal his feelings and attempt to get on with his often unwilling hosts. To weed out those who disagreed with him, he encouraged a repatriation movement by officers who had fought bravely at Narvik. It seems that a factor in their decisions was resentment at the prejudices of the uninformed local inhabitants - summed up in the phrase, 'The French let us down.'

Their dilemma was that if De Gaulle lost, his supporters would be traitors without a country. On the other hand, what was the point of being repatriated to the emasculated Armée de l'Armistice, whose main function was to guard the demarcation line between the German-occupied zone and Vichy France? The war, temporarily stalemated with the Germans unable to invade the British Isles and the British unable to do anything except sit tight, was obviously going to last several years, during which married men would not see their wives and children. A neighbour of the author, Marcel Verliat was serving as a reservist in the French navy. Landed at Portsmouth, he ate one meal of sausage and mash, washed down by a mug of long-stewed tea, in the RN barracks there. Having sampled English food, he marched back up the gangway with most of his shipmates and stayed on board until the moorings were slipped and they could return to the pleasures of *la cuisine française*. Many decisions made during this time were thus determined by personal or family reasons that had nothing to do with what was morally or politically 'right' or 'wrong'.[4]

Oddly enough, Legion recruiting seems not to have ceased

immediately after the Armistice. Journalist and author Arthur Koestler, although holding a Hungarian passport, had been a war correspondent for the London *News Chronicle* during the Civil War in Spain, where his articles earned him a spell in a fascist jail.

Having been lucky not to collect the last cigarette and twelve bullets which both sides of that conflict usually awarded irritating foreigners, he had no desire to see the inside of a Gestapo prison. On hearing of Pétain's surrender on 17 June 1940, Koestler re-invented himself as Albert Dubert, a German-speaking Swiss taxi driver from Berne, and 'volunteered' for the Legion, making it plain to the sympathetic recruiting sergeant that he wanted a ticket out of France, ostensibly to join the 'real Legion' in North Africa.

Having received no direct order in the general chaos to cease recruiting, the sergeant therefore signed Koestler on and issued a travel warrant. Other Central Europeans used to joke that a Hungarian was a man who could follow you into a revolving door and come out in front of you. Koestler qualified by somehow making his way through the chaos of three million refugees on the roads and competing for what little public transport there was. Heading for Marseilles, he was in one respect better off than the civilian refugees, who were dependent on volunteer food kitchens, because his enlistment papers at least guaranteed him a bunk and food at army camps on the way.

Reaching the Legion depot at Fort St-Jean in Marseilles on 11 August - a six-week journey that would have taken a day in normal circumstances - he was already officially an ex-legionnaire, all French forces in the Free Zone governed from Vichy having been demobilised under the terms of the Armistice agreement that took effect on 25 June. Although Marseilles was in the Free Zone, even refugees with entry visas from countries willing to accept them were not being granted exit visas to leave France until they had been screened to make sure the Germans had no objection. Koestler therefore ingratiated himself with four British soldiers on the run in civilian clothes. Together, they bluffed their way onto a ship leaving for Oran, where Baron Rudiger von Etzdorf, an anti-Nazi German ex-naval officer, spirited them away to neutral Lisbon and London.

Among less famous temporary legionnaires was Miroslav Liskutin, one of fifty qualified pilots from Czechoslovakia who escaped to France after the German occupation of their country, abandoned by its British and French allies in October 1938.

Volunteering to fly for France, he was enlisted first in the Legion and then posted nonsensically to 1 REI in bel-Abbès. Transferred into the Air Force in May 1940 Legionnaire 84202 Liskutin found himself at the time of the Armistice among a small number of French and other pilots trying to steal aircraft at Bordeaux-Mérignac airport, in which to fly to Britain and continue the fight. The ground crews, having no such option, refused to fuel aircraft for take-off, so it was by ship that these pilots finally reached the UK - in Liskutin's case to end the war a Squadron Leader sporting both the DFC and AFC.

Individual non-German refugees hiding in French uniform were small fry at that moment, but many German- and Austrian-born legionnaires were on the Gestapo's wanted list. On 17 and 20 August and again 6-9 September, a Special German Control Commission insisted that they all be handed over under the terms of Article XIX of the Armistice agreement, on the spurious grounds that they were pro-Nazi fifth columnists illegally imprisoned by the French! There were also numbers of German and Austrian legionnaires and ex-legionnaires who wanted to join the German side, whether from personal conviction or to avoid reprisals on their families in the Reich. Accordingly, at Fuveau, between Aix-en-Provence and Marseilles, ninety pro-Hitler ex-legionnaires were handed over to a Luftwaffe search team. Similarly, small parties of Italian officers were trying to locate Italian-born legionnaires for repatriation under the terms of the separate Armistice agreement signed with Mussolini. In North Africa, 320 German legionnaires demanded repatriation in August. Isolated in the punishment camp of Koléa, they were in a state of mutiny, shouting down any officer who tried to give them orders with repeated yells of 'Heil Hitler!' On 26 September and 9 October two groups totalling 996 Germans were thus assembled for repatriation, although how many were pro-Nazi and how many were coerced or volunteered for the sake of their families living in the Reich, is impossible to say.

The disparity between Berlin's estimate of the total numbers of Germans and Austrians in the Legion and the numbers actually handed over was reflected in Goebbels' personal diary as late as 8 March 1941. He was explicit that the laggards should be formed into 'rehabilitation' units to fight in Africa - in other words, penal battalions to punish them for not deserting in 1933, when the Nazi campaign of defamation of the Legion began.[5]

Whilst all the Axis-born legionnaires who wanted repatriation were allowed to depart, an uncounted number of legionnaires who did not want to return were administratively 'lost'. *Legio patria nostra* is much more than a slogan, and no Legion officer would hand over to the Gestapo legionnaires wanted for anti-Nazi activities back home or who had any other reason to think they would suffer for serving in the Legion. A 'phantom column' was therefore formed without the knowledge of Vichy or 19th Division in Oran, under whose control Sidi bel-Abbès fell. With their personal records torn up and burned, these men were given civilian clothes and became 'European Workers Detachment No 1' under 2nd Lt Chenel, the youngest officer in 1 REI, who was fresh out of St Cyr. In trucks, they travelled from bel-Abbès to Aïn Sefra and on to the punishment battalion depot at Bechar in the far south. Through Saharan sand-storms they pushed on in the suffocating heat to Bourem on the Niger River in what is now central Mali. The next stage to the French base at Bamako was relatively unadventurous. There, a special train was waiting to take them to Louga in Senegal, where a second phantom column from Fez was waiting. Its commander, Capt De Winter was delighted to hand his charges over to Chenel and return to base.

In closed railway carriages attached to a civilian train, the 'European workers' travelled to the port of Dakar, where they were hidden in a dockside warehouse, their clandestine journey already totalling nearly 4,000km. Embarked without papers on the *Cap Padaran*, they had ahead of them a voyage of another 20,000km around the Cape of Good Hope to Vietnam, where they constituted the last reinforcements 5 REI received until the end of the war. Curiously, the regiment that now protected them took its orders from the colonial government of Vietnam, which was loyal to Vichy in an uneasy cohabitation with the Japanese occupying forces under the Agreement of 30 April 1940. This recognised French sovereignty, but conceded 'certain facilities' to Japan.

On 1 July 1940, 636 of the 1,619 officers and men at Trentham Park boarded trains for Bristol, having opted to return to French North Africa. It was an emotional parting, with Monclar offering his hand to each of the thirty-one departing officers as they saluted him with last-minute excuses.[6] The occasion was marred by the guard of honour refusing to present arms as those leaving marched past. In a final sad note, when British police delivered to Bristol the 300 incarcerated Spanish legionnaires, they lay down on the dockside rather than walk up the gangway of the *Meknès*, fearing that once in Morocco they would be handed over to Franco and shot.

To erase the shame of 1 July, 13 DBLE was renamed 14 DBLE, and so remained until 4 November, when it reverted to its original designation. Caught in all this manoeuvring, James Williamson returned to camp from leave on 13 July and was advised to get rid of his French uniform and join the British army. Doing so, he became a deserter as far as the Legion was concerned - a situation only rectified when he was officially discharged on 5 April 1966![7]

Monclar's command was now down to twenty-eight officers and 900 men, who included Maj Koenig and the Georgian prince Lt Amilakvari. Even their confidence that they had made the right choice must have been badly shaken after the British Admiralty ordered Adm Somerville in Gibraltar to implement Operation Catapult on 3 July. This was the destruction of the French fleet in harbour at Mers el-Kebir, near Oran.

It was the first time since Waterloo that British weapons were trained upon French servicemen.

The decommissioning of the French ships was under way, with the boilers cold, gun turrets without power and munitions removed to stores. Reservists with homes in North Africa had already been demobilised. French navy planes had mostly been disarmed and the shells and breech-blocks removed in the coastal batteries protecting Mers el-Kebir.

Swordfish aircraft from *Ark Royal* first mined the harbour exits, to prevent any ship leaving. Somerville then presented Adm Gensoul with the ultimatum that he and his crews must either sail immediately and fight on the British side, or scuttle their ships. In fact, Admiral of the Fleet Darlan had already ordered the sea-cocks manned night and day, the officer-of-the-watch having standing orders to open them at the first attempt by Axis forces to board the vessels - as happened later in Toulon harbour.

Aboard HMS *Hood*, Adm Somerville obeyed orders as slowly as possible. At 1625hrs local time the first shell was fired by *Hood*. Although the French warships had steam up by then and could return fire with what munitions had been brought back on board, no manoeuvring was possible in the confines of the harbour without hitting each other. They were thus sitting ducks for the Royal Navy bombardment that killed a total of 1,297 French sailors, with several hundred wounded. Whilst their comrades were shrouding the corpses, three flights of Swordfish from *Ark Royal* roared in at deck level with cannon blazing, to add to the casualties.

Operation Catapult was tailor-made for Vichy propaganda. The message on posters everywhere in both zones of France was, *How can any Frenchman trust the English who did this?* Nevertheless, a trickle of newcomers reached Trentham Park from occupied France. None would have taken the risks unless highly motivated, like 2nd Lt Pierre Messmer, destined to become De Gaulle's Minister of the Armed Forces 1960-69 and Prime Minister 1972-74. At first it was hard, even for officers of this calibre, to maintain discipline - as it would be in any unit after such a traumatic schism. A frequent problem was men going AWOL owing to local girls becoming more than 'just good friends'.

Gradually, contact with the locals softened both sides' prejudices, and the choice of going or staying had weeded out the most anglophobic officers and men. De Gaulle's aloof lightning visit at the end of June had done nothing for the men's morale, but the visit to Trentham Park of shy, stammering King George VI on 25 August was an excuse to show the British monarch just how smart and disciplined French servicemen could be. It was therefore in somewhat better spirits that Monclar's little army embarked a few days later at Liverpool, destination Africa.

Chapter 29

WHICH SIDE DID YOU SAY, MISS?

West Africa, 1940; Eritrea and Syria 1941; Western Desert 1942

Saturday 31 August 1940 was one of those nights when the controllers of Britain's air defences were baffled as to how Luftwaffe bombers were finding their targets without a moon to help them.[1] The day had been the worst so far of the Battle of Britain, with forty-one RAF aircraft lost. For the fourth consecutive night, bombs were falling on the residential quarters and docks of Liverpool but, to protect his night vision, the captain of the unarmed Dutch liner SS *Pennland* was not looking back at the fires raging there. He was just praying that their glare did not reveal the wake of his ship to the German pilots overhead.[2] Incoming on his starboard beam as he made to the west past the shoals of the old wreckers' coast of the Wirral peninsula was Convoy HX 66 from Halifax, Nova Scotia - fifty-one vessels that had made it safely to the beleaguered British Isles past the U-boats and the Luftwaffe flying out of Norway.

On board the blacked-out *Pennland* were the officers and men of 13 DBLE. Her sister ship SS *Westernland* bore among its passengers Charles De Gaulle and a unique eyewitness to the ups and downs of Operation Menace - his bid to seduce the French West African colonies away from allegiance to Vichy. The only woman ever to serve with the Foreign Legion, 30-year-old Susan Travers was described as a *garçon manqué* by those who knew her.[3] Daughter of a Royal Navy officer, she was bilingual as a result of growing up largely in France, and had a reasonable grasp of German and Italian - all spoken 'with a plum in her mouth'. Her natural middle-class authority and habitual lack of feminine airs and graces ensured she was known to legionnaires of all ranks respectfully as 'La Miss'.

Travers was a better than good amateur skier and tennis-player, but what was to win her a unique fame were the steady nerves and instinctive skills that make a first-class driver. Although travelling on board *Westernland* as a nurse, her only experience of nursing had been gained in Finland with a small group of French Red Cross volunteers.[4] At the time it had seemed to her the only way to get involved in the war but, although she would do it when necessary, tending the sick was not where her tomboy heart lay.

The unarmed transports rendezvoused in the Irish Sea with their escort: HMS *Barham* and HMS *Resolution*, several destroyers and the aircraft carrier HMS *Ark Royal* as flagship of Adm Sir John Cunningham. The course they followed was a generous loop out into the Atlantic to avoid German seaplane patrols from the French Atlantic coast and reduce the risk from U-boats. After calling at the Royal Navy base in Freetown, Sierra Leone, they anchored a quarter of a nautical mile off Dakar, the capital of Senegal, in thick fog on the morning of 23 September. Things went badly from the beginning, not helped by the Vichy authorities knowing from aerial reconnaissance that *Ark Royal* - of *all* ships in the Royal Navy - was lurking just over the horizon.

After two sets of De Gaulle's emissaries had been wounded in defiance of universal military protocol, the shore batteries started shelling Cunningham's little fleet, obliging it to move out of range on 25 September. A detachment of Free French marines attempted to land and rally the local population along the coast, but were driven off after being strafed by Vichy planes.

Having been condemned to death for treason by court martial on 2 August, De Gaulle knew that his political credit was at its nadir. Should he fail to win over the African colonies, his claim to represent anyone other than himself would be proven hollow and he would join the ranks of the exiled Polish and Czech politicians in London, whose soldiers were simply enlisted in the British forces. After the humiliating rejection in Senegal, he kept to the privacy of his cabin as the convoy headed out to sea and sailed another 4,000km to the southeast.

At Douala in Cameroon he and 13 DBLE bade farewell to Cunningham's escorting force on 8 October and were welcomed by the locals, both French and native, with rapturous enthusiasm.

De Gaulle heaved more than a sigh of relief, well aware that Churchill had been prepared to dump him. He then departed for Chad and other French equatorial territories that had declared for him against Vichy, but at Yaoundé in Cameroon and Libreville in Gabon, 13 DBLE had to subdue the Vichy garrisons by force of arms. Firing on other Frenchmen reduced Monclar and many of the legionnaires to tears, but it was a job that had to be done.[5]

Other Free French forces under Col Jacques-Philippe Leclerc had prepared the way for De Gaulle in the equatorial territories. Promoted to general by him, Leclerc now led his men on an 1,800km odyssey from Chad to Tripoli on the Mediterranean coast, reducing Italian garrisons on the way to link up with British 8th Army. Having secured French West Africa with the exception of Senegal, 13 DBLE sailed right around the Cape of Good Hope and up the east coast of Africa. At Port Sudan on the Red Sea they learned that they were to take part in a little-publicised campaign to drive Mussolini's forces out of Eritrea, from where they could have caused problems for the British in Egypt and Allied traffic passing through the Red Sea.

On 8 April 1941 a mixed Anglo-French force seized the main port of Massawa, where Monclar demanded the surrender of the senior Italian officer. Admiral Bonetti threw his parade sabre sulkily into the sea, rather than graciously hand it over, only to see it rescued at low tide by an observant legionnaire and presented to Monclar as a trophy. This small campaign was important in rebuilding unit pride for the next theatre in which 13 DBLE was to see action against 6 REI in Syria/Lebanon in defiance of the Legion principle that legionnaires never fired on legionnaires.

Travers was not bothered by the thousands of men in Massawa with time on their hands and some money in their pockets. This had less to do with her rank of Legion warrant officer than Col Monclar's priority of opening a BMC, or *bordel mobile de campagne*, staffed by local women and two Italian whores.[6]

Nowhere was the war more confusing for the Legion than in Syria. In 1941, 6 REI was part of the Armée du Levant commanded by Gen Fernand Dentz who, as military commander of Paris had surrendered the capital to the Germans on 14 June 1940. His promotion to the post of High Commissioner in Syria, where he remained loyal to Vichy, earned him a death sentence at the end of the war, which he only avoided by dying in prison. The men of 6 REI were luckier. When captured, they argued quite correctly that they were professional soldiers obeying orders from their officers, who in turn were obeying instructions from their legal government in Vichy.

There had been a pro-Gaullist faction among 6 REI's officers, headed by Col Edgard De Larminat, who used the liaison mission from the British forces in Occupied Palestine as a channel to sound out British willingness to support a coup. Indications are that his following was significant until he was arrested on orders of Gen Dentz. Held in Damascus pending execution for treason, Larminat was rescued on 30 June 1940 from his prison cell by a small commando of legionnaires, who spirited him south to Palestine, where he was welcomed as an honoured guest in the officers' mess of Warwickshire Yeomanry.[7]

With him gone, other officers judged too Gaullist were either transferred back to North Africa, where they could do no harm, or understandably changed their minds about hitching their wagons to the star of a renegade colonel whose only support came from the people who had killed the defenceless sailors at Mers el-Kebir.

Although holding the acting rank of general, De Gaulle's substantive rank was colonel, and it was thus addressed that a letter he sent to the French Army High Command, explaining his actions in the summer of 1940, was returned to him in London.

Reinforcing the observation that many of the apparently political choices facing French soldiers during the war were resolved for non-political reasons Col Fernand Barre, then commanding 6 REI, put in writing much later that he had no quarrels with his brother officers in 13 DBLE. He thought that, had he been in their places, he would probably have made the same choices they had.[8] The confusion of loyalties was such that Monclar and one of his company commanders opted out of the Syrian campaign altogether because they refused to fire again on fellow legionnaires, no matter what might be the justification. Command of 13 DBLE then passed to Marie-Pierre Koenig, promoted to colonel.

The Vichy forces in Syria/Lebanon totalled thirty battalions. Against them, the Allies invaded with twenty battalions - and a confusion of reasons. Britain was invading to stop the airfield at Aleppo being used by German planes to bomb British targets in Iraq. Dentz had ordered his troops to fire on any aircraft overflying or landing in Syria, until Vichy granted landing rights in the naïve hope that it would lead to a softening of the Occupation terms. Ordered also to open Syrian ports to Axis shipping, Dentz refused.[9]

In this difficult-to-read situation, De Gaulle seems to have assumed that 13 DBLE arriving in a show of force with British support would swing the largely colonial troops garrisoning Syria/Lebanon over to his side without a shot being fired, notwithstanding Dentz' reluctant reply to an informal sounding-out that he would obey orders from Vichy.[10] With this in mind, the opening move on the Free French side was the bombardment of positions held by 6 REI with thousands of leaflets. The reply came in the form of equally denunciatory leaflets putting the opposing argument.

For the invasion of Syria the hard-pressed Allied Middle East Command cobbled together a mixed British, Indian, French and Australian force under Sir Henry 'Jumbo' Maitland Wilson - among them a squadron of Australian horse cavalry known as 'Kelly's gang'. As a kind of olive branch to the Vichy garrison in Syria of 35,000 mainly colonial troops plus aircraft and tanks, the Aussies were ordered to wear their bush-ranger hats rather than helmets 'until fired upon'. The order was greeted with coarse laughter and appropriate gestures.

Hitler's launch of Operation Barbarossa - the invasion of the USSR in June 1941 - forced him to withdraw all German aircraft and ground troops from Syria. Wearing British battle-dress and khaki pith helmets bearing a tricolour shield, 13 DBLE entered Syrian territory from what is now Jordan, taking Dar'ah in the far south and heading north towards Damascus, together with 5th Indian Infantry Brigade. On 19 June, thirteen legionnaires were killed and several others wounded in the assault on the heights of Kissoueh, controlling the southern approach to the capital, but the big test lay ahead.

On 20 June, as Damascus fell to the Allied force, a company of 13 DBLE commanded by Dmitri Amilakvari - now a major - ran smack into 6 REI at Kadam, a southern suburb of the capital. One of the Legion's most popular officers, the dashing, shaven-headed Georgian prince who affected a green cloak slashed by shrapnel in Narvik and refused ever to wear a steel helmet, halted the firing after one casualty on each side and ordered his bugler to sound *Le Boudin*. When the defenders answered with the same call, Amilakvari coolly walked across to make contact with a sergeant, a wounded corporal and five legionnaires of 6 REI, who explained that they had orders to hold until 0100 hours.

'Fine,' said Amilakvari. 'We'll leave you alone until then.' At 0105, he resumed the advance without bloodshed, but the same trick had no effect when 13 DBLE came up against 29th Algerian tirailleurs elsewhere in Kadam. They fought so tenaciously that some of Amilakvari's legionnaires had to be restrained from killing the wounded afterwards.

The record is not very clear, but it seems that Maitland Wilson tried to avoid using 'his' Legion against Dentz's, and ordered 13 DBLE to attack Baalbek in Lebanon when the focus of conflict was 200km northeast of them at Tadmuriyah, where half the 500-strong garrison was drawn from 4th Battalion of 6 REI. That Dentz had no similar qualms about using 6 REI in the thick of the fighting is borne out by comparative casualty figures: in the brief campaign 13 DBLE suffered twenty-one killed and forty-seven wounded to 6 REI's 128 killed and 728 wounded.

One of the two strong-points at Tadmuriyah, known as T2 and held by eleven men from 6 REI, surrendered to British Household Cavalry after a token exchange of fire, but strong-point T3, held by three 6 REI NCOs and nineteen legionnaires, resisted a week of attacks by RAF Regiment, yeomanry regiment personnel and elements of Glubb Pasha's Jordanian Arab Legion. On 28 June an Essex Regiment patrol found it occupied by only six legionnaires.

On 3 July after its main force of local Bedouin deserted en masse, the commander of the principal defensive position Fort Weygand sent emissaries to the Allied lines, surrendering 6 officers and eighty-seven legionnaires, mostly Russian or German.

With Tadmuriyah taken, fighting continued in Lebanon, where 1st, 2nd and 3rd battalions of 6 REI, with a high percentage of Spaniards, acquitted themselves well against combined British and Australian attackers from 6-12 July. Writing about it afterwards,

Col Fernand Barre of 6 REI said that he had not wanted to fight, but could not honourably surrender until the Allied forces had demonstrated overwhelming superiority. With Operation Barbarossa in full swing, trouble in Yugoslavia and the commitment in North Africa, Hitler had no uncommitted forces to spare for Syria. Having no chance of reinforcements, the Vichy command capitulated.

The armistice signed at Akko in Palestine on 14 July provided for the men of 6 REI to have a choice between transfer to 13 DBLE and repatriation to France. Whatever De Gaulle had thought about them rallying to his cause, he was in for a shock. Relations between officers of 6 REI and 13 DBLE were correct but frigid, many of the former considering that their opposite numbers, promoted rapidly by De Gaulle to fill the gaps on his staff, were traitors who had jumped the promotion queue. Fuelling the fires of their jealousy, the increasingly confident leader of the Free French, on a visit to Palestine and Syria, promoted Koenig to general.

Two days before the arranged repatriation date of 6 REI, the entire strength of officers and men from Col Barre down to the most junior legionnaire paraded at the *séance d'option*. Koenig had ordered Barre to withdraw so that all the men of 6 REI could make a personal choice, free from coercion. Barre refused to leave. A compromise was reached. He walked through a doorway and turned left for repatriation. The entire regiment followed him, with those who wished to stay with 13 DBLE free to turn right. To Barre's delight, all but one man followed his lead. The regiment reformed behind the regimental band and marched proudly away. It seems that although the conditions seemed to guarantee each man a free choice, there may have been an element of coercion that day, for a mystery surrounds the fact that from a nominal roll totalling 3,344 men on 8 June, only 1,233 landed with him at Marseilles. Allowing for the killed and wounded, the discrepancy was claimed by 13 DBLE to be due to 1,400 men from 6 REI deciding to join them after all. However, a more reliable estimate put the number at somewhere between 677 and 1,000 - some by desertion before the *séance d'option*, others trickling in from Allied POW camps in the theatre, and the rest from hospitals and elsewhere.[11]

With 6 REI gone, 13 DBLE settled down to one of those

strange interludes in war, during which Travers not only had an affair with Koenig, but also fell in love with him - to discover that he was deeply jealous of her previous relationships with several of his officers. Sharing his villa in suburban Beirut, she was awoken one night by a man, whom she took for him, getting into her bed. During their love-making she happened to run her hands over his head and found it clean-shaven. The equally startled Amilakvari, who had assumed he would always be welcome in her bed, scurried away with his tail between his legs on being given the news that she was now his general's mistress.[12]

In Britain by this time De Gaulle's arrogance had caused Churchill to reflect that of all the crosses he had to bear as the country's war leader, none was heavier than the cross of Lorraine - symbol of the Free French. In the Middle East the unreliability of 13 DBLE in the eyes of the Allied command made them a very doubtful asset in the war along the North African littoral, with the result that it was given - as had happened to the Legion so often in the past - the dirty jobs.

Like Koenig, Monclar was now a general, forgiven his crisis of conscience. In the levelling-up, Amilakvari was promoted to lieutenant-colonel, commanding 13 DBLE from 16 September. With the new blood acquired in Lebanon, he now led 1,771 men organised in three four-company battalions designated 1st, 2nd and 3rd Bataillon de la Légion Etrangère, abbreviated to BLE. The chosen nomenclature seemed to deny altogether the existence of the main Legion regiments sitting out the war in Algeria. Equipped by the British as mechanised light infantry, two of the battalions were re-designated demi-brigades under Lt Col Amilakvari and Col De Roux, together making up 1st Free French Brigade under Gen De Larminat, attached to Eighth Army. The other battalion was left out of the war for the moment, seemingly because the Middle East Command had not enough equipment to fit out all three.

As 1942 dawned, C-in-C Middle East Gen Sir Claude Auchinleck was busy reinforcing the Gazala Line - a series of defensive fortified 'boxes' in the Western Desert, stretching from the village of Gazala near Benghazi on the Libyan coast all the way south to an abandoned pre-war Italian fort at a map location labelled Bir Hakeim. This was in expectation of the attack that

Field Marshal Erwin Rommel launched on 20 January, sucking in much-needed reinforcements throughout that month and the next, and pushing his Afrika Korps and its Italian allies eastwards in the hope of driving the British back into Egypt and wresting from them control of the Suez Canal.

At the southern end of the line, Bir Hakeim consisted of a hexagonal 'box' of wire and trenches approximately 16km in circumference, centred on some underground rock-hewn cisterns called *bir*, no longer filled by a well that had gone dry, but on which converged several desert tracks. On 4 February Larminat's 1st Free French Brigade inherited this desolate tangle from British 150th Infantry Brigade, who were delighted to move out from a position surrounded by so many mines of all sizes and sensitivities that sand storms and even the heat often set several off in sequence.

It is possible that, somewhere on the road, the NCOs in Larminat's column recognised a familiar face in British uniform. Former Legion Sgt Brückler had been in Wehrmacht uniform a few weeks before. Wounded and taken prisoner by Commonwealth troops in the Western Desert, he had apparently been 'turned' by British military intelligence while recovering in hospital at Shallufa and was a member of a small team of German-speakers in British uniform setting off on a long-range raid on the Luftwaffe airfield at Darnah in Libya.

At the airfield, Brückler volunteered to make a solo reconnaissance, during which he 'surrendered' to the duty officer in the control tower. The officer, alarmed at the sight of a scruffy man in British uniform wearing an Arab headdress, was on the point of shooting him when Brückler gave away the rest of his group. As he told the story years later in Algeria to British legionnaire James Worden, he was decorated by Rommel and posted to the 361st Regiment, far from the line so that there would be no chance of being recaptured by the Allies. What he left out of the story is that his three surviving companions on the raid were Jewish and almost certainly sent to their deaths. Scared after the war that he would be on a list of war criminals for betraying them, he re-enlisted in the Legion under the name of Brockman. In a typically Legion closed-circuit, Worden later recounted the story to a German *adjutant-chef* who was a drinking pal - and discovered that his pal had been one of the Luftwaffe officers on duty at Darnah on the night of the raid. Part-fact and part-fiction, it makes a good yarn![13]

At Bir Hakeim, night-time temperatures went below zero; afternoon peaks could reach 50° Centigrade and sunburn was punished as a self-inflicted wound. Apart from hordes of biting flies that went mad at the approach of each sand storm arriving as a sky-high wall of black travelling at speeds of sixty miles per hour or more, the only movement in the arid waste was a continuity of dancing ochre-coloured dust-devils, of which the fine airborne particles combined with sweat or mucus to make an abrasive paste in armpit, crotch, eyes, nose and every other orifice.

In addition to the Legion, the Bir Hakeim garrison included some French marine gunners and a British Bofors anti-aircraft battery, Algerian and Moroccan light infantry, artillery from Madagascar and Mauritius, a Pacific battalion from Tahiti, some Lebanese sappers, Vietnamese auxiliaries and a black Chadian *bataillon de marche*, rumoured to practise witchcraft.

For the next three months this odd assortment of all colours and races strengthened the defences, which were nowhere near good enough in Koenig's opinion, while Travers learned the art of moving about the desert at the wheel of his command car, a Ford Utility station wagon with its side and rear windows painted over so as not to reflect sunlight. Every hour on the hour she had to stop, check the badly punished tyres and clean the clogged air filter. Koenig could not stay at a desk and spent as much time as possible at the head of two- and three-day long-range patrols known as Jock Columns - after Gen Jock Campbell, who was credited with thinking them up. The other vehicles - jeeps and Bren-gun carriers - had their Brens on a mounting that permitted use against aircraft as well as ground targets. When finding a tempting enemy target, the motto was *Shoot and scoot!*

At the beginning of April, Larminat handed command to Koenig and departed to form 2nd Free French Brigade at Bardia in Libya, unaware that he was walking away from history and that Bir Hakeim was to join Camerone on the flags of the Legion.

Chapter 30

'LA MISS' AND THE HEROES OF BIR HAKEIM

Western Desert, 1942

Two weeks later, Koenig was informed that a South African force was to take over Bir Hakeim.[1] It never happened. On 26 May came his chance to redeem the doubtful reputation earned by 13 DBLE in Syria when Rommel swung south and put Bir Hakeim on the map by handing it over to his Italian allies with the remark that they should be able to neutralise its heterogeneous garrison in about fifteen minutes.

Contact was first made by a column of M-13 Italian light tanks from the Ariete Armoured Division and the Trieste Motorised Division, who collided outside the wire with a screening party from 7th Armoured Division and 3rd Indian Brigade. After dusk, with their protectors ordered elsewhere, the defenders clearly heard the menacing squeal of Italian tank tracks and the throbbing of heavy diesel engines surrounding the box.

At dawn, Koenig's radio brought him a message from 7th Armoured HQ informing him that he was on his own, now that Rommel's attack was building up to the north. Koenig was a man of action. Although ordered to mine the safe passages through the minefields and sit tight, waiting for the enemy to come to him, he despatched several Jock columns in Bren-gun carriers to reconnoitre. They returned with the bad news that German Mk IV Panzers were already east of Bir Hakeim, cutting it off from resupply and from the nearest water.

At 0900hrs next day legionnaires on the perimeter spotted a column of seventy Italian M-13s with 75mm guns approaching in line abreast, the first wave of fifty being followed by another of twenty. Against them, the French had eleven 75mm anti-tank guns. At 400 metres' range, both sides opened fire just as the lead tank detonated a mine that put it out of action. The Italian infantry behind the tanks lost interest at this point and scrambled aboard trucks that disappeared to the rear, but the Ariete Division tanks continued coming despite losses. Six of them penetrated the defences. In the Legion's forward command post, the code books and flag were being burned with the enemy only twenty paces away when the anti-tank gunners, who had been biding their time, opened up and broke the attack.[2]

By 1130hrs the Ariete had lost thirty-three tanks - not from any want of fighting spirit. Its commander Col Prestisimone had already had two tanks shot from under him when taken prisoner in his third. Wounded, burned and wearing only underwear after tearing off his smouldering uniform, he was a worthy opponent, to whom the stocky Yugoslavian Legion padre Père Mallec gave a pair of pyjamas to wear for his meeting with Koenig. 'What went wrong?' was the gist of Prestisimone's conversation, surveying ninety of his tankers in an improvised POW cage adjacent to HQ. Once in the cage with them, after accepting Koenig's sincere apologies for having no better accommodation, he blamed Rommel for telling him it would take a quarter of an hour to roll up Bir Hakeim. 'He also told us all the mines had been lifted,' his men replied.

So many tanks had been put out of action that from a distance they looked as though simply parked for refuelling. When German and Italian trucks drove confidently up to the French wire, believing themselves to be in a friendly tank laager, their loads were a welcome addition to the French larder. The Jock columns slipped out again through the gaps and brought home a German supply convoy which had lost its bearings in a nascent sand storm, plus an even more welcome 1,000-litre tanker full of drinking water. The drivers of these vehicles were the first German POWs taken by the Legion, which was a great morale booster, but by the end of the day Koenig had an unforeseen headache in the shape of 154 Italian and 125 German prisoners to share the limited rations of the defenders, already stretched by the Jock columns liberating from their Axis captors 654 British and Indian personnel captured during the first stage of the battle.

In a ding-dong combat 15km to the north, Rommel seemed to be losing his impetus until he ordered his troops trapped in a minefield to drive right through it and attack. The resultant capture of 3,000 British prisoners and 123 artillery pieces was a severe jolt to 8th Army. Meanwhile Koenig's mobile patrols were having a field day, shooting up Axis supply columns with their 75mm guns lashed on the back of flatbed trucks to serve as home-made tank-busters.[3] In one such encounter Pierre Messmer, now a captain, brewed up fifteen German tanks, firing at the limit of range.[4] During the lull around Bir Hakeim, a French supply convoy brought in supplies from El Adem and took out with it on the return leg 'useless mouths' in the shape of POWs, released prisoners and some wounded.

A solitary staff car going in the other direction - towards Bir Hakeim - was being driven by Susan Travers. Ordered to the rear with the female nursing personnel just before the first attack, she had collected Koenig's car from a repair shop as her excuse to return, relying on her personal relationship with him to be allowed to stay, the only woman in the box. Commandeering a semi-dugout with corrugated steel roof for his Ford Utility station wagon only 200 metres from Koenig's HQ, she accommodated herself in what she called her grave, another dugout hacked four feet deep into the rock, with a sandbag wall above ground level and a canvas roof which kept the sun off her but would have been useless against shrapnel or bomb fragments.

Its sole furniture was her camp-bed purchased from the Army and Navy Stores on the Strand. Her folding canvas bath, purchased at the same time, was left in the car boot because of the water shortage. For a while until she grew lonely, she lived there day and night, eating her way through a stock of corned beef and tinned asparagus, which she consumed with the intention of leaving none for the Germans when they arrived.[5]

Until 31 May it seemed the Allied line was being held. Then the Italians made a significant breakthrough north of Bir Hakeim. Taking advantage of the lull on his own doorstep, Larminat paid an inspection visit and was impressed by all the preparations. On his departure, Amilakvari went hunting with four of the flatbed truck tank-busters, destroying several enemy tanks before being forced to return. In another fast-moving and very confusing tank battle between Panzers and British armour right outside the wire, several victims were claimed by Capt Gabriel de Sairigné's field artillery, although no one could say for sure whether they had all been enemy tanks, so bad was the visibility in the heat haze and all the dust stirred up by the tank-tracks and shells detonating.

This sort of activity might have been considered an unwise provocation, had Koenig wanted a quiet life, but he was not that kind of soldier. However, on 2 June Legion patrols were urgently recalled as two armoured columns rumbled closer from the west and north. The nearest estimate of their strength with all the supply vehicles was about 1,000 vehicles. Bir Hakeim was surrounded, bombarded from the ground and by the Italian air force throughout daylight hours. After two armoured attacks supported by infantry were halted on the southwestern perimeter by the anti-tank gunners, two Italian officers approached with a white flag. Their arrival coincided with the time-limit Koenig had been given: to hold for ten days, come what may. However when the Italian officers were taken blindfolded to his HQ he replied politely to their invitation to capitulate by saying, '*Mi dispiace*, *signori*, but tell your general we're not here to surrender.' With equal courtesy, the Italians bowed and left after congratulating him and his men on being *grandi soldati*.

Their driver having been panicked by threats on his life from malicious Italian-speaking legionnaires, the officers had to drive themselves back. Half an hour later, the first 105mm shell crashed into the French positions and, to make life even more unpleasant a sand storm blew up, reducing visibility to nil. Susan Travers sat it out in the theoretically airtight Ford, trying not to move in order to perspire as little as possible, but the men in the 1,200 slit trenches, dugouts and gun-pits had no such option. The water ration was getting critical again.

On 3 June at 0930hrs two British POWs had the unpleasant experience of being shot at by Legion sentries before they were recognised as friends approaching the wire. With them, they brought a letter on squared signal-pad paper signed by Rommel personally telling the garrison to put up white flags and walk out unarmed. Such a letter should have been addressed to the commander, not to his men, and should not have used the familiar form *Wenn ihr weisse Flaggen zeigt* - meaning, if you show white flags - which implied that Rommel was talking to men under his command. Koenig, nicknamed by his men *le vieux lapin* was not a happy bunny after reading this insulting breach of protocol. Had he needed anything to stiffen his resolve, Rommel's letter would have done it.

The Bofors battery claimed four Stukas shot down in the space of a few minutes at 1700hrs. Another unusual event that day was the landing on an improvised strip within the box of a Spitfire, whose South African pilot ran out of juice. With a tank full of truck fuel, which cannot have done the engine much good, it took off again shakily during a fortuitous lull in the shelling. A fragment of shrapnel piercing the radiator of Koenig's car, Travers managed to persuade one of the Vietnamese mechanics to dismantle it and haul it with her to the primitive workshop, where the hole was welded up. Finding her way back to the bunker, she repeatedly lost her way in the fog of abrasive dust particles.

That night a British supply convoy made it into the camp through the lines, narrowly missing on their return journey a trio of German officers who drove up at 0430hrs on 5 June with a third invitation to 'avoid unnecessary bloodshed'. Refusing even to see them, Koenig gave orders for them to be allowed just five minutes to get out of range. In their haste to depart, they drove over a mine that put their Kubelwagen out of action, leaving them to walk home in rather a hurry.

The bad news after daybreak was that an immense battle to the north had cost the British 6,000 men killed, wounded or taken prisoner - and 150 tanks. No sooner had the implications been digested - there was little else for breakfast - than the first 150mm and 210mm shells began arriving with a sound like express trains ripping through the air overhead, accompanied to the amazement of defenders and attackers alike by a light shower of rain that became a slashing downpour of hail. Immediately seeds germinated, so that the wasteland bloomed within hours beneath a sky criss-crossed by friendly and enemy aircraft so interwoven that the Bofors crew could often do nothing except watch as aircraft shot up by other aircraft plummeted down in streaks of black smoke to explode on the desert below.

Rommel now put everything he could spare into the reduction

of Bir Hakeim. Two Italian divisions, two German ones and twenty-one batteries moved in for the kill. Overhead, as many as 500 Heinkel and Savoia bombers arrived and departed in waves, dropping their loads on the French positions. At this point it has been estimated that the 3,700 men inside the wire were diverting from Rommel's main push around ten times as many enemy forces, plus a significant part of the Axis air forces in the Western Desert. In the military game of numbers, the French were winning for the first time since Narvik.

That night German sappers lifted the mines from a wide avenue through the minefields, preparatory to a major ground attack. Under cover of early morning fog and beneath a heavy overcast, the Lebanese sappers replaced them, unaware that the same fog was hiding the approach of a battery of the best German multi-purpose artillery piece of the war: the 88mm gun. They were also up against the best machine gun of the war in the shape of the rapid-firing Maschinengewehr 42, which was beginning to replace the MG 34. Recoil-operated and firing up to 1,000 rounds per minute of belt-fed 7.92mm rifle ammunition, both models dealt with over-heating by having barrels that could be changed in seconds.

As waves of tanks and infantry pressed in from south, west and north, the German 88s were now firing over open sights with barrels horizontal, blasting the only rise from which the French artillery observers had any view of the battlefield. The attack was only broken up by raids from the RAF, but no sooner had they returned to base than sixty Junkers bombers appeared overhead, dropping loads that included delayed-action land mines to hamper collection of wounded and repair of the day's damage.

Nearing desperation, with large gaps torn in his defences, Koenig ordered Messmer's company, which had been in continuous action without sleep for forty-eight hours, to act as a flying squad and plug the holes. Another raid from thirty-five Junkers took out the bunker sheltering the main French ammunition dump, a deficit that was partly offset by small, fast-moving convoys slipping between the German forces at night, bringing in supplies and taking out wounded, some of whom had lain in the open for hours because no help could get to them in daylight.

By 8 June the French had held for far longer than anyone on either side could have predicted and Rommel was now personally driving his men on, impatient to finish off this running sore on his southern flank. Although a crucial position fell to the enemy that day, still Koenig's forces held on, moving like zombies, asleep on their feet. The water reserves were down to one gallon per man. Many men had already drained the radiators of trucks and drunk the bitter, rust-coloured liquid inside after passing it through the filters of the gas masks they hoped they would not have to use for their original purpose. Shaving and washing water was similarly treated.[6] To see good food and drinkable water falling beyond the wire during an unsuccessful air drop was torture.

Thick fog shrouded the dawn of 9 June. As it cleared, four 88s and six heavy machine guns opened up from the position taken the previous day. In case any defender wondered why infantry did not follow up, the answer arrived in the shape of forty Stukas dive-bombing with their sirens screaming. The afternoon brought a raid by forty-two Junkers, after which German infantry threatened to overwhelm the French positions until broken up at the last minute by the half-tracks manoeuvring at close quarters under the energetic command of a Breton veteran from the First World War, Lt Jean Dève, nicknamed 'Dewey'.

The German counter-battery fire was pinpoint-precise by now. A shell detonated the magazine of one French gun position producing a gigantic secondary explosion. Miraculously unwounded, the sergeant immediately improvised a tourniquet on the stump of arm through which the only other survivor was bleeding to death and carried him away to safety just before the position was over-run. By now, men were taking unbelievable risks, whether in the belief that they must be immortal to have survived so long or because their judgement was destroyed by the noise and adrenalin of three weeks' sustained bombardment. When Koenig sent a crate of beer to a sergeant of 3rd Battalion whose gun crew had knocked out two mortars and a 77mm gun, the gleeful sergeant climbed onto the parapet of sandbags to yell defiance and was promptly shot dead.

The big event of the day was a successful airdrop with a container of 170 litres of water, which was immediately distributed to the wounded. Restricted to a smaller circle was the gist of a coded radio message from 8th Army, to the effect that Bir Hakeim had more than served its purpose and further resistance was unnecessary. Koenig, however, had no intention of surrendering and seeing his men in cages before being taken away to sit out the war as POWs. Nor, to his credit, was he prepared to leave his wounded behind and break out with only the able-bodied. However, there could be no question of making a mass breakout in daylight, and he needed twenty-four hours to plan and prepare the sortie by which he hoped to get the maximum numbers away to safety.

Among the few to whom he communicated the plan was the faithful Travers. He had only sought her out a couple of times in the past three months, making a point of telling her little so that, if taken prisoner and identified as his driver, she could truthfully reply that she knew nothing of his plans.

Half-asleep in her dugout, she heard him approaching and tried to smarten herself up. So exhausted that he could hardly keep his eyes open, he informed her of the breakout planned for the following night. The only preparation she had to make was to smash the windscreen of the Humber, so that it would not craze and blind her if hit by an Axis bullet.[7]

On the morning of 9 June, the first flight of enemy aircraft was unable to unload its bombs because the German and Italian positions were so close to the French ones. Ammunition of all calibres running out, 2nd Battalion drove off an Italian attack with hand grenades. At 1300hrs, 130 Luftwaffe aircraft flattened what remained of the northern perimeter and a bomb destroyed the clearly marked hospital, killing the wounded and most of the orderlies. In the artillery bombardment that followed, ten tanks advanced so tightly coordinated that shrapnel from air bursts was spattering their hulls. Again the Bren-carriers were used to blunt the attack, which was finally broken up by the cannon of a flight of RAF Spitfires that appeared in the nick of time - which was just as well because few guns were still serviceable after firing a daily average of 700 rounds each, totalling 42,000 shells during the siege.[8]

After a diversion provided by British 7th Armoured Division attacking the enemy rear, by dusk all essential preparations were in place for the breakout - not to the east in the direction of the

British rear, but to the southwest where the Axis forces were thinnest on the ground. After clearing the enemy besiegers, the idea was to swing round to the southeast and then head north for a cairn and British fuel dump known as B837. This had to be found in the darkness by picking up three red lamps shining southwards to avoid the enemy sighting them.

The news spread as legionnaires saw their officers changing into clean uniforms and using precious last drops of drinking water to shave off several days' growth of beard. Then came orders to destroy what could be destroyed and render unserviceable everything else, with 3rd Battalion given the dirty job of staying to guard the flanks of the column. Trucks and ambulances were loaded with the 200 most severely wounded men. Those who volunteered to walk included the German colour sergeant of 3rd Battalion, whose arm had been amputated only hours before.

At midnight the disengagement began as quietly as possible, not to alert the besiegers. Desert navigation, especially on such a moonless night, always had an element of luck. It seemed this was missing when Koenig's best navigator Lt Bellec led the long column of vehicles straight into a minefield. As his Bren-carrier blew up, the explosion cued the unmistakable sound of MG 34s and 42s firing at the flash. A second carrier hit another mine. Travers and everyone else held their breath. Was the secret out, or did the besiegers think they were dealing with a small party infiltrating with supplies?

Bellec clambered aboard a third carrier, realising his error. The only way out was back. In hushed tones, the wounded who could walk were ordered out of the trucks in the hope of making them too light to detonate the anti-tank mines all around. They started walking, aware that every step could blow them to hell. Equally gingerly, Travers slewed Koenig's car round in her tightest three-point turn and followed Amilakvari's car through the darkness broken by flashes as vehicles brewed up on all sides. Amilakvari's was the next to go. Edging around it, scared of setting off a mine herself, Travers took the somewhat blackened Georgian prince on board, aware that each extra passenger made it more likely that the Humber would set off a mine under them all.

Once the Germans started firing flares, speed was the only weapon. One particularly close heavy machine gun was taken out by Lt Dève driving his half-track right over it and its crew. After repeating the operation on a second machine gun, he died trying the same trick with a third. Incredibly in all the confusion of explosions, screams and enemy fire, Bellec or someone else had regained his bearings and the column slowly forged ahead through the gap in the enemy lines. With Amilakvari waving a Tommy gun beside her in the front passenger seat and firing it at any target he could see until told by Koenig to shut up, Travers kept her foot down, ignoring the bumps and potholes over which she was crashing - and her general's yells from the back seat to slow down and reduce the risk of smashing the suspension or colliding with another vehicle.

There surely can have been no other battlefield on which a woman drove to safety through minefields and enemy positions two high-ranking officers, both of whom had been her lovers - and was allowed by them to drive because she was the best of the three behind a wheel. The ultimate tribute to Travers' driving is that the only damage to the car was ruined shock absorbers, a dent in the rear where another vehicle drove into her - and eleven bullet-holes. By 0200hrs they had lost everyone else and were alone in the desert, navigating by guesswork and a pocket compass of Amilakvari's, which he had to get out of the car to use. At one of these stops, they clearly heard German voices nearby and drove straight on, never mind the compass bearing!

After dawn the absence of any other vehicle in sight convinced Koenig that his entire force must have been either wiped out or taken prisoner. Exhaustion, survivor guilt and his commander's responsibility for the men under his command all combined to crush his spirit. Travers heard him decide his duty lay in leaving her somewhere safe and turning back to give himself up, to be with his men. Happily, Amilakvari convinced him that he could not possibly give the Axis such a propaganda coup.[9]

Finally swinging east and then north, they were reasonably sure they had broken through all three siege lines, but missed cairn B837 altogether and stumbled by chance on the field workshop of a British armoured company, from where they were directed to

2nd Free French Brigade HQ. Larminat was not there, having left at dawn with two trucks and six ambulances to rendezvous with the breakout party at the cairn. With Amilakvari and Koenig stunned that they appeared to be the only successful escapees, Travers took the car to the MT section for makeshift repairs to the shock absorbers.

Her job done, she fell asleep in the shade of the car - and awoke to see a dream come true. Ambulances and vehicles of all descriptions were arriving separately and in convoys, suspensions groaning under the load of filthy, hungry, thirsty men, sitting, standing and hanging on all over them. The final cost to the Free French forces of the fighting breakout was seventy-two known dead, with twenty-one wounded and 736 missing in action, but by 1900hrs that day Koenig knew his gamble had paid off: he had managed to bring some 2,500 men of the Free French Brigade safely through the lines. Others continued to trickle in from the desert for the next three days. The Legion suffered worst. Tasked with securing the flanks of the breakout, it had least chance of getting clean away.

Both battalion majors were taken prisoner. Maj Puchois of 3 BLE was captured, hemmed in by twenty Germans, whose officer courteously invited him to hand over his empty pistol after an exemplary fight.

Withdrawn to Alexandria for refitting, Koenig and his men were hailed by the large French-speaking population. High on their heroic performance at Bir Hakeim, some officers voiced unwise criticism of the RAF, whose support they thought inadequate. Since the Desert Air Force had many other commitments, this was another irritation for the British, including one Very Important Visitor. Winston Churchill, on a morale-raising tour of hard-pressed Commonwealth troops in the Western Desert, ignored the French totally, which Koenig took as a personal snub.[10]

Nor did Gen Bernard Montgomery, the new C-in-C appointed in August to replace Auchinleck, have much affection for his French allies. However, in the autumn of 1942 as he prepared to push Rommel all the way back into Tunisia, Koenig's men, regrouped and re-equipped in two battalions totalling 1,274 men, were tasked with carrying out a diversionary raid on El Himeimat, a strongly fortified ridge dominating the Qattara Depression - a basin of salt lakes and marshes below sea-level straddling the Egypt-Libya frontier, which was impassable to military traffic and therefore formed the southern end of Rommel's line extending from the coast at El Alamein. The position was held by 400 Italian paras, well dug in and protected by minefields.

It was, as someone remarked at the time, not a job one would give to one's best friends. Because El Himeimat could only be approached across an open plain, exposed to the defenders' artillery, the decision was to attack by night, starting at 1930hrs on 23 October. Everything went wrong. Intelligence was badly out of date. As they moved into the radio shadow of the escarpment the command communications net failed, making coordination impossible.[11] Sappers cleared a path through the minefields, but when the first half-tracks of 1st Demi-Brigade stalled in the soft sand Axis artillery laid down a bombardment and German tanks appeared on the flanks. Bogged down and a sitting target, Maj Paris de Bollardière abandoned the attack, but with the radios out was unable to communicate his decision to Lt Col Amilakvari, who continued to attack with 2nd Demi-Brigade.

At dawn, more German armour counter-attacked and the Luftwaffe also showed up to strafe the Legion positions. The 2nd Demi-Brigade was under such heavy pressure that Amilakvari withdrew it into a defensive perimeter on a small rise. At 0900hrs Koenig ordered the withdrawal. On the Jock column safaris, it was normal for legionnaires to wear their white képis,[12] which were cooler than tin helmets, but Amilakvari refused even in battle to replace his black, gold braided colonel's képi with a helmet. At some point on the retreat, he caught a 105mm shrapnel fragment in the head and was killed outright. His body was wrapped in the torn green cloak and carried away by his legionnaires to the unrestrained grief of Travers and all the men who had known and admired him.

Made cynical by all the hype and PR distortion in the media, one tends to doubt the wartime adventures of Susan Travers, the girl who always wanted to be a boy. They do seem incredible - as does her military career after the war when a change of gender, on paper only, allowed the fiercely masculine world of the Legion to take her formally on its strength as an *adjutant-chef* or Warrant Officer, First Class. Among the medals she was awarded for war service was the Croix de Guerre. Early in 1956 she was also awarded the Médaille Militaire. In the courtyard at Les Invalides, standing within a few steps of Napoleon's tomb, she had it pinned to the lapel of her coat by the ageing general who had been her lover years before. Out of respect for his and his family's feelings, she never told her story until long after his death in 1970. In 1996 she was made a Chevalier de la Légion d'Honneur as her father had been, making them the only father and daughter to have been so honoured.

These, France's highest awards for bravery, are not awarded for inventing fantasy.

Chapter 31

THE STORMY REMARRIAGE

North Africa, 1942-1943;
Europe 1944-1945;
Vietnam 1945-1949

Although El Himeimat had only been a diversionary attack and the offensive as a whole was successful, Montgomery was not impressed by the Legion withdrawal after losses of only eleven killed and sixty-nine wounded, which he deemed to indicate a lack of determination. In reply, Gen De Larminat, an unhappy man who committed suicide in 1962, blamed all the problems on poor intelligence and alleged lack of British air and artillery support. Not he, but Bollardière was sacked by Koenig in an unsuccessful effort to appease Montgomery, who sent the Legion into reserve on 14 November.

This was six days after Operation Torch, the Anglo-American landings at Casablanca in Morocco and Oran and Algiers in Algeria which gave Rommel the ultimate headache of a war on two fronts in North Africa, where his Italian and German armies were now trapped between the predominantly US forces to the west and British 8th Army to the east.

The Allied landings met comparatively light resistance, with some pro-Gaullist units of the Vichy forces going through the motions but deliberately firing wide, not that this saved them from being bombed and strafed by American pilots, who could not tell the difference from the air. A squadron of Spaniards with 1 REC went further in surrendering without firing a shot.[1] Around Casablanca, resistance developed under the Pétainist Resident-General Charles Noguès when the invading forces tried to expand their initial beachheads. However, on 10 November the fighting eased and on the following day the French authorities in Morocco concluded an armistice.

In Algeria the situation was not so clear-cut, with some French troops remaining loyal to Pétain while others backed the anti-Vichy French general whom the Allies were sponsoring in North Africa, the tall, aristocratic Henri Giraud, whose reputation was unsullied by allegations of collaboration because he had been in a German POW camp until managing to escape in 1942 and making his way clandestinely to Algeria.

With Vichy C-in-C Admiral Darlan being in Algiers at the time of the invasion, the US timetable was put out of sync on 9 November by a French counterattack on the Arzew beachhead near Oran. On 11 November German and Italian commanders fearing an Allied invasion of the south of France overran the Free Zone that had been sovereign French territory governed from Vichy. They could hardly have done otherwise, but this breach of the Armistice agreement re-aligned most Pétainists in North Africa, inducing Noguès and others to assent to Darlan's proposals for a working agreement with the Allies. Brokered by American diplomats, it recognised him as political ruler of French North Africa with Gen Giraud as C-in-C of *all* Free French forces. On 13 November, this arrangement was endorsed by Eisenhower against considerable local opposition but with the backing of President Roosevelt.

De Gaulle was furious, but the deal with Darlan reflected his low popularity with the Armée d'Afrique, where fewer than 10% of officers and men recognised his authority. In any case, the Americans cared little for his feelings, given that their politically astute manoeuvre made allies of the 120,000 men of the Armée d'Afrique who might otherwise have continued fighting for Rommel.

Although the move brought the whole of French West Africa also over to the Allies, Darlan was unable to persuade Adm Laborde in Toulon to sail for North Africa while there was still time. Anti-German to the core, Laborde nevertheless understandably refused to bring his crews and vessels over to the side that had killed his friends and comrades at Mers el-Kebir. His one word reply to Darlan's signal ordering him to do so was, '*Merde!*' No less than 171 ships that could arguably have shortened the war were thus denied to the Allied cause by Churchill's ghastly miscalculation of 3 July 1940.

On 27 November 1942 the Luftwaffe mined the exits from the harbour of Toulon to prevent Laborde having any second thoughts, whereupon he implemented Darlan's previous standing orders given in August 1940. Every ship in port was scuttled to frustrate German plans to take them over. [2]

For a month, everyday life carried on much the same in Darlan's North Africa. Informers informed; people were arrested. Anti-Semitic laws remained in force. Deserters, including men who had fought for De Gaulle, were sent to disease-ridden desert punishment camps. Legion officers continued to display portraits of Marshal Pétain in their messes.

On 24 December Darlan was assassinated in mysterious circumstances by 20-year-old Fernand Bonnier, who had been given small arms training by undercover American or British officers. A coffin was ordered for Bonnier *before* his court martial, at which he confidently expected his controllers to extricate him. Instead, he was conveniently shot at 0730hrs on 26 December and buried in an unmarked grave, after leaving only a scribbled and ambiguous note on the back of a visiting card bearing the name of a prominent Gaullist. [3] His controllers have never been revealed but from this moment De Gaulle showed a flair for politics that amazed both his many enemies and his few supporters in the Allied camp, repeatedly outmanoeuvring his rival Giraud to become the leader of *all* Free France.

At the beginning of 1943 Rommel was being squeezed in the nutcracker of which the eastern claw was the British 8th Army - not including 13 DBLE, where morale crumbled again while it was held in reserve training in Tripolitania until the final stages of the Afrika Korps' retreat into Tunisia in April/May 1943. Drafted belatedly to the front during the final stages of the German collapse because they spoke the second language of the country and knew it better than any other Allied troops, they fought their way westwards. The other claw of the nutcracker, comprised of the predominantly American forces moving in from the west, had its southern flank secured by the six demoralised Legion battalions[4] of the Armée d'Afrique, given the miserable job of fighting their way eastwards in foul winter weather through the hilly and mountainous country inland.

The first to see action were the remnants of 1 REC, formed into one armoured car squadron and an infantry company which attacked at Foum el-Gouafel on 11 January, capturing 200 prisoners and thirty 47mm guns.[5] After handing over command to Gen Jürgen von Arnim, Rommel was recalled to Germany on 6 March, a sick man. On 23 March, 1 REIM - or 1st Legion Marching Regiment - was formed from troops at bel-Abbès, including men who had opted for repatriation rather than join the Free French in 1941, plus 4 DBLE arriving from Senegal.

At the beginning of May they suffered heavy casualties at Djebel Mansour against German armoured units. Tunis was captured on 7 May and Bizerta almost simultaneously. With Hitler refusing to allow any German forces to be evacuated from North Africa, von Arnim was driven to surrender on 13 May. However, at the victory parade in Tunis on 20 May Koenig and his men were obliged to march with British 8th Army[6] because French 19th Army Corps - to which the Legion 'belonged' organisationally - not only included Barre and his men of 6 REI from Syria but, more importantly, was pro-Giraud and anti-De Gaulle. The divisions within the Legion were not over yet and the partners in this uneasy remarriage had to be dragged to the altar step by step, even after the official re-integration of 13 DBLE on 1 August 1943.

An honour guard of officers and men from 13 DBLE, sent from Tunisia to escort De Gaulle, was placed under open arrest once inside Algeria and escorted back to the frontier under armed guard. Gaullist officers ran an underground railway to enable deserters in Algeria to reach 13 DBLE in Tunisia. In reply the Legion's internal Intelligence known as Bureau de Sécurité de la Légion Etrangère, or BSLE for short, infiltrated informers among the men involved. The first official transfer of seventeen officers, twenty NCOs and 180 legionnaires was given a very cold reception on arrival at 13 DBLE. Several of the officers who had sat out the war in North Africa decided to transfer out again rather than put up with the hostility of the more aggressive Gaullists.[7]

Morale in all Legion formations suffered during the ten months after the end of hostilities in North Africa. While being completely re-equipped with modern American materiel, it was also being milked of so many trained soldiers transferring to British, American and other Allied forces that Lt Col Gaultier echoed Rollet's fears after the First World War that the Legion would dwindle away to nothing.[8]

Although latecomers in the long drawn-out Italian campaign, arriving in April 1944 as part of De Gaulle's 1 DFL under Gen Diégo Brosset, 13 DBLE fought at Pontecorvo and San Lorenzo while redesignated 1st and 2nd BLE of 1 Free French Division. It also distinguished itself at Radicofani in the Val d'Orcia, where three Tiger tanks guarding the approach to the medieval castle on a high rocky spur were engaged by the machine-guns of 2nd Lt Marcel Guillot as a distraction while Lt Julian and five volunteers climbed the sheer rock-face and cleaned out the company of German infantry inside the walls with a generous helping of hand grenades.

Withdrawn from Italy in August for Operation Anvil - the Allied invasion of the South of France[9] - 13 DBLE at last traded its Cross of Lorraine shoulder patch for the Gallic cockerel, in common with the rest of the Legion, although continuing to favour the Narvik commando-style beret over the traditional white képi until the final victory parade in Paris in May 1945. On landing at 1800hrs on 16 August at Cavalaire-dur-Mer, they passed from US command to that of Gen Jean-Marie De Lattre De Tassigny, consolidating De Gaulle's position as leader of all French forces.

His determination that his troops should not be sidelined in the reconquest of France placed heavy demands of them all, including 13 DBLE. Reaching Lyons on 5 September, they took severe losses in the fighting for Autun before linking up with RMLE and 1 REC after one unorthodox answer to the manpower shortage was negotiated in August 1944 by American OSS officers, who conducted through the lines an SS unit of 650 Ukrainians. They were enlisted en masse in the Legion, where they continued to fight under their own officers in defiance of the usual practice of breaking up national groups.

The change of allegiance did the Ukrainians no good. They may have thought the Legion was now their fatherland, but the following summer they were forcibly repatriated by De Gaulle under the terms of the Yalta agreement - and shot.[10] Close to a million Cossacks and other Eastern Europeans who had been fighting not for Hitler but against Russian military domination of their homelands were similarly deprived of their rights as POWs and handed over by the US and Britain, together with their wives and children, to be executed or sent to the Gulag.[11]

Meantime, as an example of dirty tricks for a dirty campaign, during the bitter winter of 1944-45 a Legion detachment carrying its wounded on stretchers was surrounded 20km south of Strasbourg. It succeeded in returning to the French lines after a German legionnaire convinced a sentry that they were Wehrmacht reinforcements, sent to prevent the escape of the encircled French! After divulging his comrades' whereabouts, the sentry was the first to die.

Once across the German frontier, one of the German NCOs who had been shielded under a false name from the Armistice Commission - Sgt Maj Moulin's name had been Porschmann - posed as a superior officer, interrogating by telephone the Wehrmacht and SS units about to be attacked in order to determine their strength and dispositions. In another company, the young captain allowed one of his German-Jewish legionnaires half an hour to finish his own private war. Given permission to infiltrate the village where he had been born and whose inhabitants had betrayed the rest of his family to the Gestapo, the legionnaire crawled off into the darkness with ten grenades and thirty minutes' grace. The civilian inhabitants were hiding in their cellars. Ten muffled explosions were heard before he returned within the time limit, job done.[12]

Despite all the dirty tricks, casualties in what had been 13 DBLE were heavy, but no worse than in other French forces, hard driven by De Lattre to justify De Gaulle's post-war political ambitions. So it was essentially paranoia and combat fatigue that drove two 13 DBLE officers to accuse the 'other Legion' in Sidi bel-Abbès of deliberately trying to wipe them out by making sure the Gaullist units were given the most dangerous assignments. Whatever the truth of the allegation, 13 DBLE was withdrawn from the German front in March 1945 and transferred to the Alps.

When the war in Europe ended in May 1945, France had not originally been allocated a zone of occupation in Germany, so one had to be carved out of the British and US zones. There, between October and the end of the year, the Legion sent recruiting teams into POW cages, offering a choice between donning Legion uniform and staying put at risk of being tried for war crimes. Most Wehrmacht soldiers had had enough of war, but men from the *Länder* within the Russian zone of occupation and former SS men who had reason to fear prosecution if they stayed in Europe, did volunteer to the tune of 12,000.

One of these, whose war was only a little more involved than those of many others, was ex-Sgt Brückler or Brockman, who had betrayed the long-range raid on Darnah airfield in 1942. Another was Mussolini's private doctor, who enlisted and rose to the rank of *adjutant-chef médic*. In those years Legion recruiting officers did not ask too many awkward questions because France needed as many experienced soldiers as possible for another war just beginning.

More or less at the same time that 13 DBLE was transferred to the Alps, the forgotten Legion regiment in Indochina was in a parlous state. After obeying orders from Vichy not to resist the Japanese invasion, 5 REI [13] had been reinforced by the two phantom columns of 'European workers' in 1941, but the suspension of normal rotation since then had increased average age considerably. In addition, the stultifying boredom of garrison life under occupation by the Japanese had reduced combat efficiency to an all-time low. Lack of medical supplies combined to lower general levels of health by malaria, dysentery and venereal diseases. Although on paper the French forces totalling 65,000 outnumbered their Japanese occupiers two to one, most were colonial troops. Secondly, they were substantially disarmed and low on ammunition. Thirdly, the Japanese were increasingly jittery after the loss of Burma to the British and Gen Douglas MacArthur's retaking of the Philippines and capture of Iwo Jima. Contingency plans had been drawn up by the French command to deal with a rumoured Japanese plan to massacre all the Europeans in Indochina during their own withdrawal. After repeated false alarms, on the evening of 9 March 1946 many French barracks were unguarded and numerous personnel living out with their

Vietnamese wives and families. Officers and men were seized in their homes and in bars and restaurants. In Lang Son Gen Lemonnier authorised a number of his officers to accept an invitation to a banquet, where their Japanese hosts welcomed them to the strains of a jazz band - until 2000hrs, when they found themselves surrounded by armed guards. Those who resisted were shot or run through with their hosts' swords.[14]

The legionnaires were machine-gunned while singing the Marseillaise as a last gesture of defiance. One of three survivors there, Legionnaire Hardouvalis[15] managed to make it to the house of his Vietnamese *congai*. Betrayed by her neighbours, he refused to divulge the hiding place of some recently parachuted American arms and had the distinction of being forced to dig a vertical grave shorter than himself and stand in it so that his head could be hacked off to make him fit.[16]

When Lemonnier and the French Resident Camille Auphale refused to sign a surrender document, they were ordered to dig their own graves, kneeling on the edge of which they were beheaded. In Hanoi legionnaires fought to the last bullet and then with bayonets before being overpowered, the survivors being beaten, knifed and bayoneted to death. Resistance at the punishment battalion in Ha Giang was also swiftly overcome and followed by mass executions.

The young officer who had brought the phantom columns to Vietnam, Lt Chenel was nearly caught in a Hanoi hotel room, but escaped armed solely with his service revolver. Hijacking a rickshaw at gunpoint, he then stole a bicycle, and another when that broke, continuing on horseback and on foot to rejoin his men at Son La - a journey of 200km accomplished in less than three days. Chenel then launched his own war against the Japanese after being given command of 1st Company of 1st Battalion on 20 March.

It was in vain. Surprise and savagery had done their work. The French commanding general was on the run wearing no badges of rank and posing as a colonial administrator after sending a signal to De Gaulle assuring him of the intention to fight to the last man against the Japanese. Reaching the airstrip at Dien Bien Phu six days ahead of his own staff, Brig Gen Sabatier welcomed De

Gaulle's right-hand man and Intelligence chief Col Passy[17] who flew in from Calcutta, informed Sabatier of his promotion to major-general and made him the supreme representative of the government in what remained of French Vietnam.[18] Sabatier later wrote a book justifying his conduct.[19]

In northeast Vietnam soldiers like Chenel fought on, but were eventually forced to withdraw in five columns totalling 3,000 mixed troops across the Chinese border, repeatedly ambushed during a fifty-two-day epic march. Although their *congais* had been left behind to their fate, one did follow the column for 240km from loyalty to Sgt Leibner. After he was killed in a skirmish with Japanese pursuers, she gazed briefly at his body before vanishing into the jungle.

Just over 1,000 of the column survived to reach friendly territory in China suffering from beri-beri and general exhaustion. It was their good fortune that the French ambassador to Chiang Kai-Shek was Gen Zinovi Pechkoff, the ex-legionnaire, who was able to arrange repatriation to Europe via India for some of the wounded.[20] After 5 REI was formally disbanded on 1 July 1945, the fittest were then formed into a *bataillon de marche* that on 8 February began the long trek back to Vietnam, fighting their way against local warlords along what would become the Ho Chi Minh trail.

While dragging the Lang Son River to recover the breech-blocks of the 155mm guns dumped there to save them from the Japanese, the pioneers also recovered several brass-bound antique chests. When forced open, they were found to be full of mint-condition Mexican coins dated 1884 and 1885.[21] Against all the odds, after more than half a century, the *caisse noire* dumped there by Gen Herbinger during the panic withdrawal of 1885 had been recovered by its rightful owners.

Truly, 5 REI was the lost legion. De Gaulle's attitude was that they were Pétainist collaborators. In Washington, President Roosevelt had died on 12 April after saying that France had milked Indochina for one hundred years and that the people of Vietnam were 'entitled to better than that'.[22] Neither he nor his successor Harry Truman had any sympathy for the pre-war colonial administrations of their European allies. In London, Winston Churchill had been rejected as Britain's post-war leader and could do nothing to influence Washington. His successor, Prime Minister-elect Clement Attlee had sympathy neither for France nor colonialism.

Playing his own long-term game, Stalin at the Potsdam summit conference in July-August 1945 grabbed all the Baltic and Balkan countries he could to extend the only empire of the twentieth century and agreed for Britain to accept the Japanese surrender on the Asian mainland including Vietnam south of the sixteenth parallel, with Chiang Kai-Shek's Kuomintang doing the same to the north of it. Great Britain's representative at the surrender ceremony was Adm Louis Mountbatten, the Supreme Allied Commander in South-East Asia. In a secret despatch to the Foreign Office, he warned that the French would not be able to retake possession of their pre-war colony of Vietnam as though nothing had happened since 1940 because of the growth of the Viet Minh independence movement under Ho Chi Minh during the Japanese occupation.[23]

With Vietnam divided in two, while the Chinese moved into the northern half of the country British troops disembarked in Saigon during September and European survivors had the unnerving experience of seeing them rearm surrendered Japanese soldiers as a force to reimpose law and order. It may seem strange, in view of his sustained successful campaign to drive the French out of his country, that the main proponent of the return of French troops at the time was Nguyen Hai Quoc, whose *nom de guerre* was Ho Chi Minh, meaning He (Who) Lights The Way. Ho was by profession a history teacher, who saw clearly that the European powers, humiliated by the Japanese and financially ruined by the two world wars, would never regain their pre-war status in Asia. Whatever colonies they did recover would soon be lost to national independence movements - as happened in British India, Malaya and Africa and the Dutch East Indies. China, on the other hand, would never let go.

Having formed the Viet Minh[24] in May 1941 during his exile in China, Ho considered that it was - in his own words - better for his countrymen 'to sniff French arse for a short while than eat Chinese shit for centuries to come'.[25] Some of his supporters resented his agreement to 15,000 French soldiers being stationed north of the sixteenth parallel, but since the quid pro quo was the departure of 180,000 Chinese soldiers, he won that point.

Ho was a founder member of the French Communist Party and a Comintern delegate. Although led by Communists, the Viet Minh purported to be a national front organisation, open to all political persuasions. After the Japanese surrender to the Allies on 10 August 1945, Viet Minh units armed by American OSS operatives seized control of the northern capital of Hanoi on 19 August and proclaimed the independent Democratic Republic of Vietnam. Gen Leclerc did not return to Hanoi until 18 March 1946, with a token force to replace the Chinese, who were in no hurry to leave. At his side as he inspected a guard of honour was a small Vietnamese man in western suit and a floppy felt hat. This was the DRV's Minister of the Interior, Vo Nguyen Giap who had commanded the Vietnamese guerrilla forces fighting the Japanese in Vietnam since 1943.

The French-Vietnamese Accord recognised the DRV in return for it accepting the status of a member of the French Union and granting concessions to French business interests, foremost of which was the Michelin rubber company. Yet De Gaulle's High Commissioner Adm Georges Thierry D'Argenlieu denounced the Accord from the outset, placing his faith at the time in the force of French arms - which is where the Legion came into all this. D'Argenlieu was a curious character, having served in both world wars in the navy, but been a barefoot Carmelite monk in between - as he would be again after playing his part in this tragedy.

Leclerc's French and North African troops began the long push northwards from Saigon - among them 3 REI and 13 DBLE, whose commander Col De Sairigné was an early victim of a Viet Minh ambush. On 5 October, 1st and 2nd Battalions of 2 REI under Col Lorrilot landed at Nha Trang to secure the coast of Annam, or central Vietnam. Dirty tricks were the order of the day on both sides. The mixed bands of Viet Minh, Japanese soldiers and local bandits had the unpleasant habit of dum-dumming their bullets, which ensured few prisoners were taken. So 2 REI cheated in different ways, disguising the smaller and darker-skinned legionnaires as *nah qué* peasants in black pyjamas and conical hats to achieve maximum surprise.

In the famine-torn northern provinces the peasants, who had not enough food for themselves and their children, were raped and robbed by armed bands, both native and Chinese irregulars. The tension mounted until 19 November, when the Viet Minh threw down the gauntlet by cutting Hanoi's water and electricity supplies before attacking the French garrison with mortar and small arms fire. They released all the prisoners in the jails before melting away into the jungles in traditional guerrilla style. Their killing of twenty-nine French soldiers brought a savage riposte: on 23 November approximately 6,000 Vietnamese civilians were killed[26] when French warships retaliated by bombarding the defenceless port city of Haiphong - which in turn led to 600 European civilians being abducted or killed.

Like the attack on Fort Sumter that started the American Civil War, the bombardment of Haiphong was the first blow in Vietnam's Thirty Years' War: Round One, France v. Viet Minh; Round Two, USA v. NVA and Viet Cong. De Gaulle having resigned after doing his best to reunite a deeply divided country, few people in France took any interest in what was happing in their name on the other side of the planet. On 7 December two second-lieutenants disembarking at Haiphong with 2 REI were to become Legion legends. Their names were Bernard Cabiro and Roger Faulques. The French High Commissioner, Monsieur Sainteny was trying to keep the civil population calm, but the capital was surrounded by an unknown number of enemy. After being transported up-river by landing craft of the Naval Assault Division, nicknamed 'Dinasau', 2 REI's job was to find out how many and to reopen Highway One joining Hanoi and Saigon.

It was a grim Christmas with Junkers bombers inherited from the Luftwaffe parachuting ammunition to French units cut off from resupply even in the centre of Hanoi.[27] Cabiro's 1st Company suffered four legionnaires killed and two officers, two NCOs and eighteen men wounded. Steadily, the French won the upper hand, so that in temperate Hanoi, its shady villa-lined avenues laid out like a provincial town in the Midi, officers and their European wives once again played tennis and swam at the Cercle Sportif, attended Mass in the huge redbrick Catholic cathedral and concerts in their own opera house. In sweltering

Saigon, 1,200km to the south, the Continental Palace Hotel on Place Garnier - now Lam Son Square - was a chunk of Europe come adrift, with cool drinks on the terrace and air-conditioned rooms with every possible service. Prudent Europeans did not venture across the river into the Chinese city of Cholon after dark, but that had more to do with *tong* gangsterism than Communist terrorists.

Outside the main towns, the impossibility of 'pacifying' mountainous and jungle terrain without killing the entire population in which Giap's dedicated troops swam 'like fish in the water', forced the French to achieve a delusory paper progress by dotting command maps with strategically distributed 'hedgehog' forts. One of these, at Hoc Monh outside Saigon, was built by legionnaires as a fortified palace complete with dining-hall, sickbay, prison, electricity, modern plumbing and sanitation. Serving in a less luxurious 'hedgehog', Legion WO1 Eugen Brause recalled massacring human waves with well-sited machine-guns in concrete emplacements and the overpowering smell of fuel and roasted pork when the *fougasses* - tanks of napalm buried beneath the glacis - were remotely fired during an attack.[28]

Unless with its own airstrip, even the best constructed 'hedgehog' was vulnerable when replacements and supplies came in by armoured convoys on the network of *routes coloniales*, which are still the main highways of Vietnam. Highways Three and Four became death traps for all except the most heavily armed convoys. Routinely, the Viet Minh besieged a strongpoint, waited for the relief column, ambushed it and then faded away.

As in all confrontations between conventional forces and guerrillas, the anger of the soldiers boiled over in occasional killing sprees, as testified by some of the Germans who made up 60% of those involved. Describing one such excess when headless male bodies were left in a village square as a warning and women and children burned alive in their homes, ex-Cpl Günther Woitzik claimed to have been so sickened that he deserted soon afterwards. Whether it was before or after some of his comrades were found by a river where they had been swimming with eyes gouged out and penises and testicles thrust into their mouths, he was unclear. 'I always kept the last three bullets for me,' he said.[29]

Joachim Schriever not only deserted, but fought as a renegade with the Viet Minh before being repatriated to East Germany via China and Moscow in 1951. 'The Chinese were officially friendly because our countries were Socialist brothers,' he recalled. 'But privately they said, "Long-noses no good."' East German politician Erich Honecker organised a total of seven transports of Legion deserters by the same route. Some, like Schriever, were produced at Press conferences to denounce the imperialist war in Vietnam, but were afterwards destined to lifelong surveillance by the Stasi as having probably been corrupted politically during their time in the West.[30]

Legion deserter Willy Deckers recalled being greeted when his Moscow-Berlin train reached the East German border station at Frankfurt-an-der-Oder by what he thought was the Hitler Youth band to which he had belonged, only to be informed that it was the Freie Deutsche Jugend - the Communist equivalent. Afterwards, he and the others in his transport were held for months in a 'quarantine camp' ostensibly awaiting the result of their blood tests for malaria.

This was long before the Berlin Wall, so he took a chance after being released and crossed the border into the West. However, after fellow-deserter and Communist activist Jackie Holsten was imprisoned, it seemed safer to be treated as a spy in the East, so Deckers went back.[31] At the same time in the French zone of Occupied Germany, Legion recruiting teams were openly defying the German police and smuggling up to fifty young men a day across the border into France.[32]

Time, said Ho, is on our side because, since the imperialists cannot kill one of us for each child that is born, we must win in the end. At the time, less than 5% of the Vietnamese population supported the Communists, but the longer France and then the US kept the conflict going, the stronger the Party became.

The tactics of the Legion in North Africa were patently unsuitable for pursuing across flooded rice paddies and the river deltas, jungles and mountains of Vietnam an enemy who had only to cache his weapon in order to look like every other peasant. Initially, 1 REC was equipped with US M29 'Crab' amphibious vehicles. When too many men had died in these open-topped death traps, they were replaced by another modified all-terrain vehicle, the closed-in Alligator, which at least gave protection from grenades thrown by suicide volunteers during ambushes.

The disciplined Viet Minh became adept at the same technique used by the Chinese Communists against the British in Malaya: blowing up the road after the leading armoured vehicles had passed, isolating them from the rest, then raining grenades and fire from well-sited machine guns into the stalled column of civilian and military vehicles. The French High Command decided that the only way of taking the war to the enemy was to convert some of its ex-Luftwaffe Junkers bombers to drop men where they were needed, fast. The Legion formed its first paratroops with volunteers from 3rd Company of 3 REI under Capt Morin in April 1948. After training, the first Bataillon Etranger de Parachutistes, known as 1 BEP, landed at Haiphong in autumn 1948. Lt Cabiro and other officers of 2 BEP disemplaned at Than Son Nhut on 24 January 1949, followed by their men landing from the transport *Joffre* at Saigon on 9 February. Six weeks later they were in action in the central region of the country.

The equipment of both battalions was so obsolete that their unwieldy, outdated Lebel rifles had to be dropped separately to avoid injury on landing. Once on the ground the paras were thus at first armed only with combat knives until they could locate the bundles of rifles. Since parachutes were in such short supply that they had to be collected after each drop for reuse, the observant Viets made it a priority to steal or destroy them. A Legion para's first decision after landing was therefore whether to roughly repack the billowing folds of silk or to head straight for his weapon maybe a couple of hundred metres away. Even so, *la guerre aeroportée* - airborne warfare - was the trump that would win the war in Vietnam. At least, that was what the generals thought until the defeat at Dien Bien Phu taught them otherwise.

PART III

THE POST-IMPERIAL PERIOD

Chapter 32

WHO NEEDS THE LEGION NOW?

When the Evian Agreements ended the Algerian war in 1962, the consensus in many French officers' messes was that the Legion had outlived its usefulness, now that there were no more colonial wars to be fought. President Charles De Gaulle understandably dissolved 1 REP, but what saved the rest of the Legion and transformed it into a modern world-class fighting force was - according to Legion lore - former wartime *résistant* and ex-Legion officer Pierre Messmer, who was his Minister of the Armed Forces at the time, charged with reorganising all the French armed services after the generals' revolt.

Was De Gaulle a man to be swayed from his chosen path by a subordinate, albeit a much-trusted one - or was he playing a deeper game?

The world, as seen from the banks of the Seine in 1962, was becoming an increasingly monolingual planet, on which all other cultures were being submerged or swept away by a flood of Pepsi, Coke and Procter and Gamble detergents bearing with it a flotsam of Hollywood films, Y-Fronts, Playtex bras, Levi jeans and Nabisco cereal products. Later would come the totally irresistible cultural *tsunami* of transatlantic television series and the implantation worldwide of multinational companies able by secret boardroom decisions to destabilise entire countries, but in 1962 it seemed to President De Gaulle that there was still time for France and the French-speaking countries to build a politico-cultural coffer dam around themselves and keep at bay this threat to their continued independent political, cultural and commercial identity.

Francophonie is a word coined in 1880 to mean the linguistic community of France, Quebec and those parts of Belgium and Switzerland where French was the first language, plus regions like the Levant and southeast Asia, where it was the second language used for commercial and cultural exchanges by a French-educated middle class. De Gaulle's plan was to unite the fifty-plus *francophone* countries in a bloc where their common interests could be protected from what he saw as an Anglo-Saxon conspiracy to dominate the entire planet. The zenith of this policy was his speech in Montreal in the summer of 1967 ending with *'Vive le Québec libre!'* - a call to arms that did not amuse the Canadian federal government.

English-speakers take for granted the convenient pre-eminence of their language, but Arabic script is the second most widely used in the world. If every business executive had to master it for routine international correspondence, that would change our worldview. Spanish is the first language of 250 million people. Basic Spanish is easy for Europeans to acquire, but tourism and business would be very different if we were all *obliged* to learn it in order to travel abroad. Mandarin Chinese has 800 million first-language speakers and is used as a second language by millions more, but if we were compelled to master even a modicum of 15,000 Chinese characters in order to use our computers, we should see the world differently.

The examples give a measure of how disadvantaged French-speakers are and why De Gaulle wanted to revalidate what had been the language of diplomacy, respected worldwide for its precision. To some extent, his dream outlives him at today's *francophone* summit meetings bringing together the heads of state from fifty-five countries - Belgium, Benin and Burkina Faso all the way to Togo, Tunisia, Vanuatu and Vietnam - thus keeping French culture alive in those countries and encouraging trade and tourism between them for their mutual benefit.

Another aim of De Gaulle in shaping the *francophone* bloc at the time was to defuse some of the tensions in the dangerously polarised Cold War, whose two principal players in Washington and Moscow manipulated smaller countries like pawns in a game that could end in global disaster. France was a founder member of NATO but its president's hostility to American control of the Alliance would lead in March 1966 to his expulsion of NATO forces so that nuclear missiles could no longer be launched from French territory without the French government being consulted.

Since any launch against the USSR would have triggered immediate retaliation against the source of the incoming missiles, few people in France queried his decision.

In 1962, he saw interference by the Soviet bloc and the US in the domestic affairs of Third World countries as steps on the path leading to global conflict. To reduce the possibilities of French and Belgian withdrawals from their African colonies being exploited for Cold War ends, De Gaulle believed that France could become a force for peace by offering an alternative to intervention by Moscow or Washington in countries wishing to become clients of neither power bloc.

This new peace-keeping role could only be exercised after expunging the stigma of 'colonial oppressor' that attached to France's armed occupation of Algeria. With that behind her, she could play a major part in world politics again, providing she had a self-contained rapid-reaction force capable of mounting effective low-cost peace-keeping missions with very little support in the jungle, desert, swamp and mountain environments that prevail in much of the Third World.

Even in 1831 many voices had been raised against the folly of French colonial adventures. In 1962, after the war in Algeria had cost almost every family in France the life of a relative or close acquaintance, De Gaulle knew that few voters would buy into his dream - unless the rapid reaction force was officially composed of foreigners, whose deaths would lose no votes in French elections. Thank you, Marshal Soult.

The problem for Charles De Gaulle and future incumbents of the Elysée Palace after his resignation in 1969 was that a army of foreigners, whose NCOs and men were as loyal to their officers as the paras of 1 REP had been, was far too dangerous to keep on French soil, unless dismembered in such a way that all the president's men could only put the pieces together again *outside France*.

To ensure the Legion never mounted another insurrection or became the tool of another coup, its regimental depots in France were therefore separated geographically by hundreds of kilometres and all situated well distant from the capital. About as far from Paris as one can get on the mainland, 1 REI runs the main headquarters at Aubagne near Marseille. 4 RE, entrusted with training, is at Castelnaudary near Toulouse. The cavalry regiment 1 REC is at Orange, with 2 RE in Nîmes. The engineers of 1 REG and 2 REG are in Laudun and St Christol on Corsica. The most dangerous legionnaires - those in 2 REP - are confined on the island of Corsica with no means of getting to the mainland faster than the speed of an overnight car ferry. On the occasions when they are deployed elsewhere in more than detachment strength, an outsider might be forgiven for thinking that the French air force is reluctant to find aircraft for them. Across the Atlantic in French Guiana are the men of 3 REI. On Mayotte, between Madagascar and Mozambique, is the Foreign Legion Detachment designated DLEM; and in Djibouti on the Horn of Africa is that old war-horse 13 DBLE.

The Legion has not changed greatly since Messmer's massive relocation and restructuring. It currently numbers 7,699 officers, NCOs and legionnaires from 136 countries, constituting nine regiments and one independent sub-unit. With the embargo on French citizens enlisting as legionnaires long since lifted, 24% are French.

Some 10% of officers joined as legionnaires; the others are rotated to the Legion as part of their service in the French army. As to where legionnaires currently come from, at a recent induction session attended by the author, a group of thirty would-be legionnaires were ordered in French to sit down if they understood spoken French. Half of them did so. A second NCO ordered those still on their feet to sit down - this time in Russian. All of them sat down with the exception of one African and a solitary Briton. Of the thirty, on average five would make it through basic training and be posted to a regiment. The other twenty-five would fall by the wayside at some point in the six months before they were eligible to wear the coveted white *képi*.

Chapter 33

THE LEGION REBORN

By the end of 1962, 1 RE was already ensconced in its new HQ at Aubagne, with the memorial installed at one end of the parade ground and the banners and battle honours displayed in the museum and the adjacent hall of honour. At the time, 2 REP was still in Algeria, where the Mers el-Kebir enclave was to remain French under the Evian Agreements until 1968 - rather like the US base at Guantánamo on Cuba. Discipline was waning and morale low among the trained paras digging ditches around the military airfield of Bou Sfer when James Worden met up with his compatriot Simon Murray. Both men were surprised that Legion recruiting continued, although not on a scale to make up for all the desertions: Murray recorded twenty new arrivals and 136 deserters in three months.

The Bou Sfer runway ended up eighty metres shorter than planned, owing to defaulting legionnaires being ordered not to scrub floors or do press-ups, but to exercise instead their night-fighting skills by stealing sacks of cement from the heavily guarded stores of building material. The runway cement was, in their opinion, better employed making concrete bases for the tents that were 2 REP's sole accommodation that freezing, wet winter until replaced by prefabricated huts erected on the same bases the following spring.

On 10 December 1962 Gen Lefort presided over the installation of a new colonel for 2 REP and announced the regiment's new role as an elite fighting arm. Morale began to lift. In between digging ditches and drains, Murray was a member of the morale-boosting regimental shooting team and also much in demand as a pianist for dances in the officers' mess. The perimeter fence and mines had not yet been installed so he, Worden and other old hands were in the habit of wandering off-base at night to take their pleasures in the immaculately decorated brothel run by two ladies named Janine and Suzanne in the little village of Bou Sfer.

Anglo-Saxons unaccustomed to the idea of soldiers' brothels may be unaware that there is no obligation to indulge in sexual activity; many men simply go along for a drink in an atmosphere more congenial than the bar of the *foyer du légionnaire*. For those who wonder about the mutual attraction of harlots and heroes, Worden suggests that they get on well not just because they represent supply and demand in the same market but because there is an instinctive sympathy between members of the human race's two oldest professions, both despised until needed.

The main spectator sport at Mers el-Kebir was rugby, in which 2 REP's regimental team earned a reputation for seriously damaging visiting players from other French military formations. Fitness training was back on the daily timetable, including jumping into and out of inflatable assault craft in all weathers and being put ashore from submarines on waterless islands to test men's endurance and initiative in making it back to base before they died of thirst.

Based at the former penal battalion base of Bechar in the Sahara, 2 RE was guarding the French nuclear testing area. Tests concluded, the regiment moved into Mers el-Kebir until disbanded in 1968 after the base was handed over to Algeria. Meanwhile, 3 RE was posted direct from Algeria to Madagascar, for training in amphibious warfare and tropical operations. Transferred to French Guiana for jungle warfare training and guard duties around the European Space Centre at Kourou, it had an especial role at the Ariane launching site.

Initially, 4 RE moved from Tébessa way south into the Sahara to guard the oil wells around Touggourt. After its subsequent transfer to France, it became the training regiment, based in the impressive purpose-built Quartier Danjou outside Castelnaudary. Starting in summer 1963, 5 RE began sending men from Bechar to 5 RMP - Régiment Mixte du Pacifique - created for the construction and security of the Centre d'Expérimentation du Pacifique nuclear testing grounds, where among its other jobs have been vehicle maintenance, running power stations and water distillation plants there.

Despised until needed? Worden should know. Legionnaires rotated back to France from Algeria found their reception by the inhabitants of towns near their bases ranging from indifferent to downright hostile. On his first trip into Aix-en-Provence, impeccably dressed in their Sunday-best uniforms, he and friends were refused service in hotels and restaurants simply because they were legionnaires.[1] The phenomenon is not peculiar to France. Of British soldiers, Rudyard Kipling wrote:

'It's Tommy this and Tommy that - and Tommy, go away.
But it's "Thank you, Mr Atkins," when the band begins to play.'

Worden's company was tasked with reinterring the coffins of Rollet, Aage and the Unknown Legionnaire in the Legion cemetery at Puyloubier, the village run for disabled and convalescent legionnaires in the Cézanne country of Provence. He personally volunteered to dig the hole for the Unknown. It is typical of the quirky ethos of the Legion that everyone knows the identity of the Unknown Legionnaire. His name was Zimmerman, and he died in bed after completing twenty years of undistinguished service. The posthumous honour was conferred on his remains to make the point that every legionnaire merits honour, whatever his rank or personal record.

Reporting to the new HQ of 2 REP at Camp Rafalli, outside the Corsican port of Calvi, Worden announced himself by name, number, length of service and time in present rank. He had flown in the RAF during the Second World War and was aware that he was no longer a young lion. It was nevertheless a surprise to hear His new CO, Col Caillaud - who had himself served in the BEP in Vietnam - mutter to the camp commandant, 'Where are they digging up all these old bastards from?

Under Caillaud's energetic leadership, 2 REP was transformed from a conventional para regiment into the French equivalent of the British SAS. At the time, Caillaud's ideas passed for revolutionary in the French army. He believed that every man in the regiment should be equally good at several specialisations. So, the 1st Company trained in anti-tank warfare, night fighting and urban warfare; 2nd Company was for mountain and arctic warfare;

3rd Company had wet feet from amphibious operations with its own combat swimmers; 4th Company were the guys one would not want to meet on a dark night, trained in long-range penetration for intelligence-gathering and sabotage, and expert snipers. In addition, Command and Services Company provided HQ, signals, medical, repair and other facilities. The Recce and Support Company had a reconnaissance platoon, two anti-tank platoons, an anti-aircraft platoon, a mortar platoon and the pathfinder platoon. A number of legionnaires were also trained to make HALO landings in hostile territory for hostage rescue and other tasks you don't boast about to your girlfriend.

Already by 1964 Worden noticed that morale, which had suffered much from the politically motivated withdrawal from Algeria that made a mockery of all the deaths, was slowly going up again - as was the number of British legionnaires. From an estimated fifty or so in the whole Legion towards the end of the Algerian war, the figure rose in 2 REP to around 12% after the 1982 Falklands War. Indeed, Worden with Murray and compatriot Bob Wright distinguished themselves as the first trio with the same nationality to serve simultaneously as *caporals-chef* in the same regiment.

The Legion's new role envisaged by De Gaulle continued to grow in importance after his death in 1970. Contingents of varying strength have served over the years in Cambodia, Ruanda, Congo, Bosnia, Serbia, Croatia, Central African Republic, Lebanon and in Iraq during the First Gulf War. They have also been in 'other places', about which nobody talks.

Two examples of Legion intervention illustrate its modern role. The multi-ethnic Republic of Chad lies in the very heart of the African continent, surrounded by Sudan, Central African Republic, Cameroon, Nigeria, Niger and Libya. With neighbours like that, the Chadian president's appeal in 1969 for military assistance from France surprised no one. De Gaulle's reply came in the form of a tactical HQ and two rifle companies commanded by Maj De Chastenet with three Tripacer observation aircraft, an Alouette command helicopter, a Pirate helicopter gunship and six H34 transports.

Arriving in-country, Chastenet acquired vehicles locally to

transform his paras into motorised units, plus a section of horse cavalry for patrolling areas inaccessible to motor traffic. Within the first six months, the task force saw combat against rebel forces three times. The third was most spectacular. Returning in the Alouette from a courtesy visit to Am Tinan in the south of the country, Chastenet noted a rebel group of horsemen below.

Instructing his pilot to continue on course as though nothing were amiss, he radioed ahead to put his forces on alert. A section of legionnaires was heliportered to the scene, but the rebels took refuge in a wood, where the Pirate gunship came into play. By the end of the operation sixty-eight rebels had been accounted for.

On 25 October 1969 Col Jeannou Lacaze landed at the capital Abéché[2] with his staff, the regimental colours and reinforcements from 2 REP, plus a motorised company from 1 RE, permitting a rapid expansion in the scale of operations, which reached a peak in 1970 after Maj Malaterre had taken over. That October Capt Wabinski's Reconnaissance and Support Company was airlifted to the Aouzou region in the northwest, near the Libyan border. Cross-border insurgents had surrounded the Chadian army garrison of Aouzou, which was holed-up in barracks and had lost control of its airstrip 5km south of the town.

Taking a chance, French pilots touched down on the airstrip, wrong-footing the insurgents by disgorging their loads of combat-ready legionnaires before coming to a halt. Taken aback by the speed of their deployment, the Libyans made little resistance, enabling Wabinski's men to link up with the relief column approaching by road under cover of darkness. The combined force, guided by local Chadian soldiers, then attempted to cut off the insurgents' retreat into Libya via the Leclerc Pass, driving the Libyans into some remote caves.

Next day, a company of Chadian paras was flown in. Together with the legionnaires, they drove the rebels out of the caves, killing forty-one and capturing two machine guns, two assault rifles and nineteen rifles. Before the end of the operation, three more machine guns, six rifles and a hoard of compromising paperwork was also taken, at the cost of one legionnaire dead and six wounded. In the entire Chad intervention most 'casualties' were from haemorrhoids suffered by men seated in poorly sprung military vehicles crashing for long hours over corrugations of concrete-hard earth.

In the autumn of 1962, that curious hybrid 13 DBLE found itself a new home in the Republic of Djibouti on the strategic Horn of Africa, where companies from 2 REP rotated through the territory in support. The territory had voted four years earlier to remain a member of the French Union, rather than be swallowed up in the neighbouring Somali Democratic Republic.

Fourteen years later, the run-up to independence in June 1977 placed Djibouti - a state of 23,000 sq km with a population of about 600,000 - under severe pressure from neighbouring Somalia.

Hoping to end the French military presence crucial to the territory's independence, on 3 February 1976 four armed Somali terrorists hi-jacked a school bus in Djibouti City that was carrying twenty-seven children of French military personnel. At the police control post at the city limits, the terrorist at the wheel smashed through the barrier and drove off in the direction of the Somali border. Finding the crossing point blocked by a gendarmerie vehicle, the driver stood in the doorway with his pistol at the head of a boy held in front of him as a human shield, ordering the armed gendarmes to stay clear. The boy was then sent to the officer in command with the hijackers' demands that all the terrorists in detention be released, their weapons returned to them, the country granted 'independence' immediately and all French forces evacuated forthwith. Failure to comply in full was to be met by execution of all the children.

A unit of France's GIGN anti-terrorist unit was flown to Djibouti, its commanding officer offering himself as a hostage if the children were released. The deal refused, it was evening when Jehanne Bru, a civilian employee of the Djibouti base, was permitted to take food and drink onto the bus for the children.

By this time a company of 2 REP under Capt Soubirou had taken position around the bus. The terrorists insisted that the road be unblocked, after which the driver drove forward to the Somali frontier post, so that any fire-fight would risk putting the Somali soldiers on duty there in the line of fire and spark an international incident.

A further threat was issued to execute the children should the French government fail to comply with all demands. There were now three terrorists inside the bus with the courageous Jehanne Bru and the children. Another was behind it, two were patrolling near it and a sixth was on the balcony of the frontier post when three sections of 2 REP paras rushed the bus, shooting dead the two patrolling hijackers. Under covering fire from 13 DBLE snipers, Cpl Larking managed to leap aboard the bus, as did Cpl Lemoine and S/Sgt Jorand. All three hijackers on board were dead within seconds. In the shoot-out, the little girl seated on the driver's lap as a human shield died, but twenty-one unharmed children were immediately evacuated through the bus windows. Five injured children plus Jehanne Bru and the civilian driver were evacuated by helicopter to hospital in Djibouti City. Four of the children recovered, but a second girl who succumbed to wounds received in the assault was buried at Aubagne near the grave of her grandfather, a former Legion NCO.

Chad and Djibouti are territories to which little attention is paid in the English-language media, but one Legion operation made headlines all over the world. It happened in 1978 at an African mining town called Kolwezi.

Chapter 34

THE DOVE THAT WAS A TIGER

12-16 May 1978

On 12 May 1978 the name Kolwezi was familiar only to a few thousand people in the mining industry. The following day all the world's media were focusing on this typical African mining town in the Shaba province of Zaire[1], where the giant Gécamines complex employed several hundred European technicians in addition to the large African workforce. Including dependents, the European population totalled around 3,000 people, who awoke on Saturday 13 May to find themselves at the sharp end of Operation Chicapa.

Chicapa, meaning 'dove', had been chosen as the code-name by Cuban advisers in Angola, themselves controlled by Soviet advisers.[2] This was the period when Picasso's white dove was a universal peace symbol much used by Communist-front organisations, although the several thousand mainly teenage Katangan FNLC[3] rebels called themselves 'Tigers'. They had force-marched across 300km of savannah from their training camps in Angola. Armed with Kalashnikov assault rifles, Belgian FAL rifles, Israeli Uzis and American M16s, they were dressed in cast-off uniforms from a dozen or more African and European armies, their sole distinguishing mark being a small patch of blue cloth bearing a silver tiger stitched somewhere on their clothing.

The aim of the Moscow-planned invasion was to destabilise the government of Zairian President Mobutu by seizing the copper and diamond mines operated by the giant Gécamines company, which had taken over the installations and exploitation rights of the Belgian Union Minière du Haut Katanga upon the territory becoming independent in 1960. Plausible denial was assured by the Soviet controllers staying safely in Angola, leaving operational control on the ground in the hands of their Cuban subordinates, who did not join the long march across country, but arrived first-class by air, parachuting in after the town had been taken.[4]

Mothers grabbed all the food from their kitchen cupboards and hid it under floorboards and in roof spaces to prevent it being stolen by the rebels who had arrived with no provisions of their own. The more prudent Europeans filled baths and sinks before water supplies were cut off. The main anxiety at this stage was to prevent their children going outside and being hit in the exchanges of fire between Zairian FAZ troops and the rebels, who were taking no prisoners.

Zaire/Democratic Republic of the Congo

News about the scale of the invasion was radioed to the Zairian capital Kinshasa via the Gécamines base in Lumumbashi, but the government of President Mobutu did nothing. Its alibi for inaction was an invasion by Katangan rebels the previous year, when they had been stopped 100km or so from Kolwezi by the elite Kamanyola Division of the Zairian army[5], assisted by a Moroccan expeditionary force. However, this time, the government in Kinshasa showed little interest in reinforcing the FAZ troops in Kolwezi, confronting what was obviously a much larger and more determined invasion.

In the French embassy at Kinshasa, the calm and urbane ambassador André Ross was updated by his Breton military attaché Col Larzul. Larzul, never a man to waste words, informed him tersely of the destruction of every aircraft on the Kolwezi airstrip. Summoned to the presidential palace, Ross was expecting anything but Mobutu's bland assurance that he had told the Soviet ambassador to halt the invasion or be held responsible for it. For the moment, all Ross could do was pass this information back to Paris.

At 0500hrs on 14 May he managed to have a telephone conversation with a Gécamines director in Lumumbashi, learning that all the Zairian troops in Kolwezi either had been killed or had fled northwards, with the exception of a few holed up in barracks surrounded by the rebels. All this was passed on to the Belgian and American embassies.

In Kolwezi, the FNLC accused all single European males of being mercenaries hired by the Zairian army. To save money, engineer Pierre Vérot had not brought his family out to Africa. Dragged in front of a wall pitted with bullet-holes, he had to step over several bodies on the ground. Ordered to face the wall by the officer in charge of the execution squad, he refused to do so in the belief that the teenage firing squad could not kill a man looking them in the eyes. Each time he was forcibly turned around, he turned back and faced his would-be killers - until abruptly told he could go home.

Another civilian, 50-year-old Marc Fauroux was the second generation of his family to run the civil engineering firm that was the largest employer after Gécamines. Mobutu having banned the ownership of any firearms by Europeans six months previously, all Fauroux could do was impotently watch the invasion forces move into town on the Saturday and estimate their size at around 4,000. On the Sunday morning he was summoned by a little man in uniform wearing a cloche hat on which was written in ball-pen *Commanding Officer*. In his hand, the unwelcome visitor had a notebook with a long list of names and addresses.

'Are you Marc Fauroux?'

There was no point in denying it. Four armed soldiers grabbed Fauroux by the arms and marched him away. 'Where are you taking me?' he asked, as calmly as possible.

'To your trial.'

Noticing a number of armed rebels standing outside the stores in Avenue Burga, the main shopping street, obviously to deter looters, Fauroux consoled himself with this evidence of some discipline among the invaders. Then, by a burned-out French AML armoured car, he saw the first corpses, already scavenged by dogs. The 'courtroom' to which he was taken, full of rebels milling around, armed to the teeth and all shouting at the same time, put him in mind of the mob at the trial of Louis XVI, howling for the king's blood.

Accused of 'economic collaboration in the theft of the people's mineral resources',[6] he tried several times to interrupt in his own defence, but was told that he had already been condemned to death, with immediate effect. Speechless with shock, he was being led away by the firing squad when he saw one trembling rebel in violent argument with the 'judges'. Recognising him as a foreman he had employed some years before, Fauroux heard the room grow quiet as his unexpected advocate pleaded for his life. Finally the senior 'judge' smiled and grunted a brief order.

Expecting to be released, and uttering a prayer for his saviour, Fauroux was grabbed again, led outside and stood against a wall pocked by bullets with his feet in pools of fresh blood. Too shocked to even close his eyes, he heard the fire-selectors of the guards' Kalashnikovs click, saw the weapons raised – and then was showered with fragments of masonry as they emptied their magazines all around him, roaring with laughter at their joke.

Outside Kolwezi, even in Kinshasa, life went on as usual. On the Monday morning at 1000hrs, Ambassador Ross called into his office Col Larzul and Col Yves Gras – the 55-year-old head of the military mission in Zaire. He showed them a copy of a cable from the Belgian Embassy to Brussels: the Belgian expats in Zaire were now demanding that their government mount an airborne intervention to protect its citizens at risk in Kolwezi. Perhaps there would be a happy ending, after all.

That evening, Ross and Gras attended a diplomatic reception hosted by the Moroccans. On the surface, everything was normal, but they noticed the Zairian guests keeping very much to themselves and nervously checking their watches. Defying diplomatic protocol, Col Gras accosted the Belgian chargé d'affaires Mr Van Sina to ask what the Belgian government was going to do about the situation. Van Sina stammered that it was not his decision.

'There'll be a massacre, if you don't bestir your government to act,' Gras hissed at him before the Belgian could disengage himself.

Tuesday 16 May dawned rapidly, as it always does on the equator. In Kolwezi, Gras' prediction was already coming true as the rebels' discipline broke down irretrievably. They had arrived exhausted.

After three days of rest and gorging themselves on looted food and beer supplies, they saw looting and murder as their victors' prerogatives. In the European residential areas, parents converted rooms without outside windows into makeshift shelters by dragging into them mattresses and anything else that might absorb stray bullets or fragments of grenades which pierced the walls as the rebels pursued wounded Zairian soldiers or simply emptied their magazines into houses for fun.

Men, women and children, both Black and European, were dying as the rebels looted and slaughtered at will in an orgy of destruction, smashing and burning furniture and grinding toilet fittings into dust for the sheer pleasure of destroying everything of utility. Europeans who removed a vital engine part from their car to simulate a breakdown and prevent it being driven off were gunned down; others were shot after handing over the keys and left lying where they fell until packs of semi-wild dogs moved in for an unexpected feast.

After another meeting with Mobutu, still refusing to admit that the situation was out of control, Ross cabled Paris for the attention of President Valéry Giscard d'Estaing that the 3,000 Europeans in Kolwezi were now hostages of the rebels, that the summary executions and ubiquitous looting gave grounds to fear general massacres and that the situation was growing worse by the hour.

Shortly afterwards, a French resident of Lumumbashi brought the news that Kolwezi was without electricity or water and that the killings were being stepped up. Ross called the Belgian ambassador, diplomatically hinting at a French and Belgian intervention, only to be told that the 'alarmist rumours' were all exaggeration - and that the Belgian Foreign Minister was 'negotiating' with the son of Katangan secessionist Moïse Tshombe in Brussels.

Larzul's reaction was unprintable. 'Cloud cuckoo land', would have been a polite rendering. Amassing maps to plan a rescue operation, he found the dithering of the politicians in Paris and Brussels incredible. Gras likened it to a house on fire where everyone was arguing who had the right to use the extinguisher.

A few firemen were on the way. At first light, a company of Zairian paras had been dropped east of the New Town, near what had been the local HQ of the Zairian army. Shot dead in mid-air, shot on the ground before unbuckling their harness, the majority died within minutes. The few survivors fled, meeting on their way a FAZ motorised column from Lumumbashi commanded by Maj Mahele that was supposed to link up with them. In Brussels, the FNLC spokesmen were convinced that Mobutu's troops could not have managed to drop in without foreign support and announced that the paras had been European and suffered hundreds of casualties. The news was relayed worldwide by the wire services. Worse, the FNLC now declared that any further armed intervention would be met by 'grave retaliations' against the European hostages and flooding of the mines, where demolition charges had already been laid.[7]

The failure of the airdrop was the last straw for the remaining Zairian soldiers holding out in Kolwezi. Of different tribal origin from the Katangans and not even speaking the same language, they tried to make their escape in small groups, unleashing a mounting blood-lust among the rebels, who were high on their easy victory. Nor were they any longer restrained by the Cubans, who appeared to have left the immediate area of Kolwezi after raising a militia in Manika, the native town.

In the offices of the Baron-Levêque company, a number of Europeans saw laughing teenage soldiers approaching, armed with

Uzis, M-16s, Belgian FALs and the ubiquitous Kalashnikovs. Calling out that there were no Zairian soldiers inside, two pipe-laying engineers walked out, hands away from their bodies to show they were unarmed. The kids mowed them down. Turning their weapons on the men, women and children inside the building, they continued firing until every wall was covered in bloodstains, with bodies in places jammed solid in a last desperation one metre high. The only survivors were two men who had hoisted each other into the crawl space under the roof when the first shots rang out and a woman with four serious bullet wounds, who survived under a pile of dead bodies.

The hero of the day was Maj Mahele, whose untried young para recruits were about to run away at the first ambush until he stood up and opened fire, taking out one rebel sniper with a grenade and yelling at them to do likewise. Inspired by his personal courage, they yelled their ancestral battle-cry of *'Kanga diablos!'* and pushed on through several other ambushes to retake the airport after killing around a hundred rebels. Shortly after 1400hrs, the valiant major was able to radio the good news. A single counter-attack at 1800hrs, repulsed by his young troops, was their final test.

'Just as well,' Mahele commented later. 'By then, we'd run out of ammunition.'

Chapter 35

GO! DON'T GO! GO!

Operation Leopard - 17-19 May 1978

As news filtered out of Kolwezi, at 2 REP's Camp Raffali on Corsica and in the Calvi citadel which served as the officers' mess, the general consensus was that no other military unit was equipped and trained to intervene in such a situation. It was, however, extremely unlikely they would be given the job because Zaire, as the former Belgian Congo, was more closely linked to Brussels than Paris, and there were many more Belgian than French expats in Kolwezi.

At 1100hrs on Wednesday 17 May Col Philippe Erulin took a call from the HQ of 2nd Parachute Brigade in Toulouse, informing him that 2 REP was placed on operational stand-by, ready to move out in six hours' time with all equipment and vehicles. No destination was specified.

He replied, 'I need a minimum of twenty hours.' An energetic and resourceful leader of what he regarded as the best regiment of professional soldiers in the French army, he was not being negative - simply stating the obvious.

'Tell me the problems,' replied Gen Liron, at the other end of the line.

Only two months off retirement, Erulin had the regiment's state of readiness in his head, day and night. Apart from officers and men on leave, 1st Company under Capt Vergio was yomping high up in the Corsican Mountains, far from the nearest road; part of 2nd Company was in Bastia, on the other side of the island; other detachments were at Corte in the highlands of central Corsica. More of a problem was how to get back the sixty-six officers and men on courses spread out between Castelnaudary and the combat swimming course at Mountlouis-Collioure in the Pyrenees.

'Leave it to me to get all those on the mainland back to you within the time-limit,' said Liron. 'For the others, do your best.'

Before Erulin had replaced the handset, every man on the base was deafened by the alert siren ordered by the adjutant Lt Col Bénézit, who had been listening in. Civilians think that NCOs are always shouting, but there were few raised voices after the siren's wailing died away. Honed by constant exercises, every officer, NCO and man knew his place and what was required of him.

By 1700hrs every man on strength had been accounted for, with one exception. Senior medical officer Capt Jean-Noël Ferret reported a man missing. Yannick Lallemand had taken off with a company of 2 REI and was somewhere in the mountains between Porto Vecchio and the Col de Bavella. Far from AWOL, he was the army chaplain for Corsica, with a special responsibility for 2 REP, but was on the regimental roll as senior stretcher-bearer.

The quietest but busiest man on camp was Flemish Capt Stéphane Coevoet, responsible for logistics. It was his duty to get all the men onto the right planes with their light equipment and ensure that the vehicles and heavy equipment they would need on the ground reached them in time. His office was a mass of loading lists and manifestos showing exactly what each plane-load weighed. While he worked on his sums, many of the men on base were asleep in their combat fatigues, having learned long since to eat and slumber when they could.

At 1600hrs the regiment, apart from the missing chaplain, was ready. The deadline passed without news from Toulouse. Several officers had been invited to drinks by a lecturer from the University of Liège in Belgium, who was passing through Calvi. In the absence of orders to the contrary, Erulin agreed they should attend as planned. Their host, a former director of agronomy for Belgian Central Africa, knew Zaire intimately, but was unaware that his guests would be there in a few hours - as were they too, at this moment.

In Kinshasa Ambassador Ross was reading an intercepted cable from the Belgian Consul-General in Lumumbashi to his government in Brussels. 'It is increasingly urgent to intervene in order to prevent further massacres... I beg you to intervene soonest... Each hour's delay means more lives lost.'[1] For a diplomat to write in those terms to his government was rare, to say the least, so Ross immediately copied the cable to Paris, thinking, 'This will make President Giscard act.'

Three floors above him, colonels Gras and Larzul were planning a drop on Kolwezi. The obvious drop zone was the airstrip 5km outside town, which was still held by Maj Mahele's men, but that would mean the paras fighting their way slowly through the residential areas, giving the rebels ample time to kill every European in the town. There had to be a better way ...

With no aerial photographs to help, Gras' team had drawn copies of the Kolwezi area from a 1:10,000 scale regional map. Contour lines, railways and vague outlines of built-up areas were of little help in avoiding hazards like trees and high-tension lines. If the pilots of the drop planes spent too long sussing out the ground below, that too would alert the Katangans to massacre their hostages. The handful of officers in Gras' office were doing their best, but as time passed and no news came from Paris, their spirits drooped - as did those of 2 REP on Corsica, still waiting for the 'Go!'

Midnight came and went. In the ambassador's residence at Kinshasa André Ross could not sleep. The plea from Lumumbashi *I beg you to intervene soonest* rang in his head. When the telephone in his study rang, he checked his watch and saw that it was exactly midnight. With a diplomat's instinct, he guessed some deadline between Paris and Brussels had just expired.

The cool impersonal tones of the *chef de cabinet* 6,000km away said, 'The president instructs you to immediately inform the Zairian head of state that French paratroops will be dropped on Kolwezi.'

Ross breathed again and dialled the number of Mobutu's presidential palace. Passed from the switchboard to a secretary to a valet to a bodyguard, he hung on until told that exceptionally he would be put through to the citizen-president himself. Mobutu sounded enormously relieved that someone else was taking responsibility and told Ross to thank President Giscard for him.

The ambassador's next phone call was to Gras, who was put in personal command of the operation fifteen minutes later by a coded call from Army High Command in Paris and informed that the force being sent for the operation was 2 REP, effective immediately. When the anonymous voice asked how soon the drop could be executed, Gras rapidly calculated the problems and answered, 'Saturday 20 May.' He replaced the receiver with a huge sigh of relief, having worked with the BEP in Vietnam and with 1 REP and 2 REP in Algeria. After all the waiting, nothing could be better than having the Legion's paras for a job like this!

It was 0100hrs on Thursday, but Gras and his team felt the fatigue fall away, now that they could get down to some real planning. Larzul queried whether the planes for the drop would have to come from the Zairian Air Force. 'Unless the Yanks and the Belgians get into the act,' Gras replied. 'But don't count on it.' 'In that case,' said Larzul, 'the Zairians have two Transall C-160s and five Hercules C-130s.'

'How many men can they carry?'

'I'd say 500, tops. But we don't know how many bodies 2 REP is sending.'

'And what about an airborne command post?'

Long phone calls later, one of Gras' aides came back with the offer of a twin turbo-prop De Havilland CC-115 Buffalo, currently based in Kamina, for the airborne command post. In the absence of helicopters, this was the best alternative. The Buffalo offered short take-off and landing capability, had the ability to overfly the DZ slowly with good downward visibility thanks to its high wings, and it could also accommodate forty-one fully equipped paras exiting through the rear loading bay if necessary.

At 0220hrs Col Erulin was in his official villa at Calvi, changed back into his combat fatigues after cocktails with the Belgian lecturer and wondering whether it was worth going to bed. False alarms and countermanded orders were a normal part of life in 2 REP. The phone rang and he heard Bénézit say in his habitually calm voice, 'Colonel, we've just received the order to be ready to move out at 0300hrs.'

'Everyone on parade! Call in all officers off-base and all the leave men.'

'It's already been done, sir.' In the background, Erulin could hear the alert siren wailing.

Not a man on the base had to do more than lace up his boots. By the time Erulin swung in through the main gate of the camp, for once not stopping to inspect the guard, whose bugler sounded *Le Caïd* in his honour as he swept past, the sections were all at their preordained tasks, loading weapons, munitions, rations, personal packs - everything in its specified place. At 0430 the forward command jeep swept out of the main gate, at the head of a long snake of vehicles: 1st and 3rd companies, then the main command vehicles, followed by 4th and 2nd companies. At this stage, no one knew where the next few hours would take them. Was it an exercise? Was it for real? If so, where? The betting men placed even money on Kolwezi and Chad.

The military airport of Solenzara, from which take-off was scheduled, lay diagonally across the mountainous island. As the crow flies it was a journey of 160km. By road the heavily laden trucks could make it in three hours flat out, if there was no hold-up. Capt Coevoet was the man of the moment, grappling with one major problem: no aircraft had yet arrived at Solenzara. Erulin called him on the command radio net to say that Paris had just signalled the imminent arrival of five DC-8s, due to take off at 0930hrs. 'Maybe,' replied Coevoet phlegmatically. 'Or maybe not.'

Depending on the aircraft available, all his sums would have to be done again. Whilst the convoy was still en route, the mini-fleet was changed to three DC-8s chartered from UTA, a civil airline with long experience of flying African routes, one DC-8 from Transport Command and an Air France Boeing 707.

On arrival at Solenzara, officers and men were ordered to remove name tags from their fatigues. Weapons were to be stowed in the holds. By 0815 the regiment was ready, men standing at ease in sticks of eight with jump-packs in front of them, each surmounted by a steel helmet. It was hurry-up-and-wait, all over again. By 1000hrs no aircraft had been sighted, nor could the control tower enlighten Erulin what was going on. At 1130hrs the first DC-8 landed, followed closely by a smaller aircraft bearing Gen Lacaze, commanding 11th Para Division. From him, Erulin and his officers learned at last that their destination was Kolwezi, nearly 8,000km distant - after first landing at Kinshasa to board the drop aircraft.

As that first DC-8 took off at 1345hrs with enough fuel to fly direct to Kinshasa, a dusty jeep braked to a stop in front of the hangars. Chaplain Lallemand had caught up with his flock. A ripple of laughter greeted his arrival. Someone said, 'That's why the planes are late. The padre fixed it with God.'

In Kinshasa, Col Gras was fuming when Paris ordered him to advance the drop. Cutting corners could cost soldiers' lives. Saturday - so he was informed - could be too late to save the hostages. 'They waste four days talking,' he growled after putting down the phone, 'and then they want the impossible.'

He had already told Ambassador Ross that he refused to liaise with the Belgians. His opposite number in the Belgian embassy, Col Bleus had received no orders from Brussels, yet Brussels was insisting on controlling 'any operation that might take place'.[2] Even worse, someone in Brussels had leaked to the wire services the details of the planned operation. There could have been no better way of inciting the rebels to massacre all their hostages.

Beneath his urbane exterior, Ross too was angered by the stupidity that could cost so many lives. At 1800hrs, Gras was summoned to the office of Zairian Gen Ba Bia, who showed him a blue signal pad decrypt of an intercepted transmission from Nathanaël M'Bumba in Angola, ordering his troops in Kolwezi to retreat back into Angola 'after killing all the prisoners and blowing up the pumping equipment to flood the mines'.[3]

When it is a choice between the lives of civilians and those of soldiers, the decision is always the same. Hurrying back to the embassy, Gras was already working out which corners could be cut to advance his carefully worked-out timetable, and then called Paris to announce that he had brought forward the operation by a whole day.

Zaire is so vast that the last 1500km leg of 2 REP's odyssey - from Kinshasa to Kolwezi, which was in a different time zone - would take the five C-130 Hercules and two C-160 Transalls four hours' flying time. Take-off was scheduled for 0700hrs with the drop at noon local time. As if he needed another bad piece of news, during his orders meeting at 1900hrs Gras learned that the Zairian Air Force could provide no air cover for the drop because it had run out of ammunition for its Mirage jets and had to wait until more arrived from Paris.[4]

Erulin's aircraft touched down on Kinshasa's N'Djili airport at

2330hrs. The other four transports were spread out along the several routes imposed by their different needs to land and refuel. According to the control tower, the second aircraft would arrive at 0200hrs on Friday 19 May. There was no ETA for the others. The legionnaires in Erulin's DC-8 unloaded all the equipment and awaited orders. But where was Col Gras with the plans for the operation? Erulin called a briefing for 0300hrs in the hope that he would have arrived by then - and that at least one of the other three aircraft would have touched down.

By 0300hrs the second aircraft had not only landed, but already been unloaded by the passengers. However, there was still no sign of Gras and the plans. After the control tower announced the ETA of the last two planes for 0838hrs, Coevoet and Bénézit decided that the regiment would have to jump in two waves. The first would take off from Kinshasa at 0700hrs as planned, and be dropped directly on Kolwezi. The drop aircraft would then fly to the military airfield at Kamina, where they would pick up the second wave, flown there by a DC-10 of Air Zaire. The change of plan meant that, to ensure each section arrived on the ground reasonably closely grouped, its men would have to be split up among several aircraft - in the right order on every plane.

Given the delay in the arrival of the other aircraft from Solenzara, it was the best way of speeding things up, so Erulin approved the change of plan, which gave Coevoet's brain a million new problems to solve, fast. A phone call to the embassy established that Gras should have been with them long since. No one knew where he was. For want of a nail, the kingdom was lost - so says the proverb. For want of a tyre in this case, the whole complicated operation was now in jeopardy. Col Gras was furious, having burst a tyre when his jeep hit a deeper than usual pothole on the poorly maintained and unlit road to N'Djili airport. The shock having bent the bolts, making it impossible to change the wheel, all he could do was fume impotently until two Belgians passing by chance stopped and helped him to get the damaged wheel off, and fit the spare.

By 0430 he was giving his briefing for Operation Leopard, unaware that Paris had baptised the drop 'Operation Bonite'. No one had told him. Erulin and his officers listened intently as Gras' dry voice rattled off the details. The first wave of 450 men was to land on Zone A - the flying club airstrip. That comprised the command element, two companies and mortar sections. Their task was to secure the Post Office, the Hotel Impala, the John XXIII secondary school, the Gécamines hospital and the rebels' HQ. The second wave from Kamina would drop on Zone A and/or Zone B to the east of the New Town. Once the residential areas were secured, with no further danger to the European hostages, 2 REP could link up with the Zairian paras still holding the main airstrip, south of Kolwezi.

Friday 19 May was rapidly dawning. Erulin and his officers had not slept for thirty hours. As they dispersed to their companies, an alarming discovery was made. The regulation French parachutes normally used by 2 REP had been left on Corsica, to save weight. Those used by the Zairian paras were American T 10 chutes, which had no provision for attaching weapons and equipment. Erulin's men had no intention of landing in a hot DZ with their weapons dropped separately. Their predecessors had died from that disease in Vietnam. So they set to with twine, bent coat-hangers and anything else to hand, devising ways of attaching arms and equipment to the harnesses.

At 0700hrs a thick fog rose off the Congo River, reducing visibility at N'Djili to a few metres. Erulin wondered how the last two aircraft from Solenzara could land in such a pea soup? On board one of them was the medical team. While he hoped that Lallemand would be employed more often as stretcher-bearer than chaplain, to jump with neither medics nor chaplain was one more hazard to be factored into the equations of life and death.

The paras fitting themselves into the narrow pull-down mesh seats lining the sides of one of the C-130s heard the starter motor whine, and whine, and whine. Then, 'Everybody out!'

The mechanics, they learned, would need days for the necessary repair. Coevoet sweated over his loading schedules for the tenth time, working out how to fit a whole plane-load of men into the other aircraft. Meanwhile the paras, encumbered with weapons, equipment, main and ventral chutes, stood around like ungainly statues in the fog.

In the embassy, one of Gras' team answered the phone to hear a Parisian accent in Army High Command ask whether 2 REP had yet taken off. 'If not,' said the distant voice, 'the operation is cancelled. Effective immediately!'

Gras' aide muttered, 'Affirmative,' and replaced the receiver, unable to believe his ears. The rebels must have heard the broadcasts on Zairian radio announcing the drop as 'imminent'. What would happen now to the hostages?

At N'Djili airport, Coevoet had finally managed to cram the excess paras into the remaining planes. Cram was the word. Instead of being seated neatly on the seats with the dispatchers able to walk down the aisle and check everything, they were jammed against each other, side to side of the fuselage. Erulin, waddling across the hardstanding with his two chutes already on, was just about to heave himself up into the lead plane when Gras' jeep screeched to a halt at the bottom of the ladder with the counter-order from Paris.

Taking the news philosophically, Erulin disagreed with Gras that the best thing was to disembark all the paras and their equipment. Despite the discomfort and the heat once the fog had burned off, he decided they would stay loaded until midday, by which time Paris might have countermanded the cancellation.

Gras departed for the embassy to give Paris a large slice of his mind, but André Ross counselled calm, having worked out that the reason for the cancellation must be interference from Brussels. The question was, how did Brussels know details of the operation? The answer was that the Zairians had naïvely let the local Belgians in on the planning, and they had told their masters.

However, Ross was not the sort of diplomat to leave things as they stood. That a simple phone call could cancel a complex operation already so far advanced, was not good enough for him. So he took a chance and placed a call direct to President Giscard's office in the Elysée Palace. His instinct was right: far from having cancelled the drop, Giscard was expecting any minute to be advised of its outcome. Operation Leopard was most definitely back on - and a telex confirmation was on its way!

Gras was telling the Air Force general who had issued the cancellation what he thought of him when a third voice cut in on the line, interrupting him with the words, 'Take off immediate! The counter-order has been countermanded.'

With the time at 0855, the timetable was already two hours behind schedule when Erulin received a radio transmission from Gras that boiled down to one word: 'Go!'

At that moment he had only one problem. The Zairian pilots had been asked to stay near their aircraft, but were nowhere to be found. By the time they had been rounded up, one of the Transalls had developed engine trouble and the second had a flat tyre. There was another Transall, graciously made available by Citizen-President Mobutu, but this was his personal plane, fitted with bath, drinks fridge and double bed. The paras found screwdrivers to strip out the fittings, until stopped by the Zairian mechanics. 'Don't bother,' they said. 'This one also has engine trouble.'

Coevoet was beginning to think he was in a nightmare. Some Mirage mechanics appeared with an oxygen cylinder and some rubber hoses they cobbled together to get what looked like enough pressure into the flat tyre. Coevoet now had to fit eighty laden paras into each flyable aircraft designed for sixty-four men. Achieving the impossible, with the first wave crammed into four C-130s and the single C-160, the dispatchers had no idea how men bent double and crammed on top of each other could hook themselves up to the static lines over the DZ, let alone jump out of the doors in anything like normal time. The only good point was that Capt Ferret and his medical team had meantime arrived and were also crammed in like sardines, so that casualties would receive immediate attention.

It was 1040hrs when the first overloaded aircraft lifted off and clawed its way to cruising height. Inside, officers and men were laughing with relief. After all that happened, nothing else could go wrong. Could it?

Chapter 36

KILL OR BE KILLED AT KOLWEZI

19 May-6 June 1978

The first surprise after take-off was for the shivering human sardines in two aircraft to see an inverted forest of icy stalactites rapidly forming on the ceiling above their heads. The Zairian crews had forgotten to switch off the air conditioning. Politely requested to do so, they obliged, laughing. Cabin temperature jumped 25° Centigrade, melting the icicles and soaking the men below. Crammed together, unable to move even to reach the toilets, the more stoical and the more exhausted managed to doze.

Approaching the drop zone, they manipulated themselves into something like a standing position with difficulty, easing their cramped limbs. Unable to pass among them as normal, the dispatchers yelled for each man to check that those fore and aft of him were clipped on to the static line. So jammed together were the men and their equipment now that the pull-down seats were stuck, reducing usable floor-space even more. Many men could not even stand straight, but were bent beneath others or forced to crouch on the floor with several other men above them. They knew the DZ was 800 metres long. At the speed the planes were doing, the pass would last twelve seconds. How the hell would a stick of eight men extricate itself from the jumbled mass and jump in that time?

At 1512hrs the red lights came on. The doors were removed, the dispatchers hanging out of the doorways checking the land slipping past below. To their amazement, beneath them was the town of Kolwezi, with the huge open-cast mines making enormous scars in a landscape pitted with round yellow lakes of slurry. The light stayed red as they passed over the DZ close to 90° off-course. The men waiting to drop groaned in unison.

There could not have been a better way of announcing their arrival to the rebels waiting for them below.

The second pass was little better. The jump light stayed red as the pilots corrected course again. And again for another pass. At 1540hrs - after half an hour of fly-overs - the light was green and the dispatchers yelled the word everyone had been waiting for: 'Go!'[1]

With the pilots refusing to reduce speed below 400kph, the legionnaires were buffeted horizontal, spun round and round, expecting to have their necks broken by the shock when their chutes opened. Men who had jumped with American chutes before had warned them of this possibility. The first stroke of luck that day was to find that the shock was, if anything, less than they were used to, but although the canopy above them was far bigger than expected, the rate of descent was fast in the thin air at 1500 metres above sea-level.

Automatic weapons were firing beneath them, but orders were not to return fire before landing, for fear of hitting their own comrades. A louder explosion made them look up - and understand why the Zairian pilots in the lead planes had not reduced speed or altitude. An anti-aircraft shell had just missed the last plane in the formation, flying lower than the others. The French pilot at the controls was less worried by the near-miss than the fact that the preceding aircraft had not respected the drop height of 250 metres above the ground. To distance themselves from the artillery below, they had dropped high, which meant that the large propellers of his turbo-prop craft were about to carve a tunnel through a cloud of men and chutes.[2] A wrench on the controls realigned his aircraft, avoiding them by the narrowest margin.

'Go!' Dispatcher Zingraff counted the men of 3rd Company out on the second pass and counted them again below. One canopy was missing. Leaning out, he found the missing para still attached to the plane hurtling along at 400 kph and desperately hacking away at the static line with his combat knife. By gestures, Zingraff made him stop, to avoid falling far from the DZ. The C-130 not being fitted with a winch to get the unlucky man back inboard, Italian legionnaire Strata, a veteran of seven military drops and many in civilian life, hung obediently in the slipstream until the next pass, when Zingraff cut him free and watched him make a successful landing, using his ventral chute.

For the other men the jump lasted twenty seconds at most, but no one had allowed for a strong north wind blowing them away from the flying club and into the buildings of the New Town. From below streams of tracer arced up at them, slotting neat holes in the canopies - and some bodies. Houses, trees, walls rushed towards them - interspersed with three-metre-high termite mounds, as hard as concrete. All they could do, was face the wind, pull on the shrouds to empty the canopies as much as possible, close their legs, hunch their shoulders, jam elbows into the ventral chutes and relax their knees to land *roulé-boulé* like a rubber doll.

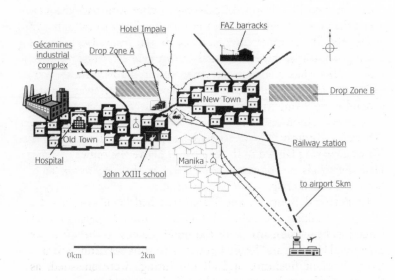

Operation Leopard, Kolwezi, May-June 1978

Those who landed in trees knew the drill, releasing their ventral chutes and rappelling down the shrouds. Erulin landed on a termitary, winded and with a gashed cheek but otherwise unharmed. Many men found themselves in elephant grass over their heads, lost for bearings until a whistle blast gave them a direction to head for. Others found themselves facing a Tiger through the dense grass stalks, at which point it was kill or be killed - the quicker finger deciding which way it went.

A mystery for Erulin was, what had happened to the eight men of his anti-tank section, dropped way off the DZ. Seven made it back spread over the next twenty-four hours; the other was already dead before he hit the ground, 2 REP's first casualty of the operation. Wrapped in his parachute by Chaplain Lallemand, his body was flown back to Corsica for burial.

The job of a radio man is to stick like a leech to his commander, come what may. Emerging from the elephant grass, Capt Gausserès wiped the dust out of his eyes, unable to find his operator, who had dropped immediately after him and weighed about the same. Where the hell was he? Unwilling to call out and attract the fire of rebels he could see not far away, Legionnaire Lacan was nearby but suspended by his canopy, caught in the topmost branches of a giant tree. He rappelled down the shrouds of his ventral, but still ended up twelve or so metres above the ground until, swinging from side to side, he managed to catch a branch and climb and slip the rest of the way to the ground. Gausserès' orderly Vittone was perhaps the luckiest man in Kolwezi, having landed in the catenaries above the railway tracks. Had the rebels not blown up the power station, he would have been barbecued crisp.

Lt Bertrand Bourgain and his section had been assigned the mission of taking the rebel HQ in the Hotel Impala. Having landed right in the gardens of the hotel, thanks to the wind, he assembled his men and headed inside. The stink was unbelievable. Every item of furniture and all the fittings were smashed, as though wild beasts had rampaged through. Everywhere, there was dried blood and what seemed to be parts of human bodies. Holding their breath and trying not to vomit, the legionnaires picked their way through the scene of violence to the cellar, where the stink of putrefaction was strongest, from swollen bodies locked together in one fly-covered festering mass.

Bourgain called Gausserès, and heard the reply: 'Black to Black One, Over.'

'Have discovered twenty or so bodies, but the hotel is empty. Over.'

The terse radio message, devoid of emotion, was relayed to Erulin, who asked, 'Black bodies, or white?' He was hoping to have news to pass on to Larzul via Gras regarding the six French military advisers rumoured to have been held in the hotel.[3]

Bourgain replied, 'Only Black, so far. Continuing search.'

Confronted with the blood everywhere, even on the ceilings, and on the window sills as though desperate wounded people had tried to throw themselves out, men vomited among the destruction. The unflushable toilets were full of blood, but nowhere was there any sign of the six advisers until a legionnaire stumbled over a notebook in which one of them had noted the progression of events, hour by hour. The last note was timed at 0800hrs. Which day, no one ever knew. It read, 'Heavy machine gun firing at the hotel.'

But where were the bodies?[4]

Gausserès was at the railway station, checking out a train of munitions intended for the Zairian army. It had never been unloaded. Sealed cars contained 81mm mortar shells, hand grenades, small arms ammunition. The intermittent sound of firing as other units came up against rebel strong-points grew louder and more sustained. At least two heavy machine guns were firing and there was the occasional *crump!* of a field artillery piece.

By a lucky chance the anti-tank corporal of the section sheltering behind debris by the bridge into the New Town had just caught up with them. Calmly, Cpl Morin allowed the first rebel armoured car to approach from Mobutu Boulevard. 150 metres, 100 metres, fifty metres ... At thirty metres, Morin squeezed the trigger. The driver of the burning vehicle was killed outright but two other rebels managed to extricate themselves and flee under cover of the smoke. A second armoured car advanced, its machine gunner hosing down the debris behind which the legionnaires crouched.

Legionnaire Solatorenzo replied with disciplined short bursts from his light machine gun to keep the heads of the men inside well down and reduce their visibility. In the middle of the road, Cpl Laroche stood with his grenade-launcher at the shoulder, sighting along it as though on a practice range and waiting with nerves of steel until he could not miss. *Paf!*

With the second armoured car immobilised and on fire, two more rebels jumped out and escaped into side streets. A rebel truck approaching through the smoke became the next target for Solatorenzo and skidded off into another side street as his bullets tore through the sides of its soft top.

All over town, Legion units were in contact, but Erulin's professional assessment was that the main force of rebels had pulled out, leaving stay-behind detachments to slow up the recapture of the town and thus delay pursuit. But perhaps they were also assassination squads. And anyway his men could just as easily be killed in a chance skirmish as in a battle. As though to make the point, as he came in sight of a group of rebels on higher ground a burst of firing forced him and the men of his mobile command post to roll fast into a ditch for shelter.

Bourgain's section pushed on from the massacre in the hotel until it ran into a heavily defended crossroads. French *caporal-chef* Lombard and Yugoslavian Legionnaire Golic were both qualified snipers. This was what they had been training for. Within minutes they had killed three Katangans. The others fled, leaving behind four weapons: M16s and Kalashnikovs. Bourgain's men next launched a volley of rifle grenades at the strongpoint in the technical school, the rebels inside fleeing rather than be outflanked by the legionnaires, and thus giving them an easy passage across the bridge into the native town of Manika. The gendarmerie building next on their list was a harder target, with Danish Legionnaire Jansen taking out several rebels at point-blank range with his machine-pistol. A Katangan appeared from nowhere behind Sgt Touami, about to fire. Before he could squeeze the trigger, Legionnaire Tavari - fifteen metres away and armed only with a pistol - had shot him dead with his first round.

Inside the Gendarmerie, Bourgain was the next to just miss requiring Chaplain Lallemand's professional services. Seeing a

Katangan pull the pin out of a grenade, preparatory to hurling it into a room full of hostages, he downed the rebel with a single burst. The primed grenade rolled across the floor towards him. 'Everybody outside!' yelled Bourgain, hurling himself through a doorway onto the ground in the courtyard, where the grenade exploded, miraculously injuring no one.

In the prison, cells were so tightly packed with hostages, both Black and European, there was no room to sit or lie down. From time to time during the previous days, men had been hauled outside and shot, relieving the physical pressure and increasing the mental stress of those still inside. Hearing the noise of combat growing nearer, and with their guards apparently gone, a number of prisoners emerged into the street - to find themselves the target for a mob of the militia raised by the Katangans' Cuban advisers and ordered to 'liberate themselves' by killing all the Whites.

Documents captured later, bore this out. Armed with sticks, machetes and knives, they raced towards the bewildered hostages.

A Zairian officer who for some reason had not been shot translated their confused battle-cries for the Europeans just in time. Desperately, they ran back into the prison, seeking shelter in the stinking cells they had just vacated, but - as in every prison - it was impossible to bolt the doors on the inside. Men tore off their filthy, blood-stained shirts and knotted them together to make a rope of sorts, lashing the door bars to the window bars. As it started to stretch, desperate men clung to the bars of the doors to stop them being wrenched open, blows from the mob's weapons raining on their hands and forearms.

Without warning, as suddenly as they had arrived, the would-be killers left. From outside, the exhausted and confused prisoners heard a voice call, '*Armée française! Sortez, les mains en l'air!*' Come out with your hands up! They were the most beautiful words the prisoners had ever heard. Unshaven men, women and children covered in blood and excrement stumbled out into the courtyard, crying with relief and joy at the sight of their liberators, arrived not a minute too soon. Weeping, hardly able to stand, they wanted to touch these men who had saved them. Some, unable to stand, clutched a legionnaire's leg or touched the toe-cap of his boot in gratitude for their lives.

Among the twenty-six Europeans and nine Blacks were Belgian and French citizens, Australians, Americans - and ex-Sgt Catena, a former Legion para. Some of the children were wounded. A little girl of five in a dress stained by her mother's blood, kept repeating, 'They killed my Mummy. They killed my Mummy.' Others had seen both parents killed before being 'adopted' by caring adults after roaming in distress through the slaughter.

Bourgain's immediate concern was to get medics for the injured and persuade the others not to leave the prison and risk walking into the fire-fights raging on all sides. 'Where are the other prisoners?' he asked. 'All dead,' someone calmer than the others replied.

Elsewhere people hiding in their barricaded homes heard legionnaires race past talking French and had to be told to stay where they were for the moment. Some of the hostages were incoherent from grief and fear; others were completely in control, offering to guide their saviours to nearby enemy strong-points.

The task of retaking the hospital had been allotted to 2nd Company, so that Capt Ferret and his team of medics had facilities for more than first aid. What they found there ruled this out for the time being. All medical supplies had been stolen or simply destroyed. Even the medicine cabinets had been smashed to pieces with rifles butts. Mattresses had been torn to pieces and beds, some with the occupants still on them, pushed down the lift wells.

By dusk, the men on the ground were wondering where the second wave had got to. So were the men in the second wave. Col Gras had made provision to transport and drop 200 men. In the event, he had to transport fifty more to Kamina, including the six NCOs and twenty legionnaires under Capt Halbert who were the super-paras of 2 REP, expert in HALO insertions. Although Operation Leopard had no call for their particular expertise, they had no intention of being left behind in Kinshasa, even if it did mean travelling seated in the gangway. The most unlikely passenger in the DC-10 bringing them to Kamina was Col Larzul, wearing an old set of unmatched combat fatigues found in the bottom of his wardrobe. He was to be Col Gras' liaison officer with 2 REP on the ground, and was still hoping against hope for news of his six men who had been in Kolwezi.

The DC-10 touched down at Kamina just before 1600hrs. Eager to get aboard the drop aircraft, the men of the second wave found their first obstacle was the lack of any means to reach the ground, six metres below the open exit doors. In typical Legion fashion, they found a simple solution: launch the emergency toboggan slides. The crew, however, ruled that out, arguing that their boots and equipment would puncture the slides. As Col Larzul peered down at the ground staff, bewildered at the arrival of so high an aircraft at this military airfield, some humorist yelled at him, 'Go!'

But it was no joking matter. If the second wave did not take off very soon, it would be too late for a drop that day, never mind that their comrades in the other companies were in combat and the hostages they had come all this way to save at increasing risk with every passing hour. An enterprising Belgian transport contractor brought in his fork-lift truck to lift ground staff up into the holds and commence unloading the paras' equipment, but no one had any idea how to get the men out of the main cabin until a set of landing steps was 'extended' by balancing on it a house-painter's ladder, down which all 250 men descended at last to the ground.

Having learned from the first wave's experience, the paras had prepared lengths of twine and wire to lash their equipment onto the American harnesses. As they were doing this, the drop planes were landing after the return leg from Kolwezi. Perhaps afraid the engines would stop altogether, the pilots did not reduce engine speed to idling. In the infernal din of sixteen turbo-prop engines that left some men deaf for two days, the second wave clambered aboard. Just over an hour after they had touched down at Kamina, they were rolling along the runway, destination Kolwezi - as they thought.

To the west, the sun was plunging below the horizon. They arrived over Kolwezi in a cloudless sky on a night of full moon. The red light on, the paras heaved a sigh of relief. This was what they had come for. Night drops were a part of their training.

'On your feet! Hook on!'

The dispatchers were aware the planes were still far too high. The leading men of the first sticks looked out into the gloom, and saw the reason why the pilots had no intention of reducing altitude. Lines of tracer curved lazily up towards them. Other bursts of tracer outlined continuing combats on the ground. Then the red light went out and the dispatchers pushed the first men back from the doors. Col Erulin, 400 metres below them, had decided not to risk a night drop. Confident that the main Katangan force was far away, and more than satisfied with the progress made by the first wave, he had cancelled the drop to save unnecessary casualties, despite knowing how frustrated the men above him would feel.

It being impossible for them to land at Kamina in darkness, the C-130s now set course for Lumumbashi with the legionnaire condemned to endure one more agony. Jammed in as they were, it was impossible to get the seats down again. Legs bent, heads twisted beneath the ceiling, they clung to each other and anything else within reach, some suffering agonies of cramp for the rest of the flight to Lumumbashi. Landing at 1930hrs, they staggered to the ground, unharnessed themselves and spent the night huddled together for warmth, lying on the concrete beneath the wings of the drop planes.

The Katangans' dislike of fighting after darkness if they could avoid it enabled Bourgain and his men to escort the hostages liberated at the prison to the technical school, where they would be easier to protect. At 2030hrs Erulin moved his HQ into the John XXIII secondary school through a crowd of civilians defying the Legion's curfew - imposed in their own interest - who had come to thank Erulin, his officers and men and President Giscard, for saving them.

Lt Col Bénézit was given the job of listening to them, calming them and trying to get them back into safety while Erulin was drawing up a balance sheet for the day's operation with Coevoet and Capt Thomas, the Intelligence officer. It was extraordinary: 2 REP had one man dead, three or four wounded and most of the anti-tank section still missing, but not yet considered MIA.

Examining the captured documents revealed that the Katangan/Angolan force had consisted of eleven battalions of 300 men, with six further battalions securing the axis of the advance. Weaponry had included Chinese 82mm mortars, 81mm French mortars and 60mm mortars.

In human terms, however, alarming reports were still coming in. Nearing the slaughterhouse scene in the offices of the Baron-Levêque Company, Capt Gausserès found the stench of corpses growing even stronger than elsewhere. He and his men were picking their way across ground literally carpeted with bodies. So advanced was the putrefaction that Gausserès estimated the killings to date from Tuesday or Wednesday at the latest. In the moonlight, here was a man's leg gnawed to the white bone by the scavenging dogs, there a woman with her abdomen torn open by them. And there, a little girl whose leg had been torn off by them. It was the children's bodies that most upset the legionnaires, torn between impulses to vomit or to weep.

Firing continued sporadically throughout the night. Shortly before the second wave was due at 0500hrs on the Saturday morning, Erulin was handing out fresh tasks to the companies already on the ground. The second wave landed without incident, watched by hundreds of Europeans enjoying the pleasure of being able to walk out into their gardens for the first time in a week.

While 3rd Company was warily entering the native town, where the militia had gone to ground and could well still be killing hostages, they received a warning that several aircraft carrying Belgian troops would shortly be landing at the normal airport, 5km outside town. As always when 'friendlies' are coming from another direction with no common radio frequencies, Erulin's concern was to avoid any confrontation between them and 3rd Company.

Despite the nights without sleep and all the unfortunate delays, the legionnaires were beginning to relax. Some joker suggested that the sun was in the wrong place here, south of the Equator. It was Gausserès' company that ran into the Belgians while taking the Protestant church in Manika. An exchange of fire was narrowly avoided, and Gausserès found himself embracing an old buddy. Belgian Capt De Wulf had been on an airborne course with him less than twelve months before. The differences of their governments forgotten, the two captains swapped details of their missions.

To Gausserès' surprise - and Erulin's dismay - the Belgians had not come to support the Legion, but simply to evacuate all

European civilians. Despite the first contact passing off without casualties, it was not long before sustained fire was incoming - from Belgians who continued firing when Gausserès leaped up and banged on his steel helmet, yelling none too politely that the rebels did not wear helmets. What a day, he thought, caught between the FNLC stay-behinds in Manika and King Baudouin's men, fresh from Brussels!

Compared with the Legion, the Belgians had arrived in style aboard American C-130s. Also on the ground at last was Col Gras' Buffalo. He was the first to learn that the Belgians had orders to evacuate the hostages and themselves within seventy-two hours. Gras was furious at the idea of leaving Kolwezi a ghost town, open to pillage and plunder of what was not already pillaged and plundered. But the Belgians would not listen. They had their orders, as he had his.

The Legion's liberation of Kolwezi continued. The shops of Avenue Burga, guarded against looters when Marc Fauroux had been dragged along to what had so nearly been his execution, were now hollow shells, in which everything had been smashed, all the fittings wrenched out and ground to dust in the street. The worst for the legionnaires and the people they had liberated was the stench and the blood. Hungry, thirsty and sleep-deprived, they trod with every step in the lifeblood of murdered people as they continued with the task assigned them: to make Kolwezi safe for normal life to resume.

The Katangans had killed Blacks and Europeans indiscriminately. Disconcertingly in the nightmare scene, the bloated European corpses, with eyes pecked out by birds and limbs half-eaten by the dogs, had turned black, while the African bodies had paled in the sunlight to a chalky grey colour.

For the wounded survivors, help was on the way. Capt Ferret found the hospital still unusable, but in the neighbouring clinic ten European doctors were doing their best to restock medical supplies. Their lives had been spared because they had operated on wounded Tigers until the retreat began. Then the rebel commanders had ordered their men to march back into Angola. Those unable to walk had been shot by their comrades, rather than be left and forced to talk.

Ferret left them to their good work and returned to the bar of the Impala Hotel, where he had improvised a sick bay. Cpl Jean Prudence, shot in the chest and a kidney, was operated on that afternoon by an Indian surgeon, assisted by a black surgeon and a French anaesthetist. That afternoon, begging medical supplies from the Belgians at the airport, Ferret was surprised to see the Belgian doctors from the clinic boarding evacuation planes. They had been *ordered* to leave. Their European patients were going with them, but there was 'no space for Blacks' aboard the evacuation aircraft - not even for the wife and children of engineer Henri Jagodinski. The Legion found them seats on another plane. By Monday, Ferret and two Zairian general practitioners were the only doctors left in Kolwezi until Ferret's No 2, Capt Morcillo, was flown in from Corsica to help out.

Combats in the neighbouring townships of Metal-Shaba, Luilu and Kapata continued for several days. On Sunday 21 May Ambassador Ross flew in to tour Kolwezi with Col Gras and make notes for a dispassionate account of events sent to Paris.

That evening President Mobutu flew in to personally thank the Legion for an impeccably executed operation.

But the Legion had not finished spilling its blood. Pulled back to Lumumbashi after handing over Kolwezi to the FAZ, Morcillo learned from civilian colleagues that people were dying in the hospital for want of blood. The Zairian soldiers refused to give any in the belief that it would shorten their lives, so 2 REP volunteered - every officer, NCO and legionnaire.

Before leaving Zaire, on 6 June - the thirty-fourth anniversary of D-Day - the regiment spent as much energy polishing equipment and cleaning uniforms as it had in fighting the Katangans. The purpose was a victory parade through the streets of Lumumbashi to the delight of the inhabitants, mostly Black with a scattering of Europeans. Erulin marched at the head of his men. The regimental song they sang in unison as they marched does not bear translation. The words are pretty awful, even in French. But the sense is fine, and the last lines are always clear: *Nous sommes fiers d'appartenir au 2e REP.*

We are proud to belong to 2 REP, they sang - and they had every right to be. To borrow a phrase from that sometime soldier

Winston Churchill, this was their finest hour. The price that had been paid amounted to five men dead and twenty men wounded.[6] The casualties' names give some idea of their origins before the Legion became their country: Allioui, Arnold, Becker, Clément, Harte, Jakovic, Marco, Muñoz, Raymond, Seeger, Svoboda ...

The above is no more than a sample of what Col Erulin's legionnaires achieved in an ultimate test of the training that bonded officers and men from so many different countries into one superbly trained fighting machine. An entire book could be written about the suffering of the hostages of Kolwezi and the heroism of the legionnaires who risked their lives to liberate the survivors, keeping a sense of humour and discipline despite all the unnecessary obstacles placed in their way by ignorance and incompetence in two European capitals.

No army in the world has ever done better, or more, in such trying circumstances. If the continued existence of the Legion needed a justification, Kolwezi was it.

Acknowledgements

Every historian of the French Foreign Legion owes an enormous debt to the knowledgeable and helpful staff of Les Archives de la Légion Etrangère in Aubagne. I take great pleasure in thanking the Commanding General of the Foreign Legion for the privilege of using the excellent research facilities at Aubagne and especially for his kind permission to photograph objects in the Legion's fascinating museum there, which is open to the public. The President of Les Amis du Musée de la Légion Etrangère, Gen Bruno Le Flem, gave me a warm welcome and valuable insights. Commandant Guyot of 1 RE displayed an encyclopaedic knowledge of Legion archives and Major Michon at the Centre de Documentation was unfailingly patient and helpful.

I also owe a great deal to ex-legionnaires and former Legion officers who generously recounted their personal experiences, to give readers the feeling of what it was like, serving in the Legion. Respecting the tradition of anonymity, I have named few of them. *Ni vu, ni connu* - as they say. Two whom I can thank by name are Brigadier Anthony Hunter-Choat, formerly Sergent Choat of 1 REP, for his generosity in writing the Foreword and making numerous constructive comments on the final draft; and Colonel Philippe Dufour, President of the Association des Anciens de la Légion Etrangère de Bordeaux, who made me an honorary ex-legionnaire on the strength of this book - an honour of which I am proud.

This book first took shape over lunch in a Gloucestershire pub with my friend and colleague Jonathan Falconer. For this revised edition, thanks go to my agent Mandy Little and at Ian Allan Publishing to Publisher Nick Grant, in-house editor Mark Beynon, copy editor Peter Stafford, Book Production Editor Matthew Wharmby and Design Manager Keith Wootton. They have all, once again, done me, and this time the Legion too, proud.

Douglas Boyd

Appendix A: Equivalent ranks

French	British	United States
engagé volontaire	recruit	recruit
légionnaire 2ème classe	private	private
légionnaire 1ère classe	lance-corporal	private first class
caporal or brigadier in cavalry	corporal	corporal
caporal-chef	-	-
sergent	sergeant	sergeant
maréchal des logis (cavalry)	sergeant	sergeant
-	-	sergeant first class
sergent-chef	staff sergeant	master sergeant
-	-	first sergeant
adjutant	warrant officer (2)	warrant officer junior grade
adjutant-chef	warrant officer (1)	chief warrant officer
major	-	-
aspirant	2nd lieutenant	2nd lieutenant
lieutenant	lieutenant	1st lieutenant
capitaine	captain	captain
commandant	major	major
lieutenant-colonel	lieutenant-colonel	lieutenant-colonel
colonel	colonel	colonel
général de brigade	brigadier	brigadier-general
général de division	major-general	major-general
général de corps d'armée	lieutenant-general	lieutenant-general
général d'armée	general	general
maréchal de France	field marshal	general of the army

Appendix B: Glossary

ALE	Les Archives de la Légion Etrangère at Aubagne
ALN	Armée de Libération Nationale - the armed wing of FLN
Arab	loosely used to mean an inhabitant of the Maghreb, including non-Arabic-speakers like the Berbers
bataillon de marche	temporary battalion for a specific operation
BEP	Bataillon Etranger de Parachutistes - Legion para battalion
bey, also *dey*	elected Turkish governor
bled	country, wilderness, also village
BMC	bordel mobile de campagne - soldiers' brothel
bo-doi	Viet Minh soldier
Boudin, Le	Most famous Legion marching song and bugle call - literally 'Black Pudding,' but variously thought to refer to the rolled blanket or overcoat, or tent roll originally carried atop the back-pack
BSLE	*Bureau de Sécurité de la Légion Etrangère* - Legion internal security
cafard	sand bug
cafard (avoir le)	be severely depressed
caïd	Arab governor, also slang for 'boss' By extension, the bugle call sounded for the colonel of the regiment
Camerone (faire)	fight to the last round
can-bo	Viet Minh political officer
colon	European settler
congai	Vietnamese wife or mistress
convoyeuse	Evasan nurse
corvée	fatigue duty

Deuxième Bureau	French military intelligence
DBLE	Demi-Brigade de la Légion Etrangère - Legion half-brigade
djebel	mountain
DZ	drop zone of a parachute operation
ETA	estimated time of arrival
Evasan	French for 'medevac'
fellagha, pl. *fellouze*	ALN fighter (usually abbreviated to 'fell')
FLN	Front de Libération Nationale - the main anti-French independence party of Algeria
GIGN	Groupe d'Intervention de la Gendarmerie Nationale - France's best-known anti-terrorist unit
gnouf	Legion prison
goum, or *goumier*	North African native infantry on French side
HALO	High Altitude Low Opening - a free-fall glide with parachute opened far from the launch plane, used in clandestine insertions
harka	an Arab war-party
harki	Algerian soldier working for French army
katiba	ALN company
képi	hard French military cap
ksar or *ksour*	a fortified village
lazaret	hospital, esp. for contagious diseases
LURP	(member of a) long-range reconnaissance team
maghrebin	North African Arab
mechta	neighbourhood of a village
pied-noir	orig. synonymous with Maghrebin, later a European settler in French North Africa
razzia	a scorched-earth raid
régiment de marche	temporary regiment for a specific campaign
REC	Régiment Etranger de Cavalerie - Legion cavalry regiment

REI	Régiment Etranger d'Infanterie - Legion infantry regiment
REIM	Régiment Etranger d'Infanterie de Marche - temporary Legion infantry regiment
REP	Régiment Etranger de Parachutistes - Legion para regiment
Rif	Part of Atlas range of mountains in Morocco
Riffian	a Berber inhabitant of the Rif region
RMLE	Régiment de Marche de la Légion Etrangère - a temporary regiment of men drawn from other units for a specific operation
RMVE	Régiment de Marche des Volontaires Etrangères - a temporary regiment of foreign volunteers
SHAT	Service Historique de l'Armée de Terre
Spahi	North African cavalryman on the French side - at first Arab, but later European
stick	a group of paras who jump together
taule	slang for 'prison'
tirailleurs	light infantry
wilaya	one of five regional commands of ALN
zouave	Algerian infantryman, later French but wearing the same Moorish uniform

List of Illustrations

1. Monument aux Morts, Aubagne.
2. Funeral of legionnaire in North Vietnam, 1950.
3. Marshal Soult.
4. King Louis Philippe.
5. Gen Achille de St Arnaud.
6. Gen Joseph Bernelle.
7. Madame la Générale Bernelle.
8. Maj Ludwig Joseph Conrad.
9. Col Granet Lacrosse De Chabrière.
10. Capt Danjou.
11. Bronze bust of Col Pierre Jeaningros.
12. Gen Achille Bazaine.
13. Alan Seeger in his poet days.
14. Alan Seeger in uniform shortly before his death.
15. Cole Porter.
16. Capt Fernand Maire.
17. Gen Paul Rollet.
18. Col Amilakvari.
19. Gen Pierre Koenig.
20. Portrait of Col Pierre Jeanpierre.
21. Four legionnaires in 1840 uniform.
22. Death of Col Chabrière at Magenta.
23. Two legionnaires in Mexico, 1862.
24. Legion mounted company fording wadi in Morocco, 1912.
25. Legionnaires with Lebel 1896 rifles in 1911.
26. Foreign volunteers march through Paris, 1914.
27. Legion HQ at Sidi bel Abbès.
28. Legion infantry in Algeria, 1935.
29. NCO bids farewell to wife and child, March 1940.
30. Legion machine gunner, France 1940.
31. Volunteers at Gare de Lyon, Paris, May 1940.
32. Legionnaires in Bren carrier at Bir Hakeim, 1942.
33. Injured legionnaire in Saigon hospital, 1950.
34. Fortified Legion camp in Vietnam.
35. Legion patrol in rice paddies, northern Vietnam, c1950.

36. Mortar company of 1 BEP at Dien Bien Phu, March 1954.
37. AMX 13 tank of 1 REC on the Tunisian border, 1958.
38. 1 REC in Algeria, 1957.
39. 1 REP paras exit a Shawnee H 21 Flying Banana in the Aurès Mountains, 1959.
40. Passing out parade at 4 RE HQ in Castelnaudary.
41. Engagés volontaires from three continents.

Abbreviations used in captions

MLE - photographed by the author in the Legion museum at Aubagne by kind permission of the Commanding General of the Foreign Legion.

ALE - documents in the Archives de la Légion Etrangère, reproduced by arrangement with the Centre de Documentation of 1 RE at Aubagne.

List of Maps

Page 21   Vietnam: the strategic Highway Four, 1949
Page 35   Province of Tonkin/North Vietnam
Page 41   French positions at Dien Bien Phu, November 1953-May 1954
Page 58   The Algerian War, 1954-62
Page 103 The Maghreb/French North Africa
Page 115 The Spanish Intervention, 1835-9
Page 175 The Mexican Intervention, 1862-3
Page 218 Tonkin/North Vietnam, 1883-92
Page 281 The Legion in France, 1914-18
Page 402 Zaire/Democratic Republic of Congo
Page 420 Operation Leopard, Kolwezi, May-June 1978

Further Reading in English

As the Notes show, books in several languages were used in the preparation of this volume. The following titles in English will be of interest to readers and should not be difficult to obtain:

F. Fleming *The Sword and the Cross* (London, Granta 2003)

T. Geraghty *March or Die* (London, Grafton 1986)

J. Harvey *With the Foreign Legion in Syria* (Fresno, Linden Publishing 2003)

C. Jennings *Mouthful of Rocks* (London, Bloomsbury 1990)

S. Murray *Legionnaire* (London, Sidgwick & Jackson 1978)

T. Pakenham *The Scramble for Africa* (London, Abacus 1992)

D. Porch *The French Foreign Legion* (London, HarperPerennial 1992)

S. Travers *Tomorrow to be Brave* (London, Corgi 2001)

M. Windrow *French Foreign Legion 1914-45* (Botley, Osprey Publishing 1999)

J. R. Young and E. Bergot *The French Foreign Legion* (London, Thames & Hudson 1984)

Notes and Sources

1. All translations are by the author, unless otherwise attributed.
2. All reasonable steps have been taken to trace copyright owners. If any copyright has nevertheless been infringed, please communicate with the author, care of the publisher, so that this may be corrected in subsequent editions.
3. Abbreviations used below:
   SHAT - document at the Service Historique de l'Armée de Terre;
   ALE - document in the Archives de la Légion Etrangère.

Introduction
1. *'Il sentait bon le sable chaud'*
2. *' ... devenu fils de France, non par le sang reçu, mais par le sang versé.'*
3. *Vous autres légionnaires sont soldats pour mourir, et je vous enverrai là où on meurt.'*

Chapter 1
1. The French-built main roads, known as the *routes coloniales*, are still the principal arteries of the Vietnamese road network. Since many of them were used by the US later and renamed Highway One, etc, they are thus referred to in this book, and not as RC 1, RC 2 following French usage.
2. P. Bonnecarrère *Par le Sang Versé* (Paris, Presses de la Cité 1989), pp. 388-390.
3. SHAT 10 H 1142 18 August 1950.
4. Bonnecarrère, p. 418.
5. An alternative version is that, to overcome lack of radio communications owing to terrain and meteorological conditions, a written order was dropped to Lepage from a light spotter plane flying beneath the low cloud cover.
6. Bonnecarrère, pp. 431-2.
7. Bonnecarrère, p. 421. The incident is interesting as it corroborates Charton's statement that the locals were not coerced into coming along, nor used as a human screen.
8. Bonnecarrère, p. 422.
9. Bonnecarrère, p. 426-7.
10. B. Cabiro *Sous le béret vert* (Paris, Plon 1987), p. 252.
11. Gen R Huré and Gen H. de la Barre de Nanteuil, quoted in T Geraghty *March or Die* (London, Grafton 1986), p. 287.
12. Cabiro, p. 256.
13. Historian Philippe Devillers in *Les Brûlures de l'Histoire* broadcast on FR3 TV 26 April 1994
14. then called Bône.
15. See pp. 410-11 of Memorandum for the Secretary of Defense by the Chairman of the Joint Chiefs of Staff dated 28 August 1953 entitled 'Subject: The Navarre Concept for Operations in Indochina,' summarising the paper *Principles for the Conduct of the War* in Indochina submitted by Navarre to Lt-Gen O'Daniel, Chief of US Military Mission in Vietnam. Accessible in The Pentagon Papers, Gravel Edition on www.mtholyoke.edu/acad/intrel/pentagon/doc17.htm.
16. See p. 8/18 of the doctoral thesis prepared in 1991 by Maj Harry D. Bloomer for United States Army Marine Corps University Command and Staff

College *An Analysis of the French Defeat at Dien Bien Phu*, accessible on www.globalsecurity.org/military/library/report/1991/BHD.htm.
17. Bloomer, pp. 3/18 & 12/18.
18. Devillers in *Brûlures.*

Chapter 2
1. C. Jacquemart in *Le Figaro* 7 May 2004.
2. E. Bergot *Les 170 Jours de Diên Biên Phu* (Paris, Presses de la Cité 1979), pp. 45-8.
3. Ibid, p. 52.
4. Ibid, p. 53.
5. Ibid, p. 57.
6. Devillers in *Brûlures.*
7. Bergot, *170 Jours*, pp. 60-61.
8. Bloomer, pp. 14-18.
9. P. Grauwin *Doctor at Dienbienphu* (London, Hutchinson 1955), p. 169 (abbreviated by the author).
10. Ibid, p. 278 (abbreviated by the author).
11. Ibid, p. 156 (abbreviated by the author).
12. Geraghty, p. 293.
13. Ibid, p. 294.
14. Devillers in *Brûlures.*
15. L. Greisamer in *Le Monde* 13 July 2004.
16. Ibid.
17. E. Bergot *Convoi 42* (Paris, Presses de la Cité 1986), p. 91.
18. Bergot's *Convoi 42* describes the ordeal in fictional form to avoid using real names.

Chapter 3
1. The end of the Second World War in Europe.
2. Reasonable estimates put the figure at 6,000. Radio Cairo claimed 50,000 dead.
3. S. Stora *Histoire de la Guerre d'Algérie* (Paris, Editions La Découverte 2004), p. 15.
4. Ibid, p. 18.
5. D. Porch *The French Foreign Legion* (London, HarperPerennial 1992), pp. 572-3.
6. An abbreviation of *fellagha*, plural *fellouze.*
7. Interview with the author.
8. Interview with the author.
9. In his speech to the House of Commons 4 November 1956.
10. P. Sergent *Ma Peau au bout de mes Idées* (Paris, La Table Ronde 1967), pp. 154-6, 242.
11. P. Aussarès *Pour la France* (Paris, Editions du Rocher 2001), pp. 265-7.
12. Stora *Guerre d'Algérie*, p. 25.
13. Ibid, p. 27.
14. S. Murray *Legionnaire* (London, Sidgwick & Jackson 1989), p. 172.
15. Interview with the author.
16. J. W. Worden *Wayward Legionnaire* (London, Futura 1989), pp. 94-6.
17. Ibid, pp, 104-5.

18. Ibid, p. 104.
19. Ibid, p. 105.
20. Ibid, p. 177.
21. Aussarès, p. 267.

Chapter 4
1. *La Guerre d'Algérie en Photos* (Paris, EPA 1989), p. 46.
2. Ibid, p. 61.
3. French grenades had longer fuses than US ones. When the latter were issued to men unaccustomed to them, things became 'interesting.'
4. French name, Philippeville.
5. Cabiro, p. 330.
6. Murray, pp. 131-4.
7. Cabiro, pp. 357-60.
8. Ibid, p. 362.
9. Murray, pp. 135-8.
10. *La Guerre d'Algérie en Photos*, p. 111.
11. Worden, p. 112.
12. Cabiro, pp. 365-8.
13. Ibid, p. 371-3.
14. Murray, p. 172.
15. Ibid, pp.169-81.
16. Stora *Guerre d' Algérie*, p. 90.
17. Ibid, p. 90 adds another 16,378 to this category.
18. Figures extracted from official reports and quoted in Stora, pp. 15, 25, 32, 34.
19. Stora *Guerre d'Algérie*, p. 90 quotes Renseignements Généraux figures giving 15,000 victims of internecine feuds and another 2,000 ALN killed by the Tunisian and Moroccan armed forces.
20. *La Guerre d'Algérie en Photos*, p. 90.
21. It was called *la guerre des sables*-the war of the sands.
22. The *départements d'outre-mer* and *territoires d'outre-mer,* known as DOM TOMs.

Chapter 5
1. *L'Histoire de Guillaume le Maréchal ed.* P Meyer, vol III, Paris 1901, p. 171.
2. Stora *Histoire de l'Algérie Coloniale* Paris, La Découverte 2004, p. 12.
3. *Chronique de France et des Français* Paris, Larousse 1987, p. 837.
4. Col P. Azan *L'Armée d'Afrique 1830-1852* Paris, Plon 1936, p. 124 (author's italics).
5. SHAT Xb 725, 16 July 1831.
6. Porch, p. 6.
7. SHAT Xb 726 30 June 1831 (author's italics).

Chapter 6
1. The full name *el djazaïr beni Mezghana* means 'the islands of the sons of Mezghana,' whose four islets were linked to make the early harbour walls.
2. R. C. Anderson *Devils, Not Men* (Newton Abbot, David & Charles 1988), p. 30.
3. J. Wellard *The French Foreign Legion* (London, André Deutsch 1974), pp. 23-4.
4. Meaning 'west' in Arabic.

5. Anderson, p. 31.
6. *L'Aiglon*.
7. He had also been Napoleon's Minister of Police.
8. Col P. Azan *L'Armée d'Afrique* 1830-1852 (Paris, Plon 1936), p. 47.
9. SHAT Xb 725 1 December 1832.
10. Azan *L'Armée d'Afrique* pp. 80-81.
11. Ibid, p.50.
12. SHAT 764, 1 January 1884.
13. Gen P. A. Grisot and Lt E. Coulombon *La Légion Etrangère de 1831-1887* (Paris, Berger-Levrault 1888), p. 97.
14. C-A. Julien *Histoire de l'Algérie Contemporaine* (Paris, PUF 1964), p. 272.
15. Wellard, p. 12.

Chapter 7
1. Porch, p. 27.
2. Wellard, p. 41.
3. Porch, p. 34.
4. Wellard, p. 45.
5. Anderson, p. 35.
6. Azan *L'Armée d'Afrique* p. 251.
7. Ibid, p. 307.
8. Wilhelm von Rahden *Wanderungen eines alten Soldaten* (Berlin, Alexander Duncker 1851), Vol III, p. 251 (Author's abridged translation).
9. Azan L'Armée d'Afrique, p. 523.
10. G. Bapst *Le Maréchal Canrobert* (Paris, Plon 1913), Vol I, p. 357.

Chapter 8
1. A St-Arnaud *Lettres du Maréchal St-Arnaud* (Paris,Calmann-Levy 1864), p. 139.
2. St-Arnaud, p. 131.
3. Porch, 61 (abbreviated by the author).
4. Porch 64-5.

Chapter 9
1. P. Azan *Par L'Epée et par la Charrue. Ecrits et Discours du Général* Bugeaud (Paris, PUF 1948), p. 112.
2. Lady Duff Gordon *The French in Algeria* (London, John Murray 1855), p.26.
3. *Archives d'Outre-mer* 18 June 1842, quoted in Porch, 76.
4. Bapst, Vol I, p.255.
5. J. de la Faye *Souvenirs du Général Lacretelle* (Paris, Emile Paul 1907), pp. 1-2.
6. Formerly Mogador.
7. P. de Castellane *Military Life in Algiers* (London, Hurst & Blackett 1853), Vol I, p. 237-8.
8. Wellard, p.14.
9. Porch, p. 82.

Chapter 10
1. *Chronique*, pp. 893-7.
2. There is an excellent account with maps and photographs on http://www.xenophongi.org/crimea/war/alma/alma.htm.
3. In the work known as *rei militaris institute*.

4. See account on http://www.xenophongi.org/crimea/war/balaklava/balabat.htm.
5. See inter alia http://www.lourmel-algeriefrancaise.com/un%20peu%20d'histoire.htm.
6. Porch, p. 126.

Chapter 11
1. Count G. de Villebois-Mareuil 'La Légion Etrangère' in *La Revue des Deux Mondes*, Vol 134 1896, p. 876.
2. Porch, p. 133.
3. Porch, p. 127.
4. Anderson, p. 40.
5. Grisot and Coulombon, pp. 565-70.
6. SHAT Xb 778.
7. Of Irish stock, but born a French citizen.
8. C-J. Zédé, quoted in Porch, p. 129.
9. Ibid, pp. 129-30.
10. Porch, p. 130.

Chapter 12
1. Porch, p.136.
2. Geraghty, p. 82.
3. G. Diesbach de Torny *Notes et Souvenirs* (unpublished MS), ALE, p. 50.
4. *Légion Etrangère Historique Sommaire - avril 1864* (ALE).
5. C-J. Zédé in *Carnets de la Sabretache* No 371 July-August 1934.
6. For a full account of the engagement from both Mexican and French sides, plus directions for finding Camarón, see the Spanish-language site of Bernardo Massieu and Marco Couttolenc - http://www.prodigyweb.net.mx/bservin/batalla_camaron_veracruz.htm.

Chapter 13
1. The Museum of the Foreign Legion at Aubagne has a remarkable collection. Open to the public, it is, to borrow the *Guide Michelin* expression, well worth the journey.
2. Personal communication from Brig Hunter-Choat.
3. *Légion Etrangère, Historique Sommaire 'avril 1864'* (ALE).
4. J. A. Dabbs *The French Army in Mexico 1861-67* (The Hague, Mouton 1963), pp. 230, 268.
5. Geraghty, pp 91-2.

Chapter 14
1. Now Hradec Králové, Czech Republic.
2. Grisot and Coulombon, pp. 317-26.
3. Ibid.
4. *Chronique*, p. 933.
5. *A corps d'armée* at the time was between 25,000-30,000 men.
6. *Chronique*, p. 933.
7. Porch, p. 165.
8. Quoted in Geraghty, p. 101.

Chapter 15
1. Porch, p. 165.
2. Grisot and Coulombon, p. 338.
3. Also referred to as *fédérés*.

4. French bitterness at these harsh terms led to the vengeful Treaty of Versailles in June 1919 that sowed the seeds for World War 2.
5. *1er Régiment Etranger 1867-72* (ALE).
6. They still are subject to military law. In a recent Internet forum, a Paris fireman was advised by a serving legionnaire to complete his contract before trying to join the Legion, since it would otherwise treat him as a deserter.

Chapter 16
1. Geraghty, p. 111.
2. Porch, p. 208.
3. M. Poulin *L'Admiral Courbet, sa jeunesse, sa vie militaire et sa mort* (Limoges, Ardant 1888), p. 67.
4. Meaning, the beautiful island.
5. H. MacAleavy *Black Flags in Vietnam* (New York, Macmillan 1968), pp. 257-8.
6. Le Père Pralon *Lionel Hart, engagé volontaire* (Paris, Retaux-Bray 1888), p. 189.
7. Called la Rivière Claire by the French.
8. Pralon, p. 128.
9. Sometimes transliterated as Li Xan-Phuc or Luu Vinh Phuoc.
10. C. Hubert *Le Colonel Dominé* (Paris, Berger-Levrault 1938), p. 66.
11. M-E. Dominé *Journal, 28 February*, quoted in Porch, p. 217.

Chapter 17
1. Author's abridged translation.
2. SHAT 3H 10, 22 April 1885 (Négrier Report).
3. A-P. Maury *Mes Campagnes au Tonkin* (Lyon, Vitte & Peyrusssel 1888), p.194-6.
4. Bôn-Mat *Souvenirs d'un Légionnaire* (Paris, Messein 1914), pp. 177-9.
5. J. P. Le Poer *A Modern Legionary* (New York, Dutton 1905), p. 145.
6. Bôn-Mat, p. 181.
7. Maury, p. 199.
8. Col Tournyol du Clos in *La revue de l'Infanterie* No 525, Vol 89, 1 May 1936, p. 859.
9. L. Huguet *En Colonne: Souvenirs d'extrême-Orient* (Paris, Flamarrion (undated), p. 109.
10. E. Bolis *Mémoires d'un sous-officier* (Courrier de Saône et Loire, Châlon-sur-Saône 1905), p.61.
11. C. Meyer *La vie quotidien des Français en Indochine 1860-1910* (Paris, Hachette 1985), p. 259.
12. A. Sylvère *Le Légionnaire Flutsch* (Paris, Plon 1982), p. 64.

Chapter 18
1. Porch, pp. 245-7.
2. F. Martyn *Life in the Legion from a Soldier's Point of View* (New York, Scribner's 1911), pp. 184-5.
3. Sir R. Burton *A Mission to Gelele, King of Dahomey* (London, Routledge and Kegan Paul 1966), pp. 261-4.
4. Also spelled 'Whydah' by English-speakers.
5. Martyn, p. 195.
6. Capt Jacquot *Mon Journal de Marche de Dahomey* (unpub. MS), quoted in Porch, p. 257.
7. The Hotchkiss was a gas-operated heavy machine gun introduced in France in 1892. Possibly the confusion is because the *Opale* was firing both shells from her cannon and the Hotchkiss as well.
8. Jacquot, quoted in Porch, p. 257.
9. Geraghty, p. 129.
10. Martyn, p. 197.
11. H. P. Lelièvre *Campagne du Dahomey* (unpub. MS, ALE), p.27.
12. J. Bern *L'éxpédition du Dahomey* (Sidi-bel-Abbès, Lavenue 1893), p. 60.

Chapter 19
1. Now called Kodok.
2. See G. Drower *Heligoland: the true story of German Bight* (Thrupp, Sutton 2002).
3. E. F. Knight *Madagascar in Wartime* (London, Longmans Green 1896), p. 162.
4. Then called Tamatave.
5. Then called Tananarive.
6. Then called Majunga.
7. Porch, p. 277.
8. Rollet papers (ALE), quoted in Porch, p. 303.
9. E. Reibell *Le Calvaire de Madagascar* (Paris, Berger-Levralt 1935), p. 104.
10. Lt G. L. Langlois *Souvenirs de Madagascar* (Paris, Charles Lavauzelle 1897), p. 116.
11. Langlois, pp. 123-4 (Author's abridged translation).
12. Reibell, p. 119.
13. Porch, p.275.

Chapter 20
1. Known as *l'affaire des fiches*.
2. Geraghty, p. 140.
3. F. Fleming *The Sword and the Cross* (London, Granta 2003), p. 169.
4. *Le Temps*, 2 May 1901.
5. *The Times*, 29 April 1901.
6. Ibid.
7. J. Germain and S. Faye *Le Général Laperrine* (Paris, Plon 1922), p. 98.
8. Fleming, p. 171.
9. Geraghty, p. 145.

Chapter 21
1. Geraghty, p. 146.

2. *al mamlakah al Maghribiyah.*
3. Sgt Lefèvre *Les Mémoires du Sergent Lefèvre à la Légion Etrangère*, (unpub. MS at ALE, pages not numbered).
4. Ibid.
5. See images on www.ecpad.fr.
6. Lefèvre - author's abridged translation.
7. Porch, pp. 323-4.
8. Ibid, p. 293.
9. E. Rosen *In the Foreign Legion* (London, Duckworth 1910), p. 229.
10. Ibid, pp. 239-40.
11. Herson report (SHAT 1H 1015).
12. The consequences of Bülow's oversight caused his resignation on 26 June 1909.
13. Geraghty, p. 151.
14. Sylvère, p. 203.
15. An interesting summary from *The Handbook for the Diplomatic History of Europe, Asia and Africa 1870-1914*, published in Washington DC by the Government Printing Office in 1918, is available on www.mtholyoke.edu/acad/intrel/boshtml/bos135.htm.
16. Figures disputed in SHAT 3H 148, 12 March 1913.

Chapter 22
1. French title, *Du Côté de Chez Swann.*
2. legal name, Frédéric Sauser.
3. M-C. Poinsot *Les Volontaires Etrangers ... en 1914-15* (Paris, Dorbon-Aine 1915) pp. 12-13.
4. Wellard, pp. 83-4.
5. Poinsot, pp. 31-2.
6. Including 6,500 Alsatians and Lorrainers, 4913 Italians, 3393 Russians, 2396 Germans and Austro-Hungarians, 1,867 Swiss, 1,462 Belgians, 1380 Greeks, 1369 Czech/Slovakian citizens, 979 Spaniards, 600 Americans from both hemispheres, 595 Turks, 591 Luxembourgers and 379 Britons.
7. B. Cendrars *La Main Coupée* (Paris, Folio 1974), p. 141.
8. A. Seeger *Letters and Diary of Alan Seeger* (New York, Scribner's 1917), p. 154.
9. J. Reybaz *Le 1er Mystérieux: Souvenirs de guerre d'un légionnaire suisse* (Paris, André Barry 1932), pp. 16-17.
10. K. Todorov *Balkan Firebrand* (Chicago & New York, Ziff Davis 1943), p. 50.
11. Seeger Letters and Diary, p. 153.
12. Not just because of the vastness of the country, the poor railway network and the inefficiency of civil administration. There were also the personality problems of the Russian command. C-in-C Grand Duke Nikolai knew nothing of War Minister Sukhomnlinov's elaborate Plan 19 for a pre-emptive strike into East Prussia that would take the pressure off the French on the western front. In any case, the grand duke was not on speaking terms with his army commanders; even Russian wireless communications were sent uncoded, and thus constantly intercepted by the Germans.
13. Against troops including the BEF on the French left.
14. That is, 4th Bataillon de Marche of 1 RE.
15. On 2 January.
16. In May 1915.

Chapter 23
1. Cendrars, pp. 31-2.
2. The popular name for French infantry, meaning literally 'hairy ones', from their often unshaven appearance in the line.
3. Seeger *Letters and Diary*, p. 69; also P. A. Rockwell *American Fighters in the Foreign Legion 1914-1918* (Boston & New York, Houghton Mifflin 1930), pp. 47-9.
4. Cendrars, pp. 182-4.
5. Ibid, pp. 312-14.
6. A. Seeger *Poems* (London, Constable 1917), p. 173.
7. Many self-declared Russians were officially Polish, Romanian, etc, depending on where the frontiers were at the time of their birth or enlistment.
8. L. Poliakoff *Histoire de l'Antisemitisme ... 1870-1933* (Paris, Calman-Lévy 1977), p. 294.
9. *Le Crappouillot* (issue of August 1934) cites on p. 49: 216 executions in 1914; 315 in 1916 and 136 in 1918. The figures are impossible to verify, although with even so respected a historian as the American Douglas Porch being refused access to the relevant archives, it would seem they come close.
10. An excellent hour-by-hour account is to be found on the website of *Les Bulletins de l'ASMAC* under the heading *La Légion Etrangère sur le front de Champagne*.
11. E. Morlae *A Soldier of the Legion* (Boston & New York, Houghton Mifflin 1916), pp. 51-4.
12 Ibid, pp. 32-3.
13. Anderson, pp. 57-8.
14. Porch, p. 334.

Chapter 24
1. J. Mosier *The Myth of the Great War* (London, Profile 2002), pp. 236, 241. German losses were consistently grossly inflated by both French and British High Commands throughout the war to 'justify' the enormously higher Allied losses.
2. Just to the west of exit 13 on the A1 motorway; Belloy-en-Santerre lies to the east of the same junction.
3. *Jeune legionnaire, enthousaiaste et énergétique, aimant passionnément la France, engagé volontairement au début des hostilités et faisant preuve d'un courage et entrain admirables, glorieusement tombé le 11 juillet 1916 devant Belloy-en-Santerre. A Bel-Abbès 24 juillet 1924, le colonel Boulet-Desbareau, commandant le 4ème Régiment Etranger.*
4. Geraghty, p. 186.
5. SHAT 24N, 2912 (RMLE 23 April 1917, p.12).
6. The ridge was so named for the road *(chemin)* built along it for the daughters of Louis XV to enjoy the magnificent views over the countryside in both directions when visiting the Countess of Narbonne in her château nearby. It was, of course, the view that made the ridge so important to both sides.
7. Col Bouchez's report of 26 July 1918 in Rollet papers at ALE (abridged translation by the author).
8. Rollet papers, undated (ALE).
9. Porch, p. 376.

10. Founded on 20 April 1916, the squadron was an anomaly because there were more qualified French pilots than planes for them to fly. However, Escadrille Lafayette was credited with 199 'kills.' Ex-legionnaire pilots included Kiffin Rockwell, who shot down two German aircraft before being killed in combat during 1916, and Edward Genet, killed by anti-aircraft fire in April 1917. The black professional boxer Eugene Bullard, who did not 'fit' in this WASP squadron, was posted to 107th French Infantry Regiment to get rid of him. One of the generation of black musicians who enriched French musical life between the wars playing jazz in Paris nightclubs, he re-enlisted in 1940 and was wounded in the French retreat that summer before being evacuated to the US.

11. J. Green Memoirs of *Happy Days* (New York & London, Harper and Brothers 1942), pp. 182-3.

12. Personal file of Cole Porter at ALE.

13. *Quatre ans il a peiné, saigné, souffert. / Et puis, un soir il est tombé dans cet enfer. / Qui sait si cet inconnu qui dort sous l'arche immense / mêlant sa gloire épique aux orgueils du passé / n'est pas cet étranger devenu fils de France, /non par le sang reçu mais par le sang versé ?*

14. *Liste nominative* (unpub MS at ALE).

Chapter 25

1. Porch, p. 386.

2. General Mordacq *Le Ministère Clemenceau. Journal d'un Témoin* (Paris, Plon 1931), vol III, p. 328.

3. SHAT 3H, 93.

4. A derogatory term equivalent to 'kraut'.

5. Promoted lieutenant, he served until 1939.

6. J. Weygand *Légionnaire* (Paris, Flamarrion 1951), pp. 218-19.

7. SHAT 34N, 310 *(Historique du Régiment 1921 à 1934)*.

8. It did not work because men preferring a civilian brothel would avoid the penalty for contracting VD there by afterwards going with one of the girls in the BMC, to ensure their names were on her list when they reported sick. If already infected, they infected her and her subsequent clients.

9. B. Stuart *Adventures in Algeria* (London, Herbert Jenkins 1936), p.18.

10. J. Martin *Je suis un Légionnaire* (Paris, Fayard 1938), p. 177-8.

11. J. Brunon *Le Livre d'Or* (privately published), p.454.

12. A. R. Cooper *Born to Fight* (Edinburgh and London, Blackwood 1969), p. 166.

Chapter 26

1. Published in London by Sampson Low, Marston & Co (no date).

2. Wellard, p. 95.

3. *Engagés volontaires* still accomplish remarkable odysseys to reach a recruiting office. The author interviewed in the Police Commissariat at Hendaye a young Armenian would-be recruit who had walked all the way from his home country - a distance of around 4,000 kilometres, crossing frontiers by night and surviving on the leavings thrown away at fast-food outlets.

4. 'Ex-Legionnaire 75,645' *Slaves of Morocco* (London, Samson Low, Marston & Co 1938), pp. 144-6 (abridged by the author).

5. *La Tragédie de Médouina* in 'Vert et Rouge No 28', 1950, pp. 40-45.

6. Porch, p. 392.
7. *epitoma rei militaris*, the treatise on warfare written by Flavius Vegetius Renatus (fl. fourth century CE) was still studied at St Cyr in 1894 when Rollet was a cadet there.
8. Wellard, p. 96.
9. Ibid, p. 101.
10. J. Harvey *With the Foreign Legion in Syria* (Fresno, Linden Publishing 2003), pp. 86-7 (orig. pub. London, Hutchinson 1928).

Chapter 27
1. Porch, p. 454.
2. Legion magazine *Képi Blanc* No 490 of May 1989, p. 28.
3. They probably included the sender of the postcard reproduced as Plate 28. The mis-spelled and ungrammatical message on the back is addressed to Pierre Genty, c/o Madame Genty at La Vigne St René, in Côtes du Nord. It reads: 'At Valbonne on the 7th. My dear little one, two words to tell you I am in good health and I hope my card finds you the same. I am going on leave Tuesday or Wednesday but you can write to me at home. It's only for seven days - afterwards it's the front. But don't worry about me, I hope to see you before leaving for the front. (illegible) I leave you for a moment. (signed) He who loves you and thinks of you.'
4. *Képi Blanc* No 490 of May 1989, p. 47.
5. Z. Szajkowski *Jews and the Foreign Legion* (New York, KATV 1975), pp. 74-5.
6. Porch, p. 464.
7. P. Johnson *A History of the Modern World* (London, Weidenfeld and Nicolson 1983), quoted in Geraghty, p. 217.
8. Although the number includes 1,500 German sailors rescued from Kriegsmarine ships, that still leaves the defending ground forces outnumbering the attackers by two to one.
9. P-O. Lapie *La Légion Etrangère à Narvik* (London, John Murray 1941), pp. 30-34.
10. Anderson, p. 70.
11. C. Favrel *Ci-devant légionnaire* (Paris, Presses de la Cité 1963), p. 164.

Chapter 28
1. Anderson, p. 70.
2. Ibid.
3. Porch, p. 471.
4. French vessels in British ports were permitted to leave unhindered until 28 June.
5. P. Carell *Afrika Korps* (Paris, J'ai Lu 1963), p. 278. 2,000 of these men did serve in Rommel's Afrika Korps, initially in labour battalions until reassigned to his infantry, some of them seeing action against 13 DBLE fighting on the Free French side at Bir Hakeim in 1942.
6. G. de Sairigné *Carnet de Route de Lieutenant Gabriel Sairigné: 1 July* (Unpub. diary in ALE archives).
7. Anderson, p. 71.

Chapter 29
1. The *Knickebein* technology being used was simple triangulation. Luftwaffe bombers followed one radio beam to the point where it was intersected by another from a different bearing directly over the target.

4. De Sairigné, p. 42.
3. Geraghty, p. 269.
4. S. Travers *Tomorrow to be Brave* (London, Corgi 2001), pp. 60-63.
5. Ibid, p. 78.
6. Ibid, p. 105.
7. Geraghty, p. 222.
8. Unpub. letter of Colonel Barre dated 1 October 1981 in ALE archives.
9. C. Buckley *Five Ventures* (London, HMSO 1954), pp. 46-7.
10. Ibid, p. 44.
11. A-P. Comor *L'Epopée de la 13e demi-brigade de la Légion Etrangère 1940-45* (Paris, Nouvelles Éditions Latines 1989), pp. 161-2.
12. Travers, pp. 146-61.
13. Worden, pp. 49-50.

Chapter 30
1. Travers, p. 189.
2. Geraghty, p. 243.
3. See photo in Travers, p. 208.
4. Geraghty, p. 245.
5. Travers, pp. 202-5.
6. Ibid, p. 207.
7. Ibid, pp. 208-11.
8. Geraghty, p. 259.
9. Travers, pp. 218-28 and Koenig quoted in Geraghty, p. 265.
10. H. Amouroux *La Grande Histoire de France sous l'Occupation* (Paris, Laffont 1979) Vol IV, pp. 268-9.
11. Porch, p. 484.
12. See various photos in Travers, p. 208.

Chapter 31
1. A. Perrot-White *French Legionnaire* (London, John Murray 1953), pp. 182-97.
2. C. Williams *The Last Great Frenchman* (London, Little Brown 1993), p. 200.
3. Ibid, p. 204.
4. From 50,000 men in 1940, Legion strength excluding 13 DBLE had fallen to 18,000. See Porch, p. 490.
5. Anderson, p. 79.
6. Porch, p. 485.
7. Ibid, p. 493.
8. SHAT 12P 83 of 10 March 1945.
9. Blamed by many Allied leaders for slowing down the main invasion in the north, with the result that Stalin was able to grab most of central and southeastern Europe.
10. Comor, pp. 285-7.
11. See N. Tolstoy *Victims of Yalta* London, Hodder and Stoughton 1977.
12. Personal communication to the author.
13. Since 1930 all Legion units in Vietnam had been grouped under 5 REI, which thus became the Indo-Chinese regiment.
14. Anderson, p. 85.
15. He was sometimes called Tsakiropoulos, possibly a confusion of his real name and the name under which he had enlisted.

16. P. Sergent *Les maréchaux de la Légion* (Paris, Fayard 1987), p. 369.
17. Real name Dewavrin.
18. Sergent *Les maréchaux*, p. 363.
19. G. Sabattier *Le Destin de l'Indochine* (Paris, Plon 1952).
20. Anderson, p. 85.
21. Sergent *Les maréchaux*, p. 194.
22. Geraghty, p. 270.
23. Lord Mountbatten *Report on Post-Surrender Tasks* London, HMSO quoted in M. Arnold-Foster *The World at War* (London, Thames Methuen 1983), p. 323.
24. The full title was 'Viet Nam Doc Lap Dong Minh Hoi', meaning League for the Independence of Vietnam.
25. J. P. Harrison *The Endless War* (New York, Columbia Univ 1989), p. 109.
26. An exact figure was never published.
27. Cabiro, p. 130.
28. interviewed on camera in *Les Légionnaires allemands dans la Guerre d'Indochine* transmitted on Arte-TV 9 February 2005.
29. Ibid.
30. Ibid.
31. Ibid.
32. Ibid.

Chapter 32
1. On reorganisation, the infantry regiments dropped the 'I' from their designation.

Chapter 33
1. Worden, p. 156.
2. Formerly Fort Lamy.

Chapter 34
1. Zaire is now called Democratic Republic of Congo. Shaba was formerly Katanga, a province of the Belgian Congo until 1960.
2. Front National de Libération du Congo, headed by Nathanaël M'Bumba.
3. Under the aegis of the Soviet-Cuban Committee chaired by Castro's brother Raul, and co-ordinated by Soviet generals Vassili I. Petrov and Sergey Sokolov, Cuban destabilisation operations were ongoing in Algeria, Angola, Benin, Congo Republic, Equatorial Guinea, Ethiopia, Guinea, Libya, Sierra Leone, Tanzania and Zambia.
4. P. Sergent *La Légion saute sur Kolwezi* (Paris, Presses de la Cité 1978), p. 86.
5. Trained by North Korean instructors.
6. Sergent *Kolwezi*, p. 55.
7. Sergent *Kolwezi*, pp. 82-4.

Chapter 35
1. Sergent *Kolwezi*, p. 107.
2. Ibid, p. 130.
3. Ibid, p. 131.
4. Ibid.

Chapter 36

1. Sergent *Kolwezi*, p. 150.
2. Ibid, p. 151.
3. Ibid, p. 229.
4. Reported killed by some unreliable witnesses, but claimed by the Katangans to have been abducted as hostages into Angola. The truth was never established.
5. Sergent *Kolwezi*, p. 169.
6. Ibid, p. 227.

Index

Note: ranks given are highest attained.

Aage, Lt Christian, Prince of Denmark, 82, 316, 321-3, 396
Abbas, Ferhat, 82
Abd al-Aziz, Sultan of Morocco, 254, 261-2, 272
Abd al-Hafid, Moulay, 272-3
Abd el-Kader, 103, 107-10, 124-6, 130, 132, 135, 137, 254
Abd el-Krim, 323, 325, 327-30
Action Service, 61, 81
Agadir Incident, 272
Aiglon, son of Napoleon I, 104
aircraft, 30, 32-3, 35-6, 40, 43-9, 51, 53, 68-9, 75, 350-2, 355, 365-8, 374, 385, 388, 397-8, 411-19, 425-7
Aït Ahmed, Hocine, 82
Alba, Gen Manuel, 185
Aleksandr II, Tsar of Russia, 156-7
Alessandri, Gen, 25
Algeciras Conference, 262-3, 266
Algeria, 56-83, 90-1, 100-111, 123-142, 186, 193, 198, 212, 349-50
Allenby, Gen Edmund, 329
Alleg, Henri, 63
Alsace and Lorraine, 208, 210, 278-9, 291
Amazons, Dahomeyan, 235, 238-40
American Civil War, 170, 186
Amilakvari, Lt Col, 321, 344, 349, 355-6, 358, 363, 369-72
André, Gen Louis, 252
Anschluss, 335
Anthoine, Gen, 302
Arago, Maj, 201
Armée d'Afrique, 133, 140, 149, 197, 206, 244, 257, 376
(see also Chasseurs d'Afrique, Spahis, Zouaves)
Armée de Libération Nationale - Algeria (ALN), 58-61, 64, 66-9, 71-2, 80, 83,
Armée du Levant, 353
Attlee, Prime Minister Clement, 383
Aubagne, 82,
Auchinleck, Gen Sir Claude, 358, 371
Aumale, Duke of, 135

Auphale, French Resident Camille, 381
Aussarès, Gen Paul, 61, 67, 81

Ba Ahmed, 254
Ba Bia, Gen, 413
Bacri and Busnach, 90
Bailloud, Gen, 266
Bakunin, Mikhail, 200
Bandera (Spanish Foreign Legion), 312, 323-4
Bangerter, Legionnaire, 301
Bao Dai, Emperor of Vietnam, 37
Barre, Col Fernand, 354, 357
bashi-bazouks, 148
Bataillons d'Afrique, 111, 141, 147, 229, 273
Baux, Col Jean-Louis, 118
Bazaine, Maria de la Soledad, 150, 190, 211
Bazaine, Marshal François-Achille, 120, 150, 159, 189, 192, 196, 198, 202, 211
Beau Hunks film, 316
Bedeau, Lt Col Alphonse, 117, 125-7, 129
Behanzin, King of Dahomey, 235, 237, 239-41
Belkacem, Krim, 82
Bellec, Lt, 369-70
Ben Bella, Ahmed, 60, 82
Benedetti, Count Victor, 194-5
Bénézit, Lt Col, 409, 411, 414, 427
Bengoechea, Legionnaire, 283
Berbers, 262, 273, 323-5, 334
Berg, Cpl Evariste, 183, 185
Bergot, Capt Erwin, 40, 55
Bernelle, Gen Joseph, 107, 111, 113, 115-8
Bernelle, Madame la Générale Tharsile, 116-7
Berthezène, Gen Pierre, 103
Bertrand, Col, 255
Besson, Col, 338
Bethouart, Gen Marie-Emile, 340-1, 343
Bey Hadjj Ahmed, 124, 126, 137
Bichemin, Maj, 256

Bigeard, Col Marcel, 39, 50
Black Flags / Pavillons Noirs, 216, 218-25, 230
Blanc, Sgt, 40-1
Blanqui, Louis-Auguste, 200
Bleus, Col, 413
Blum, Prime Minister Leon, 193
Bobillot, Sgt, 219-22
Bolis, Sgt Ernest, 231
Bonetti, Adm, 353
Bonetti, Pascal, 308
Bôn-Mat, Legionnaire, 228-9, 232
Bonnelet, Capt, 260
Bonnier, Fernand, 376
Borelli, Capt, 82, 219, 225-7
Borgnis-Desbordes, Gen, 230
Bouchez, Col, 306
Boudiat, Mouhammed, 82
Boulet-Desbareau, Col, 297
Boumoudienne, President Houari, 82
Bourbaki, Gen Charles, 204-6
Bourgain, Lt Bertrand, 421-7
Bourguiba, President Habib of Tunisia, 33
Bouzian, caïd of Zaatcha, 140
Boxer, Adm, 152
Boyer-Resses, Maj, 344
Brause, WO1 Eugen, 386
Bréa, Gen, 139
Brest-Litovsk Treaties, 303, 307
Brière de l'Isle, Gen Louis, 224-5, 227, 230
British Expeditionary Force (BEF), 277
British Legion (in Spanish intervention), 115, 117, 136
Brockman, Legionnaire, see Brückler
Brosset, Gen Diégo, 378
brothels, see prostitution
Brothier, Maj Albert, 33, 338
Bru, Jehanne, 399-400
Brückler, Sgt, 359, 380
Brundsaux, Capt Paul (Loum-Loum), 235, 248, 253, 319
Brunon, Jean, 319
Brunswick, Sgt Félix, 203, 207
Buchoud, Col, 68
Buffalo game, 22, 23
Bugeaud, Gen Thomas, 108-9, 123-5, 132-133, 135

Bureau Arabe, 140
Bureau de Sécurité de la Légion Etrangère (BSLE), 377
Burton, Sir Richard, 235
Butterworth, Frank, 307

Cabanier, Rear-Adm Georges, 36,
Cabiro, Capt Bernard, 33, 39, 44, 46, 55, 74, 76-9, 385, 388
cafard, see depression
Caillaud, Lt Col, 396
Cambas, Col Angel, 182
Camerone / Camerone Day / Camarón, 50, 51, 68, 78, 167-9, 178-85, 319, 360
Campbell, Gen Jock, 360
Canrobert, Gen François, 122, 142, 147, 150, 156-7
Carbillet, Capt, 330
Carbuccia, Gen Jean-Luc, 141, 146
Carlota, consort of 'Emperor' Maximilian, 186, 191
Carpentier, Gen Marcel, 24, 31
casualties (and treatment of), 26, 30, 38, 49, 51, 67, 118, 120-1, 124, 127, 129, 140, 142, 151-2, 154-8, 160, 163-4, 168, 179, 181-3, 188, 190-1, 193, 201, 204, 209, 214-5, 220-2, 224-5, 229, 239, 250-1, 260, 264, 265, 280, 290, 294, 297-8, 301, 304-6, 308-9, 342, 355-6, 371, 385, 398, 421, 430-1
Cat Bi naval airbase, 34,
Catena, ex-Sgt, 425
Catteau, Legionnaire, 168, 181-2, 225
Cavaignac, Gen Louis-Eugène, 139
Cavaignac, Godefroi, 139
Cavour, Camillo, 161, 164
Cendrars, Blaise, 275, 277, 283, 285, 287, 294
Challe, Gen, 69, 74-5, 77, 79
Cham, Lt, 107
Chanzy, Gen Alfred, 210
Charles X, King of France, 89, 91-4, 101, 109
Charton, Col Pierre, 24-9
Chassepot, Antoine-Alphonse, 197
Chasseurs d'Afrique, 104, 106, 110, 151, 197, 313
Chenel, 2/Lt, 348, 381-2

Chiang Kai-Shek, 38, 382-3
Churchill, Prime Minister Sir
    Winston, 353, 358, 371, 375, 382,
    431
Clauzel, Marshal Bertrand, 123-5
Clemenceau, Prime Minister Georges,
    255, 310
Clinchant, Gen Justin, 206
Code of Honour, 320
Coevoet, Capt Stéphane, 409, 412-27
Cogny, Gen, 36, 38
Cohn-Bendit, 'Red Danny', 79
colonial troops, 32, 39, 42-3, 45, 48,
    50, 64, 68, 75, 130, 137, 147, 159,
    197, 200, 219, 224, 240, 243, 276,
    280, 291-2, 295, 307-8, 323, 326,
    329-30, 331, 333, 360, 384
Combe, Col Michel, 106, 126, 127
Combes, Emile, 252
Commune, Communards, 207-10
Communist International
    (Comintern), 384
communist legionnaires, 337-8
Communist Party of France (PCF),
    337, 384
Comonfort, President Ignacio, 170
congais, 231-2, 381, 382
Conrad, Col Joseph, 110-11, 117-21,
    125
Constantin, Legionnaire, 168
coolie-tram, 221-2
Cot, Lt Col, 294
Courbet, Adm Amédée, 216-8
Crimean war, 144-160, 168
Cuckoo game, 22-3, 314
Cunningham, Adm Sir John, 352

Dahomey campaign, 234-42
Daladier, Edouard, 278
D'Amade, Gen Albert, 267, 269
Damrémont, Gen Charles, 125-6
Danjou, Capt, 82, 166-8, 170, 175,
    177-80, 183-4, 219
D'Argenlieu, Adm Georges, 384
Darlan, Adm of the Fleet François,
    350, 375-6
Darmuzai, Col, 72, 76, 78
De Barrail, Gen François, 136
Debré, Prime Minister Michel, 77,
De Brian, Maj Paul-Aimable, 188

De Castellane, Count Pierre, 136
De Castries, Capt, 214
De Chabrière, Col Granet, 162
De Chastenet, Maj, 397-8
Deckers, Legionnaire Willy, 387
De Fleury, Lt Gen Rohault, 126
De Foucauld, Charles, 257
De Galard, Geneviève, 46-7, 49-50,
    52-4
De Gaulle, President Charles, 31, 71-
    2, 75, 77-81, 340, 343-5, 351-3,
    357-8, 375-9, 381-2, 385, 390-2,
    397
De Gramont, Foreign Minister
    Antoine, 194-5
Degueldre, Lt René, 81
Dejean, Ambassador Maurice, 43
Dejoinville, Adm, 135
De la Croix De Castries, Gen
    Christian, 34-5, 38, 42-3, 45, 49-51
De la Marmora, Gen, 155
De Lambert, Maj, 22, 23
De Lanessan, Governor-General
    Antoine, 232
De Larminat, Col Edgar, 354, 358-60,
    363, 371, 374
Delarue, Chaplain, 61,
De Lattre De Tassigny, Gen Jean-
    Marie, 31-3, 79, 327, 378-9
demi-soldes, 96
De Musis, Maj Salomon, 97, 106, 107
De Négrier, Brig Oscar, 213-4, 215-6,
    224, 227, 229, 230, 267
Dentz, Gen Fernand, 353-5
De Palladines, Gen Aurelle, 203-4
depression, state of, 136, 322
Depression, The, 314
De Roux, Col, 358
De Sairigné, Col Gabriel, 364
De Sampigny, Maj, 299
Desert Song operetta, 334
desertion, deserters, 65, 81, 106-7,
    119, 130-1, 136, 188-9, 376, 386-7,
    394
Desmichels, Baron Louis, 108, 109
Désorthès, Col, 268
De St-Arnaud, Marshal Achille, 128-9,
    143, 146-7, 150
De St-Germain, Maj Charles, 140-1
De Suzzoni, Col Raphaël, 198

De Torny, Capt Gabriel Diesbach, 173
Deuxième Bureau, 53, 61-3
Deval, French Consul in Algiers, 90
Dève, Lt Jean, 367, 370
Deville, Maj, 299
De Villebois-Mareuil, Count Georges, 153
Dewavrin, Col André, 382
De Winter, Capt, 348
De Wulf, Capt, 428
Dey Ahmed Khodja, 90
Dey Ali Khodja, 90
Dey Hussein, 90, 94
Dey Omar, 90
Diaz, Capt, 219, 221
Diaz, Porfirio, 188
Dien Bien Phu, 20-55, 119, 166, 221, 381, 388
Diguet, Maj François, 229
Dodds, Gen Alfred-Amédée, 236-7, 239-41
Dominé, Maj Marc-Edmond, 217-9, 221-2, 225
Don Carlos, Spanish Pretender, 113
Doty, Legionnaire Bennett, 331-2
Dreyfus, Capt Alfred, 252
Drude, Gen André, 273
Druzes, 329-33
Duchesne, Gen Charles, 219, 244-51
Dufour, Col, 71
Dunant, Henri, 164, 220
Dupuis, Jean, 215
Duriez, Lt Col, 299-300, 302
Durmoustier, 2/Lt, 116
Duval, Gen, 57

Eden, Sir Anthony, 61
Edward VII, 270
Eisenhower, Gen Dwight, Allied Supreme Commander, 375
Eliot, T. S., 292
Elkington, Lt Col John Ford, 294
Entente Cordiale, 145, 262
Erulin, Col Philippe, 408-30
Escadrille Chérifienne, 326
Esterhazy, Ferdinand, 252
Etienne, Eugène, 213, 237
Eugénie, consort of Napoleon III, 196, 199

Evans, Lt Gen George de Lacy, 115, 117
Evian Agreements, 125, 390, 394
executions, 67, 188, 208-10, 228, 291, 303, 338, 342-3

Faber, Cpl François, 283
Farnsworth, Legionnaire Henry, 277, 283, 294
Fashoda Incident, 243-4
Faulques, Maj Roger, 26, 29-30, 44, 385
Faurax, Maj Marius-Paul, 234, 238-9
Fauroux, Marc, 403-4
Favre, Foreign Minister Jules, 206, 208
Favrel, Legionnaire Charles, 342
Fels, Sgt Maj, 42
fells, 59, 62, 64-5, 69
Fenton, Roger, 153
Fernando VII, King of Spain, 112
Ferrary, Lt Col André Camille, 116, 121
Ferret, Capt Jean-Noël, 409, 429-30
Ferry, Prime Minister Jules, 227, 230
First World War, 270, 273-306
Flatters, Col Paul, 254
Foch, Gen Ferdinand, 305
Forces Armées Zaïroises (FAZ), 402-6
Forey, Gen Elie-Frédéric, 172-4
Forget, Maj, 28
Formosa /Taiwan, 217-8
Francis II, Emperor of Austria, 136
Franco, Col Francisco, 323, 344
francophonie, 390-1
Franco-Prussian War, 193-211
Franz (Francis) Ferdinand, Archduke, 274
Franz Joseph, Emperor of Austria, 171, 182
Free French Brigade, 2nd, 371
Free French Division, 1st, 378
French, Gen Sir John, 276, 278
Friedrich Wilhelm, Crown Prince of Prussia, 198-9
Front de Libération Nationale - Algeria (FLN), 57, 60-2, 70, 329
Front de Libération Nationale du Congo (FLNC), 401-6, 429
Frossard, Gen Charles-Auguste, 198

Galliéni, Marshal Joseph, 233, 250, 261
Gallifet, Gen Gaston-Alexandre, 210
Gambetta, Minister of War Léon, 199-200, 203, 205-8
Gambiez, Gen, 46, 75, 333
Garcin, Marius, 125
Gardy, Col Paul, 52, 333
Garibaldi, Capt Bruno, 281
Garibaldi, Giuseppe, 191, 205, 281, 282
gas, poison, 287, 293, 304
Gaubert, Maj Clavet, 97
Gaucher, Lt Col, 41-2, 44,
Gaultier, Lt Col, 378
Gausserès, Capt, 421-2, 429
Geneva Conventions, 164
Gensoul, Adm, 349
George V, 274, 294
Germans serving in Legion, 32, 42, 49, 65, 74, 80-1, 113, 117, 169, 186-7, 199, 202, 208, 267, 273, 276, 310, 322, 334, 338-9, 347-8, 369, 379
Germann, Capt, 300
Giap, Gen Vo Nguyen, 20, 24-5, 29-32, 34, 38-9, 43-4, 51, 384, 386
Gilles, Brig Jean, 38, 42
Giovanelli, Col, 224-5
Giraud, Gen Henri, 375-6
Giscard D'Estaing, President Valéry, 405, 410, 416
Godot, Lt, 75
Golic, Legionnaire, 423
Gouraud, Gen, 75
Gras, Col Yves, 404-25, 430
Grauwin, Maj Paul, 47
Green, Julian, 307
Grisot, Gen Paul, 194, 205
Groupe d'Intervention de la Gendarmerie Nationale (GIGN), 399
Guderian, Gen Heinz, 335
Guillot, 2/Lt Marcel, 378
Guiraud, Col Maurice, 39, 50, 72, 73
Guizot, Prime Minister François, 138
Gyulai, Gen Franz, 162

Haig, Field Marshal Douglas, 278
Haiphong bombardment, 385
Hajj Ahmed, Bey of Constantine, 124

Halbert, Capt, 425
Hardouvalis, Legionnaire, 338
Harispe, Gen Jean, 120-1
harka, 263-4, 266
harkis, 60, 62-3, 83
Hart, Legionnaire Lionel, 218
Harvey, Legionnaire John, 331-2
Haussman, Baron Georges, 165
Hebig, Capt Johan, 119
hedgehog fortresses, 32, 38, 386
Herbillon, Col, 141
Herbinger, Lt Col Paul Gustave, 229-30, 382
Herson, Gen, 268
Highway Four, 20, 22, 24-5, 27-8, 30-1, 58, 386
Highway One, 385
Highway Three, 386
Hinderschmidt, Legionnaire, 222
Ho Chi Minh, President of Vietnam, 31, 37, 51, 383, 387
Hohenlohe Regiment, 89, 92, 94, 100
Holsten, Legionnaire Jackie, 387
Honecker, Erich, 387
Hunter-Choat, Brig Anthony, 185
Hussein al-Ibni, Sharif of Mecca, 329-30

Ignatiev, Gen, 307
Imbert, Jules, 264
International Tribunal, the Hague, 271-2
Irribarren, Gen, 120,
Isabella II, Infanta of Spain, 112
Ismail Pasha, Gen, 148
Italians serving in Legion, 33, 169
Italian intervention, 161-4, 168
Itzkowitz, Eliahu, 54

Jacquet, Colonial Secretary Marc, 43
Jacquot, Lt, 238-9
Jagodinski, Henri, 430
Jannin, Prefect of Police, 75
Jansen, Legionnaire, 423
Jeanningros, Col, 166, 174, 176, 179, 183
Jeanpierre, Col Pierre, 26-7, 29-30, 59, 66-9, 81
Jiménez, Mexican cavalry commander, 178

Joffre, Marshal Joseph, 292, 298
Jonnart, Célestin, Governor of
    Algeria, 257, 261
Jorand, S/Sgt, 400
Jouhaud, Gen, 75
Juárez, President Benito, 170, 184,
    187-8, 191
Julian, Lt, 378

Kabyles, 208, 246, 250
Kemmlet, Legionnaire, 304
képi, as official headgear, 317-8
Khader, Mohammed, 82,
Kipling, Rudyard, 396
Kisling, Moïse, 283
Kitchener, Lord Horatio, 243
Klems, Sgt Joseph, 324-5, 334
Koenig, General Marie-Pierre, 344,
    349, 354, 357-8, 360-71, 374
Koestler, Arthur, 346
Kolwezi, 401-31
Konrad, orderly Ulrich, 178
Kress, Sgt, 28-9
Kretchatisky, Brig Boris, 313
Krupp, Alfred, 197, 205
ksar, 259, 264, 265

Laborde, Adm, 375-6
Lacan, Legionnaire, 421
Lacaze, Gen Jeannou, 398, 412
Lacoste, Resident Minister Robert, 59,
    61
Lacretelle, Charles-Nicolas, 135
Lafayette squadron, 285, 307
Lai, Legionnaire Casimiro, 176, 178,
    183, 185
Lainé, Lt Ramón, 180
Lalande, Col André, 39
Lallemand, Chaplain Yannick, 409,
    413, 415, 421
La Miss, see Travers, Susan
Lamoricière, Gen, 137, 254
Landriau, Capt, 332, 333
Langlais, Lt Col Pierre, 45
Langlois, Lt Gustave, 248, 250
Laos, 34, 35, 42, 51, 53
Lapeyre, Lt Pol, 326
Lapie, Capt Pierre-Olivier, 341
Larking, Cpl, 400
Laroche, Cpl, 423

Larzul, Col, 403-10, 422-6
Lawrence, T. E., 329
Le Boeuf, Minister for War Edmond,
    196-8
Leclerc, Gen Jacques-Philippe, 353,
    384
Lefèvre, Sgt, 263, 265-6
Lefort, Gen Jacques, 81, 342, 394
Légion d'Orient, 330
Légion franche étrangère, 89,
Legion organisation
    1831-40: 1st Btn, 103, 2nd Btn, 103;
    4th Btn, 103, 107, 110-12, 117, 130;
    5th Btn, 103, 107, 110-11, 117; 6th
    Btn, 103-4, 106-7;
    1840-1856: 1Reg, 140, 146, 161-2;
    2Reg, 135, 141, 146-7, 162, 164-5;
    (as Foreign Brigade in Crimea),
    146-160;
    1862-1884: (as single foreign
    regiment) 165, 166-172, 193; 5RE,
    199-200, 202, 204 (reabsorbed
    1870);
    1884-1920: 1RE, 234-5, 242, 255,
    260, 263, 266, 268, 271, 273, 276-7;
    2RE, 234, 242, 256, 259, 264, 268,
    271, 273, 276-8
    after 1920: 1BEP, 25-7, 29-30, 33,
    39, 42-3, 46, 50, 52, 388, 411;
    1RE/REI, 59, 66, 313, 318, 326,
    331, 347-8, 392, 394, 398; 1REC,
    64, 313, 330-3, 337, 374, 377-8,
    387, 393; 1REG, 393; 1REP, 59, 61,
    63, 66-7, 69-76, 80, 83, 185, 390,
    392, 396, 411; 2BEP, 33, 43, 46, 48-
    50, 52, 388, 411; 2RE/REI, 43, 52,
    59, 313-4, 324, 333, 384, 385, 393,
    395; 2REC, 314, 337; 2REG, 393;
    2REP, 59, 64, 72-4, 76, 77-8, 80,
    393, 394-5, 397, 398, 399, 400, 408,
    410-31; 3RE(I), 22, 24, 27, 30, 46,
    52, 59, 64, 65, 70, 74, 78, 295, 313,
    384, 388, 393, 395, 397; 4DBLE,
    377; 4RE/REI, 59, 313, 318, 330-2,
    393, 395; 5RE/REI, 46, 59, 70, 314,
    348, 380, 382, 395; 6RE/REI, 314,
    353, 354-7; 11REI, 336-8; 12REI,
    337-8; 12DBLE, 65; 13DBLE, 32,
    39, 41, 42, 44, 46, 48-9, 52, 59, 62,
    74, 337, 339-41, 343-4, 351-7, 361-

Index

373, 377-80, 384, 393, 399-400,
(re-designated 14DBLE 1 July–
4 November 1940 and also 'LE'
to distinguish it from the Vichy
regiments in North Africa);
21RMVE, 336-9; 22RMVE, 33,
336-9; 23RMVE, 336-9; 24RMVE,
336-9; operational formations, inc
bataillons and *régiments de marche*
and detachments, 186-7, 204, 234-5,
277, 280-306, 329, 337, 377-8, 382-
3, 395
Legion, Roman, 86
Leibner, Sgt, 382
Lelièvre, Legionnaire Henri-Paul, 238
Le Livre d'Or, 319
*Le Livre d'Or des Légionnaires Morts
pour la France au cours de la Grande
Guerre 1914-1918*, 308
Lemeunier, Col, 50
Lemoine, Cpl, 400
Lemonnier, Gen, 381
Léonard, Legionnaire, 168
Leopold, Prince of Hohenzollern-
Sigmaringen, 194
Leopold I, King of Belgium, 187, 189,
197, 199
Lepage, Lt Col Marcel, 25-7, 29
Le Pen, Lt Jean-Marie, 61, 63
Let, Maj, 256
Ligne Morice, 64
Liron, Gen, 408-9
Liskutin, Sqdn Ldr Miroslav, 347
Liu Yung-Fu, 220, 225
Lloyd George, Prime Minister David,
298
Lombard, Cpl-chef, 423
Lorrilot, Col, 384
Louis II, Prince of Monaco, 283, 321
Louis XVI, King of France, 90, 404
Louis XVIII, King of France, 89-90
Louis-Philippe, King of France, 75,
92-4, 106, 111, 113, 117-8, 121-2,
135, 138, 145, 185, 319
Luders, Gen, 159
Lyautey, Marshal Louis, 261-3, 272-3,
283, 310-12, 322, 325, 327-8

MacArthur, Gen Douglas, 380
MacCarthy, Oscar, 257-9

MacMahon, Marshal Edme, 134, 136,
162, 198
Madagascar campaign, 244-51
Mader, Sgt Maj Max-Emmanuel, 301,
305
Maginot Line, 335
Magnin, Cpl Charles, 177
Magrin-Vernerey, Lt Col Raoul,
see Monclar
Mahele, Maj, 406-10
Maine, Cpl, 168, 182, 185
Maire, Maj Fernand, 300, 319, 324,
336, 337
Maitland Wilson, Gen Sir Henry,
355-6
Malaterre, Maj, 398
Mallec, Chaplain, 362
Mammaert, Cpl, 216-7
Mangin, Gen Charles, 306
Mannerheim, Gen Carl, 314
Manue, Legionnaire Georges, 338
Manurien, Capt, 300
Marchand, Capt Jean-Baptiste, 243
Maria Cristina, Regent of Spain, 112
Marie-Amélie, Queen of France, 138
Marie-Antoinette, Queen of France,
138
Marolf, Lt, 291
Marredo de Gomez, Juana, 181
Martin, Legionnaire Jean, 318
Martinez, Lt Col Antonio, 162-3
Martyn, Lt Frederic, 234-5, 238-9,
240, 247
Masselot, Lt Georges, 337
Massone, Lt, 214
Massu, Gen Jacques, 61, 63, 67, 69, 71
Maudet, 2/Lt Clément, 167-9, 175,
181-3, 185, 225
Maury, Legionnaire, 228
Maximilian, 'Emperor' of Mexico,
(born, Archduke Ferdinand
Maximilian Joseph), 172, 186, 189,
191
Mehl, Capt, 216
Mendès-France, Prime Minister
Pierre, 54, 57
Mendizábal, Prime Minister Juan, 115
Menshikov, Prince A. S., 148-53, 157
Mers el-Kebir, 75,
Messmer, Prime Minister Pierre, 78,

363, 366, 390
Mexican intervention, 166-191
Milán, Col, 168, 174, 179, 181-3
Millan Astray y Terreros, Col Jos
   311-12
Minié, Capt Claude-Etienne, inventor
   of eponymous ammunition, 149
Ministère de la Marine, 93, 94
Mitterand, President François, 61, 67
Mobutu, Citizen-President of Zaire,
   401-5, 410
Molé, Count Louis-Mathieu, 117, 126
Monclar, 340-1, 343-4, 349, 353, 358
Monroe Doctrine, 171, 187
Montgomery, Field Marshal Sir
   Bernard, 371
Montagu-Stuart-Wortley, Col, 270
Moore, Lt Thomas Parr, 136
Morcillo, Capt, 430
Mordacq, Gen Jean, 310
Morin, Capt, 388
Morin, Cpl, 422
Morin, Délégué Général, 75
Morlae, Legionnaire Edward, 293
Morny, duc de, 170, 189
Moroccan Division, 290, 292, 298,
   304-5, 306
Moroccan Liberation Army, 327
Morocco, 59, 135, 253-273, 322, 333-
   4
Morzicki, Sgt, 179-81
Moulay Hassan I, Sultan of Morocco,
   254
Moulay Jussef, 273
Moulay Moustafa, 258, 260
Moulin, Sgt Maj, 379
Moulinay, Capt, 219, 222
Mountbatten, Adm Louis, 383
Murray, Cpl-chef Simon, 73-4, 76, 80,
   394, 397
Mutiny, 74-8, 307

Napoleon I, Emperor of France, 89-
   90, 109, 112, 132, 149
Napoleon III, formerly Prince Louis-
   Napoleon Bonaparte, 139, 142, 145-
   147, 151, 155-61, 164, 169, 171-3,
   185, 187, 189-90, 194, 196, 198
National Guard, 203, 207
Naval Assault Division (Dinasau), 385

Navarre, Gen Henri, 33-6, 38, 42, 45,
   51, 298
   French navy, 217, 245
Nguyen Hai Quoc, see Ho Chi Minh
Nicot, Col, 35
Niessel, Gen, 327
Nikolai I, Tsar of Russia, 144, 146,
   156
Nikolai, Grand Duke and C-in-C of
   Imperial Russian armies, 286, 307
Nivelle, Gen Robert, 298, 302-3
Noguès, Gen Pierre, 374-5

Ochsenbein, Gen Johann, 155, 161
Odintsoff, Col, 313
Ollivier, Prime Minister Emile, 196
Operation Albatross, 51
Operation Anvil, 378
Operation Atlante, 36
Operation Blücher, 304
Operation Bonite, see Operation
   Leopard
Operation Castor, 36
Operation Catapult, 349
Operation Chicapa, 401-30
Operation Menace, 351
Operation Leopard, 408-31
Operation Petsamo, 340
Operation Regattas, 42
Operation Torch, 374
Operation Vulture, 49
Opium, 39, 232, 233
Oraa, Gen Marcelino, 120
Organisation Armée Secrète (OAS),
   60, 72, 74, 80-1
Oudinot, Col, 110

Pal, Legionnaire, 271
Palin, Ray, 67
Palladines, Gen Aurelles, 203-4
Palmerston, Prime Minister Lord, 152
Panmure, Lord, 152
Papon, Maurice, 80
Pâris De Bollardière, Gen Jacques, 62,
   372, 374
Parisian Volunteers, 103,
Passy, see Dewavrin
Pavillons Noirs, see Black Flags
Pechkoff, Gen Zinovi, 280, 382
Pégot, Maj, 42, 44

Pein, Maj Théodore, 282-3, 289
Pélissier, Marshal Aimable (duc de Malakoff), 137, 157, 159
Pérez, Tomás, 21, 22
Pétain, Marshal Philippe, 298, 303, 305, 308, 327-8, 343, 345, 375-6
Peter the Great, 144
Peter I, King of Serbia, 321
petroleum, 59, 254
Picot, Georges, 329
Piroth, Col Charles, 34-5, 45, 221
Poincaré, President Raymond, 276, 280
Pointurier, Lt, 259
Porschmann, see Moulin, Sgt Maj
Porter, Cole, 308
porteurs de valises, 63
POWs, 52-4, 58, 310, 357, 362, 364, 368, 379, 380
Prestisimone, Col, 362
Princip, Gavrilo, 274
prisoners, (see also POWs), 52, 69, 116, 137, 214, 294, 297, 305, 342, 363
prostitution / brothels, 26, 28, 43, 49, 50, 73-4, 78, 315, 328, 353, 395
Prudence, Cpl Jean, 430
Przybyszewski, 283
Puchois, Maj, 371
punishment, 73, 116, 129-30, 267, 269, 271, 315
Puyloubier, 184, 396

Quartier Viénot, see Sidi bel-Abbès
Querville, Adm, 75

RAF, 368, 371
Raglan, Lord (and forces under his command), 147-50, 156
Rainilaiarivony, consort of Ranavalona, 244, 250
Ranavalona, Queen of Madagascar, 244, 249-50
razzias, 132-3, 137, 140, 256, 271, 302, 333-4
recruiting, 155, 164, 172, 185-6, 189, 199, 205, 210, 267, 306, 309, 314, 330, 346, 380, 387, 394
Red Cross, 164
refugees, 26, 31, 132-4, 189, 210

Rembert, Capt, 162
Revers, Gen George, 20-22, 24, 30
Revoil, Paul, 272
Reybas, Jean, 277
Robertson, James, 153
Roches, Leon, 125
Rockwell, Legionnaire Kiffin, 285
Rollet, Gen Paul, 82, 246, 302, 306, 315-9, 378, 396
Rommel, Field Marshal Erwin, 359, 364-5, 367
Roosevelt, President Franklin, 375, 382
Rosen, Erwin, 267
Ross, Ambassador André, 402-16, 430
Rousselet, Capt, 116-7
Rovigo, Duke René Savory, 105
Royal Navy (British), 145, 151-2, 263, 286, 340, 350, 352
Russell, William, 152

Sabatier, Gen, 381-2
Sainteny, French High Commissioner Jean, 385
Salan, Gen Raoul, 33, 64, 69, 75, 77
Salisbury, Foreign Secretary Lord, 244
Sarrail, Gen Maurice, 286-7, 330
Saussier, Capt Gustave, 176,
Schaeffer, Maj, 230
Schriever, Legionnaire Joachim, 387
Second Republic, declaration of, 138-9
Second World War, 314
Seeger, Alan, 277-8, 285, 292, 296-7, 298
Sections Administratives Spécialisées (SAS), 70
Selchauhansen, Christian, 260
Senes, Ensign, 219
Sergent, Capt Pierre, 68, 77
Seroka, Lt Joseph, 140
Servan-Schreiber, Jean-Jacques, 62
Service de Documentation Extérieure et de Contre-Espionage (SDECE), 58, 60-1, 72
Shervington, Col Charles, 244
Ships: HMS Ark Royal, 349, 352; HMS Barham, 352; Breslaw, 91; Cap Padaran, 348; Cintra, 269; Finistére, 173; Galilée, 267; HMS Hood, 350; Joffre, 388; Meknès, 349; Mitrailleuse, 219, 220; Monarch of Bermuda, 340;

Mytho, 236; *Opale*, 239; *Panther*, 272; SS *Pennland*, 351; USS *Philadelphia*, 101; *Porthos*, 331; *Primaguet*, 245; HMS *Resolution*, 352; *Riga*, 269; HMS *Rip Van Winkle*, 151-2; *Sphynx*, 100; *St Louis*, 173; *Ville de St Louis*, 236; *Wagram*, 173; SS *Westernland*, 351-2
(Sidi) bel-Abbès, 52, 73, 77, 81, 133, 140, 184, 227, 235, 262, 277, 313, 315, 319, 331, 347-8, 377, 379
Sidi Slimane, 214
Sidi Muhammed, Sultan of Morocco, 254
Silvestre, Gen Manuel, 323, 325
Simonot, Lt, 67, 69
Sisowath Monireth, Crown Prince of Cambodia, 321
smala, 132, 135
Solatorenzo, Legionnaire, 423
Solenzara air base, 412, 414
Somerville, Adm, 349, 350
Sou, Marshal, 233
Soubirou, Capt, 399
Soult, Marshal Nicolas, 93-5, 112, 129, 133, 161, 165, 392
Soustelle, Jacques, 57
Spahis, 140, 206, 256, 260, 263, 273, 313, 327, 333-4
Spanish Civil War, 346
Spanish intervention, 112-122
Stalin, Joseph, 383
St-Marc, Maj Elie Denoix, 73, 74, 77
Steoberg, Legionnaire Tirbald, see Streibler
Stoffel, Col Christophe, 97-100, 189
Strata, Legionnaire, 420-1
Streibler, Legionnaire Thiebald, 225
Sultan al-Atrash, 331
Susbielle, Capt, 259
Sweeney, Charles, 326-7, 336
Sykes, Sir Mark, 329
Syria, 330-33, 343
Szabo, Lt, 342

Tasnady, Sgt Maj, 66, 70
Teitgen, Paul, 62
Tennyson, Alfred Lord, 151
Théatre des Opérations Extérieures (TOE), 311

Thiers, Prime Minister Adolphe, 112, 117, 138, 195-6, 203, 208
Thomas, Capt, 427
Tisserand, 2/Lt, 260
Tissier, Sgt Maj, 260
Todleben, Gen, 153
Tonel, Sgt Maj Henri, 177
torture, 61-3,
Touami, Sgt, 423
Travers, Susan, 351-2, 358, 360, 363-73
Trezel, Gen Camille, 109-11
Trochu, Gen Louis, 199
Truman, President Harry, 382
Tscharner, Capt, 297
Tshombe, Moïse, 406

Vaillant, Minister for War Jean-Baptiste, 160
Valée, Marshal Sylvain, 126-7, 129, 132
Vauchez, Capt, 260
Vaury, Legionnaire, 221
Vegetius, 150
Vergio, Capt, 408
Vérot, Pierre, 403
Vézinet, Gen, 75
Victoria, Queen of England, 145, 151
Viénot, Col, 157
Viet Minh, 20, 22-5, 28-9, 31-2, 35, 39-40, 42-3, 48-52, 383-5, 387-8
Vietnam, 20-55, 215-33, 348-9, 380-8
Vigy, Gen, 263, 265
Vilain, 2/Lt Jean, 168-9, 174, 181
Villebois-Mareuil, Count Georges, 153
Vittone, Legionnaire, 421
Voirol, Gen, 95, 106
Völkerrechtsbund zur Bekämpfung der Fremdenlegion, 268
von Arnim, Gen Jürgen, 377
von Benedek, Gen Ludwig, 192
von Bismarck, Prime Minister Otto, 193, 195, 197, 203, 206
von Bolt, Lt Ernst Milson, 173-4, 203
von Bülow, Chancellor Bernhard, 270
von der Tann, Gen, 200, 203-4
von Etzdorf, Baron Rudiger, 346
von Heinleth, Maj Adolf, 200-1
von Hohenberg, Sophie, 274

Index

von Ludendorff, Gen Erich, 304
von Manteuffel, Gen Edwin, 146, 205-6
von Moltke, Gen Helmuth, 192, 196-7, 279
von Moltke the Younger, Gen Helmuth Johannes, 279-80
von Rahden, Baron Wilhelm, 120
von Roon, Count Albrecht, 196
von Schlieffen, Count Alfred, 274, 279
Voyron, Brig Emile, 247

Wabinski, Capt, 398
Wadell, Maj, 299
Weaponry, 38, 40, 42, 44-5, 48-52, 64, 69, 149, 154, 156, 161, 192, 197, 199, 200-1, 205, 207, 217, 219, 238, 244, 257, 263, 279-80, 284, 287-8, 293, 300, 323-4, 337-8, 360-1, 363-8, 378, 382, 384, 386, 387-8, 401, 407, 419, 427
Wellington, Duke of, 147
Wensel, Legionnaire, 168, 182
Western Desert, 358-373
Wilhelm, Crown Prince, 270
Wilhelm I, King of Prussia, 194
Wilhelm II, Kaiser, 262, 270
Williamson, Legionnaire, James, 342
Willoughby, Gen Digby, 244
Woitzik, Cpl Günther, 386
Worden, Cpl-chef James, 64-5, 78, 359, 394-7
Wren, P. C., 256
Wright, Cpl-chef Bob, 397

Ysquierdo, Capt, 69

Zédé, Lt Charles-Jules, 162-3, 174
Zeller, Gen, 74-5, 79
Zeralda Camp, 75, 77, 80
Zimmerman, the Unknown Legionnaire, 396
Zingraff, Despatcher, 419
Zouaves, 103, 142, 147, 158, 162-3, 197-8, 200, 204, 263, 273, 286, 290
Zumalacárregui, Col Tomás, 113
Zurell, Cpl, 30, 39, 41